O9-AIE-129

SHADOW WARRIORS

ALSO BY KENNETH R. TIMMERMAN

Countdown to Crisis

The French Betrayal of America

Preachers of Hate

Shakedown

Selling Out America

The Death Lobby

Weapons of Mass Destruction

Poison Gas Connection

SHADOW WARRIORS

THE UNTOLD STORY OF TRAITORS, SABOTEURS, AND THE PARTY OF SURRENDER

KENNETH R. TIMMERMAN

NEW YORK

Published in the United States by Crown Forum,
an imprint of the Crown Publishing Group,
a division of Random House, Inc., New York.
www.crownpublishing.com

Library of Congress Cataloging-in-Publication Data
Timmerman, Kenneth R.
Shadow warriors : the untold story of traitors, saboteurs,
and the party of surrender / Kenneth R. Timmerman.—1st ed.
p. cm.
Includes bibliographical references and index.
1. Iraq War, 2003—Moral and ethical aspects. I. Title.
DS79.76.T56 2007
956.7044'38—dc22 2007023036

ISBN 978-0-307-35209-5

Printed in the United States of America

10 9 8 7 6 5 4 3

First Edition

For Diana, Simon, and the next generation of citizens and spies

CONTENTS

Therefore put on the full armor of God, so that when the day of evil comes, you may be able to stand your ground, and after you have done everything, to stand.

—Ephesians 6:13

SHADOW WARRIORS

PROLOGUE

THE UNDERGROUND

Some have called it the CIA's greatest covert operation of all time.

It involved deep penetration of a hostile regime by planting a network of agents at key crossroads of power, where they could steal secrets and steer policy by planting disinformation, cooking intelligence, provocation, and outright lies.

It involved sophisticated political sabotage operations, aimed at making regime leaders doubt their own judgment and question the support of their subordinates.

It involved the financing, training, and equipping of effective opposition forces, who could challenge the regime openly and through covert operations.

The scope was breathtaking, say insiders who had personal knowledge of the CIA effort. All the skills learned by the U.S. intelligence community during fifty years of Cold War struggle with the Soviet Union were in play, from active measures aimed at planting disinformation through cutouts and an eager media, to *maskirovka*—strategic deception.

It was war—but an intelligence war, played behind the scenes, aimed at confusing, misleading, and ultimately defeating the enemy. Its goal was nothing less than to topple the regime in power, by discrediting its rulers.

Many Americans believe this was the CIA's goal during the 1990s, when the Agency had "boots on the ground" in northern Iraq, working with Iraqi opponents to Saddam Hussein. Most patriotic Americans probably hope that the CIA today has such an operation to overthrow the mullahs in Tehran, or North Korean dictator Kim Jong Il.

But the target of this vast, sophisticated CIA operation was none of them.

It was America's 43rd president, George W. Bush.

Many Americans look at the war in Iraq and understandably feel that something has gone dreadfully wrong. Given the way our political system works, the first person they blame is the president of the United States. After all, he is the commander in chief. As Harry Truman famously said of his role in the blame game of American politics, "The Buck Stops Here." So aren't Americans right to hold Bush accountable for the failures of his administration? And wasn't that the main message of the November 2006 elections?

The short answer, of course, is yes. But the truth is far more nuanced, because it is based on information that is not widely available to the public—or when available, information that has been systematically ignored, denied, or purposefully misconstrued by the president's political opponents and their cheering section in the elite media.

Take the whole question of Saddam Hussein's efforts to build weapons of mass destruction and his ties to terrorist groups. The fear that Saddam would have handed chemical, biological, or nuclear weapons to a terrorist group for use against the United States drove President Bush and his advisors—and everyone else who saw the intelligence—to conclude that the United States had no option but to remove Saddam's regime.

After the devastation of the 9/11 attacks, no U.S. president could have failed to act against Saddam once it became clear that the Iraqi dictator would not disarm voluntarily, as required by seventeen United Nations Security Council resolutions. At the time those decisions were made, in the fall of 2002, no one doubted the intelligence, not U.S. allies overseas or even the president's opponents in Congress.

But as you will learn in this book, some of that intelligence was cooked—not by the Bush administration but by its opponents—in an extraordinary covert operation that has never been revealed until now (see Chapter 5). The goal was to lay the groundwork for a political assault on the president of the United States, and by extension, against America and on American troops serving in harm's way. *Bush lied, people died!*

You will learn that from the very start the president's original war plans were undermined by officials at the State Department and the CIA, who shifted that strategy from liberation to occupation, and in so doing helped to spark the insurgency that caused the deaths of more than 3,000 American servicemen. Four years later, as this book appears, we are stuck with a war that the president never desired and never planned, while those who bear direct, personal responsibility for the train wreck of events have faded back into obscurity.

You will learn of arsenals of weapons of mass destruction (WMD) that Saddam and his allies moved or destroyed shortly before the fighting began, to hide them from the coalition. You will learn, too, that there was extensive evidence that Saddam Hussein was funding and training a variety of terrorist groups on Iraqi soil, giving rise to legitimate fears that he might give WMD to terrorists to use against us. But since the war, this evidence—which has been supplemented by masses of documents and audio recordings seized in the aftermath of the invasion—has been dragged through the mud and its purveyors discredited (see Chapters 9, 14, and 17).

Many of the shadow warriors involved in this extraordinary campaign to impeach the truth have succeeded until now in keeping their role in these events hidden. They are professional bureaucrats, staff directors, intelligence operatives, National Security Council professionals, former ambassadors, and career diplomats. I will name many of them in this book for the first time, so Americans can judge their actions by the light of day.

Others—such as Senator Carl Levin (D-MI), Senator John D. "Jay" Rockefeller (D-WV), Senator Chuck Hagel (R-NE), and General Brent Scowcroft—are public personalities. Until now they have managed to obscure their role in subverting the U.S.-led war against the terrorists who attacked us on September 11 through political subterfuge, outright lies, and a complaisant media.

This book will correct the record and expose their maneuvering.

After President Bush was elected to a second term in November 2004, Secretary of State Colin Powell called a town meeting at the State Department in Washington. Faced with a sea of Kerry-Edwards stickers in the parking lot and hearing tales of open insubordination from his aides, Powell decided to confront the problem head-on. "We live in a democracy," he said. "As Americans, we have to respect the results of elections." He went on to tell his employees that President Bush had received the most votes of any president in U.S. history, and that they were constitutionally obligated to serve him.

One of Powell's subordinates, an assistant secretary of state, became increasingly agitated. Once Powell had dismissed everyone, she returned to her office suite, shut the door, and held a mini town meeting of her own. After indignantly recounting Powell's remarks to her assembled staff, she commented, "Well, Senator Kerry received the *second highest* number of votes of any presidential candidate in history. If just one state had gone differently, Senator Kerry would be President Kerry today." Her employees owed no allegiance to the president of the United States, especially not to policies they knew were wrong, she said. If it was legal, and it would slow down the Bush juggernaut, they should do it, she told them.

Here was an open call to insubordination. And she was just one among many mid-level government managers, at State and elsewhere, making similar calls to their employees.

Even under the stewardship of Donald Rumsfeld, the Pentagon was filled with mid- and top-level managers who hated Bush and secretly worked to undermine the policies of his administration. At a time when the president was fighting against sagging opinion polls because of the war, for example, a Democratic Party political hack was chosen to run the critical Coalitions for the War office, even though she openly boasted that she had voted against Bush twice. Her boss, Undersecretary of Defense Eric Edelman—one of the architects of the Iraq War, and a former aide to Vice President Dick Cheney—felt she shouldn't be judged on her political opinions.

While the overwhelming majority of public servants take pride in serving their president loyally, whatever his party affiliation, a dedicated core of shadow warriors were determined to use their position to destroy him. Edelman wasn't alone among Bush administration managers in his naïve belief that all public servants would put their nation above politics.

Addressing a joint session of Congress on September 20, 2001, just nine days after the September 11 attacks, President George W. Bush warned about the coming war with the terrorists and the regimes that backed them.

"Americans should not expect one battle, but a lengthy campaign, unlike any other we have ever seen," he said. "It may include dramatic strikes, visible on TV, and covert operations, secret even in success."

Today, many of those stories are no longer secret—not because the Bush administration has decided to declassify them but because they were leaked by shadow warriors to a hostile media in an effort to undermine the president, embarrass America's friends overseas, and thwart the ability of the United States to wage the war on terror. Such efforts go way beyond partisan differences or a legitimate debate over policy.

During a previously unreported trip to Turkey, then–CIA director Porter Goss witnessed the damage firsthand. He had gone to seek approval for U.S. overflights of Turkey in the event the United States decided to launch a preemptive attack on Iranian nuclear facilities, but he was summarily rebuffed by his Turkish counterparts. "You Americans can't keep secrets," the Turks told him.

Details of virtually every covert U.S. intelligence tool used in the war on terror began winding up on the front pages of the *New York Times* and the *Washington Post.* Former Democratic senator Zell Miller called the leaks a "second cousin to treason" and accused CIA dissidents of waging a "sting operation" against the Bush administration at the expense of national security. Until now, however, there has been no public outcry against the shadow warriors who were responsible for these travesties. They have hidden their tracks well.

This book is the story of these extraordinary attempts, carried out in time of war, to undermine a sitting president of the United States as he sought to defend the nation from military and terrorist attack. For the shadow warriors, nothing was sacred beyond this goal. They were willing to expose top-secret U.S. intelligence operations, aid and abet America's enemies, and work covertly to ensure failure in Iraq, all to achieve their goal of defeating the presidency of George W. Bush.

As I will show in this book, at times the motivation of the shadow warriors was purely personal, the result of some long-ago slight, real or imagined, borne in silence for years. Thus, I will tell the extraordinary story of two titans of the Bush administration who fought for control of the U.S. intelligence community. Unbeknownst to one of them, his rival bore him a grudge from college days that went so deep he was willing to gut a major component of U.S. intelligence in order to exact vengeance some fifty years later (see Chapter 19).

The elite media likes to portray itself as above the political fray. They are "investigators," just out to find "the truth." Their role is to probe the powerful to expose lies and hidden agendas. After all, most government secrets are not classified because they are vital to national security but because they are embarrassing to our political leaders. Right?

Well, sometimes.

The hidden bias of the elite media has been exposed in a spate of recent books. But how many readers are aware that beyond just bias, many reporters feed from secret troughs, tapping into an underground network of sources and informants whose agenda runs counter to what most of us would consider the national interest?

When the *Washington Post* runs a story about the CIA's "secret prisons" by Dana Priest (see Chapter 10), do they publish a disclaimer informing readers that the reporter is married to a left-wing political activist who for thirty years has specialized in generating public opposition to the government of the United States of America and has publicly opposed any form of covert action? Or when they run a story by Walter Pincus that lashes out at some failure by the Pentagon's Defense Intelligence Agency, do they tell you that Pincus is married to a woman who was a Clinton administration political appointee and a steady donor to Democratic candidates and the Democratic National Committee (DNC), who had burrowed into the State Department Bureau of Intelligence and Research (INR), a tiny group of analysts that has no spies and is well known in the intelligence community for second-guessing everybody that does?

Or when the *New York Times* publishes a story by James Risen exposing a highly classified National Security Agency program to intercept the communications of suspected terrorists, do they ever tell you that Risen once coauthored a book glorifying (and exposing) covert U.S. intelligence operations with Milt Bearden, a former CIA covert operative? As chief of the Soviet/East European Division of the Directorate of Operations, Bearden sent a still infamous cable to CIA chiefs of station worldwide when the Berlin wall collapsed telling them to "stand down" their spy networks against the Soviet Union because the Cold War was over. ("And guess who is still spying on us today?" a retired station chief who had received Bearden's cable commented to me wryly.)

On December 1, 2000, Jesse Jackson brought his troops to Washington for the first day of the Supreme Court hearings on the Florida election recount. "Racist! Fascist!" Jesse's horde shouted to groups of pro-Bush demonstrators.

Jackson was back ten days later, when the Supreme Court heard oral arguments in *Bush v. Gore.* "If this court rules against counting our vote, it will simply create a civil rights explosion," he said. "People will not surrender to this tyranny. . . . They will not stand by and accept this with surrender." Jackson's inflammatory words were dangerously close to a call for insurrection. Over the next several weeks—indeed, even after the inauguration—Jackson repeated them in rallies all across the United States.[1]

It was no surprise that Democrats were gunning for George W. Bush from the very first day of his presidency. Most pundits chalked it up to payback for the impeachment of "their" president, Bill Clinton.

What they didn't realize at the time was that Bush's enemies had no intention of giving up, and called on their supporters to create what amounted to an underground resistance movement within every agency of the United States government. To them, Bush was an illegitimate president whose authority they could not accept.

In small ways and large, Bush's opponents did their best to thwart his actions as president. During the weeks before they left office, for example, the Clinton team enacted hundreds of "midnight regulations," ramming through last-minute rules in areas where they had failed to win congressional approval to enact their policies.

Each of the last-minute rules was carefully tailored to help a Clinton friend or harm an enemy. Some regulations were merely silly, covering the type of desk chairs private businesses were required to buy for their employees, or the proper size of the holes manufacturers must put in Swiss cheese. But some had serious implications.

Most notable was Clinton's one-minute-to-midnight agreement to join the International Criminal Court. Under that treaty, which Clinton signed on December 31, 2000, without the advice and consent of the United States Senate, U.S. servicemen could be brought before an international court at the behest of a foreign enemy of the United States, for actions carried out in wartime under the lawful orders of their commanders. It took nearly eighteen months to walk that one back.*

Within hours of the inauguration, White House chief of staff Andrew H. Card Jr. imposed a sixty-day review period for rules that had not yet gone into force. But beyond that, the Bush team shrugged off the Clinton efforts as little more than a nuisance, the cost of power under our political system.

It was a huge mistake, for which they are still paying the price.

George W. Bush never got the first rule of Washington: People are policy. He allowed his political enemies to run roughshod over his administration through a vast underground he never dismantled and never dominated. *Shadow Warriors* tells this story—the when, the where, the how, and especially the who—for the first time.

---

*Undersecretary of State John R. Bolton, the poster boy of all the Left loved to hate, officially informed UN secretary-general Kofi Annan on May 6, 2002, that the United States considered Clinton's signature null and void and did not consider itself a party to the treaty.

CHAPTER ONE

A BATTLE ROYAL

Frank Ricciardone was a career diplomat, but he had no illusions to whom he owed his allegiance. In 1999, he had been appointed as the secretary of state's special coordinator for the transition of Iraq. It was a new position, with no real precedent in U.S. history. Although Ricciardone owed his title to the Iraq Liberation Act (ILA), an overwhelmingly bipartisan piece of legislation passed by Congress in 1998, he owed his *job* to President Bill Clinton's secretary of state, Madeleine Albright. He knew how Washington worked.

Now, in January 2001, he began to ingratiate himself with his new political masters at the Bush White House and the State Department over long lunches and private meetings. An Arabist by training (I first met Ricciardone in Jordan, where he was posted in the early 1990s), he overwhelmed them with his detailed knowledge of Iraq and the Iraqi opposition. "I was sitting at the Turkish border counting refugees," he said, referring to a period the Republicans called "the debacle." This was August 1996, when Clinton abandoned the Iraqi opposition and allowed Saddam Hussein to smash their safe haven in northern Iraq, murdering hundreds of fighters and forcing tens of thousands more to flee across the border.

Because he had seen the sufferings of Iraqis up close, he told Bush administration officials, "this is a mission I believe in."

But in fact, Ricciardone's mission from the very start had been something quite different. He ensured that no viable Iraqi opposition would emerge to lay claim on U.S. government support, because that is what Albright, Clinton, and Democrats in Congress secretly wanted.

In other words, his job was to make sure the Clinton administration could break the law, with no one the wiser.

Clinton and Albright believed they could keep Saddam Hussein "in his box" through United Nations sanctions, which they saw as a cost-free policy. As long as U.S. forces in the region encircled Iraq, and the U.S. Air Force enforced "no-fly zones" in the north and the south of Iraq, Saddam Hussein posed no strategic threat to the United States, they argued. He might massacre his own people, send $25,000 checks to encourage suicide bombings by Palestinians, and dabble with al Qaeda operatives, but those were mere "nuisances" the U.S. could handle.

The real threat to the United States, they felt, was Ahmad Chalabi, an Iraqi political genius who chaired the Iraqi National Congress (INC), a coalition of opposition groups based in northern Iraq. Chalabi and the INC were seeking to enlist U.S. help in overthrowing Saddam Hussein.

Dr. Chalabi was many things. He came from a family of prominent Iraqi politicians who had held office in democratically elected governments before the takeover by Saddam Hussein's Baath Party in 1958. He had a Ph.D. in mathematics from the University of Chicago, but early on went into business and made a fortune introducing Visa card services to the Middle East in the 1970s.

Yet Chalabi was also a master lobbyist, who understood the American political system better than most American politicians. Almost singlehandedly, he convinced an overwhelming majority of the House and Senate to approve the Iraq Liberation Act of 1998, which authorized the U.S. government to spend $97 million per year to train and equip an Iraqi Liberation Army, and to spend additional funds to support the INC and other opponents of Saddam.

Frank Ricciardone's mission was to stop Ahmad Chalabi at all costs, because he could drag the United States into a war.

With the change of administrations, Ricciardone knew that his new political masters were divided. Some, such as Deputy Secretary of Defense Paul Wolfowitz and Undersecretary of State John Bolton, were strong Chalabi supporters. They believed that the military plan Chalabi had developed with the help of the former commander of U.S. Special Forces, Lieutenant General Wayne Downing, was sound. (The Downing Plan called for training and equipping two heavy brigades of Iraqi fighters—10,000 men—and helping them to establish beachheads in the Kurdish-controlled north and the Shia-dominated southern parts of Iraq, backed by U.S. airpower, then gradually moving on Baghdad as Iraqi units loyal to Saddam began to defect.)

But Ricciardone knew that the Joint Chiefs of Staff hated the plan (they favored a more robust use of American forces that would head directly for Baghdad, the "center of gravity" of Saddam's regime), and that both the State Department and the CIA hated Chalabi—with a passion. Differences over how to deal with Iraqi dictator Saddam Hussein and what role the U.S. should give Chalabi and the Iraqi National Congress became a battle royal within the national security establishment well before President Bush took office in 2001. Positions had been staked out, allies gathered, and elaborate strategies mapped out by both sides. The new administration never fully grasped the deep, visceral opposition to their plans within the entrenched bureaucracy.

Ricciardone could be beguiling. He told his new political masters, "I really want to see these programs go forward. But the INC has got to be business-like."

It was a ploy that Ricciardone and a small group of career State Department officers—Rebecca J. King, Kathy Allegrone, and Filo Dibble—already had used with success to make sure that no significant amount of the $97 million initially authorized by the Iraq Liberation Act ever got spent.

In 1999, for example, Congress appropriated $8 million in Economic Support Funds to help the INC expand its operations in Iraq, Europe, and the United States. But the INC only received $267,000 of that money—and it was used not to recruit fighters for the Iraq Liberation Army but to hire American consultants imposed on the INC by Ricciardone and his staff to rewrite INC grant proposals. In 2000, an additional $8 million was left unspent, with only $850,000 going to the INC. By the time the Bush administration came in, $3.2 million had been paid to a Landover, Maryland, company called Quality Support, Inc., for the sole purpose of organizing conferences, setting up a luxurious office the consultants could use in London (the INC already an office there), and so-called "administrative services."[1]

In one boondoggle organized at Ricciardone's behest, Quality Support brought 300 Iraqi exiles to New York for a "national assembly" in October 1999 that cost U.S. taxpayers $2.1 million, or $7,000 per head.

Why did it cost so much? For one thing, in a move reminiscent of Hillary Clinton's Travelgate fiasco, Quality Support insisted on buying all the tickets through their own travel agent at well above the going rates.

One INC member offered to buy his own ticket from Los Angeles to New York for the conference for $344. Quality Support refused, and insisted on overnighting him a full-fare ticket that cost U.S. taxpayers $1,800. INC members in London offered to buy tickets for under $500, but Quality Support turned them down, giving the business to their own travel agent, who charged an average of $2,000 per ticket. "Those payments went through the State Department audit without a hitch," INC executive board member Sherif Ali bin Hussein al Hashimi told me. "But when it came to our budget, Kathy Allegrone," the State Department officer who was managing the INC account, "argued day and night with us over an eight-dollar rounding error," he said.

That was how the shadow warriors worked. They knew all the ins and outs of the bureaucratic process. Like the lawyers in Charles Dickens's *Bleak House*, they knew that if they could delay things long enough their opponents would probably forget what the fight was all about.

"The INC had problems with their bookkeeping," another Ricciardone deputy told me in February 2001, in response to my question about why the congressionally appropriated funds were never spent on their intended purpose against Saddam. "Until just recently, they had no legal standing. We had to get them incorporated before they could receive funds under the program. That's why the money had to be paid out through consultants."

Put simply, it was a crock.

"Quality Support's mandate was to pile up money on the street and burn it," INC advisor Francis Brooke told me. But if you only read the version of these events that has appeared in the *Washington Post* or the *New York Times*, you would be convinced that the INC was wasting vast amounts of U.S. taxpayer money.

Ricciardone was unhappy when I called him to inquire about Quality Support and why more money was not getting to the Iraqi opposition.

"Rather than looking at Quality Support, I'd like to see someone investigate all that money that's been going to John Rendon," he said. *Wink wink, nod nod.* "And you know where that's coming from!"

Of course I did. The Rendon Group's contract with the CIA was one of Washington's worst-kept secrets. But because it *was* still secret, people could characterize it any way they wanted.

And they did.

CHALABI

But wait a minute, I can hear Bill O'Reilly saying. This Chalabi character is a crook!

Wasn't he arrested by U.S. agents in Baghdad in 2004 and accused of selling intelligence to Iran?

Wasn't he the one who fabricated the evidence on Saddam's WMD to suck us into a war we didn't need?

Jane Mayer called him "The Manipulator," in a feature story that appeared in *The New Yorker. Newsweek* even put him on the cover, calling him a "convicted felon," "one of the great con men of history," and "Bush's Mr. Wrong."[2]

Left-wing blogger Steven Clemons of the New America Foundation suggested a "citizen's arrest . . . for this duplicitous intel swindler who has undermined America's interests and helped cause thousands of deaths among Iraqis as well as among American, British and other forces."[3]

And that's just for starters. If you Google "Ahmad Chalabi" and "crook," you'll get over 33,000 hits. If you Google his name and the word "fraud," you'll get over 70,000. But the media has steadfastly refused to tell Chalabi's side of the story. Instead, they have taken a series of elaborate CIA smears to the bank.

So before we get any further let me tell you about the other side of Ahmad Chalabi, as well as my fifteen-year relationship with him, so readers can evaluate Chalabi, the CIA, and my own biases as we proceed with this part of my story.

I spent much of the 1980s as a reporter in Iraq, discreetly interviewing Western arms dealers and the chiefs of Iraq's WMD programs. I came away from that experience with a healthy respect for the ability of a seemingly Third World country such as Iraq to take technology from wherever it was available and cobble together deadly new weapons. In the West, our weapons look like highly polished jewels. In Iraq, you could cut your hand open by rubbing it against the rough-edged welds of locally made rockets and missiles. The extended-range SCUDs Saddam Hussein sent crashing into Israel in early 1991 might have looked like flying garbage cans, but they still wrought havoc on Israeli civilian populations, which was precisely their purpose.

During the Gulf War in 1991, I became a vocal critic of the first Bush administration, admonishing it in the *Wall Street Journal* for failing to finish the war by marching on to Baghdad. I also criticized it for failing to punish foreign companies selling weapons production technology to Saddam Hussein.

My 1991 book, *The Death Lobby: How the West Armed Iraq*, detailed the involvement of more than 450 mainly Western firms in helping Iraq to build an indigenous weapons industry capable of producing long-range ballistic missiles, chemical and biological weapons, and nuclear warheads. *The Death Lobby* received extensive coverage in the United States when it was released—in part, I recognize now in hindsight, because it was critical of a Republican president, George H.W. Bush.

The Death Lobby also attracted the attention of Rolf Ekéus, the chief UN arms inspector in Iraq, who called it "our bible" and gave it to team leaders looking for undeclared WMD sites in Iraq; and of Jules Kroll, a former New York prosecutor who invented a whole new industry now known as business intelligence. Kroll had won a multimillion-dollar contract from the government of Kuwait to track down Saddam Hussein's secret fortune, estimated by some sources to be somewhere between $5 billion and $10 billion. And he wanted my help.

I flew to London to meet with Kroll's team of investigators in April 1992, and one of the first people they wanted me to talk with was Ahmad Chalabi. Why? Because outside of Saddam's inner circle, Chalabi knew more about Saddam Hussein's murky financial dealings than anyone else then alive.

I had briefly met Chalabi a few months earlier in Paris at a conference organized by the Rendon Group (yes, with CIA money) that exposed Saddam Hussein's brutal human rights record. We heard firsthand testimony from family members of victims of Saddam's intelligence services; tales of opponents of the regime dipped into vats of nitric acid, who were told with a laugh that if they cooperated they would be tossed in quickly, but if they refused they would be kept alive as long as possible so they could feel the acid eating up their flesh.

For years, Chalabi had been working against Saddam while operating one of the Middle East's largest private financial institutions, Petra Bank. He developed close ties to Jordan's King Hussein, Crown Prince Hassan, and King Fahd of Saudi Arabia, while using his banking credentials to track Saddam's money. Now he was coming out into the open.

"I knew that since 1985, Iraq was in dire financial straights," he told me as we sat together for hours in his tiny Card Tech Services office on Cromwell Road in a somewhat seedy section of southwest London. "I knew the extent of the debt, and the massive cash requirements of Saddam to buy new weaponry," he said. "I was aware that a big credit squeeze on Iraq was coming. I could see large overdrafts in U.S. banks—Irving Trust, Chase—and large politically motivated loans from Arab banks such as UBAF and the Gulf International Bank, GIB. This was the Achilles' heel of Iraq."

Later, when I learned of the fabulous stories told about Chalabi and the hundreds of millions of dollars he allegedly extorted from Petra Bank,

I thought back to this first meeting—and to others subsequently—and wondered why I had never seen the trappings of his supposed "vast" wealth? Where were those Savile Row suits the *New York Times* always mentions whenever it spits out Chalabi's name? Where were the $2,000 Gucci loafers? The gilt bathroom fixtures? The crystal chandeliers? In truth, his tiny office was shabby, sweaty, and busy. As for Chalabi himself, he picked up the thread of his tale in between hurried phone calls in English and Arabic, barking orders, signing papers brought in by an assistant, always affable, never losing his train of thought. From time to time, his eyes twinkled as he recounted some particularly spicy exploit from his double life—as a banker dealing with Saddam's billions and as an opposition spy.

Already in 1985, he told me, he had become aware that Saddam Hussein had turned in a massive way to the Atlanta, Georgia, branch of the Banca Nazionale del Lavorro (BNL), which was borrowing half a billion dollars a day just to keep its Iraq loans afloat. "I helped to expose this and felt very good when BNL was shut down on August 4, 1989," he told me, even though his own Petra Bank had been raided by the Jordanian military at the request of Saddam Hussein just two days earlier. With Jordanian tanks and Iraqi intelligence officers surrounding his offices in Amman, Chalabi was forced to flee Jordan, hiding in the trunk of Crown Prince Hassan's personal car. "The Jordanian military had orders to deliver me to Saddam," he said.

For becoming a target of Saddam Hussein's goon squads, the CIA labeled Chalabi a "con man" and a "convicted felon." In support of that charge, they dragged out a trumped-up 1992 "indictment" of Chalabi, handed down in absentia by a kangaroo court in Jordan at a time the Jordanian prime minister was known to be working hand-in-glove with Iraqi intelligence. Chalabi has always disputed the charges against him, and pointed out that Jordan never filed extradition papers against him with any other country, allowing him to travel freely in the years to come.

But when Jordan's King Abdullah II continued to smear Chalabi in public and in closed-door meetings with President Bush, Chalabi filed a civil suit in U.S. District Court against the Kingdom of Jordan in August 2004 to get the indictment annulled and hundreds of millions of dollars of the bank's assets returned. He alleged that the Jordanian government, the former prime minister, and the former governor of the Central Bank "schemed to falsely claim that Petra Bank . . . was in financial trouble" as part of a conspiracy to have him "kidnapped . . . tortured and killed" by

Iraqi intelligence. In addition, he said that recently discovered information would establish that the Jordanian government and its accomplices "had taken the missing money from Petra Bank and still hold it today, concealed in a disguised bank account." He also alleged that the defendants were conspiring with "certain employees and agents working for the CIA" to spread false information that Chalabi was working on behalf of the government of Iran, and had "attempted to induce the United States itself to bring criminal charges against Chalabi on false information." Those were hefty charges against a sovereign state that Chalabi's lawyer, John Markham, told me were backed up by hard documentary evidence.[4]

The origins of this dispute go back to the mid-1980s, but it is still being played out today. The Jordanians were furious that Chalabi had exposed Jordan's back-door deals with Saddam Hussein, including a scheme to provide falsified end-use certificates to the United States for Iraqi arms purchases during the 1980s. Out of revenge they sought to destroy him, and convinced powerful allies in the CIA and the White House to help. The Jordanian government continued to feed the U.S. media with lies about Chalabi even as the lawsuit crawled through the U.S. judicial system. The case was still pending as this book went to print.

During our first face-to-face meeting in London, Chalabi displayed an authentic insider's knowledge of the secret workings of Saddam's international finances. Details it had taken me months, and sometimes years, to learn about the BNL banking scheme, for example, Chalabi knew like the back of his hand. He said that he believed Saddam invaded Kuwait in August 1990 because he was unable to make payments on his latest arms purchases from France, a tip I was able to confirm later from French defense industry sources. "In March 1990, I gave a paper at a conference at Chatham House in London on the Iraqi debt," he told me, with that distinctive twinkle in his eye. "I said—only partly in jest—that the only way for Saddam to resolve the debt crisis was to invade Kuwait."

Many times over the next fifteen years, I spent several days virtually camped out in Chalabi's London offices, talking to him, to his intelligence chief, Aras Habib, and to his top aides, Francis Brooke, Zaab Sethna, and Entifad Qanbar. When Chalabi obtained new information from defectors the INC managed to spirit out of Iraq, I would fly over from Paris or from Washington to get in-depth briefings and whatever documents he could release. Not once, in all the years we knew each other, did he make a false claim for these defectors. From the start, he made it clear they had only partial knowledge, and that their information was only the starting point for additional investigation that I should perform on my own.* But you'd never know that by reading the attacks on Chalabi that regularly appear in the press.

HIS FATHER'S FARM

To understand the real Ahmad Chalabi and the ongoing war in Iraq, you need to understand the past. You need to understand that Iraq once had a representative government that provided political and personal freedoms to its people. And you need to understand how that experience was burned into Chalabi's soul as a young man.

Chalabi vividly remembers the day in July 1958 when Iraqi army officers, allied to the Baath Party of future dictator Saddam Hussein, stormed his father's farm along the Tigris River north of Baghdad. They were looking for his older brother, who was a cabinet minister in the government of Nuri Said, the last prime minister of a free Iraq.

"One of the officers put a pistol to my mother's head, asking her where she was hiding my brother," Chalabi recalls. "When she refused, I volunteered to go with them in my brother's place. I soon regretted it. I was only thirteen."

That type of spontaneous bravura has marked Chalabi's life ever since. Although his portly figure and Ph.D. in math might make him appear more at home in a corporate boardroom, he showed that same type of extraordinary courage on the battlefields of northern Iraq in the mid-1990s, at times physically separating troops of warring Kurdish factions as he attempted to work out a truce between their leaders. (Since the liberation of Iraq, Chalabi has gone repeatedly, unarmed, into Najaf and other cities where U.S. officials feared to tread, to jawbone warlords and Shiite religious leaders into cooperating with the coalition authorities. Chalabi supporters claim that the CIA has repeatedly tried to assassinate him during these trips, including a near-miss in August 2005, when one of his bodyguards was killed. On November 18, 2006, he survived yet another assassination attempt, when his convoy was attacked on the road from Baghdad

*He expressed the same reservations to the CIA, but apparently they had lost the art of debriefing defectors after Milt Bearden stood down the Directorate of Operations networks fighting the KGB.

to Salahuddin in the north. Although three of Chalabi's aides were killed, he emerged unscathed.)

In Chalabi's Iraq, Saddam Hussein was an aberration, not the inevitable consequence of some mythical incompatibility of Arabs and democracy, as the CIA and the State Department still believe to this day. Freedom was part of Chalabi's genes.

Soon after the 1958 revolution, Chalabi's parents sent him to Britain to finish high school. He went on to MIT, where he met the sons of Shiite Muslim leader Ayatollah Mohsen Hakim, the top religious authority in Iraq. In 1965, he was invited, along with his father, by King Faisal of Saudi Arabia for the pilgrimage to Mecca, where he first met Faisal's younger brother, who later became King Fahd.

When Saddam Hussein engineered a second military coup in 1968, Chalabi was already active in the democratic opposition. In the summer of 1969, right after taking his Ph.D. from the University of Chicago, he flew to Tehran to meet with the shah of Iran's top intelligence advisor, General Nematollah Nassiri, and with Mullah Mustafa Barzani, an opposition leader of the Kurds in northern Iraq. "Nassiri told us he had a secret agent in Baghdad who was going to lead a coup, but it turned out their group had been infiltrated by Saddam," Chalabi said. "The CIA fell into the same trap twenty-five years later."

The coup plotters were hanged in Baghdad's Revolution Square in 1970. But the shah didn't give up. For many years, Iran continued to supply money and arms to Mullah Barzani, whose Kurdish peshmergas fought bloody hit-and-run battles with the Iraqi army. Years later Barzani's son, Massoud, took over his father's group and joined Chalabi's Iraqi National Congress to fight Saddam. It's just one more example of the stunning depth and breadth of Chalabi's connections. And yet the CIA and the State Department persisted in calling him "an exile" with "no roots in Iraq," who was "out of touch" with ordinary Iraqis.

In the early 1990s, when the United States was still providing military protection from Saddam to a Kurdish "safe haven" in northern Iraq, Chalabi convened a meeting there of Iraqi tribal leaders, hoping to win their support in the fight against Saddam. "As we sat down to eat, they gave me a petition with their demands," Chalabi recalled. "I went to the bookshelf, and found an album on Iraqi history that contained an almost identical letter sent to the government in 1934. I pointed out to them that it had been signed by their grandfathers." Chalabi's own grandfather was a member of Parliament at the time, and went on to become a cabinet minister in 1944. "In a way, I told them, we were picking up where our grandfathers left off."

LIBERATED ZONE

After Saddam's forces brutally crushed the spring 1991 uprising, driving more than a million Iraqis into forced exile in neighboring Iran and Turkey, the Bush 41 administration convinced the United Nations to establish a "safe haven" for the Kurds in northern Iraq and a no-fly zone to protect the Shias in the south. Meanwhile, Iraqi opposition groups began to coalesce, and in 1992 formed the INC as a leadership coalition comprising the seven main Iraqi opposition parties. With U.S. backing, the INC twice conducted elections in northern Iraq that the State Department termed "reasonably fair and free," and established a government under Chalabi's leadership.

Problems with the INC coalition began almost immediately. The leaders of two rival Kurdish factions, Massoud Barzani and Jalal Talabani, traveled to Washington in 1993 seeking the appointment of a high-level State Department emissary who could help them overcome age-old clan rivalries and cement their fragile experiment in democracy. (In addition to the power-sharing arrangement, they were squabbling over how to divide lucrative customs tariffs on the borders with Turkey and Iran.)

But the Clinton administration had other fish to fry. As one State Department official who met with the Kurdish leaders told me at the time, "we're not going to hold their hands."

Fighting between the two Kurdish factions began in March 1994, and continued intermittently for more than a year. Chalabi did his best to keep the coalition together, at one point personally standing in front of an armored column sent to capture Barzani at his headquarters in Salahuddin. "You'll have to capture me first," Chalabi told the rival militia leader.

Undersecretary of State Peter Tarnoff and his deputy, David Litt, promised Chalabi the United States would help finance an INC peacekeeping force to stand between the Kurdish militias, but that aid never came. After the summer of 1994, Barzani began receiving arms from Iran, helping him to stave off collapse against his better-armed rival.

WHY THE CIA HATES CHALABI

Through patient negotiations, Chalabi managed to get the two rival Kurdish groups to cease fighting each other, and in early 1995 they began planning the INC's first military operations against Iraqi government forces.

But on March 3, the day before the attack was planned to start, CIA officer Bob Baer rushed to Chalabi's headquarters in Salahuddin with a cable from National Security Advisor Tony Lake.

> "THE ACTION YOU HAVE PLANNED FOR THIS WEEKEND HAS BEEN TOTALLY COMPROMISED. WE BELIEVE THERE IS A HIGH RISK OF FAILURE. ANY DECISION TO PROCEED WILL BE ON YOUR OWN."[5]

"The U.S. had promised air support," Chalabi recalled, when he first told me this story in 1998. "And now Lake is accusing us of trying to embroil the U.S. in a protracted war against Saddam, and told us we were on our own."

Despite the last-minute betrayal by the Clinton White House, the INC and Talabani's forces defeated two Iraqi army divisions in a series of brief encounters to the west of Irbil, with many top Iraqi officers defecting to the INC. "The operation was a stunning success," former CIA officer Warren Marik told me. "I personally interrogated two Iraqi brigade commanders. We felt we had the Iraqi army on the run."

The telex from Tony Lake was only the tip of the iceberg. Back in Washington, intrigues were brewing. Unbeknownst to Chalabi, the CIA had decided to throw its weight behind the *Wifaq*, a group of former Baathists, deserters from Saddam's cause, who claimed to have a significant following within the Iraqi army and Saddam's inner circle.

Known in English as the Iraqi National Accord, or INA, the *Wifaq* promised the Americans they could topple Saddam from within, while placating skittish neighbors such as Turkey and Saudi Arabia who feared the opposition would split the country along ethnic lines, with a Kurdish state in the north and a Shiite Muslim state in the south.

The INA offered a "silver bullet" solution, replacing Saddam with a Sunni-led military junta while maintaining Iraq's central government structure. When the *Wifaq* learned of the INC military plans for early March 1995, it hurriedly dispatched General Adnan Nuri to Washington, where he met with the head of the CIA's Near East Division, Steven Richter. General Nuri told Richter that the *Wifaq*'s chances of pulling off a coup would be ruined if the United States allowed the INC offensive in the north to go forward. He warned the Americans that Chalabi and the INC were trying to suck the United States into a full-blown military confrontation with Saddam. It was this warning that prompted the frantic telex from Tony Lake to Bob Baer and Ahmad Chalabi on the eve of the INC offensive. After their initial success on the battlefield, the INC stood down. Yet *Wifaq*'s promised coup never materialized.

One year later, in March 1996, Chalabi received alarming news from an agent the INC had recruited within Saddam's Special Security Organization. Iraqi intelligence had captured sensitive communications equipment, including jammers and a "burst" radio, from agents working for the INA. The equipment had been supplied by the CIA, and was to have been used to jam Saddam Hussein's ability to communicate with his security forces during yet another *Wifaq* coup under preparation. The "burst" radio was to communicate between the coup plotters in Baghdad and their control officers in Amman, Jordan.

To Chalabi it was clear that Saddam intended to let the plot bubble on so he could round up as many of his enemies as possible, while embarrassing the Americans in the bargain. Chalabi decided to warn the U.S. government, and immediately set out on the long and perilous journey out of northern Iraq.

When he reached London several days later, he called his old friend Richard Perle, a top Pentagon official during the Reagan administration and now a key neo-conservative strategist.

"Richard, I need to see you urgently," he said. "Something terrible is about to happen."

"Can you tell me what this is about?" Perle asked.

"I can't speak over the phone," Chalabi said. "I'm flying to Washington tomorrow. Can you meet me?"

"Of course," Perle said.

Chalabi arrived the following evening and immediately went to see Perle. He laid out what he knew, and the terrible danger awaiting America and its agents. "You've absolutely got to warn them, Richard," he said.

"You're right," Perle said. "Let me see if I can get to Deutch."

The next morning, Perle phoned CIA Director John Deutch, who was a personal friend, and said he had critical information to convey but that it was too sensitive to discuss over the phone. Deutch suggested Perle come to the exclusive Cosmos Club in downtown Washington, D.C., where he was scheduled to give a luncheon speech that day. "Meet me there a half hour ahead of my speech," he said.

In a dark-paneled parlor off the elegant dining room, Perle briefed the CIA director on what Chalabi had told him the night before. The CIA plot against Saddam Hussein had been compromised. Key members of the secret organization had been captured and were now under the control of Iraqi intelligence. The Iraqis were maintaining communications with the CIA team in Amman as if nothing had happened. Deutch needed to understand that whatever they were telling the CIA team on the ground was false.

Deutch understood what Perle was saying, but he was preoccupied. "I'm going to send Tenet to talk to you," he said. "You should give him all the details."

George Tenet, an affable former Democratic staffer on Capitol Hill, had just come over to CIA as the number two man, after running intelligence programs for Clinton at the National Security Council. He was a political operator, not an intelligence officer. His main skill was a keen sense of how Washington worked. Tenet came to Perle's tiny office at the American Enterprise Institute in Washington later that afternoon. In the meantime, Perle managed to get more details from Chalabi of exactly how the coup plot had been compromised. Tenet listened carefully for well over an hour, as Perle told him just how bad it was.

We've got to get Chalabi to brief John and our top guys who are handling this whole thing, Tenet said. He needs to lay this out in person.

Tenet knew that John Deutch had no intention of giving Chalabi a fair hearing, but he wasn't going to tell Perle that. The offer to meet the Iraqi face-to-face was intended to keep Perle from going off the reservation. The last thing Deutch wanted was to have Richard Perle and his American Enterprise Institute friends pissing all over the Agency in Congress or in the media. Tenet made clear that because they would be discussing operational details Perle was not cleared for, Chalabi should come alone.

"I fully understand," Perle said.

To make the meeting more discreet, Deutch summoned Chalabi to his hideaway office in the Executive Office Building next to the White House. Deutch brought Steve Richter, the head of Middle East Operations, as well as "Ron," the operations officer assigned to work with Chalabi and the INC. When Chalabi began to go into details of the INA coup plot, Richter stopped him and asked "Ron" to leave the room. He wasn't cleared for the INA operation—nor was Chalabi, for that matter.

Richter was furious. He had never liked Chalabi or his operation in northern Iraq, and now here he was blundering into Richter's highly classified operation to overthrow Saddam Hussein like a mad dog with rabies.

The meeting did not go well. "They scoffed at the information, and said everything was under control," Chalabi told me later. Richter's reaction was indicative of what the CIA had become: rather than thanking Chalabi for giving him a timely warning about an operation gone sour, he chose to shoot the messenger.

The Clinton White House and the CIA favored a coup in Iraq because they saw it as another cost-free solution, like the UN sanctions. If it failed, America could pretend not to have been involved. If it succeeded, the United States would recognize the new government in a heartbeat. Run by Baathist military officers, the new government would show no more tolerance toward domestic dissent than Saddam Hussein had shown. But it would cooperate with the United States to find and destroy Saddam's hidden WMDs, which was all that counted. "The CIA always liked toadies," Perle commented when he related this story to me later.

The decision to go with the generals was a political one, not based on U.S. strategic interests. It was all about Bill Clinton's 1996 reelection campaign. Deutch and Tenet had recently come back from a White House meeting with Clinton, who was eager to find a way to insulate himself from Republican attacks that he was weak on national security. *Bring me the head of Saddam*, Clinton told Deutch. *I want to hold up his f—king head at the convention*, he shouted, meaning the Democratic National Convention that would renominate him for the office of president of the United States.

To CIA officer Warren Marik, who was on the ground in northern Iraq when the White House pulled the plug on the INC later that year, the story was sadly familiar. "Clinton's National Security Council got this idea of an officer on a white horse capable of pulling off a coup," he told me.

Three months later, the ax fell, just as Chalabi had predicted. Saddam arrested the three sons of General Muhammad Abdullah Shahwani, a recently retired senior officer, who were serving as couriers between the coup plotters in Baghdad and the *Wifaq* and their CIA control officers in Amman. Just to rub salt in the wound, the Iraqis used the CIA encrypted "burst" radio to send Koranic taunts to the father in Amman, mocking him for having trusted "infidels."*

Buoyed by his success in besting the Americans, Saddam executed the three sons and many others involved in the plot, then turned to the INC-controlled enclave in the north, which still was considered a

---

*Shahwani, a Turkoman, would return after the liberation of Iraq as the new head of Iraqi intelligence.

UN-protected safe haven. Forging a secret alliance with Kurdish Democratic Party leader Massoud Barzani, Saddam moved his troops and tanks northward on August 30, 1996, in direct violation of UN Security Council resolutions. Barzani personally escorted the commander of Iraq's 10th Army division into Irbil, where INC headquarters was located. When asked to justify his actions two years later, Barzani called his pact with Saddam a matter of survival. "Regimes have always been killing our people," he told me. "We are still here because we have defended our people as best we could."

Chalabi's intelligence chief, Aras Karim Habib, was speaking to Chalabi on a satellite telephone as the Iraqi troops advanced on a private residence they had leased as a safe house from a widow in Irbil. "I was broadcasting live reports of the Iraqi advance when all of a sudden an Iraqi patrol burst into the house," he told me. "I hid behind the kitchen door, a loaded pistol in my hand, ready to kill them and then myself." An Iraqi soldier peered into the kitchen, but was called back at the last minute by his commanding officer. *It's just a widow's house*, he said. *Let her be.*

The next day Aras and other INC officials fled in a convoy to the Turkish border, but had to turn back because Iraqi troops had chased the UN monitors out and were now in control of the area. That same day, the Iraqis took ninety-six captured INC fighters to the small town of Qushtapa, a dozen miles south of Irbil. As the villagers gathered round, the Iraqis lined their prisoners up against a wall and executed them in cold blood. It was a gruesome message to Barzani, who was Saddam's ally of the day. Some fourteen years earlier, Saddam's half brothers had rounded up several thousand male members of the Barzani clan in the same town and carted them away in military trucks. They have never been seen since. Qushtapa was full of memories for Barzani. This was Saddam reveling in his Godfather role.

The fall of Irbil was a bitter defeat for Chalabi and the INC.

But for John Deutch and George Tenet and Steve Richter at the CIA, allowing Saddam to smash the free Iraq enclave led by the INC was all about payback. Chalabi had shown the CIA to be like the Emperor with No Clothes. He had exposed their failed operation—not to the public, but to the CIA director and his deputy in person—and they would never forgive him for it. "The CIA hated Ahmad Chalabi because he was always coming out with information they didn't have and that is later confirmed," a former Bush administration official told me.

From that point on, the CIA adopted an "ABC" policy: Anybody-But-Chalabi.

A few years later, during a chance encounter in a Fairfax restaurant in December 1998, Tenet admitted to Chalabi and an aide that he was behind the smears then making the rounds in the press. (These were essentially the same stories one still hears today: Chalabi was a crook, a convicted felon, an agent of Iran. The most absurd and most persistent rumor of all was that Chalabi was responsible for compromising the failed 1996 coup.)

Let's bury the hatchet, Tenet said. *We've got work to do. We need your guys on the ground.*

Tenet's immediate problem was highly embarrassing. The United States and Britain had just completed a four-day campaign of air strikes against Iraqi WMD sites, known as "Desert Fox," but because Saddam had kicked the UN arms inspectors out, the United States had no one on the ground to judge the effectiveness of the bombing. After the Gulf War, the United States realized that many of the targets they had bombed in Iraq had been plywood fakes—fake tanks, fake missile launchers, fake radar units. Chalabi had been showing reporters, including me, a detailed bomb-damage assessment pulled together by his men in Baghdad and on the ground at bombed-out weapons sites in northern Iraq. George Tenet needed Chalabi and his men to rescue the wounded reputation of his boss, Bill Clinton, who was being accused of a "wag the dog" operation in Iraq to deflect public attention from his impending impeachment trial.

Like so many things with George Tenet, his offer to "bury the hatchet" was all talk. He took Chalabi's bomb-damage assessment and distributed it around Washington as the CIA's own. Now his boss could turn to the media with a straight face and say that his December 1998 bombing campaign in Iraq had been both necessary and effective, not just a publicity stunt.

Despite Chalabi's continued willingness to cooperate, the CIA spread slime about him for years to come. As left-wing blogger Steven Clemons would write in 2005, "the word from many I know in the CIA is that Chalabi was the person who tipped off Saddam Hussein before a [1996] coup attempt against the Iraqi leader. The CIA had cut Chalabi out of the action—because of misinformation that Chalabi had allegedly passed on and irresponsible management of sensitive information. For that, Chalabi tipped off Hussein."[6] It was a scurrilous lie, of course, but it went unchallenged, because few people knew the real story of what actually happened, which I have related here for the first time.

The CIA also continued to support groups such as the *Wifaq* that claimed they could pull off a palace coup against Saddam, despite repeated failures, while undermining Chalabi's INC, despite its record of success in northern Iraq.

The battle royal over Iraq went far beyond the reputation or the actions of one man. It involved two different concepts of America's role in the world, two different value systems, two different views of the Middle East. One believed in stability; the other believed in freedom. One propped up Arab dictators who subjugated their people, as long as they maintained America's access to oil; the other believed that Arabs, like Americans, aspired to live in freedom, and that long-term stability could only result from relationships of mutual interest entered into by free and sovereign peoples. For many years—well before 9/11 or the invasion of Iraq—Ahmad Chalabi was the touchstsone of this battle.

Former national security advisor Brent Scowcroft typified the foreign policy establishment and its rejection of the Bush agenda. So did his former boss, the president's father. In a bitter exchange with Condoleezza Rice in 2003, Scowcroft berated her and the president for promoting freedom.

"Condi, you're not going to democratize Iraq," he said. Rice replied that he was "just stuck in the old days," and said that the president was determined to change fifty years of U.S. policy that tolerated an autocratic Middle East. "But we've had fifty years of peace," Scowcroft moaned.[7]

Fifty years of peace, imagine that. During that time, we've had five major Arab-Israeli wars, two Palestinian intifadas, the introduction of the suicide bomber as a preferred weapon of terrorist regimes, the 1979 revolution in Iran, the seizure of the U.S. embassy in Tehran, a 444-day hostage crisis, the U.S. embassy bombing in Beirut in 1983, the murder of 241 U.S. Marines later that year, the taking of U.S. hostages in Lebanon in the 1980s, Saddam's invasion of Kuwait in August 1990, the Gulf War, the first World Trade Center bombing in 1993, the bombing of two U.S. embassies in Africa in 1998, the USS *Cole*, and 9/11—and the list is by no means exhaustive.

But for the shadow warriors, these were but skirmishes—a small price to pay, apparently, for maintaining the status quo of big business, big interests, and Arab oil.

CHAPTER TWO

THE SPOOKS' WAR

Two and a half months after the 9/11 attacks, a tiny CIA unit commanded by decorated operations officer Gary Berntsen had tracked Osama bin Laden and the top al Qaeda leadership to a cave complex at Tora Bora, in the White Mountains on Afghanistan's rugged eastern border with Pakistan. Although Pakistani president Pervez Musharraf had pledged to deploy Pakistan ground troops to prevent bin Laden from escaping, they were slow to arrive.

Camped at the base of the forbidding snow-covered mountain range with an Afghan tribal force led by a Pashtun warlord named Nuruddin, Berntsen realized that at the rate they were advancing, bin Laden was going to escape. "We need U.S. soldiers on the ground! We need them to do the fighting! We need them to block a possible al Qaeda escape into Pakistan!" Berntsen thought frantically as he watched the al Qaeda men slip away. But when he called for reinforcements to CENTCOM commander General Tommy Franks, who was in charge of the Afghan campaign, he got a resounding no. Franks was willing to send B-52s with 15,000 pound "daisy cutter" bombs to pound the al Qaeda caves, but he refused to send troops. The 1,200 troops he had on the ground by that point in Kandahar already had their hands full. "Let the tribals do it," he told Berntsen.[1]

Berntsen's account of the battle of Tora Bora is devastating. The opportunity to get bin Laden and the top al Qaeda leadership when they were all assembled in one place would never come again. Or so it appeared.

Franks continued to play the good soldier, taking blame for that failure upon himself. That was not the case with Berntsen's superiors at CIA.

They leaked the whole story to the *Washington Post* on April 17, 2002, well before Berntsen came home to publish his eyewitness account.

"We had a good piece of SIGINT," or signals intelligence, an unnamed official told the *Post*.[2] The leakers told the story of bin Laden addressing an apology by radio to his troops for having led them into a trap, before splitting them into two groups and leading half of them to safety to the north. Some reports said a group of them then fled to Iran.[3]

The disclosure was clearly aimed at embarrassing President Bush and Defense Secretary Rumsfeld, who were constantly being asked what had happened to bin Laden. At a Pentagon briefing the day the leak appeared, Rumsfeld repeated what Franks's spokesman, Rear Admiral Craig Quigley, had told the *Post*. "We have never seen anything that was convincing to us at all that Osama bin Laden was present at any stage of Tora Bora—before, during or after," Quigley said. "I know you've got voices in the intelligence community that are taking a different view, but I just wanted you to know our view as well. Truth is hard to come by in Afghanistan."

That was too much for Deputy CIA Director John McLaughlin, who had seen the bin Laden intercept and read all of Gary Berntsen's angry reports from the field. "We knew they'd scatter to Pakistan, or Iran, or Somalia, or Sudan, or Syria, or Yemen. They might go to Indonesia," he said. "Once they dispersed, that was really the start of the 'war on terror' as we know it. A war that we were just then learning how to fight—and the one we're still fighting."[4]

The theme McLaughlin sounded would become a familiar routine from top CIA officials over the next two and a half years. Don't blame us. Blame Bush.

THE FIRST "SECRET" PRISONER

One of the first terrorists to scatter was Ibn al-Sheikh al-Libi, a Libyan-born al Qaeda member who reportedly ran the al-Khaldan training camp, one of bin Laden's largest facilities in Afghanistan. Captured in Pakistan on November 11, 2001, with help from the CIA, he was interrogated initially at the Kandahar airport. Sometime in December, it appears, he was flown out for safekeeping to the USS *Bataan*, an amphibious assault ship where other detainees were then being held.[5]

The capture of al-Libi posed a unique problem for the United States government. Unlike John Walker Lindh and the Taliban fighters captured on the battlefield in Afghanistan, al-Libi had no affiliation with a state. By no stretch of the imagination was he covered by the Geneva Conventions, as government lawyers argued that the Taliban fighters should be.

Newsweek later reported that FBI officials on the ground in Afghanistan had tried to retain control over al-Libi, and clashed with the CIA team in Afghanistan. The FBI wanted to interrogate al-Libi in a controlled fashion, alternating inducements and gentle pressure, and didn't like what they were hearing about the CIA's threats to turn him over to the Egyptian government for torture. The CIA officer who was handling al-Libi appealed to his boss back in Washington, counterterrorism chief Cofer Black, who took the case to Tenet directly. Tenet, in turn, appealed to the White House, which ruled in his favor. Al-Libi's mouth was duct-taped shut, and he was taken to the airport to be sent to Cairo. "So we lost that fight," a former FBI official said.[6]

Thus began the saga of the CIA's "secret prisons." When details of the prisons began to leak in May 2004, including their whereabouts and the top-secret proprietary companies used by the CIA to shield the ownership of aircraft used to transport the al Qaeda detainees, former Agency operatives protested that they had been forced to carry out illegal operations against their will.

"This is not what we do," one twenty-five-year veteran of the clandestine service told me. "The vast majority of our guys are opposed to torture. It's not who we are. And it's bad business."

In one published account, McLaughlin and his partisans simply reinvented history and blamed Rumsfeld for forcing CIA to set up the secret prisons. Tenet had gone to Rumsfeld in the autumn of 2001 asking DoD to help with the growing number of al Qaeda captives, they claimed, but Rumsfeld was unmoved and said that DoD was "not getting into the prison business." Tenet's team greeted the news of Rumsfeld's purported refusal with "groans of disbelief. 'Once again, we're the default—left holding the bag,' said one. 'This is not what we're good at,' said another."[7]

At best, these are selective, self-serving recollections. Remember that the Defense Department opened a high-security prison at Guantánamo Bay, Cuba, in January 2002, that took in hundreds of high-value al Qaeda prisoners who had been captured on the battlefield. If the CIA truly felt so bad about holding prisoners in secret, they could have shipped their detainees to Gitmo and been done with it.

At worst, they demonstrate a willingness on the part of top CIA officials to betray the secrets of their own agency and their own government at a time when they believed it would do maximum political damage to the president of the United States.

A "PRIVATE WORD" WITH TOMMY FRANKS

Senator Bob Graham (D-FL) was eager to take up that CIA offer to blame Bush.

Thanks to the defection of Vermont's Republican U.S. senator Jim Jeffords on May 24, 2001, the Democrats now had a one-vote majority in the Senate (50 Democrats, 49 Republicans, and 1 Independent—Jeffords). On June 6, the day Jeffords's party-switch became effective, Graham became chairman of the Senate Select intelligence committee. In that position, he was one of two U.S. senators briefed on every sensitive counterterrorism operation being planned or carried out by the U.S. government.

He was briefed on the battle of Tora Bora as it took place, and was well aware that high-value prisoners were being taken to Camp X-Ray in Guantánamo. He was also briefed on the intelligence they provided to their interrogators about the 9/11 plot.

On February 19, 2002, Graham met with General Franks at MacDill Air Force Base in Tampa, Florida, for a briefing on the war in Afghanistan. MacDill was the home of the U.S. Central Command, CENTCOM, which had responsibility for all military operations in the Middle East and South Asia.

Graham says he had never met General Franks before, and he was surprised when the Army four-star asked him to join him for a "private word" in his office after they had gone through the PowerPoint briefing on Afghanistan in the amphitheater.

"Military and intelligence personnel are being redeployed to prepare for an action in Iraq," Franks confided to Graham. Even the CIA's Predator drones, which were operated by the Air Force, were being redeployed to the Iraq theater, he said. "What we are doing is a manhunt," Franks complained, referring to the continuing Afghan operations. "We're better at being a meat ax than finding a needle in a haystack. That's not our mission, and that's not what we are trained or prepared to do."

Graham said he was "stunned" to hear this from General Franks, but remember the date. By this time, the Taliban had been smashed, al Qaeda had been scattered to the winds, and a pro-American government led by Hamid Karzai was taking shape in Kabul. Of course it was time to redeploy. But that's not how armchair general Bob Graham saw it.

"The more I thought about it, the more furious I became. Victory against al Qaeda was in our grasp, and we were releasing the pressure," he wrote.[8]

As Graham told me later, he believed "the Bush administration had a mind-set that it wanted to go to war with Saddam Hussein without regard to the relative severity of his threat."

Graham said if he had been in charge (and he ran for president in 2004), he would have focused on "several evils in the Middle East that were more threatening to U.S. interests than Iraq."

Among his potential targets? "We skipped over Iran, which was much further along in its development of WMD than Iraq has turned out to be. We skipped over Hezbollah, which is probably going to be the shock forces of Iran in its support of the Shiites. We skipped over Hamas, which now has taken over the Palestinian government. All those were clearly greater threats to the U.S. than Iraq, but we decided to not only spend our resources on Iraq but pay the price on ignoring the greater threats, and that price is now being paid."

So imagine this: With Senator Graham as president, the United States would have left Saddam Hussein in power but would have waged war against Iran, Syria, Lebanon, and the Palestinian Authority, because they all were run by terrorists or harbored terrorist groups.

And he thinks we angered the rest of the world by taking out Saddam Hussein?

"TOMORROW IS ZERO HOUR"

Congressional Democrats have always excelled at conducting hard-hitting political investigations, a skill their GOP colleagues seem to lack. The Democrats know how to use all the tools available to congressional committees—even when they are in the minority—to subpoena documents and testimony from government officials, corporate honchos, and whomever they decide to paint as Villain-of-the-Day.

Their bloodlust for impeachable acts committed by the Reagan White House during the Iran-Contra scandal outlasted Reagan's presidency by four years! Similarly, an investigation launched early in 2001 into potential "secret agreements" between Vice President Dick Cheney and oil industry executives at White House energy task force meetings during the early months of the administration simmers along to this day. Allegations that Cheney still works for Halliburton (he was CEO of the oil field services company until 2000) and profits personally from their contracts in Iraq can be found all over the Internet, fueled by documents obtained by Democratic congressional investigators and Judicial Watch, and by the heavy breathing of elected Democrats such as Senator Carl Levin and Representative Henry Waxman.* By comparison, Republican investigations into Whitewater were halfhearted and inconclusive, while the impeachment hearings of Bill Clinton were an utter failure and totally missed the real scandal of the Clinton years, which was the sell-off of military secrets and technology to Communist China.

By going after Cheney and the inner workings of the White House before 9/11, the Democrats were casting about for potential scandals that could throw the new administration off-balance. As time went on, and these efforts became more organized and involved the compromise of national security secrets, they became a conscious effort to undermine and subvert the elected government of the United States, carried out by a legion of shadow warriors.

A glimpse of things to come occurred within hours of a closed-door hearing on June 19, 2002, that was part of the first 9/11 inquiry, conducted jointly by the Senate and the House intelligence committees.

That morning, the Joint Inquiry heard Lt. Gen. Michael V. Hayden, then director of the National Security Agency, testify about al Qaeda messages the NSA had intercepted on September 10, 2001, but had not translated until the day after the September 11 attacks.

"The match begins tomorrow," one of the messages read. "Tomorrow is zero hour," went another.

The messages were dramatic, and the Democrats jumped all over them as evidence that the Bush team had missed a vital warning of the impending attacks. Just hours after General Hayden completed his closed-door testimony, his classified remarks—including the text of the NSA intercepts—were broadcast on CNN by reporter David Ensor.

Senator Bob Graham, who was the Senate chair of the Joint Inquiry, acknowledged the leak, which he told me made him "livid." But he blamed it inexplicably on a White House effort to "sabotage" the 9/11 investigation, an allegation he admitted made him look like "a conspiracy theorist."

CNN's David Ensor credited their Capitol Hill producer, Dana Bash,

*The Halliburton attacks intensified during the war in Iraq, and have rarely been challenged. Few Americans realize, for instance, that more than a hundred Halliburton employees have been killed in Iraq, or that the company has actually lost money through its reconstruction contracts in Iraq.

with the scoop. What he didn't report was that Bash was married to a top Democratic staff lawyer working for House intelligence committee cochair Jane Harman (D-CA).

"As committee counsel, Bash's husband would have had access to all the sensitive intelligence," a former committee staffer told me. "He didn't have to leak classified information to his wife—just give her enough information so she could ask sensitive questions that would embarrass Bush, and there couldn't legally be any questions." That's not necessarily what happened in this instance, but it was how the shadow warriors operated.

The leaked NSA intercepts were all over the *Washington Post* and *USA Today* the next morning, and provided ammunition to Democrats who accused the Bush administration of having missed the warning signs of the September 11 attacks. But if they were a White House effort to stymie the Joint Inquiry, they failed. Democrats and Republicans asked the FBI to investigate the source of the leak, and continued their inquiry into the 9/11 attacks as if nothing had happened.

In the end, no indictments were ever announced. Indeed, if a member of Congress was the source of the leak—and remember, CNN cited congressional sources for the information—then no punishable crime had been committed. (The only punishment for members of Congress who divulge classified information is for their party leadership to remove them from the intelligence committee.)

INTELLIGENCE MATTERS

After 9/11, classified intelligence information increasingly became a part of the American political discourse.

How many people had ever heard of the President's Daily Brief (PDB) before the 9/11 Commission hearings? And yet today it has become an article of faith that President Bush ignored an explicit warning, contained in the August 6, 2001, PDB, that Osama bin Ladin was planning to use civilian airliners as weapons and crash them into major U.S. buildings. (When the White House finally declassified the PDB in its entirety, it turned out to have contained no such warning—only the misleading title "Bin Laden Determined to Strike in U.S.")[9]

Then–national security advisor Condoleezza Rice accurately described the PDB article when she told the 9/11 Commission that it contained mostly "old intelligence." Even its opening line showed it was a backgrounder, not a sizzling new intelligence item. "Clandestine, foreign government, and media reports indicate bin Ladin since 1997 has wanted to conduct terrorist attacks in the U.S.," it read. Bush's reaction was that it contained no "actionable intelligence," nothing that even *suggested* an imminent attack. "It said Osama bin Ladin had designs on America. Well, I knew that," Bush said. "What I wanted to know was, is there anything specifically going to take place in America that we needed to react to."[10]

Intelligence mattered, as Senator Bob Graham liked to say. And increasingly, Democrats showed themselves willing to use it—and to leak it, when it fit their political purposes, to attack the president of the United States.

Three months after the NSA leaks, Senator Carl Levin—who also sat on the Senate intelligence committee and the Joint Inquiry—blasted the White House for not declassifying the identity of the operational planner of the 9/11 attacks, Khaled Sheikh Mohammed, whom he said had been known to the intelligence community "since 1995." Levin vowed to use the Joint Senate-House Inquiry into the 9/11 attacks, on which he sat, to officially reveal the terrorist's name and his role in the 9/11 plot—a move that could have compromised efforts then under way by the CIA and Pakistani intelligence to capture Mohammed in Pakistan. Levin argued that Mohammed's name and role were already known to the press, so it made no sense for them to remain classified.[11]

In the end, Levin backed off from his threat to give high-profile exposure to Mohammed, and the CIA nabbed him together with other top al Qaeda operatives at a safe house in Rawalpindi, Pakistan, in January 2003. The U.S. government detailed Mohammed's role in the 9/11 plot almost immediately upon his capture, making a mockery of Levin's contention of a political cover-up.

But can anyone think for an instant that Khaled Sheikh Mohammed would have stayed put in Pakistan if Senator Levin had revealed in public that the CIA was hot on his trail, as had been his intention? The fact that Levin could conceive of doing so clearly shows that he placed partisan political gain well before the national interest.

CHAPTER THREE

SECRET OFFICE IN THE BASEMENT

Deputy Undersecretary of Defense William J. Luti was a Navy captain with an attitude. With a Ph.D. in International Relations from the Fletcher School at Tufts, a stiff white mustache, and boundless energy, he had gone from driving an amphibious assault ship to driving a desk without ever slowing down. A protégé of former House speaker Newt Gingrich, Luti snagged a job at the White House working for Vice President Dick Cheney at the beginning of the Bush administration, then became the Pentagon's point man for postwar planning in Iraq. With a biting wit and encyclopedic knowledge of the Middle East, Luti was not just brilliant: he was a dedicated neo-con, a man who believed in the freedom agenda.

This was not just any war that he was helping to plan: it was a just war, a war that embodied the best of America, a war for freedom against a ruthless tyrant that had the potential of transforming the Middle East.

Luti's immediate boss, Undersecretary of Defense Douglas Feith, asked him to set up an "in-house policy shop" to develop postwar plans, which they called the Office of Special Plans.

Wary of congressional subpoenas from the likes of Levin and the new Democratic cochair of the Senate intelligence committee, Senator John D. "Jay" Rockefeller IV (D-WV), Luti kept his operation low-key. The last thing they wanted to do was alert Senate Democrats or the media that they were planning a war. Those were his standing orders from his bosses, Doug Feith and Deputy Defense Secretary Paul Wolfowitz.

"We are a *policy* shop, a consumer of intelligence, not a producer of intelligence," Luti would repeat to anyone who visited his office. Almost immediately, however, word leaked out that a secret "intelligence unit" had been set up in the Pentagon by neo-conservative ideologues, whose goal was to "cook" intelligence proving that Saddam Hussein was involved in the 9/11 attacks. The shadow warriors had struck again. Reporters and congressional staff started firing off questions about a "secret office in the basement," down by the Pentagon ramp.

There was a tiny intelligence analysis unit—"two guys and a computer," Luti called it—that Feith had tasked with taking an independent look at existing intelligence products on Saddam Hussein's ties to international terrorist groups, including al Qaeda. Officially known as the Policy Counter-Terrorism Evaluation Group (P-CTEG), it was separate from Luti's war-planning operation, although it reported through him.

Dana Priest of the *Washington Post* phoned Luti one day in the fall of 2002 as those rumors of a secret intelligence unit reached their peak. "You're down by the ramp, right?" Luti almost burst out laughing. She actually believed in the loony-tunes story being pushed by the Lyndon LaRouche types about a secret office in the basement. "You're confusing two guys and a computer with the DoD policy shop," he told her.

It was too late by the time Luti realized that he had a mole in his office, a shadow warrior.

One of the first people detailed to work under him in the newly created Office of Special Plans was Air Force Lt. Col. Karen Kwiatkowski. Just one year from retirement, Kwiatkowski was an Africa specialist, and not eager for her new assignment. "At this point," she wrote later in *The American Conservative*, "I didn't know what a neo-con was or that they had already swarmed over the Pentagon, populating various hives of policy and planning like African hybrids, with the same kind of sting reflex."[1]

Kwiatkowski began leaking information about the Office of Special Plans to *Executive Intelligence Review*, the publication of conspiracy theorist and aspiring presidential candidate Lyndon LaRouche. At one website associated with the LaRouche organization, her posts were signed "Deep Throat Returns." Laced with irony and heavy breathing, they painted a picture from the inside of an administration hell-bent on waging a war for oil, on behalf of a silent Israeli partner ("Greater Zion," as she called it). It was just the type of conspiracy thinking that flourished around LaRouche, who called the Bush administration neo-cons "Children of Satan" and claimed they aimed to "unleash an attempted step-wise fascist takeover of the USA from within."[2]

Michael Rubin, now a fellow at the American Enterprise Institute, worked in Luti's office at the time, and had this to say about Kwiatkowski:

> Kwiatkowski did serve in the Pentagon prior to the war, as did I, as did approximately 23,000 others. But Kwiatkowski was not involved in Iraq policy. Her reminiscences fall more into the realm of fiction than fact. I worked in the Office of Special Plans (OSP), charged with some aspects of the Iraq portfolio. My job was that of any desk officer: Writing talking points for my superiors, analyzing reports, burying myself in details, and drafting replies to frequent letters from Congressmen John Dingell and Dennis Kucinich. I was a participant or a fly-on-the-wall at many post-war planning meetings and accompanying video teleconferences. One person I never met was Kwiatkowski. This should not be surprising. Kwiatkowski was an Africa specialist who was the point woman for issues relating to Morocco. Just as I never attended meetings relating to Western Sahara, Kwiatkowski was not involved in Iraq policy sessions.[3]

The rumors about his office made Luti think of a virus jumping from the animal kingdom to humankind. First it appeared on the LaRouche websites, then it made the jump to the mainstream press, thanks to people like Seymour Hersh, who "didn't bother to check their facts," he complained.

Luti took me down to see the "secret office in the basement" at the start of the Iraq War. As his staff grew to sixteen, he had been given overflow space in a former storage area off a first-floor corridor. (Although technically it was the Pentagon "basement," most of the cubicles had windows—I checked.) Oh yes, and that James Bond–esque title: Office of Special Plans? In retrospect, Luti admitted that was probably a mistake. Luti and Feith were worried when they set up the new unit in August 2002 that if they called it the Postwar Iraq Policy Office it would undercut the president's efforts to find a diplomatic solution to the standoff with Saddam Hussein.

Over the next two years, Luti and his office would be accused of many things, most of them fanciful. Senators Rockefeller and Levin alleged they were secretly working on behalf of Israel. As source, they cited an article in the left-wing weekly *The Nation*, which asserted that Luti and his team were "coordinating their terrorism assessments with a rump unit established last year in the office of Prime Minister Ariel Sharon of Israel." Luti dismissed it as "Church committee stuff," a congressional witch hunt.

Given the efforts by Senate Democrats to handcuff every member of his office and frog-march them to the brig, it's a wonder Luti and his team got any war planning done at all.

But they did.

For one thing, Luti's analysts were tracking extensive evidence that Saddam's family and senior members of his regime were planning to leave the country as soon as U.S. forces attacked. "We see money being transferred out of the country. We see exit routes being planned. The extreme pressure we are bringing to bear is beginning to have a noticeable effect throughout the ranks of the senior leadership," they told me in February 2003, well before the first shot had been fired. This led them to forecast (accurately) that the "major combat operations" phase of the war would be short.

Working with CENTCOM planners, Luti's office pulled together a detailed strategic framework for how the United States would help Iraqis to run postwar Iraq, which they called "Phase IV." In December 2002, the initial concepts were turned over to an operational planning team based in Qatar, Joint Task Force IV (JTF-IV). The planning team "included representatives from the Departments of Defense, State, and Treasury; USAID; CIA; and, from the White House, staff of the National Security Council and the Office of Management and Budget," OMB director Joshua B. Bolten told the Senate Foreign Relations committee later. It also included representatives from the United Kingdom, Canada, and Australia, as members of the coalition. (So much for the notion that George W. Bush "went it alone.")

The detailed blueprint for the postwar period became known as OPLAN Iraqi Reconstruction. Nearly 300 pages long, it was activated at the end of April 2003 by USCENTCOM OPORD 10-03. Postwar reconstruction was split up into seven broad areas: coalition building, security, rule of law, civil administration, infrastructure, governance, and humanitarian assistance. Each area had its own set of detailed plans.

The security piece, for example, including plans to rebuild the Iraqi police, the border patrol, and the army, as well as the creation of a facilities protective service and a separate Iraqi civil defense corps. Recruitment goals were set, and budgets allocated.[4]

Although the plans were not classified, and top Pentagon officials briefed reporters in detail, the elite media continued to blast out their pre-agreed message. Bush had launched the wrong war in the wrong place, with *no plan* for after the shooting stopped. No one seemed to care that those accusations were untrue, starting with senior editors in major newsrooms. USCENTCOM OPORD 10-03 was rarely mentioned, directly or by allusion.

ON THE FLOOR OF THE METROPOLE

Up in his fourteenth-floor suite of London's Metropole hotel, National Security Council envoy Zalmay Khalilzad was holding court. It was mid-December 2002, and he had come off an earlier success in Afghanistan, where he had helped fledgling Afghan groups to conduct a *loya jirga*—or political conference—that ultimately led to the creation of an Afghan unity government to replace the Taliban. President Bush had now asked him to do the same thing with the Iraqi opposition. As the president's personal envoy he had tremendous authority, and he knew it.

Advising him were the CIA's Ben Miller, who had been detailed to the National Security Council to work Iraq, and the State Department's Tom Warrick, who had been conducting think-tank sessions for several months with Iraqi intellectuals for the State Department's Future of Iraq Project. Both opposed the Bush administration's plans to overthrow Saddam and replace him with a free Iraqi government. Both hated Ahmad Chalabi and the Iraqi National Congress with a passion.

Skilled at operating in the shadows, they advised Khalilzad to use the London meetings to stall for time. Chalabi and his supporters in Congress were clamoring for the United States to recognize a government in exile. String it out. Be noncommittal, Miller advised Khalilzad. Refer back to your principals, say they want to keep their options open.

The truth was, a government in exile was the last thing the CIA and the State Department wanted to see emerge from London. If that happens, my guys are going home, Miller said. (It was an open secret by that time that the CIA had paramilitary teams inside northern Iraq, where they were training groups of Kurds in guerrilla warfare, even if they had no one in Baghdad itself.)

Khalilzad reveled in all the trappings of power. He was surrounded by State Department Diplomatic Security officers, immediately visible because of the telltale earpiece communications devices they wore. One by one, he worked his way through the roster of the 330-odd delegates to the Iraqi leadership conference, summoning around 80 of them individually for private interviews in his suite.

He called them "listening sessions." But several of the Iraqis who responded to his summons felt differently. "He was auditioning us," several of them told me shortly after the conference ended. "Khalilzad and Ben Miller were looking for candidates who could lead a coup against Saddam."

They were also creating jealousies, playing favorites, meeting with delegates who had never seen a U.S. official before, while shunning known political leaders for whom Washington had become a second home in hopes of discrediting them. It was the CIA's ongoing search for a *deus ex machina*, an easy out, the man on the white horse who would defeat Saddam.

Downstairs, a very different scene was unfolding inside the conference hall. It was noisy, chaotic, with delegates huddling in small groups to caucus as others delivered impassioned speeches about the future of their country, free at last from the dictator, Saddam Hussein.

Making his way from group to group without any of Zal Khalilzad's security men was the Pentagon's Bill Luti. "Here's the number-three guy at the Pentagon, working the floor of the conference hall like it's the Republican convention," one of Chalabi's deputies told me.*

Chalabi was in the midst of a massive recruiting drive. The first of some 5,000 Free Iraqi Forces, culled from among INC supporters in the United States, Canada, Britain, and New Zealand, were then undergoing basic military training in Texas. More were scheduled to receive training as military scouts in Hungary by special arrangement with the Pentagon. Luti applauded their efforts, and looked forward to a "Liberation of Paris" moment in Baghdad, when Chalabi's troops would lead U.S. armored columns into the Iraqi capital to be greeted as liberators.

Such at least was the original plan when Congress first passed the Iraq Liberation Act (ILA) in 1998. "When we started all this, we were thinking in terms of the Reagan doctrine," a senior White House official told me. "Stand up a liberation army, use local forces, not a 150,000-man U.S. invasion force."

With U.S. air cover, those local Iraqi forces would liberate pockets of territory in the north and in the south of the country and establish a free Iraqi government run by Chalabi's INC with seats reserved for leaders from the inside who were prepared to come forward as the "rolling liberation" of their country began.

But the State Department and the CIA had a different idea. They

---

*While Luti was certainly not "number three" at the Pentagon, he was number three when it came to planning for postwar Iraq. The other two were Deputy Secretary Paul Wolfowitz, and Undersecretary Doug Feith.

didn't want a liberation. Democratic government was too messy, too hard to control, and it terrified America's friends in the Arab world, especially in Jordan, Egypt, and Saudi Arabia. And besides, Chalabi was considered too "unreliable."

As neo-conservative strategist Richard Perle told me at the time, both State and CIA were dead set against supporting individuals and groups they could not control, "and Ahmad Chalabi is a pretty independent-minded fellow. If he wasn't, he couldn't lay claims to leadership—and the State Department can't stand that, and the CIA even less."

Perle was an outspoken supporter of Chalabi and his Iraqi National Congress, the fractious alliance that included every major Iraqi opposition party then in existence, from the ethnic Kurdish groups who had been running their safe haven in northern Iraq since 1992 to the Iranian-backed Islamic Dawa Party. Also joining the INC big tent were former Baathists of Iyad Allawi's Iraqi National Accord, the *Wifaq* whose failed coup Chalabi had exposed in the spring of 1996.

"The U.S. interest is in removing Saddam's regime, not just Saddam himself," said Perle. "One of the problems with a coup is that it entails by definition a group of people who are close to Saddam. If their motive for acting against Saddam is to assume the reins and carry out the same policies, then a coup would be a very bad thing," he told me just after that December 2002 London conference ended.

The *New York Sun* singled out the CIA's Ben Miller for particular criticism. "Mr. Miller invested years in planning failed military plots and coups in Iraq," the *Sun* wrote in a lead editorial on January 22, 2003. "There's no indication he has ever been committed to the democratic Iraqi opposition."

They were right.

"Whose side are they on?" a frustrated Chalabi aide complained, when it became obvious that Khalilzad and Miller would oppose the declaration of a provisional government during the London conference, as the Iraqis were clamoring to do. "You'd think they were trying to help Saddam."

The delegates in London elected a sixty-five-member "follow-on committee," composed of leading members of all the various opposition groups, from communists, Islamists, and Kurds to Republicans, former Baathists, and even monarchists. The leadership committee included representatives of virtually all of Iraq's leading tribes as well—the al-Dulaimi, the Shamar, the al-Jubouri, the al-Jumaily, the al-Bazzaz, the al-Shami, and the al-Shalaan.

Not only was it hard to imagine a more representative group of

Iraqis, *the names on that list have formed the backbone of every Iraqi government since liberation.* These were the future leaders of a free and democratic Iraq. Period. But the CIA and the Department of State were intent on not recognizing their legitimacy.

"It's not that State and CIA were evil," another former administration official directly involved in these deliberations told me. "It's just that their whole bureaucracy was opposed to regime change and they did everything possible to throw wrenches and banana peels in front of it—and, once we got rid of Saddam, to make sure it would never happen again, for example, in Syria or Iran."

Worried that the London conference had bolstered Chalabi and his supporters, the State Department set its grant officers to work. Under the direction of David Pearce, the director of the Northern Gulf Affairs Office, State desk officers again whittled away at the INC grants. Money pledged to the INC to operate Liberty TV to broadcast into Iraq was withdrawn, forcing them off the air. The INC newspaper was shut down. Training programs were cut. And the recruitment of Iraqis to serve as liaison officers to U.S. forces on the ground was scaled back, all at a time when the White House was preparing the American people and U.S. troops for war.

"This is going to cost American lives," a State Department auditor who reviewed the INC programs and bemoaned the cuts told me at the time.

When Liberty TV went off the air—because the State Department reneged on a $25,000 funding commitment at the last minute—the Pentagon replaced it with an expensive program known as "Commando Solo" to broadcast Pentagon news briefings and other information in Arabic into Iraq. "Commando Solo" was a modified Boeing 737 aircraft, equipped with an onboard transmitter. To reach its audience, it had to fly across Iraqi territory, where it was vulnerable to Iraqi antiaircraft fire.

Two months before the London conference the State Department's Office of Inspector General had already issued a scathing report accusing Pierce and other Northern Gulf Affairs officers of negligence, gross incompetence, and mismanagement of the INC programs. Any problems the INC had encountered resulted from the fact that it "has operated without a grant agreement since June 1, 2002, and lacks funding to meet financial obligations incurred since that date," the OIG report concluded.

For the entire second half of 2002, for example, Senator Patrick Leahy (D-VT) had placed a "hold" on all funding to the INC, in response to a quiet request from the State Department. Near Eastern Affairs bureau officer Yael Lempert told the inspector general that her bosses "would appreciate any assistance the OIG could provide with NEA's desire to shut down the INC," according to minutes of an internal meeting on May 17, 2002.[5] To INC supporters elsewhere in the administration, who were powerless to walk back a Senate hold, the goal was clear: "State and CIA are hoping to divide the leadership of the INC, and to pit the different groups against one another in competition for U.S. funds," one supporter said.

Because they couldn't control Ahmad Chalabi and the INC, the State Department, the CIA, and their backers in Congress tried to destroy them through bureaucratic subterfuge, congressional maneuver, and negative leaks to the press.

It was shadow warfare of the deadliest sort. As we will see in the next chapter, it ultimately would cost thousands of American lives.

STATE WINS, AMERICA LOSES

The White House was furious with press accounts that revealed the State Department's underhanded dealings with Chalabi and the INC. Shortly after the London conference, President Bush called Secretary of State Colin Powell to the White House to chew him out.

When Powell returned to the State Department, he was "not a happy camper," a source close to him said. His anger was felt all the way down through the ranks to the desk officer in charge of the INC grants. But Powell's tirade—delivered by his deputy, Richard Armitage—had just the opposite effect from that intended.

Instead of removing the bureaucratic roadblocks in the way of funding the INC, the shadow warriors reinforced them.

Grants officer Anna Mary Portz flew from Washington to London on January 23, 2003. The INC leadership was told by the State Department that she was coming to hammer out new funding arrangements, in response to the inspector general's findings and on orders "from the boss." Instead, she met with INC leaders for all of thirty minutes, to inform them that the State Department had decided to pull the plug on the INC military recruitment program. "They don't know what they want, and they won't admit to having made mistakes," a stunned INC official told me shortly after that meeting, referring to Portz and the State Department.

The United States was just weeks away from war in Iraq, and now

State Department underlings were tossing aside the strategy carefully developed over a period of years and endorsed by their political bosses to put an Iraqi face on the liberation.

I can reveal here that the State Department intervened with the government of Turkey before the war, to get them to refuse transit visas for 1,000 recruits for the Free Iraqi Forces who needed to travel from northern Iraq through Turkey to the United States, where they were to receive advanced military training. The INC had recruited another 3,000 soldiers among Iraqi refugees living in Iran, but their candidacy was rejected by the CIA, who convinced the CENTCOM commander, General Tommy Franks, that they were Iranian spies. (The CIA accusation that Chalabi was somehow working behind our backs with Iran would surface repeatedly, always at a critical moment, and always without substance.)

"We wanted the ILA [Iraq Liberation Act]," a senior administration official told me later. "An Iraqi force, an Iraqi face. Instead, we gave State the responsibility for implementing the ILA, and allowed them to sabotage it. We never even overturned [Clinton-era defense secretary] Bill Cohen's order that prohibited using ILA funds for lethal force training. It was a joke."

Worse than a joke, the failure by the Bush White House to resolve the policy debate raging within the bureaucracy before going to war was a strategic error of historic proportions.

"The problem was not too much Chalabi. It was too little Chalabi." This was a refrain I heard repeatedly at the White House, the Pentagon, and in Congress. Cheney himself told confidants at one point that his greatest regret in Iraq was not Abu Ghraib, but failing to move more aggressively with the Iraqi forces, way before liberation, to implement the ILA.

The White House knew the shadow warriors were sabotaging their plans and yet did nothing to stop it.

Timidity? Incompetence? Gross mismanagement? Call it what you will. The results were foreseeable.

CHAPTER FOUR

PREPARING FOR WAR

Shahriar Ahy was an Iranian-American considered by many who had worked with him as an absolute genius. A banker by trade, Ahy went on to become a political strategist with top-drawer connections. During the 1980s, he was close to CIA Director William Casey, and tried to transform Reza Pahlavi, the playboy son of the former shah of Iran, into a gutsy resistance leader. When that failed, Ahy masterminded a grassroots "referendum" movement inside Iran that attracted international attention as a peaceful means of deposing Iran's ruling clerics. No one doubted Ahy's political genius; unfortunately for his place in history, he was a Karl Rove without a George W. Bush.

Ahy had better success in business. After the fall of the Berlin Wall, he launched an investment fund specializing in buying up assets in the newly independent Baltic states. In the mid-1990s, he brokered the Saudi takeover of United Press International, and went on to become a top advisor to the chairman of the Saudi-backed Middle East Broadcasting Centre, MBC, which operated out of Dubai's Media City.

Like anyone with connections to top Republicans in Washington, D.C., Ahy had suspected for some time after September 11 that the United States was preparing to depose Saddam Hussein. But it wasn't until a rubber-chicken dinner on December 6, 2002, to honor former president George H.W. Bush, that Ahy realized U.S. military operations were imminent.

"I was talking with former CIA director Jim Schlesinger when it suddenly dawned on me: we were going in," Ahy recalled. So he turned to an aide standing next to Lieutenant General Richard B. Myers, chairman of the Joint Chiefs of Staff, and asked if anyone had a copy of the video the

United States planned to broadcast on Iraqi television during the first hour after toppling Saddam Hussein.

Myers overheard his question, and seemed curious. "The what?" his aide asked.

"The video," Ahy said, slightly louder this time. He explained that he worked with a group of Arab broadcasters, many of whom were Iraqi, who would be willing to help the American effort. "If somebody can get me a copy of what you're planning to broadcast when you reach Baghdad, I'll bring in the best experts from the region and see if we can improve it for you," he offered.

But Myers drew a blank. Nobody had ever spoken to U.S. military leaders about any video.

Ahy explained. "The most critical thing is that first hour of broadcasting on state television. Every time there's been a coup in the Middle East since the beginning of TV, the coup plotters have always had their video ready to go. Saddam did it in 1979. Qaddafi did it in Libya. Nasser did it in Egypt. The whole idea is to paint a picture for the people right off the bat that what you're doing is the best thing that ever happened to them—and especially, to make sure *they* understand that you have total control over the situation."

Myers clearly was intrigued. He nodded to his aide, who turned to Ahy and asked him if he could do a paper for them explaining the concept.

Good Lord, Ahy thought. A paper. They are not ready for anything.

He never did the paper, and no one ever asked him about it again. But the more he learned over the next few months, the more he realized that the United States had completely failed to plan the media war. And without it, he knew they were bound to fail.

STAGING IN THE NORTH

After New Year's, the INC leadership moved back into northern Iraq, where they had been based on and off for the past eleven years. The plan going forward was to hold yet another leadership conference, this time in the northern Iraqi city of Salahuddin in early February 2003. The INC wanted to transform the Follow-on committee from London into a provisional government, ready to fly to Baghdad as soon as Saddam's regime collapsed. Even David Phillips, a State Department consultant who was unofficially liaising with the Iraqis and opposed their plans, acknowledged the unanimity of view among the Iraqis. "Iraqis agreed on one critical point: None would tolerate a U.S. military occupation or the appointment of a U.S. viceroy to govern Iraq," he wrote later of this period. "Jalal Talabani expressed the sentiments of all Iraqi opposition figures: 'If we don't accept an Iraqi general, how are we going to accept a U.S. general?' "[1]

But Khalilzad and the CIA's Ben Miller did their best to stall, still hoping they could entice a group of officers close to Saddam into removing him from the scene through a coup.

I talked to INC officials almost daily during this period, trying to get into northern Iraq to cover the opposition conference and then to join the INC troops as they marched south to Baghdad for the liberation.

The early sticking point, I was told, was the Turks. They had sealed the border into northern Iraq—especially to reporters—at the request of the U.S. State Department. State didn't want journalists to see the extent of CIA paramilitary training operations in the north, or to learn that they were actively funneling money to Sunni tribal leaders in hopes of promoting a coup.

Another key concern at this point was Saddam Hussein's chemical and biological weapons—that's right, the WMDs that reporters and congressional Democrats now insist that "everyone" knew did not exist. (And it wasn't Chalabi and the INC that provided fake intelligence of recent production of chemical weapons stockpiles; it was the CIA's own navel-gazing analysts, who created it out of whole cloth, as a July 9, 2004, report by the Senate Select intelligence committee would discover.)

The Pentagon was so worried that Saddam would use WMD against U.S. forces that battlefield commanders required U.S. troops to wear cumbersome chemical and biological weapons protection gear up until they reached the outskirts of Baghdad. They also fretted that Saddam would use chemical weapons against Iraqi opposition forces then staging in the north, and issued public warnings to Iraqi commanders by dropping leaflets and by broadcasting warnings in Arabic on all available radio frequencies. "Our message is very clear," a senior Pentagon planner told me at the time. "If they use WMD against their own population, they will be hunted down and tried as war criminals—most likely, by the U.S. military, right on the spot."

The Kurds were desperate with worry. They had already been victims of Saddam's chemical weapons in 1988, when the Kurdish village of Halabja was annihilated in a chemical weapons attack by Iraqi troops. They had no civil defenses, or even chemical weapons detection gear, and feared massive civilian casualties if Saddam attacked.

"We're most concerned by the possible covert deployment of chemical warfare or biological warfare agents," said Mike Amitay, the executive director of the Washington-based Kurdish Institute, a nonsectarian and nonpolitical group that promoted Kurdish interests. "Things like poisoning wells, or sending in human disease carriers. For example, all the milled flour sold in the North goes through government warehouses in Baghdad. There are absolutely no tests or quality control on food."

For CENTCOM commander Tommy Franks, the WMD threat figured at the top of the daily 3x5 war-planning cards he drew up to list the main battlefield and strategic challenges. "One of our main concerns was that the Iraqis might try to preempt our attack by launching WMD strikes against our massing troops," he wrote in his memoir. King Abdullah II of Jordan warned Franks in Amman on January 23, 2003, that "the Iraqis are hiding chemical and biological weapons." Egyptian president Hosni Mubarak reinforced those claims. "General Franks, you must be very, very careful. We have spoken with Saddam Hussein. He is a madman. He has WMD—biologicals, actually—and he will use them on your troops." On the very day that the president gave the order to go to war, CENTCOM intelligence told Franks that Iraqi forces were "training to operate in a weapons of mass destruction environment," and that they had intercepted communications among Iraqi units that "indicated their concern with 'chemicals and toxins.' *Since the Iraqis know we won't use WMD*, I thought, *their preparations must mean they will.* I had no doubt WMD would be used against our forces in the days ahead."

Once fighting began, Franks tells of numerous occasions when he received operational intelligence reports of Iraqi preparations to launch poison gas attacks. On April 1, 2003, American and British forces discovered hundreds of chemical and biological protection suits and masks in Iraqi barracks in Al Samawah and in Basra. "This wasn't some forgotten load of surplus equipment from the Gulf War twelve years ago. This was brand new gear, state of the art, never used," Franks wrote. After presenting these reports, Franks's chief intelligence officer told the CENTCOM commander, "I don't think it's going to be long before the troops get chem'd."[2]

On February 4, 2003, Chalabi told me by satellite phone from northern Iraq that the Turks were telling him they had no problem in allowing me and other journalists who were waiting on the Turkish side of the border to cross into northern Iraq with the official U.S. government delegation. The only sticking point was that no one could get a straight answer from Khalilzad as to when he intended to move into the north.

The reason was simple: His intention was to stall indefinitely. Instead of moving forward with another Iraqi opposition conference that they knew would only ratify the results from London, Khalilzad and Ben Miller convoked the leaders of the two major Kurdish parties to Ankara to read them the riot act.

If the Kurds continued with Chalabi and went forward with this provisional government idea, the Turks were going to invade northern Iraq, Khalilzad warned. They would use the pretext of preventing a humanitarian disaster to take over the entire region.

If there was one thing the Iraqi Kurds feared almost as much as Saddam Hussein, it was the Turks. When Jalal Talabani and Massoud Barzani returned to northern Iraq and spread the word of Zal's latest warning, they were visibly frightened.

Kanan Makiya, one of the sixty-five-member Follow-on committee and a close advisor to Chalabi, blasted Khalilzad and Ben Miller in an op-ed that appeared in London's *Observer* on February 16, 2003.

Makiya's voice had extraordinary weight. He was not just any Iraqi intellectual. In the 1980s, writing under a pseudonym for fear of Saddam's thugs, he had penned an extraordinary insider's account of life under Saddam that changed the way people thought about Iraq. His book's title, *Republic of Fear*, soon became the term of art used to describe Saddam's regime.

The two Americans had unveiled a plan during the Ankara meetings that set aside ten years of work with the Iraqi opposition and instead proposed to appoint "an unknown number of Iraqi quislings palatable to the Arab countries of the Gulf and Saudi Arabia" to advise a U.S. military government in Iraq, Makiya revealed.

> "The plan is the brainchild of the would-be coup-makers of the CIA and their allies in the Department of State. . . . Its driving force is appeasement of the existing bankrupt Arab order, and ultimately the retention under a different guise of the repressive institutions of the Baath and the army."

The biggest mistake the State Department and the CIA always made was to support the "anti-imperialists" and the "anti-Zionists" of the Arab world, rather than the partisans of "core human values of self-determination and individual liberty," Makiya believed. He came within a hair's breadth of calling the plan by its name: sabotage.

"Is the President who so graciously invited me to his Oval Office only a few weeks ago to discuss democracy, about to have his wishes *subverted* by advisors who owe their careers to those mistakes?"[3] (Author's emphasis.)

The State Department and the CIA had just changed the entire post-war strategy, without so much as informing the White House or the Pentagon. It amounted to a secret coup. But with all eyes on Saddam Hussein, no one besides Makiya, Chalabi, and the *Wall Street Journal* editorial board seemed to notice.

From Ankara, in mid-February Khalilzad and Miller flew to Dubai, where they met the man they were hoping would be the cornerstone of their new plan: former Iraqi foreign minister Adnan Pachachi. Now in his eighties, Pachachi claimed to have close ties to "dissident Baathists" inside Iraq and to Sunni tribal leaders. Pachachi personified everything that Makiya and the INC abhorred. He was close to the governments of Saudi Arabia, Jordan, and Egypt, longtime friends of Saddam, who saw him as a bulwark against the aspirations of Iraq's majority Shiite population. He also was rabidly anti-Israeli and often anti-American. "He's an embarrassment," a top INC official told me via satellite phone when he learned that Khalilzad and Miller were going to meet Pachachi in Dubai. "He's a former Baathist who lives like a millionaire in the UAE. He thinks the whole issue is Palestine."

"He's been out of the game for years," a top advisor to Kurdish leader Jalal Talabani told me. "Nobody supports Pachachi. I don't know why he's being brought in."

The Americans convinced Pachachi to write a scathing op-ed that appeared in the *Financial Times* on March 3, 2003. It rejected the efforts to pull together a "government in exile," because it "ignores the aspirations of massive anti-Ba'athist forces inside the country." He went on to cite "reliable surveys" of Iraqi public opinion—in a country that had never allowed a public opinion poll—that indicated "strong antipathy" to any government "parachuted in from abroad." Instead, he advocated a form of direct U.S. military rule, with Iraqis in an advisory role—precisely the plan that Khalilzad and the CIA's Ben Miller were now promoting.[4]

To force the hand of the Americans, Chalabi and leaders of the two main Kurdish parties went off to Tehran, to coordinate their uprising against Saddam with the Iranians.

It was a typical piece of Chalabi bravura. He was not America's man; he had other options.

By the end of February, Khalilzad finally realized he had lost his power play and agreed to allow the Salahuddin conference to proceed. One hundred fifty journalists were waiting by this point on the Turkish side of the border, trying to get into northern Iraq. To dampen expectations that the meeting would give birth to a government-in-waiting, the United States asked the Turks to keep the border sealed. They obliged.*

AIRLIFT TO THE SOUTH

General Franks hated the idea of using the Free Iraqi Forces. He was a war planner, not some kind of polyglot kindergarten teacher. How could he be certain that these ragtag Arabs, who professed loyalty to Chalabi and his Iraqi National Congress and could hardly clean a rifle, weren't totally infiltrated by Saddam? After all, they spoke Iraqi!

Franks made it clear that he wanted no part of the Free Iraqi Forces (FIF), and that contrary to the plans announced by Pentagon politicians, such as Deputy Secretary Paul Wolfowitz, he wasn't going to be riding shotgun to the liberation of Baghdad with some friggin' WOG in the driver's seat!

Franks had not set out to undo a key administration policy. On the contrary: he had agreed, against his better military judgment, to dramatically scale back the size of his expeditionary force, and was even prepared to make do without the 4th Infantry Division, which the Turks never allowed to land and transit their territory. In his original war plans, leaked

---

*There was an additional, unrelated reason why the United States wanted to keep the Turkish border sealed and free of journalists. The FBI, working with a U.S. Army officer who had agreed to play along, had staged an elaborate deception operation codenamed "April Fool," which General Tommy Franks describes on pages 434–36 of his autobiography. The idea was to stage the "sale" of an outdated CENTCOM battle plan, stamped "Top Secret/Polo Step," to a senior Iraqi intelligence officer, sources directly involved in April Fool told me. Those plans called for a massive U.S. attack from the north through Turkey, using the 4th Infantry Division, then blocked off the coast of Turkey by Turkey's Islamist government. The FBI-led deception aimed at convincing Saddam that the 4th Infantry still planned to open a second front, and that Turkey's objections to U.S. troops transiting its territory were disinformation planted by the Americans. The plan worked. As Franks himself noted, Saddam kept thirteen divisions deployed to the north of Baghdad fully expecting a U.S. attack from that direction, even though his generals were pleading for reinforcements to repel the ongoing U.S. attack from the south. General Franks was never told of the FBI involvement in Operation April Fool, my sources said.

purposefully to the Iraqis, the 4th ID was to form the pincer movement against Baghdad from the north.

He could live without the 4th ID. He was a good soldier. He just wasn't *insane.* And it was insanity to bring possible Saddam agents to his side of the front lines, where they served absolutely no military purpose. None.

But as U.S. troops began approaching Baghdad and realized they had no Arabic speakers who could serve as a liaison with local security forces and with the Arabic-speaking population, Franks began to change his tune. His deputy, Lieutenant General John Abizaid—an Arabic speaker himself, whose parents were Lebanese immigrants—started screaming that they needed the FIF as scouts to help U.S. units enter Iraqi towns and cities.

Based on Abizaid's recommendation, CENTCOM airlifted 700 of Chalabi's troops from Irbil in the north to an abandoned Iraqi air base in Nasiriyah in the South during the first week of April 2003.

Chalabi's daughter, Tamara—the only woman in the group—dubbed their accommodations "Camp Desolation." The bombed-out barracks had no windows or roofs or any of the amenities Saddam's troops had once enjoyed. There was nowhere they could escape the 100-degree heat or dust-clogged winds. But they were exhilarated.

Although they weren't allowed to take an active role in the fighting, the INC said they would do whatever Franks wanted them to do. For the most part, they served as liaison between U.S. forces and local tribal leaders, handing out humanitarian supplies and protecting U.S. military supply lines.

"We'll go wherever General Franks orders us to go," Chalabi aide Zaab Sethna told me by satellite phone from Nassiriyah. "The tribal leaders are happy to see Iraqis serving with U.S. troops," he added.

Back in Washington, the vice chairman of the Joint Chiefs of Staff, U.S. Marine general Peter Pace, had nothing but praise for the FIF troops. "These are Iraqi citizens who want to fight for a free Iraq, who will become basically the core of the new Iraqi army once Iraq is free," he said on ABC's *This Week.*[5]

If only it had been true.

Behind the scenes, the CIA's Ben Miller was working hard on Franks and on his deputy, General David D. McKiernan, who was in charge of all allied ground forces in the Middle East. "Ben Miller whispered in McKiernan's ear and turned him against the FIF," a senior Pentagon official involved in the war planning told me. Without them, there was no Iraqi face on the liberation, and no core on which to form the new Iraqi army. It was another victory for the shadow warriors and a devastating loss for America.

CHAPTER FIVE

THE NIGER CAPER

The Bush administration's enemies stepped up their attacks on U.S. policy even as coalition troops were staging to march toward Baghdad.

International Atomic Energy Agency chief Mohamed ElBaradei joined the assault, flying across the Atlantic from Vienna specially to deliver testimony at the UN Security Council on March 7, 2003. It was a moment in the spotlight he intended to relish. His agency, the UN's "nuclear watchdog," was going to take a bite out of the britches of George W. Bush. He might not prevent the United States from toppling Saddam, but he would make the effort more painful.

This is the same Mohamed ElBaradei who stunned fellow UN inspectors in the spring of 1991, just after Saddam's defeat in the Gulf War, by telling them he was sure that Iraq had no clandestine nuclear weapons program and was hiding nothing from them.

I know this for a fact, he said, after his inspection team had emerged from a frustrating encounter with the Iraqis. They have sworn this to me as brother Arabs. They would not lie to me! he insisted.

If ElBaradei had realized one of the inspectors had a portable tape recorder and was taping his words as they traveled in the UN bus back to their Baghdad hotel, he might have been more careful about what he said. As it was, his willingness to be conned by his "brother Arabs" became legendary among the inspectors and among U.S. officials who were hoping the brand-new UN inspection process could be tweaked into something that could become a model to use in other hard-case countries, such as Iran or North Korea.

Like Hans Blix, his former boss at the IAEA who was now the overall UN arms inspector in Iraq, ElBaradei was not a nuclear scientist but an international lawyer by training. For sixteen years he worked as an Egyptian diplomat, then "graduated" in 1980 to become an international bureaucrat. He moved to Vienna in 1984 to work for the IAEA, one of the cushiest of all UN agencies.

Like Blix, too, ElBaradei always appeared eager to find an excuse for the proliferators. After all, they almost always came from Third World countries, which looked at the United States, with its vast arsenal of nuclear weapons, as the enemy. Of course they wanted to have nuclear weapons! He believed that the real goal of the IAEA, the agency he now headed, ought to be to convince the Americans to reduce their arsenal, end their nuclear hegemony, and allow Third World countries equal access to nuclear technology.

Saddam Hussein didn't present a clear and present danger to the United States—or to anyone else, ElBaradei believed. If the world was facing a danger, it was from the attitude of people like George W. Bush, who preferred action to negotiations.

UN VERSUS BUSH

ElBaradei knew that most of his listeners—not just within the Security Council chamber but also on international television—looked up to his agency as the ultimate authority on all things nuclear. They were endowed with tremendous prestige, because their inspectors were the only ones on the ground who actually had physical access to Saddam's nuclear facilities.

He also knew that his analysis of Saddam Hussein's nuclear intentions was based *almost solely* on what those inspectors reported, whereas the U.S. intelligence community's assessment of Iraq's WMD programs, released in part in October 2002, used all the data at ElBaradei's disposal *plus* a huge amount of other information, including NSA intercepts of Iraqi military communications, defector reports, and satellite imagery the United States was not willing to share with the IAEA.

In reality, ElBaradei was just presenting a point of view, an opinion. But he saw no reason to dwell on that. His goal was to cast doubt on the claims presented to the Council just one month earlier by Secretary of State Colin Powell, that Saddam Hussein had resumed his WMD programs.

Powell had boiled it down to just three items that he argued provided fresh confirmation that Saddam Hussein "remains determined to acquire nuclear weapons."

The first involved "repeated covert attempts to acquire high-specification aluminum tubes from eleven different countries." Powell was well aware that some analysts doubted that the tubes were intended to be used as uranium-enrichment centrifuges. The skeptics were more inclined to accept Saddam's cover story that these expensive, high-strength tubes made of a corrosion-proof alloy were being imported to make 81mm artillery rockets. As "an old Army trooper," Powell said, he found it odd that the tubes were "manufactured to a tolerance that far exceeds U.S. requirements for comparable rockets. Maybe Iraqis just manufacture their conventional weapons to a higher standard than we do, but I don't think so." Even the skeptics agreed that the aluminum tubes *could* be used to make centrifuges, he added.

Also troubling were the negotiations in 1999 and 2000 with firms in Romania, India, Russia, and Slovenia to purchase a plant to produce special magnets, similar to those used in uranium gas centrifuges.

The third disturbing item was an Iraqi effort to buy machines used to balance gas centrifuge rotors—the six-foot-high tubes that must be "tuned" so they can spin at speeds up to 1,000 revolutions per second. Any imperfection and the centrifuge will spin off its axis and crash—with the impact of a 2,000-pound bomb. If by chance the rotor is loaded with nuclear material, a centrifuge crash can be catastrophic.

In all the confusion and hype of the past few years, most people forget just how cautious was the U.S. case that Saddam was continuing to pursue nuclear weapons work. Powell concluded that while people would continue to debate the issue, "there is no doubt in my mind, these illicit procurement efforts show that Saddam Hussein is very much focused on putting in place the key missing piece from his nuclear weapons program, the ability to produce fissile material."[1]

But to ElBaradei, Powell's briefing was just intelligence, based on supersecret stuff whose sources the United States would never reveal, whereas his update to the Council was based on *information.*

The UN nuclear chief began his presentation by demonstrating the breadth and extent of his database. Since Saddam was forced to reopen his weapons plants to UN inspections three months earlier, the IAEA had conducted 218 nuclear inspections at 141 sites, "including 21 that have not been inspected before," ElBaradei said. Agency inspectors had deployed a mobile radiation detector across 2,000 kilometers of Iraq, visiting

75 facilities, including military garrisons and camps, truck parks, and residential areas, not just declared weapons plants, looking for signs of undeclared nuclear activity.

Agency inspectors had also begun to conduct interviews with Iraqi nuclear scientists, although progress there was more modest. The Iraqis had turned over "a considerable volume of documentation" on issues of particular concern, including the aluminum tubes, the attempts to procure magnets, and Iraq's "reported attempt" to import uranium from Africa, he said.

That last item caught Powell's attention. He knew exactly where ElBaradei was going. The alleged import of uranium from Niger was one of the items the CIA had briefed him on in February when he was prepping to address the UN. Thankfully, his briefer at the Agency—Deputy Director John McLaughlin—told him "there were doubts about the Niger report," so he cut it from his presentation.[2] ElBaradei was trying to sandbag him, just as French foreign minister Dominique de Villepin had done in January.*

ElBaradei went on to minimize U.S. concerns over the aluminum tubes, while virtually dismissing the whole issue of the centrifuge magnets and the balancing machines as too minor to merit serious attention. At any rate, they were technical issues. And Mohamed ElBaradei was content to leave technical issues to the specialists. He wanted to get into the politics—the one area supposed to be off-limits to the IAEA.

The IAEA chief was well aware of the controversy brewing over the alleged purchase by Saddam of uranium yellowcake from the central African republic of Niger. An impoverished former French colony, Niger had two large uranium mines, both managed by the French, and was actively seeking new clients. The U.S. ambassador to the United Nations, John Negroponte, first mentioned the Iraqi attempt on December 19, 2002. President Bush referred to it in his January 28, 2003, State of the Union speech, carefully basing himself on British intelligence reports.

But ElBaradei knew better.

In his determination to slow the American war machine, ElBaradei had secretly diverted resources from the task of investigating WMD sites in

*I wrote about de Villepin's lies to Powell in *The French Betrayal of America* (New York: Crown Forum, 2004; pp. 12–16). Villepin led Powell to believe France would endorse military action against Iraq, but then turned around on January 20, 2003, and sandbagged him in public, declaring that France would "never" agree to a UN Security Council resolution endorsing the use of force.

Iraq to pursue a case he believed could become a political embarrassment for the U.S. president. Today, he was ready to drop the bombshell.

The whole Niger story was a sham, he said. For starters, Iraq had provided a "comprehensive explanation of its relations with Niger," and described to IAEA satisfaction the visit by an Iraqi official to Niger in February 1999. (ElBaradei declined to mention that the Iraqi official in question, Wissam al-Zahawie, was a well-known figure in Iraq's nuclear weapons establishment and had been Iraq's representative to the IAEA in the late 1980s.[3] Minor detail.)

The Niger story was based on documents that described an agreement between Niger and Iraq for the sale of 500 tons of uranium, allegedly concluded in July 2000. IAEA investigators had acquired copies of these documents and, with the help of "outside experts," had determined that they were forgeries.

"[T]here is no indication that Iraq has attempted to import uranium since 1990," ElBaradei concluded.[4]

There it was. The United States had been duped by "forged documents," and the entire case against Saddam Hussein was a hoax.

When it was Colin Powell's turn to respond to ElBaradei's presentation, the U.S. secretary of state recalled the UN agency's less-than-sterling track record. "As we all know," he said, "in 1991, the IAEA was just days away from determining that Iraq did not have a nuclear program. We soon found out otherwise. IAEA is now reaching a similar conclusion, but we have to be very cautious."

But Powell knew the damage was done. What he didn't know was just how hard ElBaradei had worked and would keep on working to counter the U.S. effort to oust Saddam.

The next day, ElBaradei met with *New York Times* reporter Felicity Barringer to reinforce his message. He revealed that the IAEA had hired outside forensic experts, who "found anomalies in the signatures, the letterhead and the format" of the Niger documents, which made it clear they were forgeries.

Asked to speculate who might have had an interest in creating such forgeries, ElBaradei said there were "a lot of people who would be delighted to malign Iraq. It could range from Iraqi dissidents to all sorts of other sources," he said.

Malign Iraq: Saddam himself couldn't have put it better.

The *Times* was so pleased with ElBaradei's story, they ran it on the front page of the Sunday edition.[5] What ElBaradei didn't tell the *New York*

Times—or anyone else, for that matter—was that his "investigation" of the forged Niger documents had been helped along by the State Department, by the CIA, and by U.S. senator Carl Levin, the Democrats' top gun on the Senate Select intelligence committee.

AN INSIDE JOB

Tipped off that the CIA recently had acquired actual copies of the Niger documents and that they were probably forgeries, ElBaradei had a top deputy, a former French nuclear weapons designer, Jacques Baute, request copies through State Department channels on January 6, 2003.

On January 13, 2003, an analyst with the State Department's Bureau of Intelligence and Research (INR) sent an e-mail to several colleagues outlining why he thought "the uranium purchase agreement probably is a hoax." He indicated that one of the documents purporting to be an agreement for a joint military campaign by Iraq *and* Iran was so ridiculous that it was "clearly a forgery."

But those analysts never shared their doubts with Powell or the White House. In an address to the World Economic Forum in Davos, Switzerland, on January 26, 2003, Powell asked rhetorically, "Why is Iraq still trying to procure uranium and the special equipment to transform it into material for nuclear weapons?" His own State Department analysts were now sandbagging him.

Unbeknownst to Powell or the White House, Senator Levin was hovering in the wings, just waiting for the president to fall into the trap. Through his intelligence committee staff, Levin kept in regular contact with "dissenters" at INR and at CIA, who kept him apprised of what they were learning about the Niger forgeries and how they had been handled within the intelligence community. Levin knew this was the potential weak point in the administration's case against Iraq, and he prepared to exploit it to the hilt.

The morning after President Bush included a reference to Iraq's attempts to purchase uranium in his State of the Union speech on January 28, Levin shot off a letter to the CIA asking them to detail "what the U.S. intelligence community knows about Saddam Hussein seeking significant quantities of uranium from Africa."

Levin has since made a cottage industry out of the president's "sixteen words" referring to the Niger uranium deal, and used them as the pretext for a four-year investigation by the Senate Select intelligence committee of the Bush administration's use of prewar intelligence.[6]

As Tenet notes in his book, "Later some would allege that this handful of words was critical to the decision that led the nation to war. Contemporaneous evidence doesn't support that, but just try convincing people of that today."[7]

The real question is not whether the administration "lied" about the prewar intelligence. The Robb-Silberman Commission on the Intelligence Capabilities of the United States Regarding Weapons of Mass Destruction, which delivered a 610-page report on the subject in March 2005, stated categorically that the CIA continued to believe in the authenticity of the Niger documents when Bush made the speech, and that "no one in the Intelligence Community had asked that the line [the famous sixteen words] be removed." The CIA continued to claim that it never actually *looked* at the documents until after the scandal broke, because they had other sources for the conclusion that Saddam Hussein was seeking significant quantities of uranium from Africa.[8]

A later Senate Select intelligence committee report, issued on May 25, 2007, revealed that "the Intelligence community used or cleared the Niger-Iraq uranium intelligence *fifteen* times before the president's State of the Union address and four times *after*, saying in several papers that Iraq was "vigorously pursuing uranium from Africa" [emphasis in the original].[9] According to Richard Perle, Sir Richard Dearlove, who was head of British intelligence at the time, insisted over breakfast in Cambridge, Massachusetts, in early 2007 that he still stood by the original story. "Dearlove told me that the basis he used for the assessment that Iraq was seeking uranium from Niger had nothing to do with the bogus documents," Perle told me.

The real question was whether the Niger documents were a plant, an elaborate sting operation by the president's enemies aimed at leading him into an error they would later claim he had known about all along; and whether certain elements at the CIA knew about the forgeries from the start but conveniently refused to inform their superiors until it was too late.

ITALIAN CON MAN, FRENCH SPIES

His French intelligence handlers gave him the code name Giacomo. They provided him with a regular stipend, a secret rendezvous point in Belgium, and a business front in Luxembourg. In exchange, he helped the French discover how their partners in the Niger uranium mines were cheating them.

Rocco Martino, aka Giacomo, had served many masters. A former Italian policeman, he had worked for Egyptian intelligence and the Italian military, and in 1996 became a paid informer for the French Direction Générale de la Sécurité Extérieur (DGSE). In 1999, he provided his French intelligence clients with genuine documents that revealed how Niger planned to expand trade with Iraq, apparently through clandestine uranium sales.

"I have the honor to inform you that the Iraqi Embassy to the Holy See in the person of His Excellency Wissam Al Zahawie, Iraq Ambassador to the Holy See, will set out on an official mission to our country as the representative of Saddam Hussein, President of the Republic of Iraq," Niger's ambassador to Rome, Adamou Chekou, informed the foreign ministry in Niamey on February 1, 1999. "His Excellency will arrive in Niamey on Friday 5 February 1999 at approximately 18:25 aboard Air France Flight 730 originating in Paris."

The DGSE paid Giacomo handsomely for this batch of authentic Niger government documents, and asked for more. "That's my job," Martino said later. "I sell information."[10]

The French continued to express interest in Niger, so Martino looked for more documents. Through an old contact at Italy's military intelligence agency, Colonel Antonia Nucera, he hooked up with a sixty-year-old Italian secretary at the Niger embassy. She was on the books of SISMI (Servizio per le Informazione e la Sicurezza Militare) as a paid informer, code-named La Signora. Colonel Nucera introduced the two in February 2000 at a Rome café. Martino, who at sixty-two was tall and slim and sported a silver mustache, knew exactly how to appeal to her. He brought her a box of chocolates for her birthday, turned on the charm, and reportedly offered her money. La Signora soon became his informant.

"I limited myself to supplying Martino with copies of embassy documents in which there were traces of Niger agreements, in particular with Iraq," she later told Rome judge Franco Ionta.

Over the New Year's holiday in 2001, burglars broke through the reinforced steel door of the fifth-floor apartment in Rome's Mazzini Quarter that housed the Niger embassy and ransacked the place. When he reported the break-in to the police on January 2, 2001, Second Secretary Arfou Mounkaila said the burglars must have been drunk. Papers were strewn everywhere. File cabinets stood open. But nothing of value had been stolen. Whoever the burglars were, they had taken only a steel Breil watch and three small vials of perfume.

At least, so he thought.

Shortly after that break-in, the fake Niger documents began to appear. According to some accounts, Martino forged the documents himself, using letterhead and official seals obtained from the Niger embassy. According to others, SISMI forged the documents using stolen letterhead and seals and had Martino peddle them to the French, the Brits, and the Americans. Martino insists he only learned belatedly that the documents were forgeries, and that he had acquired them as part of a legitimate intelligence transaction with La Signora. As for La Signora, she admitted to Judge Ionta that she was working for SISMI as an informer and that she always had provided authentic Niger embassy documents to Martino, not fakes.

It would have been a real comic opera, if the stakes hadn't been so big.

"I began to have my suspicions about Rocco Martino after the theft in the embassy in 2001," said La Signora. What tipped her off was Martino's insistence on having a copy of a Niger-Iraq uranium contract that didn't exist. "Martino always told me that if ever he got hold of an eventual contract between the two parties he would have gained a considerable sum from a certain intelligence company in Brussels to which he belonged."[11] Everyone understood she was referring to French intelligence, the DGSE.

In the summer of 2001 Martino delivered the forged contract between Niger and Iraq for the purchase of 500 tons of uranium to his DGSE handler in Brussels, Jacques Nadal. (Italian intelligence photographed the handoff and later leaked it to the press.) Even the French foreign ministry weighed in to support the sting, the Senate intelligence committee discovered later. During a November 22, 2002, meeting with State Department officials, "the French Ministry of Foreign Affairs Director for Nonproliferation said that France had information on an Iraqi attempt to buy uranium from Niger," the report found. "He said that France had determined that no uranium had been shipped, but France believed the reporting was true that Iraq had made a procurement attempt for uranium from Niger."[12]

Once they realized their fingerprints were all over the fake Niger uranium documents and what appeared to be a sting operation against the U.S. government, the French tried desperately to deny all involvement. In an unusual move, they even sent out former top DGSE counterspy Alain Chouet to claim that the DGSE had never made contact with Martino before 2002.[13]

THE CIA HAND

But while the French probably caused the documents to be forged, they were not alone in perpetuating the fraud that was aimed at undermining President Bush's credibility, burying the very real information about al-Zahawie's 1999 trip to Niger, and stopping the war in Iraq. Top CIA officers, Italy's SISMI, and even Italian Prime Minister Silvio Berlusconi also played an active role in perpetuating the Niger-Iraq uranium sting.

Berlusconi mistakenly thought he was helping Bush. The CIA officers I will name below sought to undermine him.

Berlusconi was returned to office in contested elections in May 2001. After the September 11 attacks, the naturally pro-American Berlusconi was eager to show his support for America and for the U.S. president. When French president Jacques Chirac and Tony Blair were received in the Oval Office right after 9/11, Berlusconi became desperate for equal treatment, and his eagerness to please the Americans was felt throughout his administration. "I want to tell President Bush that Italy is ready to do whatever its allies ask," he told a cabinet meeting before leaving for Washington.[14]

On October 15, 2001, the day Berlusconi finally met with Bush in the Oval Office, the new head of SISMI, Nicolò Pollari, briefed the CIA Rome station chief on the alleged Niger-Iraq uranium deal. Pollari knew he had to play his cards close to his vest, because signatures and names had been altered on the Niger documents. So rather than give the doctored documents to CIA station chief Jeff Castelli, he let him look through them and scribble a few hasty notes on their content.

Castelli's report back to his CIA division chief in Langley later that day formed the basis of the first intelligence report circulated by the Directorate of Operations "indicating that Niger planned to ship several tons of uranium to Iraq."

> The intelligence report said the uranium sales agreement had been in negotiation between the two countries since at least early 1999, and was approved by the State Court of Niger in late 2000. According to the cable, Nigerien President Mamadou Tandja gave his stamp of approval for the agreement and communicated his decision to Iraqi President Saddam Hussein. The report also indicated that in October 2000 Nigerien Minister of Foreign Affairs Nassirou Sabo informed one of his ambassadors in Europe that Niger had concluded an accord to provide several tons of uranium to Iraq.[15]

Castelli's division chief, Tyler Drumheller, apparently deemed the report so important that he forwarded it for inclusion in the daily Senior Executive Intelligence Brief, which was widely circulated within the administration. (The Office of the Vice President used articles in the SEIB in drafting initial versions of Colin Powell's UN presentation.) The item appeared on October 18, 2001, and was titled "Iraq: Nuclear-Related Procurement Efforts."

Pollari went back to Castelli three days later with a page-and-a-half note, explaining that the "information comes from a credible source," a reference to the SISMI informant, La Signora. Later, he provided Castelli with a transcription of the forged Niger-Iraq agreement, which Castelli also sent back to Drumheller. That follow-on report was circulated within the U.S. intelligence community on February 5, 2002.

Castelli forwarded three reports on three separate occasions to Drumheller. After he retired from the Agency in February 2005, Drumheller became an outspoken critic of the Bush administration, and claimed that Castelli considered the Niger reports "bullshit."

Neither Castelli nor Drumheller ever tried to expose them as forgeries, however. On the contrary: their reporting *helped to validate* the forged Niger documents, as the Robb-Silberman Commission investigating U.S. intelligence on Iraq's WMD programs later found.[16]

It was an extraordinary accomplishment by the shadow warriors. They had taken the fakes and laundered them through the system, all the while claiming their innocence.[17]

Meanwhile, Rocco Martino went to London, where he delivered a copy of the Niger documents to MI6. British intelligence contributed its own reports to Washington based at least in part on the faked documents. These reports also flowed through the CIA's European division chief, Tyler Drumheller. This created the illusion of multiple, independent reporting streams on the alleged deal. Bush ultimately relied on the British reports, summarized in a public dossier released by Prime Minister Tony Blair's office in September 2002, for the basis of the sixteen words on Iraq's uranium procurement efforts that made its way into his State of the Union message in January 2003.

Greg Thielman saw all of these classified intelligence reports as director of the Office of Strategic, Proliferation, and Military Affairs in the State Department's Bureau of Intelligence and Research (INR). Once the scandal broke, he told the leftist Italian daily *La Repubblica* that he had seen through the scam from the start.

"Well, I have an idea for you," he told reporters Carlo Bonini and

Giuseppe d'Avanzo, when they asked about SISMI's role in spreading the doctored documents. "SISMI, like the CIA and the entire Anglo-Saxon intelligence community, is ready and willing to satisfy the hawks in the U.S. administration."

But Thielman's description didn't fit the likes of CIA officers Jeff Castelli or Tyler Drumheller, who opposed the "hawks of the U.S. administration." It was another careful piece of subterfuge by the shadow warriors.

After leaving INR in September 2002, Thielman revealed his true colors, going to work for the Democratic staff of the Senate intelligence committee. By this point, Levin was gearing up to spring his trap. And all the while this extraordinary intelligence coup against the president by CIA and State Department intelligence officers and their accomplices in Congress was being set in motion, no one pursued the very real contacts between Saddam's nuclear advisor, Wissam al-Zahawie, and the Niger government.

DRUMHELLER CAUGHT IN A LIE

On October 7, 2002, as the United Nations began debating in earnest the case for war against Iraq, Rocco Martino tried again to peddle the Niger file, this time to Italian journalist Elisabetta Burba. He had sold documents to her before, so when he phoned her saying he had something "very hot," she agreed to take him to an expensive restaurant in Rome, where he passed her an envelope with documents he said "proved" that Saddam Hussein had purchased yellowcake from Niger.

Burba's editors at the newsweekly *Panorama* were skeptical, and insisted she get the documents vetted before they shelled out Martino's asking price of 15,000 euros (then worth around $15,000). They arranged for Burba to meet with a press officer at the U.S. embassy in Rome two days later, where they were joined by an unnamed embassy official who worked for CIA station chief Jeff Castelli. The Americans told Burba they were not in the business of verifying documents for journalists, but asked if they could have a copy of the documents. If anything popped up, they'd get back to her.

That is how the fake Niger documents wound up in Thielman's old State Department office, and how word of them reached Senator Levin's staff. But while the State Department's intelligence bureau put out an internal note on the forgeries, they never reported up the food chain to Colin Powell or the White House.

Nor did Jeff Castelli, the CIA station chief in Rome. According to Tyler Drumheller, Castelli paid little attention to the documents when they finally landed on his desk, because he "already knew" they were forgeries. The Rome station chief "was not the most organized guy in the world," Drumheller explained in his kiss-and-tell anti-Bush memoir.

This is the same CIA station chief who had reported back to CIA headquarters on three separate occasions after being briefed on the Niger file by SISMI, and who was being asked almost daily by headquarters if he had any new information. And yet, if Drumheller is to be believed, he was so incurious that he never even looked at the actual documents when a subordinate dumped the file obtained from the Italian journalist on his desk.

Republicans on the Senate Select intelligence committee felt so strongly about Drumheller's apparent willingness to play fast and loose with the facts that they took the unprecedented step of correcting several of his public statements in their "Additional Views" to a September 2006 report.[18]

Was it just incompetence? Perhaps. There was plenty of that to go around, as both the Senate panel and the Robb-Silberman Commission found.

But one incontrovertible fact stands out: At the center of the two intelligence mistakes concerning Iraq's WMD programs that were most hyped by the president's political opponents—the Niger documents, and an Iraqi defector code-named CURVEBALL (whose story I tell in Chapter 19)—sat one man: Tyler Drumheller, who wears his opposition to the Bush agenda as a badge of pride.

LARRY JOHNSON AND VIPS

As U.S. and coalition troops were poised to pour across the border into Iraq from the south, administration opponents redoubled their effort to sabotage the war effort, undermine the troops, and expose highly classified intelligence operations. Aiding their efforts was a former CIA officer named Larry C. Johnson, who joined the Clinton administration after an undistinguished career in the CIA's clandestine service.

Larry Johnson's last government job was at the State Department's Office of Counterterrorism, where he compiled statistics that went into the annual redbook, *Patterns of Global Terrorism.*

Johnson was best known for an opinion piece that appeared in the *New York Times* on July 10, 2001, where he claimed that the terror threat against the United States had been blown way out of proportion by "politicians of both parties" and by "bureaucracies in the military and in intelligence agencies that are desperate to find an enemy to justify budget growth."

The hype had reached such alarming proportions that Americans were "bedeviled by fantasies about terrorism," he wrote. "They seem to believe that terrorism is the greatest threat to the United States and that it is becoming more widespread and lethal." Worse: Americans "almost certainly have the impression that extremist Islamic groups cause most terrorism. None of these beliefs are based in fact."

Larry Johnson couldn't get over it. Americans *actually believed* that Muslim fanatics wanted to kill them! How silly. The facts were quite different, and were being swept under the carpet by a new administration of Republican yahoos.

The terrorism redbook for 2001 presented statistics for the final year of the Clinton administration, and the trendlines were all positive, Johnson argued. Attacks were down, and most of those had occurred in places such as Colombia, where the violence was "less about terrorism than about guerrillas' goal of disrupting oil production to undermine the Colombian economy."

He ticked off the most significant incidents, which included the bombing of the USS *Cole* (no mention of bin Laden or al Qaeda as the culprits), attacks on a McDonald's in France, and attacks against U.S. oil companies.

For Larry Johnson, the conclusion was clear: "If you are drilling for oil in Colombia—or in nations like Ecuador, Nigeria or Indonesia—you should take appropriate precautions; otherwise Americans have little to fear."

Thank you, Larry, for those great insights. Except for Byron York of *National Review*,[19] reporters who flocked to Larry Johnson as a terrorism expert in the following years conveniently forgot this extraordinary display of analytic myopia.

On March 14, 2003, Larry Johnson and a band of former colleagues who had a few things to teach Democrats about the fine art of Bush-hating, issued an appeal to active-duty intelligence officers.

Calling themselves Veteran Intelligence Professionals for Sanity, or VIPS, they knew that many of their former colleagues were hopping mad because Bush administration officials and the press had been bashing the CIA for its failure to "connect the dots" that led up to 9/11. The CIA was being made to take the blame, whereas the real culprits were at the FBI, VIPS argued. After all, the FBI had on their payroll a confidential informant named Abdussattar Shaikh, who turned out to have been the landlord of two of the 9/11 hijackers, Khalid al-Mihdhar and Nawaf al-Hamzi, during their stay in San Diego in 2000. "The terrorists were living under the nose of an FBI informant, and somehow the connection was never made because the right questions weren't being asked," Senator Bob Graham (D-FL) wrote later.[20]

And that was not the only clue the FBI had missed. There was the July 10, 2001, memo from Phoenix, Arizona, FBI agent Kenneth Williams, who suggested the Bureau investigate the high number of Middle Eastern men enrolled in flight schools, and the famous refusal by FBI headquarters to allow FBI field officers to search the computer of Zaccarias Moussaoui, which, it turned out, contained clear indications of the 9/11 plot. The FBI was blind as a bat, and yet the CIA continued to take the rap.[21]

VIPS members proudly evoked Daniel Ellsberg, the Vietnam-era whistleblower who leaked the top-secret Pentagon Papers in 1971 to the *New York Times* and went on to become a counterculture icon of the Left. They urged intelligence-community employees "to break the law and leak any information they have that could show the Bush administration is engineering the release of evidence to match its penchant for war." The VIPS appeal was quickly picked up by wacko left-wing websites, who evoked the "Bush crime family" and claimed that the beheading of U.S. citizen Nicholas Berg by al Qaeda terrorist Zarqawi in Iraq was "actually" a conspiracy by the CIA to "send a message" to antiwar elements in the United States that they had better not criticize President Bush, or else they would suffer a similar fate.[22] (Psychoanalysts have a word for such fears: paranoia.)

The administration's intelligence on Iraq "has been cooked to a recipe, and the recipe is high policy," said VIPS member Ray McGovern, a former CIA Soviet analyst who now worked at Servant Leadership School, an inner-city outreach ministry. "That's why a lot of my former colleagues are holding their noses these days."

McGovern claimed that when he left the Agency in the late 1980s, then CIA director Bill Casey had cooked a similar stew, fueling the fires of the Cold War by refusing to acknowledge McGovern's prescient view that the Soviet Union was on the verge of collapse. In fact, it was Casey and President Reagan who argued forcefully that Communism *could* be rolled back and that the Soviet Union had feet of clay—against the accommodationist advice of CIA Soviet analysts such as Ray McGovern, who claimed that the Soviet Union was here to stay.

What did Ronald Reagan and George W. Bush have in common? They were both Republicans, and they both held views of America's strategic enemies than ran directly counter to the conventional wisdom of the U.S. intelligence community. In addition to Larry Johnson and McGovern, other VIPS members included Ray Close, a former CIA station chief in Riyadh, who continued to work as a consultant in Saudi Arabia, and Patrick Eddington, a CIA analyst who resigned in the 1990s after accusing the government of hiding the extent of Saddam's chemical weapons use during the Gulf War. They regularly published their manifestos at the far-left website CounterPunch.

In a sanctimonious "memo" to President Bush on March 18, 2003, VIPS said the Niger uranium documents were so crudely forged they could not possibly have been the work of the "legendary expertise of CIA technical specialists" or of their British colleagues. "We find ourselves wondering if amateur intelligence operatives in the Pentagon basement and/or at 10 Downing Street were involved and need to be called on the carpet."

There it was again: the secret office in the basement.[23]

At this point, however, the leakers and the naysayers were gaining no traction. The war in Iraq had just begun, and support for the president and the war on terror were high. An NBC News/Wall Street Journal tracking poll conducted from March 29 to March 30, 2003, showed the president's approval rating stood at 66 percent.[24] Democrats had just voted a war-powers resolution on the basis of the National Intelligence Estimate they had asked the CIA to prepare, and were anxious to wrap themselves in the flag.

After all, the nation was at war.

CHAPTER SIX

LIBERATION WOES

As Chalabi and the Free Iraqi Forces were choppering down from northern Iraq to Camp Desolation, some 175 miles south of Baghdad, Lieutenant General (ret.) Jay Garner was pushing into Iraq from Kuwait, at the head of a veritable army of relief workers and humanitarian aid supplies.

For all the administration's critics who whined, like Senator Joe Biden, that the Pentagon had "no plan" for how to handle Iraq after major fighting was over, Jay Garner was supposed to be the answer. He headed an outfit known as the Office of Reconstruction and Humanitarian Assistance (ORHA), undoubtedly one of the most obscure agencies in a government known for bureaucratic arcana. Garner came into Iraq bearing the 300-page OPLAN 10-03, the postwar reconstruction blueprint that Bill Luti and his Office of Special Plans had developed along with the CENTCOM strategic planners at Joint Task Force IV.

Garner was well known and well liked by the Iraqi opposition, having directed U.S. relief operations among the Kurds after the first Gulf war. He was a straight shooter, direct, but also humbly aware of his own limitations. Secretary of Defense Donald Rumsfeld had given Garner two assignments: handle the flood of refugees fleeing whatever disaster Saddam set in motion as he pulled the pillars of his temple around himself, and stand up a new Iraqi government that could quickly take over running the country.

Rumsfeld made it crystal clear: the United States had no intention of occupying Iraq. Our job, he said repeatedly, is to get rid of Saddam and create the conditions for the Iraqis to take over.

When U.S. troops reached Baghdad on April 8, they found a situation significantly different from what they had expected. Many of the surprises were good. Turkey didn't come (as Khalilzad had threatened); Israel didn't come; Iraq didn't split apart immediately into three warring regions, as the CIA had predicted. Saddam didn't manage to set his oil fields on fire (he had rigged some of the wellheads with explosives, just as he had done in 1991, but U.S. special forces secured the oil fields before he could give the order to blow them). There was no ecological disaster, no massive refugee crisis, no shortage of food or medical supplies. Luti and the CENTCOM planners had foreseen just about every possible contingency—except for the ones that actually arrived.

The worst of the surprises—the massive looting, and later, the insurgency—were the direct result of what several top officials told me was "faulty intelligence provided by the CIA" on the way the Iraqi army and police would react as the regime collapsed.

The United States never expected it would have to fulfill the functions of the police and the army after Saddam's regime fell. The idea, as one official put it, was for the coalition to "cut off the head of the snake but leave the body."[1]

Instead, after the United States removed the Baath party stooges who ran the police and the army under Saddam, both institutions simply collapsed. Where they had expected to capture entire army units intact, U.S. troops instead found empty uniforms, neatly piled in rows, some even with their rifles carefully set alongside. The Iraqi soldiers had apparently been ordered by their officers to simply change into civilian clothes and go home, despite repeated warnings broadcast in Arabic by the Commando Solo aircraft and millions of leaflets telling Iraqi soldiers to lay down their arms, remain in uniform, and stay in place.

"We didn't dissolve the Iraq army," Luti said later. "The Iraqi army dissolved itself." And yet, the State Department and the CIA quickly spawned a myth among the media that Pentagon "ideologues" had somehow given a demobilization order to the Iraqi army, and that this mistake had spawned the insurrection. "It was unwise and not well-thought-out and not well informed as a policy," former U.S. ambassador Robin Raphel, a State Department shadow warrior on Garner's staff, said later.[2] In his controversial and much-disputed memoir, George Tenet claimed that the U.S. military leaflets ordered the Iraqis to "simply lay down their arms and go home."[3]

What actually happened was quite different. General Franks ordered Iraqi troops on April 10 to "remain in uniform at all times. Maintain unit integrity and good order and discipline in your units."[4] In his autobiography, Franks later wrote, "I wanted to see those defeated enemy troops kept in coherent units, commanded by their own officers, and paid in a combination of humanitarian assistance food and cash . . . [and] put to work for the Coalition on reconstruction."[5] As for the police, "the CIA told us that all we had to do was lop off the top layer of leadership, but when we did we found that the corruption went so deep that we had to start from scratch," Luti said. "Was that a mistake? You bet. But it was a mistake based on faulty intelligence."

Similar mistakes based on faulty intelligence led the United States to overestimate the status of Iraq's infrastructure. "We were told that Saddam Hussein kept on putting money into the power system, into the water and the sewage systems. But once we got in, we discovered there hadn't been any investment for the past thirty-five years," Luti told me. "Saddam Hussein used electricity and water as political tools. He'd turn it on and off, especially in the Shiite areas. If the Shia misbehaved, he'd put feces into the water and send it into Sadr City. It's incredible."

Luti was not exaggerating. Dean G. Popps, the principal deputy assistant secretary of the Army in charge of Iraq reconstruction projects, told the *Washington Times* later that the Army Corps of Engineers was "in shock" when it reached Iraq right after the liberation. Not only were sewage plants serving Sunni areas in Baghdad not working; Sadr City had no sewage system whatsoever. "Some slam the Americans because there is sewage in Sadr City," Popps said. "Please."[6]

While noting that a new Iraqi government "would require significant outside assistance to rebuild Iraq's water and sanitation infrastructure," prewar intelligence generally painted a rosy picture. "A surviving remnant of Iraq's civil authority could move quickly to repair damaged infrastructure, especially if outside assistance were available," a National Intelligence Council report prepared under the direction of analyst Paul R. Pillar concluded. This key report, declassified in April 2007 and subsequently released by the Senate Select intelligence committee, convinced war planners, including General Tommy Franks, to "leave the lights on" in Baghdad during the Allied bombing campaigns, so it would be easier to rebuild the country after the war.[7]

MURDER IN NAJAF

On April 10, just two days after U.S. troops entered Baghdad, the CIA brought moderate Shiite cleric Seyed Abd-al-Majid al-Khoie back to Iraq. The descendant of one of the most prominent Shiite clerical families in the region, al-Khoie had been quietly helping the anti-Saddam forces for many years from his base in London and was a member of the sixty-five-member Follow-on committee.

Now the CIA wanted him in Najaf, where he could issue religious rulings in favor of the coalition, and calm rumors stoked by Iran that the United States planned to install a puppet government in Baghdad. The CIA promised him they would give his supporters key provincial governorships in exchange for his cooperation.

As it turned out, a different CIA team had made the same promises to thirty-year-old firebrand cleric Moqtada al-Sadr, who was working hand-in-glove with the Iranians.*

The Iranians had long identified al-Khoie as a mortal enemy, because he opposed Islamist government. Now they saw their opportunity to take him out. When he arrived with his CIA bodyguards on the steps of the Imam Ali Shrine in Najaf, one hundred miles south of Baghdad, Moqtada al-Sadr was waiting for him with a horde of armed followers. In the extraordinary melee that ensued right there on the steps of the mosque, al-Khoie was stabbed more than a dozen times. When his CIA bodyguards pulled their Glock pistols to intervene, they stood face to face with another group of CIA bodyguards, similarly armed, who were protecting al-Sadr.

You're Mr. Mayeek? one of the CIA officers guarding al-Khoie said in amazement, seeing another American. He had heard the name of Muqtada al-Sadr's bodyguard pronounced by the Iraqis around al-Khoie, and had just assumed he was Iraqi.

Yeah. Actually, it's Mike, the other CIA officer said.

The CIA has never explained why it was protecting Moqtada al-Sadr in the immediate aftermath of the liberation, or given any accounting of the large amounts of cash it distributed to a variety of Sunni tribal sheikhs just before and after the liberation.

"The CIA was spreading money to the tribes to foment an uprising against Saddam," former Pentagon official Michael Rubin—now an American Enterprise Institute scholar—told me. "They were giving money in particular to the Dulaimi tribe and others in the Sunni Triangle. After the

*Iranian dissidents told me that Sadr was the nephew of Iranian president Mohammad Khatami, which explained in part why he spent so much time in Iran. Khatami's wife, Zohreh, was the sister of Moqtada al-Sadr's father. Both were siblings of famous Iranian cleric Imam Moussa Sadr, who "disappeared" while on a visit to Libya in 1978. Moussa Sadr is credited with having launched Lebanon's Amal Movement, a precursor of today's Hezbollah.

liberation, we found that insurgents were coming from the Dulaimi tribe. So the CIA was actually paying the terrorists. They spread millions of dollars this way."

I found this difficult to believe, but Rubin insisted that he had been in a position at the Pentagon—and then at the Coalition Provisonal Authority (CPA) in Baghdad—to see this as it was going on. "Some of those tribes were paying people to kill Americans using CIA money," he added.

In Michael Rubin's view, the CIA was "out of control." No wonder they constantly sought to blame Bush for the failures in Iraq. They desperately needed to cover up the trails leading to their own deadly errors.

PRESIDENT BUSH WEIGHS IN

After meeting with Chalabi and local Iraqis in Nasiriyah on April 15, General Garner made his way to Baghdad a week later, still upbeat. As he sat down to host a second large gathering of Iraqis on April 28—some three hundred Shiite and Sunni Muslim clerics, tribal chiefs, Kurds, and other delegates—he sketched out the goals and the expectations of the United States now that Saddam Hussein was gone.

"The reason I'm here is to create an environment in Iraq that will give us a process to start a democratic government and begin that process so that we can have a government that represents the freely elected will of the people," Garner said.

That meeting ended with a call by the Iraqis to hold a national conference in two weeks that would select the members of an interim government. Hearing the news, President Bush was ecstatic, and traveled to Dearborn, Michigan, home to a large Iraqi-American community, as a bearer of good news:

> Whether you're Sunni or Shia or Kurd or Chaldean or Assyrian or Turkman or Christian or Jew or Muslim [cheers and applause]—no matter what your faith, freedom is God's gift to every person in every nation. [Applause]
>
> As freedom takes hold in Iraq, the Iraqi people will choose their own leaders and their own government. America has no intention of imposing our form of government or our culture. Yet we will ensure that all Iraqis have a voice in the new government and all citizens have their rights protected. [Applause][8]

That was how it was supposed to work. But on the ground, the battle royal that had split the policy and intelligence community in Washington was now being played out in real time—and with real weapons.

It was the forces of dictatorship and the status quo versus the president's freedom agenda. And now it was coming to crunch time.

AN IRAQI CASSANDRA

Kanan Makiya had become a close advisor to the INC, and had developed good personal ties with the leaders of all six member parties of the coalition.

As a professor of political science at Brandeis University, who had wrestled to get funding for the Iraq Research and Documentation Project that assembled two million pages of documents on regime human rights abuses by the Baathist regime, he also understood how Washington worked. For years he had been battling the State Department and the CIA, because of their preference for dictators over democrats.

He didn't like what he was seeing in Baghdad or in the predominantly Shiite south during those first weeks after the liberation, and flew to Washington to sound the alarm.

At stake was not just a personal squabble between Zal Khalilzad or Ben Miller and Ahmad Chalabi, but fundamentally different views of Iraq's future.

"There is a view that deep down does not believe a democratic Iraq is possible," he told reporters at the National Press Club. Khalilzad and Ben Miller had actively intervened to prevent the seven-man Iraqi leadership council, elected at the Salahuddin conference at the end of February, from moving down to Baghdad, he revealed.

The chaos, the looting, the proliferation of local militias all grew out of this fundamental political logjam, he argued. Instead of empowering Iraqis to stand up a national government, State and CIA were "still trying to preserve certain elements of the Baath party," he said.

Part of the problem was naïveté on the U.S. side, an attitude of letting a hundred flowers bloom. The U.S. military took a tolerant approach toward many of the local militias and new local police forces as the expression of Iraq's newfound freedom. "To my mind, this is not democracy, but a recipe for chaos," Makiya warned. "You don't have democracy merely because the tyrant is gone. What you have in today's Iraq is a people waking up from a deep dark nightmare and horrendous experiences, coming out into the light of day and quite naturally not knowing quite how to behave."

Added to that were the actions of General Garner, who had taken a number of senior Baathists under his wing to run key government ministries, because they seemed to be the only ones still standing who knew where things were. Garner's actions contributed to the misconception that only former Baathists could turn on the lights.

Before the United States started experimenting with various new political formulas, Iraqis needed law and order, Makiya argued. They needed policemen in the streets—a new police force, with new uniforms. They needed an end to looting, an end to chaos, an end to the insecurity.

Under the Iraq Liberation Act of 1998, the INC was supposed to train the backbone of a new security force in Iraq. But because of sabotage by the State Department and the CIA, only sixty-eight—sixty-eight!—members of this new security force had ever received training in Hungary.

"So Chalabi set up on his own the Free Iraqi Forces, set them up and trained them in northern Iraq and got them flown to southern Iraq, where the local commanders on the ground have said they have been very effective in finding weapons caches and people," Makiya said. A senior Pentagon war planner dismissed the FIF as "Chalabi's pick-up team."

Chalabi turned over command of the FIF to CENTCOM, which promptly disbanded them. "Those 700 troops were the only Iraqi partner in the coalition. Think about that!" Makiya said. "We have a war of liberation that has no Iraqi component, and the only component that might have spoken in the name of the Iraqi people was shunted aside because of infighting here in Washington."

Tens of thousands of volunteers were pounding down the doors of INC offices all across Iraq to join a new, free Iraqi security force. "We need to bring them in," Makiya said.

The alternative, he warned, would be massive bloodshed, starting in the south, where Iranian-backed militia groups were already imposing themselves by force.

When an Egyptian reporter asked him what had happened to the "Iraqi president," Makiya did a double take. "You mean Saddam?" But then he addressed what he believed was the fundamental issue. For years, he said, Arabs had looked to Saddam's regime as a source of pride, when instead it should have been a source of shame.

"So why is there this smear campaign against Ahmad Chalabi? Because deep down, the type of Iraq he would represent is radically different from the type of regime that has been peddled by the Arab intelligentsia for the past fifty years."

Those were stinging words, even he admitted. "I am not in the business of making Arab governments happy," he added. "Nor should any self-respecting Iraqi government be."[9]

INFILTRATION

The State Department considered that same "Arab intelligentsia" to be its client. Its cherished causes—the eradication of Israel, the diminution of U.S. influence in the Middle East, the appeals to Arab unity, the fear of Islamism—became the cherished issues championed by the Arabists at Foggy Bottom. If the Arabs wanted dictators, let them have them. After all, they came from a different culture. We just didn't understand.

It was multiculturalism on an international scale. And just as multiculturalism in America became an excuse for the "soft bigotry of low expectations"—racism bred on a belief that "others" were not as capable or as interested in achieving freedom—on the international level it became an excuse for dictatorship.

President Bush called it "the freedom deficit." Those speeches of his didn't play well at Foggy Bottom.

Robin Raphel, the former U.S. ambassador, had served in the Arab world. She *understood* Arabs. And what she saw as she worked her way into the inner circle around Jay Garner while he was still staging in Kuwait made her almost want to laugh. Those idiots—those ideologues!—actually believed what they were saying! Freedom in the Middle East? You've got to be kidding!

The problem, she would say later, was de-Baathification. The neocon "ideologues" had swallowed the line they were getting from Kanan Makiya and Ahmad Chalabi, exiles who for decades had been critical of Saddam Hussein for his "racist" ideology. The Baath was just an Arab nationalist party like any other. All that nonsense about Saddam's uncle, Khairallah Tulfah, and his so-called "racist" treatise ("Three Whom God Should Not Have Created: Persians, Jews, and Flies") had been twisted way out of proportion. Saddam Hussein was just a bad boy from a small town who had managed to put together the meanest bunch of thugs Iraq had ever seen. Full stop.*

The "de-Baathification" process that was set in motion during the very first days after liberation "left a fair amount of bad blood," Robin Raphel said. "A lot of people had read about denazification, took a lot of different lessons from it. But we were in my view insufficiently humble about our lack of understanding about the Baath Party and why people were members and the structure and how senior you had to be to be a serious Baathist and so on. We just didn't understand it very well."[10]

And so the neo-con "ideologues" made Mistake Number One: they cracked down on the Baath Party, and made enemies of several hundred thousand Iraqis, from teachers to government employees to former torturers in Saddam's many-headed secret police. Robin Raphel and the State Department Arabists believed that if the United States was going to invade Iraq, it should have left the Baathists in charge. All that mattered was getting rid of Saddam. It was the CIA's search for a military strongman who could lead a palace coup all over again.

But Ambassador Raphel was not content to just sit back and watch the "fiasco" of freedom blossom beneath her nose: with a small core of career foreign service officers who managed to land top jobs in Garner's Office of Reconstruction and Humanitarian Assistance, she actively worked to stomp it out, sabotaging the liberation as best she could. In an extensive postwar interview, she proudly took credit for rolling back the "mistakes" of the neo-cons, whether they were U.S. government policy or not.

The shadow warriors within the Coalition Provisional Authority stuck together, she admitted later. They moved cautiously, quietly, "under the radar screen," because the neo-con political "minders" were everywhere.

But they had staying power. For example, when the White House sent free-market economists to Baghdad early on to help privatize the vast state-owned economy, Robin Raphel says, she and her colleagues "just laughed." The free-market economists "came and went and that was that.

*Raphel and other Foggy Bottom analysts would ignore specific warnings from Chalabi and Makiya that the Baath Party's very nature made it a particularly dangerous foe. Saddam and the Baath Party founders cut their teeth in clandestinity after the party's first defeat at the hands of the communists following the 1958 revolution. It was while he was fleeing for his life to Damascus and, later, to Cairo that Saddam Hussein understood that he had to create a robust structure of underground cells that would resist even the most vicious secret police—or a foreign occupier. Anyone who thought the Baath was simply going to fade away was in for a shock, Chalabi, Makiya, and other Iraqi victims of the Baath believed. That is why they argued for a far more sweeping de-Baathification campaign. They believed the Baath had to be pulled up by its roots.

Or they learned that wasn't what was going to happen." Socialism was in Iraq to stay.

First they managed to discredit General Garner, by planting stories with a willing media that suggested he was "in way over his head." Then they got appointed as his replacement one of their own.

Washington Post reporter Rajiv Chandrasekaran, who sympathized with their cause, noted that the anti-Bush shadow warriors who occupied Saddam's former palace in Baghdad referred to themselves as "Donkeys in the Desert."[11]

MEDIA DISTORTION

The extent to which the U.S. media present in Baghdad after the liberation willfully distorted what was taking place on the ground only gradually became apparent.

The main themes in the post-liberation headlines were all of a piece: looting, chaos, lawlessness, and growing resentment of the American occupiers.

Reading the words of his press colleagues made *New York Post* correspondent Jonathan Foreman sick. He was struck by the resoundingly friendly reception Baghdad residents gave U.S. troops. "[T]he intensity of the population's pro-American enthusiasm is astonishing, even to an early believer in the liberation of Iraq," he wrote. He cited example after example where soldiers were greeted by local residents, welcomed into their homes, brazenly flirted with by young Baghdadi women—treated, in short, like the liberators they were.

"But you won't see much of this on TV or read about it in the papers," he wrote. "To an amazing degree, the Baghdad-based press corps avoids writing about or filming the friendly dealings between U.S. forces here and the local population—most likely because to do so would require them to report the extravagant expressions of gratitude that accompany every such encounter. Instead you read story after story about the supposed fury of Baghdadis at the Americans for allowing the breakdown of law and order in their city."

Yes, the looting was extensive. But most of it was the work of Baghdad's poor, who were taking advantage of the demise of Saddam Hussein and his Baath Party cronies to loot government ministries and the elite neighborhoods and homes of yesterday's oppressors, most of whom had fled.

Coverage of the looting in the U.S. press included outright lies.

Foreman was embedded with the 4th Battalion of the 64th Armored Regiment, 3rd Infantry Division, along with David Zucchino of the *Los Angeles Times*.

One day the two of them accompanied their scout platoon on patrol into an upscale residential area of Baghdad, where houses that had belonged to top Baath party officials had been ransacked and taken over by looters. One noteworthy former local resident was Qusay al-Hussein, the dictator's son, whose house had been destroyed by a U.S. JDAM munition.

Foreman struck up a conversation with Dr. Ali Faraj al Salih, a cardiologist trained in Scotland, when Zucchino, "a fine, experienced foreign correspondent," walked over and began taking notes.

> "I asked Dr. Ali if he'd had any trouble with looters. 'No,' he replied, 'I have guns, with license from the government. And I have two bodyguards.' 'Have you always had the bodyguards?' I asked him. 'Oh yes,' he said.
>
> "But Zucchino's April 22 article in the *L.A. Times*—headlined 'In Postwar "Dodge City," Soldiers Now Deputies'—reports 'Dr. Ali Faraj, a cardiologist, stood before his well-appointed home and mentioned that he has hired two armed guards,' as if the doctor had been driven to this expense by unrest following the arrival of the Americans."

It was just typical of the willful distortion of facts on the ground, Foreman said. It almost seemed as if the press corps were "solidly on the side of those who grew fat under the Saddam regime."[12]

"WE JUST LOST THE INFORMATION WAR"

Former Voice of America director Robert Reilly still lies awake at night when he recalls those early weeks after the United States ousted Saddam Hussein. Reilly had been tapped by Jay Garner to stand up an Iraq Media Network on D-Day Plus One, the day after the invasion, "so Iraqis could talk about Iraq to Iraqis."

An old Cold Warrior, Reilly believed America needed to have a strategic information policy, to counter an enemy willing to spread lies and disinformation. Tall, flinty, and telegenic, Reilly could be smooth in public. When he shopped his idea in Washington in late 2002, Garner jumped at it and asked him if he was ready to deploy to Baghdad. Reilly agreed.

The shadow warriors set to work almost immediately.

Reilly's first stop, in late December 2002, was London, where the U.S. embassy had set up meetings for him with a number of Iraqi journalists. At the top of the list was Siamand Othman, a prominent Iraqi commentator and editor. When he learned that Reilly was supposed to be meeting with Othman, the CIA's Ben Miller, still at the National Security Council in Washington, phoned the embassy and ordered them to cancel all Reilly's appointments. "That was my introduction to civil war," Reilly quipped later.

Miller's objection? Othman was "too close" to Ahmad Chalabi, even though he was not part of Chalabi's organization or media projects—and in fact had become vice president of United Press International at a time when UPI had been bought out by Saudi interests. "People hated Chalabi with such intensity they were willing to scuttle the whole project just to prevent Othman, a perceived Chalabi associate, from playing a role in it," Reilly told me.

A skilled bureaucratic infighter, Reilly fought back, and eventually convinced Deputy National Security Advisor Stephen Hadley to get the NSC staff to back off. Othman provided detailed proposals for documentary TV programming, which Reilly said he found "brilliant." Working with Shahriar Ahy and MBC in Dubai, Othman proposed that they train Iraqi journalists in Media City, a free-trade zone recently set up by the ruler of Dubai to attract international media organizations. He also suggested that they consider an exchange with MBC and another friend of Ahy's who headed the Lebanese Broadcasting Corporation, to acquire a video bank of U.S.- and Arab-produced programs and movies. The beauty of the whole deal was that Ahy and his friends were prepared to give the United States access to the programming for free, in exchange for four to six minutes per hour of advertising time. It wouldn't cost U.S. taxpayers a dime.

Reilly phoned Ryan Henry back in Washington for a final heads-up before he was scheduled to fly to Dubai to hammer out the details of the contract. "That was a big mistake," Reilly says. Henry, who had just been named chief deputy to Undersecretary of Defense Doug Feith, was a closet Clintonista, "who never revealed his past work on Capitol Hill for a Democrat when he was hired at the Pentagon," according to the *Washington Times*'s Bill Gertz.[13] There was no way Ryan Henry was going to sign off on a project that might actually make the United States' liberation of Iraq look good. He ordered Reilly by phone to cease and desist.

The excuse Henry used was that it was "too early" to allow commercial programming into Iraq. But as Reilly soon discovered, the Department of State had hired Beltway contractor SAIC to manage the media project, and neither had any interest in saving U.S. taxpayer dollars. (Ryan Henry had been a top executive at SAIC before coming to the Pentagon.) SAIC assigned Reilly a retired colonel named Michael Furlong as project director. Furlong shared the State Department's intense dislike for Chalabi and the INC.

When they deployed to Kuwait in early 2003, Reilly wanted to start hiring Iraqis so they could fill the broadcasting vacuum after the liberation, but Furlong kept dragging his heels, ostensibly because of Othman's involvement. Also applying the brakes was a female Arabist from the State Department's Bureau of Near Eastern Affairs, who told Reilly he didn't need to bring Iraqi journalists from London because there were "plenty of talented Iraqis" in Iraq he could hire.

"I guess she wanted us to hire Baghdad Bob," Reilly said, referring to Saddam's information minister, who became a comic figure when he swore on live television that American troops were being "slaughtered" and would "never enter" Baghdad, just as the first U.S. M1A2 Abrams tanks could be seen on the live CNN feed, moving down the street behind him.

Thanks to the State Department's efforts to kill the Iraqi Media Network, not only did the United States fail to produce the "first hour" of video aimed at convincing the Iraq people of the benefits of the U.S.-led liberation, as Ahy had suggested to General Myers's aide a few months earlier: the United States also allowed Iran to step in and fill the vacuum. By the time U.S. troops reached Baghdad, on April 9, 2003, the Iranian regime was pumping two professional TV stations and dozens of Arabic-language radio stations into Iraq that were spewing out rabid anti-American propaganda 24/7, and no one except Reilly, Chalabi, and a few others such as Hudson Institute scholar Constantine Menges back in Washington were paying attention.

Phoning Washington for help was surreal. "Don't you understand we're in f—ing foxholes over here and these programs are our ammo?" Reilly told his bosses back in Washington. But there was no way they were going to approve his proposals to jump-start the Iraqi Media Network by hiring qualified journalists or acquiring Arabic-language programming. For whatever reason, the State Department and the CIA insisted that Reilly hire former Baathists. When Ahy saw those initial broadcasts, he just shook his head. "They could read from a sheet of paper, but that was it. They couldn't even follow an audit cue," he said.

Margaret Tutwiler, the former State Department spokesperson for James Baker, got involved right after the liberation when Reilly moved to Baghdad with Garner and the ORHA. By that point, he was trying to set up an Arabic-language newspaper, called *Somer*, that would appear twice weekly. He had recruited as editor Hasan al-Alawi, the dean of Iraqi journalists in London. When Reilly explained that he intended to bring al-Alawi to Baghdad, Tutwiler put down her foot.

I'm not going to let you have this thing run by exiles, she exclaimed. We need to recruit new people, from the inside.

Reilly couldn't believe what he was hearing. *What would you prefer, tombstones?* he thought. It was the same problem all over again. If you wanted to work with people who had remained inside Iraq during Saddam's reign, either they had been corrupted by the regime—in order to survive—or they had no significant experience of any use. And the Iranians were real pros, beaming world-class programming in Arabic into Iraq aimed at turning Iraqis against America.

Because of the infighting, neither project went forward during those initial weeks, and the Iranians succeeded in dominating the airwaves. ORHA managed to stand up a radio station in Kuwait during the first weeks of the liberation that it fed via satellite to a transmitter in Oum Qasr, Iraq's port along the Kuwaiti border. But it didn't have the power to reach Baghdad.

In the meantime, the White House turned to Clinton-protégé Norman Pattiz, the head of media giant Westwood One. Pattiz was a member of the International Broadcasting Board of Governors, and became infamous for destroying the Arabic and Persian-language freedom radios that had been funded by Congress in the late 1990s, and replacing them with Westwood One–style music and "feel-good" stations called Radio Sawa and Radio Farda. "Pattiz and his crew believed that Britney Spears and MTV won the Cold War," Cold Warrior Constantine Menges told me shortly before he died in July 2004. "They wanted to get rid of all political programming and just do pop music. Ridiculous!"

ORHA bought stock TV programming from Westwood One, put Arabic subtitles on it, and beamed it into Baghdad. "We pissed away millions of dollars that way, broadcasting live press conferences and Hollywood soaps," Reilly said.

Ever persistent, Reilly made one more attempt to pitch an independent Iraqi Media Network. He went directly to the new viceroy, L. Paul "Jerry" Bremer, soon after he arrived in Baghdad on May 12. It was a big blow-up meeting.

"We already have a television station," Bremer said. We've got, what?"—he turned to his chief aides, Clay McManaway and Hume Horan—"six-seven hours a day?"

"We're getting creamed by the Iranians," Reilly said. "They're all over us, day and night, with anti-American propaganda. And that's not to mention al Jazeera and al Arabiya, the Arab satellite channels."

Bremer picked up Reilly's proposal. "Let me make one thing clear," he said, waving the papers to emphasize his words. "I never want to hear about this proposal again. Is that clear? I-never-want-to-hear-about-this-again," thumping the air with the pages. Then he tossed it into the trash.

Out in the palace, Reilly turned to Garner. "We've just lost the information war," he said. "Every rooftop in Baghdad has got a satellite dish. And guess what they're watching? Not us."

Garner commiserated with Reilly. Look, he said. I'll repitch this to Jerry once he cools off.

But he never did. Just days later, Garner was gone.

Later, looking back, Reilly recalled a key meeting he had with Pentagon spokesman Larry DiRita in Kuwait, before he moved to Baghdad in April with General Garner. After hearing Reilly's plans to train Iraqi television reporters and to help Iraqis establish independent newspapers that would respect Western reporting standards, DiRita just shook his head. We're not going to do that, he said.

Why not? Reilly wondered.

Because we're not going in there to hang around. We're just going in there and getting rid of Saddam, and then we're going to leave.

DiRita was right. That, in fact, was the plan, and it was Donald Rumsfeld's intention. But those plans were about to change.

CHAPTER SEVEN

THE VICEROY COMETH

On May 5, 2003, General Garner announced in Baghdad that he expected to hand over the reins of Iraq's day-to-day administration to an interim Iraqi government "within ten days." Indeed, that had been the plan from day one.

For Ahmad Chalabi and the other six members of the Iraqi Leadership Council (ILC) who had been elected by their peers to steer Iraq from dictatorship to democracy, Garner's announcement was a vindication. Free at last! After all the hardship, the self-doubt, the political infighting in Washington, the threats, and the physical danger of the past twenty years, they were finally on the verge of achieving their goal of winning freedom for their country.

Chalabi had taken up quarters in the Baghdad Hunting Club in the well-to-do Mansoor neighborhood with a retinue of bodyguards and political aides (contrary to press accounts, Chalabi was actually renting the premises and had made an agreement with the Board of Directors of the club to protect it from looters, which he did). His offices became the hub for the ILC. For all the faded luxury of the surroundings, the air-conditioning didn't work, the plumbing was approximate, and Chalabi's aides needed to jury-rig a refrigerator out back near a broken fountain by hooking it up to a generator.

Bremer says he was on his way to work at the Pentagon when Garner's announcement led the 6 A.M. newscast. He was so stunned that he almost drove off the George Washington Parkway.

"I knew it would take careful work to disabuse both the Iraqi and American proponents of this reckless fantasy," he wrote in his account of his time as the American viceroy of Baghdad.[1]

Reckless fantasy. The words are clear enough. But Bremer was much more careful when he had lunch with President Bush alone at the White House the following day. They retired to a small private dining room off the Oval Office, with the French floor-to-ceiling windows open in the hot May afternoon to the South Lawn.

This was the first of many private moments the two men would spend together over the next year. Bremer claimed that he and Bush quickly established a rapport as fellow highly competitive athletes, although they had been strangers until then. Bush had taken up mountain biking, and did weight training while in the White House. Bremer competed in triathalons and ran marathons. Several years Bush's senior, the sixty-two-year-old Bremer was a vain man and prided himself on his hard stomach and jet black hair. They picked at a salad of pears and greens as they discussed the future of Iraq. Bremer used all his political skills to make Bush feel that his demands were Bush's own.

Instead of blasting Garner and his proposed "early transfer of power" to the Iraqi Leadership Council, Bremer insisted that the president give *him* full authority while in Baghdad. He spoke at length about the need not just for elections but also for creating the social "shock absorbers" that back up a civil society—a free press, trade unions, political parties, professional organizations. "These, I told the president, are what help cushion the individual from an overpowering government."

Bush's response, according to Bremer, was not an outright embrace of Bremer's formula for changing course in Iraq—for that is what he was proposing by canceling the transfer of power Garner had just announced. It was typical broad-stroke Bush, big-picture stuff. "I understand," Bremer says the president told him. "And I'm fully committed to bringing representative government to the Iraqi people. We're not going to abandon Iraq."

What is significant about this encounter is what Bremer does *not* tell Bush. By his own account, he does not tell the president that he was getting ready to leave for Baghdad *determined to bring a crashing halt to the march toward democracy* that had been under way since the first elections in Iraqi Kurdistan in 1992.

This is not what Eric Edelman, who later replaced Doug Feith in the Pentagon's number-three job, had in mind when he pitched Bremer as a possible replacement for Jay Garner. At the time, Edelman was working as the principal deputy assistant to Vice President Dick Cheney. He and other top administration officials believed they needed someone running the show in Baghdad who could get along with the CIA and the State Department, since they would need both to rebuild Iraq.

It remains one of the tragic ironies of postwar Iraq that the United States was in many ways the victim of its own success—what Tommy Franks had called "catastrophic success." Because the military campaign had gone so well—the three-week war wasn't exactly a "cakewalk," but it wasn't far from it—the United States was now facing expectations from the Iraqi people for massive economic assistance. In his thirty-five-year rule, Saddam Hussein had built more palaces than schools, roads, or power plants.

Bremer had come to the conclusion that the United States needed a rapid change of direction. The Rand Corporation had just completed a study forecasting a need for 500,000 foreign combat troops to handle postwar security—more than three times the number than deployed in Iraq. When Bremer forwarded the Rand study to Rumsfeld with a note suggesting he give it favorable attention, the secretary of defense never replied. Although he had known Rumsfeld for decades, Bremer quickly convinced himself that the secretary of defense didn't get it. He believed that Rumsfeld's scorn for the media's obsession with the looting of Baghdad "concealed the first ripple of disquiet along the Pentagon's E-Ring, where the secretary's senior civilian and military staff responsible for postwar Iraq was beginning to confront the reality of occupying a large Muslim nation in the heart of the volatile Middle East."[2]

Bremer was a creature of the State Department and aspired to become secretary of state or national security advisor after his mission in Iraq, senior administration sources told me. His worldview regarding Iraq was in stark contrast to that of his political bosses. He told his wife, Francie, when he was first offered the job in Baghdad, that he was going to be "running the occupation of Iraq."

But neither Rumsfeld, Cheney, nor Bush had ever talked about *occupying* Iraq. They had talked about *liberating* Iraq. Bremer kept these views to himself until it was too late.

SHOWDOWN AT THE HUNTING CLUB

Bremer decided to pick his fight almost as soon as he arrived in Baghdad.

Waiting for him was a small team of U.S. officials—he called them his "governance team"—led by a State Department Arabist, Ryan Crocker, and a former staffer for Democratic senator Daniel Patrick Moynihan, Meghan O'Sullivan, who had burrowed into the bureaucracy and was now a career State Department employee. Bremer clearly fell under her charms.

She was "well-organized . . . a personable young woman, Boston Irish, with red hair and a cheerful laugh." Bremer says he found her "brilliant," having earned a Ph.D. in political science from Oxford University.[3]

She was also a political adversary of everything the Bush administration stood for. As a deputy to Brent Scowcroft protégé Richard Haas at Policy Planning, she had coauthored the State Department's disastrous "smart sanctions" policy, which was aimed at reinforcing, at least in theory, the Clinton administration sanctions on Iraq. The idea was to remove from UN controls a broad range of civilian goods, while focusing international interdiction efforts on arms, spare parts, and high-technology goods. But in practice, when Colin Powell announced that the United States was considering these changes the entire UN sanctions regime simply collapsed. The experience helped to convince Bush and Cheney after 9/11 that they had to force the issue with Saddam, first at the United Nations, then if necessary by war.

Working with them was Roman Martinez, a twenty-five-year-old Cuban-American with a Harvard degree, who had been sent to Baghdad by Bill Luti as his eyes and ears. What Luti didn't realize was that what Martinez saw and heard he discussed first with Meghan O'Sullivan and Ryan Crocker before reporting back to the Pentagon. All three of them—whom Bremer quickly adopted as his own brain trust—were determined to send the Iraqi Leadership Council into the dustbin of history.

Bremer was positively gloating when he told them of his decision to "fire" Chalabi and his "small group of exiles." Crocker asked him when he planned to break the news to the ILC.

> "Tomorrow afternoon," I said. "In the morning, I'll be good cop when I sign the de-Baathification order. Then, during my five o'clock meeting with the leadership crowd, I'll let them know that we're not about to turn over the keys to the kingdom."[4]

Bremer knew that Chalabi and the Iraqi Leadership Council were furious with Garner over his decision to keep a number of top Baathists at key government ministries, so he expected them to react favorably to his de-Baathification order. To make his "bad cop" routine go more smoothly, however, Bremer sent British ambassador John Sawers to the Hunting Club, where Chalabi and the other six members of the Iraqi Leadership Council were waiting to get the nod from the new viceroy of Baghdad.

Ambassador Sawers had arrived in Baghdad just the day before Bremer, but had already come to the conclusion that the Garner era had been a "disaster." After just four days in Baghdad, he wrote a scathing memo to Prime Minister Tony Blair claiming that Garner was "out of his depth" that was widely quoted by the left-wing press. He and Bremer saw eye-to-eye on how to deal with the Iraqi opposition, but he thought it was best to break the news diplomatically.

"There's been a change of plans in Washington," he said.

"We can see that," Chalabi agreed, gracious, but wary. "The president has sent a new representative. We welcome this."

"You don't understand," Sawers said. "The NSC principals have decided that it's not the right time to transfer sovereignty to a provisional Iraqi government. They believe we need more time to build democratic institutions, to lay the groundwork for a more broad-based leadership group."

"Broad-based?" Chalabi feigned astonishment, and went around the table, introducing his partners. Jalal Talabani and Massoud Barzani, the leaders of the two main parties in Iraqi Kurdistan, between them represented around 15 percent of the population. Ibrahim al-Jaafari, leader of the Shiite Islamic Dawa Party, and Hamid al-Bayati, spokesman for the Supreme Council for the Islamic Revolution in Iraq (SCIRI), represented the two main factions among religious-minded Shias, who all together accounted for another 60 percent of the population. He himself was a secular Shia, as was Dr. Iyad Allawi, whose Iraqi National Accord also included a number of prominent former Baathists.

"The only people not represented here are the supporters of Saddam Hussein," Chalabi said. "Is that what Ambassador Bremer is referring to?"

Sawers was diplomatic, but insistent. The coalition was envisaging more of an advisory role for the Iraqis. There were issues of stability, of Iraq's Arab neighbors. Bremer had asked him to give the ILC a heads-up that they were *not* going to get the nod that afternoon.

Slowly, the message sank in.

"Okay," Chalabi said finally. "In a way you're doing us a favor. Now *you're* going to have to take the blame for everything that goes wrong."

It was a phrase that no one would forget in the years to come.

IN SADDAM'S PALACE

Bremer wasn't shy about his imperial pretensions. After deputizing the British ambassador as his messenger boy to summon the Iraqis to Saddam's palace, he wrote that he "personally thanked each 'guest' for accepting our invitation."

The American royal "we" was inviting prominent Iraqis as guests in their own country. No one could criticize Jerry Bremer for being shy.

The Iraqis went out of their way to thank the coalition for having liberated their country. Patriotic Union of Kurdistan leader Jalal Talabani warned Bremer that the coalition could yet squander its military victory "by not conducting a rapid, coordinated effort to form a new government."

In Bremer's book, Talabani is one of a "small group of exiles" who were out of touch with Iraq. But Talabani had been in northern Iraq for much of the past twelve years, in the U.S.-protected UN safe-haven. After Bremer returned to the United States, Talabani went on to become Iraq's elected president and continued to serve in that position when this book went to press.

Others issued similar polite warnings, as Bremer sat stonily, visibly unmoved. "With respect, Ambassador Bremer, I must remind the CPA of the promises made in the past month about the establishment of a transitional government in a few weeks' time," Chalabi said, looking over toward Jay Garner. Zal Khalilzad had promised the Iraqis at his last meeting with them, on May 2, that the United States planned to transfer power to them as soon as he returned from consultations in Washington. The mention of his former rival sent Bremer over the top.

"I reject the idea that the coalition is stalling," the viceroy said forcefully. "As I have said, the process will be incremental and must have as its goal a truly representative group. This body is not representative. There is only one Arab Sunni leader among you," Bremer said.[5]

Four months later, speaking to PBS's *Frontline*, Bremer was quick to downplay the accounts given by Chalabi and others on the Iraqi Leadership Council of the promises that had been made to them by presidential envoy Zal Khalilzad.

"I don't know what other people may have said," Bremer said. "But the fact of the matter was there was no way there was going to be an early Iraqi government. It simply was not possible. Anybody who thought it was possible obviously wasn't sitting here on the ground looking at a city on fire. . . . This was obvious to anybody with eyes."[6]

That confrontation in the Baghdad Hunting Club, and later at the palace, where Bremer had set up shop, effectively changed the U.S. presence from liberation to occupation and lit the spark for the insurgency that continues today. Bremer simply dismissed the INC as "exiles" and told them that the transitional government they thought they would be heading was being stood down.

"I told those five people, the leaders of those five parties, exactly that on the evening of May 16, at my first meeting with them," he told *Frontline.* "I said, 'You people don't represent this country, and you're going to have to now broaden yourselves if you want to be considered the basis of a transitional government.' "

Bremer's contempt for the Iraqi leadership was such that he couldn't even count how many of them he had summoned to his office in the palace as his "guests." (In his book, he names all seven of them.)

Bremer may have been acting out of monumental hubris or just plain incompetence, rather than out of any desire to undermine the Bush administration's strategy of liberating Iraq from dictatorship and rapidly standing up a representative government. But his unilateral, imperial decision followed the advice of the State Department and the CIA, over the objections of the Pentagon and White House strategists who thought they had the president's ear. "We were stunned when we heard what Bremer had done," a senior advisor to the president involved in planning the war and its aftermath told me in June 2007. "This decision of his just came out of the blue."

A former top Pentagon official, long involved with Chalabi and the INC, agreed. "Chalabi's enemies hated him so much they were prepared to deny Iraqi sovereignty to prevent him from gaining power, whereas Chalabi's friends were ready to accept any solution that gave Iraq sovereignty with or without Chalabi," he said. "We weren't pushing for a particular role for Chalabi. It's Chalabi's critics who made him the issue, not his friends. The objective was not to impose Chalabi, but Iraqi sovereignty."

By firing Chalabi and the Iraqi Leadership Council, all hope for a quick restoration of Iraqi sovereignty effectively ended. Kanan Makiya believes this is where the insurgency began. It didn't start as "resistance to occupation," he told PBS *Frontline.*

> It's Mafia-like tactics by the remnants of the Baath Party, which are quickly fusing into fundamentalist, Islamist, Wahhabi-leaning parties. There's a dangerous, dangerous convergence. The very al Qaeda–Saddam connection which got so discussed before the war is materializing before our very eyes. I see it in the leaflets that these fedayeen put out. The language is al Qaeda language now. So there's a very interesting sense in which all of that is coming home to roost.

Thanks to Bremer and his imperial-style rule, unemployed former Baathists, Sunni tribesmen, and Shia militiamen made common cause with foreign jihadis against the United States instead of doing the far more natural thing, which would have been to join in the reconstruction of their country. Bremer's decision to cut Iraqis out of their own future just four days after he arrived in Baghdad set in motion the insurgency and directly caused the deaths of more than 3,500 U.S. military personnel.

More than four years later, the same men Bremer dismissed so imperiously as "unrepresentative" are today running Iraq as democratically elected leaders.

It was all a terrible waste.

Garner, who was at the meeting in Saddam's palace, left Baghdad a few weeks later, and on June 18, 2003, met with Defense Secretary Donald Rumsfeld at the Pentagon and told him it was a "terrible mistake" to have dismissed the Iraqi Leadership Council.

"Jerry Bremer can't be the face of the government to the Iraqi people. You've got to have an Iraqi face for the Iraqi people," he reportedly said.[7]

But for Rumsfeld, history marched in one direction. The decision had been made, and there was no walking it back. If it was a mistake, as Garner said, then the United States was going to have to live with it.

Richard Perle believes Rumsfeld deserves his share of blame as well. "The strategy all along was to stand up an interim government," he told me in November 2006. "Bremer knew that. But when he gets out there he says, It can't be done, they're not ready for prime time. And that's the end of that. Nobody fights it."

Even Rumsfeld decided to "wash his hands," Perle said. "Rumsfeld began to take a very restrictive view of his responsibilities. He was there to fight the war, not to worry about the politics of the postwar administration. If it looked political, he just wasn't interested. History will fault him for it."

MISSED OPPORTUNITIES

The incompetence of Bremer's inner circle was as great as his own arrogance.

People like Meghan O'Sullivan, Bremer's attractive, red-haired "brainiac," and Dan Senor, his spokesman, had never served or even traveled in the Middle East before. "The closest they ever came to the region before the CPA was watching *Lawrence of Arabia*," a former Arabic-speaking colleague said. And yet, they would accompany Bremer on many of his most sensitive forays to meet with Iraqi leaders.

Not long after Bremer arrived in Baghdad, he decided to visit the *husseiniyeh* of prominent Shiite cleric Mohammad Baqr al-Sadr in the Al-Kadhimiya neighborhood north of Baghdad. On the first attempt to find the religious center, Bremer's bodyguard's got lost. (As unbelievable as it may sound, neither the U.S. military or the CPA had accurate street maps of Baghdad for several weeks after the liberation.) On the second attempt, using an Arab translator as guide, they finally found al-Sadr's compound. Accompanying Bremer were Ryan Crocker, Hume Horan, and Meghan O'Sullivan, who was dressed American-style, with free-flowing hair and a revealing open shirt. Sadr's assistant, who spoke no English, was appalled when he saw her and tried to protest, but Bremer swept him aside and marched into the religious complex.

No wonder Sadr gave them a frosty reception. O'Sullivan had just marched into a Shiite shrine without even covering her head. Perfectly normal, perhaps, for a young American woman entering a church or a synagogue on Fifth Avenue. But for the Iraqi cleric, it was not just an affront to traditional customs but a personal humiliation as well. It reinforced the impression beginning to build in Baghdad that the Americans had come not to liberate Iraq but to occupy it. He could not even control what happened in his own compound.

Once Bremer made it clear he was the new ruler of Iraq, tribal leaders from around the country flocked to Baghdad to pay tribute. They would arrive in small groups at the Assassins Gate, the main entry to the palace, and Bremer's staff would send a translator to see what they wanted. Some brought live chickens, or cakes. Others had composed poetry in Bremer's honor, just as they had done for Saddam. The translator would offer them tea—something the Americans never did—and listen.

In June 2003, a group of tribal sheikhs from predominantly Sunni al-Anbar Province came to the palace. This was before a single bullet had been fired by Sunni insurgents. Bremer wouldn't receive them, so they spoke with an aide through one of his translators.

Let us tell you why we supported Saddam Hussein, the sheikhs said. It wasn't out of love. It wasn't because we were Baathists. It was because he paid us. Every three months we would come here to the palace and he would give us money, and we would go back and pay the imams and tell them what to preach. That was how the system worked. We did it to survive.

The tribal sheikhs said they were ready to pledge loyalty to Bremer in the same way, but they wanted three things in exchange. The first was money they could distribute to their clans. The second was an understanding that they would remain in charge of the tribal criminal justice system when it came to "honor" crimes. If someone from one clan killed a member of another clan, they wanted to mete out justice. Come to us, and we will handle it, they said. But if you Americans get involved, then both clans will unite against you.

In exchange, they would police their own people, to ensure there were no attacks on U.S. forces. If anyone from our area lifts a finger against you, then you must punish us. That's the deal.

The third thing they wanted was jobs. The sheikhs complained that the Americans were bringing in foreigners to drive trucks in their country. Why? they wondered. How would you feel if your government brought in Canadians or Mexicans to drive trucks in the United States? We want to be part of the reconstruction.

Bremer's aide promised that he would pass on the message. The sheikhs agreed to return in a week's time to hear Bremer's response.

Reports on the sheikhs' offer were typed up and circulated to Bremer and his staff. For the most part, they just elicited shrugs. There was no way the United States was coming to Iraq to enshrine some backward system of tribal justice, most felt. The Defense Intelligence Agency objected that they couldn't possibly allow Iraqis to drive supply trucks, because that way they would know U.S. military movements. And that was that.

The sheikhs returned to the palace the next week, and were told that Bremer had rejected their proposed agreement.

They never repeated the gesture of deference to the new American occupiers. Instead, they threw their support behind the jihadis and the former Baathists, who were sending out feelers to them from their safe havens just across the border in Syria. And, of course, even without supplying drivers for U.S. convoys, they knew all they needed to know about U.S. military movements and were able to attack them at will.

FROM LIBERATION TO OCCUPATION

The final nail in the coffin was UN Security Council Resolution 1483, which was adopted on May 22, 2003. It declared that the United States was the "occupying power" in Iraq and informed Iraqis that they were no longer a sovereign nation.

Bremer said it was just a technicality, drafted at the request of the State

Department lawyers. But the entire Iraqi Leadership Council (now relegated to a consultancy role by Bremer) found it so shocking that they asked Chalabi to travel to Washington in mid-June to discuss it with their supporters in Congress.

When Bremer learned of Chalabi's plans, he arranged with the Pentagon to give live, video-conferenced testimony to the House Armed Services committee on June 12, 2003, the very morning that Chalabi arrived in Washington, and then to brief the press right afterward on recent developments in Iraq.

None of the reporters asked him about his decision to dismiss the Iraqi Leadership Council, and he didn't volunteer the information. He insisted, however, that UNSC Resolution 1483 called for the establishment of an "interim administration" of Iraqis handpicked by the occupation authority. He made it sound as if Iraqis had never engaged in politics before.

> "The political council will be made up of some twenty-five to thirty Iraqis from all walks of life and from the various strands of Iraqi society: men, women, Shia, Sunnis, Kurds and Arabs, tribal leaders, Christians, Turkomen, urban people, et cetera, professionals. That group is the subject of some rather intense consultations that we're undergoing right now with people from all of those walks of life."[8]

I met with Chalabi that afternoon inside the U.S. Capitol, where he was being hosted by Representative Chris Cox (R-CA), the chairman of the Republican Study Group.

In the public part of that meeting, the Washington press corps blasted Chalabi and the Iraqi National Congress for having presented "fake" defectors to the United States with "fabricated information" about Saddam's WMD programs.

Reporters said that the CIA had found that INC defectors were "imposters" who had "no knowledge" of Iraqi weapons programs. So what do you have to say for yourself, Mr. Chalabi?

Chalabi knew a put-up job when he saw one, but he responded patiently nonetheless. The INC had presented "three main defectors," he explained. The first was put in the U.S. Witness Protection Program on December 17, 2001, "because his information was considered so valuable. He was an engineer who built WMD sites."

I was familiar with the source, whose information the INC had shared with me after he was whisked off for safekeeping by the CIA. The individual, whose name I knew, was not a weapons designer—and the INC had never claimed that he was. He was a contractor whose job was to apply specialized coatings to the insides of small, secret facilities to prevent radioactive, chemical, or biological emissions from leaking. Because of that specialty, he was given access to a wide range of sites, some of them installed in the cellars of ordinary houses. His information was priceless and was subsequently corroborated by CIA and DIA postwar assessment teams. "The Intelligence Community has never deemed Source One to be a fabricator and has not recalled his reporting," a detailed Senate intelligence committee review concluded.[9]

The second source had provided information on the mobile bioweapons labs, information that was corroborated by a non-INC source and used by Secretary of State Colin Powell in his United Nations presentation on February 7, 2003.*

The third source provided information on Atomic Vapor Laser Isotope Separation (AVLIS), a process used to enrich uranium, and was still cooperating with the INC.

"There was no hyping, and no information that was unsubstantiated," Chalabi said. "If anyone was at fault, it was the intelligence community. We turned over to them whatever we found. It was their job to evaluate the intelligence."

Later, in Representative Cox's walnut-paneled private office down an unmarked corridor deep inside the U.S. Capitol, the conversation shifted back to political developments in Iraq.

Chalabi said he was concerned because Bremer seemed to be "changing his mind" every other day. "We outlined the process just short of the election of a provisional assembly," he told Cox. "All that is now on the back burner." Instead, Bremer was now saying he wanted a handpicked Iraqi council in six months. "That's a long time in politics." He laughed.

Then he became deadly serious. The attitude toward U.S. troops in Iraq had changed dramatically in recent weeks now that the United States had sponsored a UN Security Council resolution that acknowledged the United States as the "occupying power."

Iraqis were "shocked and bewildered" by UNSC Resolution 1483, Chalabi told Cox. "Bremer told us the resolution had been drafted by the lawyers. Maybe so. But remember that President Bush announced that the United States was coming as liberators, not as occupiers. We don't think

---

*The non-INC source, code-named CURVEBALL, was brought to the U.S. intelligence community by the Germans, who later claimed they had warned that they believed he was lying. A great deal has been written about CURVEBALL, most of it false. I will deal with this source in greater detail in Chapter 19.

the United States should lose the moral high ground. We need a strong statement from the White House" reiterating the U.S. goal of helping Iraqis move toward self-governance.

Chalabi gave his mischievous grin. "We're told it was the French who pressed the hardest to get that resolution," he confided.

Cox chuckled at the mention of the French. No one needed to be reminded of the obnoxious strutting and preening of French foreign minister Dominique de Villepin when the United States sought UN approval for coalition military action against Saddam. Cox agreed to raise the issue with the president's advisors.

While he was careful not to attack Bremer personally, Chalabi warned that the decisions Bremer had taken to stop the political process in Iraq were having a disastrous effect. "The Iraqi people must have a political process, immediately," he insisted. "If you deny that, you open the door to people who speak about resistance against the U.S. occupation. The process we have been advocating is not a U.S. or a Pentagon process but an Iraqi process of enfranchising the Iraqi people immediately after liberation. The last thing we need is a handpicked U.S. governing council."

And yet, that is exactly where Bremer was now headed.

Privately, aides to Chalabi told me that they were bemused at the way they were being treated in Baghdad by the U.S. military. "CENTCOM has been raiding our headquarters, arresting our people," they complained. "We'd go to the house of a senior Baathist to arrest someone or look for documents, and then twenty minutes later the Americans would come and arrest us! It was clear the houses were being watched by other Baathists."

It was less clear why U.S. forces would arrest the INC members and not the Baathists. Think of it for a moment: The United States had, as potential allies, an indigenous Iraqi political movement that was pro-Western and that favored free elections and a free-market economy. That movement had thousands of operatives on the ground who were Iraqi, who knew the neighborhoods and knew how to ask the right questions to gather valuable intelligence on where top Baathists were hiding and where key documents had been stashed. And yet, Bremer and the occupation authorities turned against the INC rather than use their services, out of concern that they would alienate the Baathists who had been defeated in war.

It was a stunning waste, which over time would become tragic.

Earlier that day, a U.S. Apache helicopter was shot down in northern Iraq by insurgents. Referring to this latest attack, Chalabi revealed that

U.S. field commander Lieutenant General David D. McKiernan had rejected proposals to establish an Iraqi security force under U.S. command that could have prevented this and other attacks.

Chalabi said he had repeatedly proposed establishing an Iraqi force that would handle looters, battle the remnants of the Baath Party regime, and help reduce U.S. casualties, but that "U.S. commanders don't want to see Iraqis with guns."

The INC proposal would create Iraqi units under U.S. command and supervision. "There would be ten Iraqis to one American," Chalabi said. "All our units would patrol jointly with the Americans." Such patrols, he added, would greatly reduce U.S. casualties. In the six weeks since President Bush had declared an end to major hostilities on May 1, one U.S. soldier was being killed by enemy fire in Iraq every day.

"There is no need to increase the deployment of U.S. forces in Iraq to guarantee security," Chalabi said. "Building up the Free Iraqi Forces will allow the United States to begin withdrawing forces and to cease being targets of terrorists. Why don't you let us fight these bastards?"

Both Bremer and the commander of U.S. forces, Lieutenant General John Abizaid, turned him down. And not a single Democrat in Congress—so eager today to withdraw U.S. troops from Iraq—said a word.

THE INSURGENCY BEGINS

By now the insurgency had begun, fueled by al Qaeda, Iran, and Syria. But U.S. commanders and political leaders had not yet recognized its potential to create chaos, nor had the media.

The American public stood firmly behind the president and the war. By the end of July 2003, the NBC News/Wall Street Journal tracking poll showed Americans giving Bush a 56 percent job approval rating. When asked if they believed the United States had "made the right decision" to use military force against Iraq, a Pew Research Center poll found that 67 percent of those surveyed thought the president had been right. That would soon change.

One sour note was beginning to creep into the polling data. When *Newsweek* asked a group of 1,003 adults on July 10–11, 2003, if they approved or disapproved of the way Bush was handling the situation in Iraq, 39 percent now said that they disapproved. This was a sharp spike from the previous poll, conducted in May, when only 29 percent disapproved.

On this question, Bush's numbers would never recover.

Two years and nearly two thousand American dead later, the U.S. military finally began to adopt Chalabi's proposals and to focus on training Iraqi security forces, although they continued to shun Chalabi and refused to allow his supporters join the new force. But with the intervening explosion of sectarian fighting and death squads and Iranian-backed militias, the task had become many times more difficult.

In December 2006, the Baker-Hamilton Iraq Study Group released its long-awaited report, which they claimed presented a bipartisan consensus for drawing down the U.S. troop presence in Iraq in favor of U.S.-trained Iraqi security forces. The report pointedly ignored the entire 2003–2005 period, when the key mistakes that fostered the insurgency were made.

Iraqi foreign minister Hoshyar Zebari, a top aide to Kurdish leader Massoud Barzani, reinforced the importance of Bremer's historic error in an interview with the *Wall Street Journal.* "The biggest mistake, honestly, if you go back, was not entrusting the Iraqis as partners, to empower them, to see them do their part, to fill the vacuum, to have a national unity government."[10]

Instead, Jerry Bremer, on the advice of the State Department, the CIA, and even some at the Pentagon, decided simply to push the Iraqis aside and establish imperial rule.

The Greek tragedies of Sophocles and Aeschylus are full of characters who are powerfully drawn toward a certain course of action by their character, temperament, or belief despite being warned that those same actions were likely to unleash devastating consequences. I do not judge Jerry Bremer's mistake from the comfort of hindsight, but on the basis of the knowledge and the advice he was given at the time. Jerry Bremer, through his arrogance and his ability for self-delusion, refused to listen.

Henry Kissinger was chatting with an acquaintance in the green room at Fox News in May 2003, shortly after Bremer's appointment to Baghdad was announced. You must be pleased, the acquaintance said. Bremer was then president of Kissinger & Associates.

But Kissinger just shook his head. *Jerry Bremer*, he said. *Always number two, never number one. The president is making a huge mistake.*

It was a tragic mistake—for Bush, for Iraq, and for the cause of freedom.

CHAPTER EIGHT

JOE WILSON LIES

Few Americans have ever heard of C. Edward Bernier, and for good reason. At the peak of his professional career, he was the head of the United States Information Service office in Islamabad, Pakistan, and spokesman for U.S. embassies in Saudi Arabia and Egypt, not exactly positions that thrust him into the limelight back home.

Bernier came out of retirement in February 2003 at age sixty-eight to take one last job: as a shadow warrior in Lieutenant General Jay Garner's Office of Reconstruction and Humanitarian Assistance (ORHA) in Kuwait. He was hired by the International Resources Group, a headhunter working for ORHA on contract to the U.S. Agency for International Development (USAID), and paid $685 per day as a media consultant. ORHA wanted his help in generating positive stories about the war, and in advising U.S. military commanders on Muslim culture.

But Bernier didn't like what he saw, especially once U.S. troops liberated Baghdad. Garner's team was exhilarated by the reaction of ordinary Iraqis, who greeted the first U.S. troops as liberators. "I was disgusted, it was denigrating," he said later. He was especially upset that he was being given orders by younger superiors "with zero background in the region."

After just three months on the job, Bernier quit and returned to Hilton Head Island, South Carolina, a resort and retirement community best known as the site of Bill Clinton's Renaissance Weekend retreats in the early 1990s. There, he boasted to friends that he had earned close to $30,000 a month while using his time in theater "to dig up stuff" to be used against the war effort and the president.[1]

Bernier's wife, Geraldine, was the president of a Democratic Party club and a prolific writer of anti-Bush letters to the *Island Packet*, the local newspaper. She wrote to oppose the war in Iraq at the very moment her husband was earning $685 a day in Kuwait, staging to go to Baghdad. "I am deeply saddened that our leaders resorted to a long-planned, preemptive war, rather than continuing to pursue multilateral diplomatic and deterrent efforts," she wrote in a survey of reader opinion published on March 23, 2003. "One would hope also that those who made and support the decision to go to war will show the same levels of resolve and resource commitment . . . to address the myriad problems facing millions of Americans at home."[2]

As he discussed what he had seen with his politically active wife, Bernier came up with an idea. He framed it in a mass e-mail he sent on June 10, 2003, to former foreign service colleagues.

"Dear friends," he began. "As the news continues to report no weapons of mass destruction, as Osama bin Laden remains somewhere out there, as Saddam Hussein has not been found, is it not time to ask ourselves how and why the American public has put up with lying from this administration for such a long time? Is there something we can do, can start? Can we launch a campaign that might grow to greater proportions that would remind our fellow Americans that George W. Bush has lied, and continues to lie to the world and to the American people?

"A bumper sticker that says: 'Bush lies,' for example? An e-mail campaign? Collecting funds for a national television ad pointing out Mr. Bush's lies? What else?"

Bernier asked the recipients of his message to forward it to "all you know," and to send him their ideas. (His message wound up at *Insight*, which then called him to verify the contents.)

Bernier says he did nothing more to generate the *Bush Lied, People Died!* campaign beyond this single e-mail, but ideas have a way of taking off through the Internet beyond the wildest expectations of their original authors. Within weeks, websites devoted to "Bush Lies" sprang up, and bumper stickers were printed and sold in huge quantities to Bush opponents from coast to coast.

THE AMBASSADOR WEIGHS IN

Two days after Bernier sent his "Bush Lies" e-mail, *Washington Post* reporter Walter Pincus revealed that the CIA had sent a "retired U.S. ambassador" to Niger in February 2002 to investigate an alleged Iraqi purchase of uranium. His report back to the CIA supposedly "disputed" a "key component of President Bush's claim" in his January 2003 State of the Union address that Saddam Hussein had revived his nuclear weapons program.[3]

It was a leak of the first order, and the *Post* properly gave it front-page treatment. Pincus sourced the information to "senior U.S. officials" and a "former government official," who spoke on condition that the name of the former ambassador not be disclosed.

No wonder Pincus included that caveat. It was the ambassador himself—the CIA's "special envoy"—who had leaked the story to him, in an effort to discredit the president of the United States.

Joseph C. Wilson IV, a former U.S. ambassador to the African state of Gabon, had been watching the steadily mounting controversy over Saddam Hussein's WMD programs for months, and believed he had information that could tip the scales against the president. So he began by leaking anonymously to the *Washington Post*, as he subsequently admitted to Senate investigators.[4]

He had seen the infamous Niger uranium documents, he told Pincus. He concluded that the "dates were wrong and the names were wrong," and that they must have been forged. Despite this, the president continued to include the claim that Iraq had attempted to buy uranium in Niger in speeches and statements and various fact sheets, knowing full well that it was false, Wilson insisted.

When he saw the story going nowhere, Wilson decided to take the plunge, and penned a 1,452-word op-ed showcased in the Sunday edition of the *New York Times* on July 6, 2003.

Titled "What I Didn't Find in Africa," Wilson's story began with a bombshell: "Did the Bush administration manipulate intelligence about Saddam Hussein's weapons programs to justify an invasion of Iraq? Based on my experience with the administration in the months leading up to the war, I have little choice but to conclude that some of the intelligence related to Iraq's nuclear weapons program was twisted to exaggerate the Iraqi threat."

It was a classic kiss-and-tell memoir. Wilson revealed the inner workings of the Bush administration "lies" about Iraq, from the point of view of someone who had participated in them. It was a great story—if only it were true.

It would take more than a year before the patchwork of lies, half-truths, and innuendo purveyed by Ambassador Wilson was finally debunked in an exhaustive investigation by the Senate intelligence committee. But in the meantime, the damage was done.

In his *New York Times* op-ed, Wilson said that in February 2002, he was asked by the Central Intelligence Agency to travel to Niger to investigate "a particular intelligence report" that documented the sale of uranium to Iraq by the Niger government. Although the CIA had agreed to pay his expenses, he said he donated his time "pro bono," and that "there was nothing secret about my trip."

The CIA wanted him to "check out the story so they could provide a response to the vice president's office," after Vice President Dick Cheney had raised questions about it, he wrote.

His message was clear. *The Evil Dick Cheney was behind it all.*

Once he arrived in Niger's capital, Niamey, Wilson says, he met with U.S. ambassador Barbro Owens-Kirkpatrick, then "spent the next eight days drinking sweet mint tea" and meeting with former government officials and others involved in the uranium business. "It did not take long to conclude that it was highly doubtful that any such transaction had ever taken place."

And that is what he reported back to the CIA and to the State Department African Affairs Bureau, Wilson wrote.

"When I saw Wilson's name on that *New York Times* article, I said, what's this? Isn't that prohibited?" a White House lawyer told me. Every person working for the CIA, even the contract workers known as "green badgers," was required to sign a nondisclosure form, which prohibited them from writing about their activities without pre-clearance from the CIA Publications Board. "But when we called over, it turned out that Wilson had never been asked to file the nondisclosure form. We were stunned. He was the only one in CIA history who was given such license," the White House lawyer exclaimed.

Former CIA operations officers also took note. "It was highly unusual," said one thirty-year veteran of the Operations Directorate, a former station chief in Europe and South America. "Both Tenet and McLaughlin—then CIA director and his deputy—said they knew nothing about Wilson's little escapade. So who signed off on it? Jim Pavitt? Steve Kappes? Someone had to give their approval." Pavittt still headed the Directorate of Operations when Wilson was sent to Niger, and Kappes was then his deputy. Both were at odds with the Bush White House.

The implication was clear. Someone at CIA had made a conscious decision to waive every security procedure on the books to allow Wilson to leak a classified operation to the media, without even the knowledge of the CIA director himself. It had all the trappings of a sophisticated disinformation operation, orchestrated and approved by shadow warriors within the Agency itself.

The *New York Times* op-ed instantly catapulted Wilson onto prime-time television, where he became the darling of the anti-Bush media. Within days, the story line had jelled: Vice President Cheney had sent Joe Wilson to Africa to get the dope on Saddam but then covered up his report, because he didn't like what Wilson had found.

However, a Senate intelligence committee investigation subsequently found information that directly contradicted nearly every critical point of Wilson's story.[5]

- The vice president's office not only had *no role* in sending Wilson to Niger, it had *never been told* about his mission or been briefed on his findings. In fact, it was *Wilson's own wife, Valerie Plame,* a CIA weapons analyst, who recommended him for the job. (p. 74)
- Wilson's oral debriefing to the CIA on March 5, 2002, did not debunk the intelligence reports of a potential uranium deal with Saddam. Instead, he spoke of "expanding commercial relations" between Niger and Iraq, which the CIA interpreted—as did former government officials Wilson spoke to in Niger—as meaning uranium sales. (p. 43)
- Wilson confirmed that an Iraqi commercial delegation (which was led by Iraqi nuclear expert Wissam al-Zahawie) had come to Niger in February 1999. The CIA report on the Wilson trip, issued on March 8, 2002, concluded that "the delegation wanted to discuss uranium yellowcake sales."(p. 43)
- Instead of proving Saddam had never tried to purchase uranium from Niger, in the eyes of most analysts *Wilson's report "lent more credibility to the original Central Intelligence Agency (CIA) reports on the uranium deal,"* the committee concluded. (p. 73)
- Wilson's trip and the CIA report that was based on his debriefing were stamped "Secret." In addition, Wilson was granted an "operational clearance" up to the Secret level by the CIA for this mission, thus raising a question about the legality of his *New York Times* op-ed. (p. 41)

And then there was his claim about the forged documents. The Senate committee found that Wilson had "never seen the CIA reports" and had "no knowledge of what names and dates were in the reports." He admitted that he may have "misspoken" to the *Washington Post* reporter when he said he had seen the documents and concluded that they were forged. "He also said he may have become confused about his own recollection after the IAEA reported in March 2003 that the names and dates on the documents were not correct."(p. 45)

Even the *Washington Post* finally admitted, three years later, that "Mr. Wilson was the one guilty of twisting the truth," not the president, and that Wilson's report "*supported the conclusion* that Iraq had sought uranium" from Niger.[6]

But just like corrections buried deep inside the *New York Times*, the truth about Joe Wilson's trip to Niger came too late and received too little attention to have much impact on the public debate. The damage had been done.[7]

PLAMEGATE

To counter Wilson's false allegations to the media, the White House decided to declassify portions of the October 2002 National Intelligence Estimate on Iraq's WMD programs, and instructed Cheney chief of staff I. Lewis ("Scooter") Libby to brief reporters on background on the Niger evidence. Separately, and apparently without speaking to Libby, veteran Washington journalist Robert Novak accurately mentioned that the person who had recommended Wilson for the Niger mission was not Vice President Cheney but Wilson's own wife, Valerie Plame, "an Agency operative on weapons of mass destruction."*

It was the kind of Washington insider's tidbit that was Novak's stock-in-trade. But in this instance, his name-dropping would have far-reaching consequences.

Two days after his fateful July 14, 2003 column appeared, left-wing commentator David Corn—a friend of the Wilsons—lobbed the first mortar at the White House. Corn's article carried the unambiguous title "A White House Smear." It began rhetorically:

---

*Despite Novak's accurate reporting, the myth that Cheney was behind Wilson's trip to Niger was repeated by the Left at every opportunity. Even Pulitzer Prize–winner Ron Suskind fell for it in his 2006 book on Cheney, *The One Percent Doctrine* (New York: Simon & Schuster). "Wilson had been sent by the CIA, at the behest of Cheney, in February 2002," he wrote on page 243 in his account of Wilson's Niger trip. That was just one of many untruths Suskind would repeat in his sophisticated attempt to smear the Bush administration.

> "Did senior Bush officials blow the cover of a U.S. intelligence officer working covertly in a field of vital importance to national security—and break the law—in order to strike at a Bush administration critic and intimidate others?"

Ever since the unsuccessful assault on the Cheney energy task force in early 2001, the Democrats had been seeking to attack the president by going after the aides who gave him confidential advice in the White House. That effort finally gained traction with the Valerie Plame affair.

Although it was Corn who effectively blew Plame's cover (Novak had never mentioned she was undercover, and indeed, later said he wasn't aware that was the case),* Corn was never hauled before the grand jury by the special counsel, U.S. Attorney Patrick Fitzgerald. But virtually the entire White House staff was forced to submit to the Fitzgerald inquisition (as was Novak, who appeared four times). Top White House staff members were told to stop talking to reporters, and had to hire private attorneys and pay for them out of their government paychecks. Karl Rove was repeatedly threatened with indictment, and was so preoccupied by his legal woes that he focused on nothing else for months, colleagues said. Libby, the only one who was actually indicted—not for leaking her name, but for allegedly lying under oath to the grand jury about it—raised more than $2 million for his defense, but still faced a mountain of legal fees.

Even as the devastating impact on the White House became clear, the man who later admitted responsibility for the leak of Valerie Plame's name to Novak—Deputy Secretary of State Richard Armitage—remained silent. Right before his eyes, the president was getting mugged. All Armitage had to do was call for help, and yet he did nothing.

"I understand why Armitage wouldn't say anything," one White House staffer who was questioned by Fitzgerald said. "But we now know that Armitage told Powell that he suspected he was the source of the leak early on. Why then did Powell never come to the president and say, hey, it was Richie. There's no need to put your administration through a witch hunt. It just tells you something about [Powell] that he never did."

The Bush-hating press loved it, and created an entire cottage industry around "Plame-gate." Both *Newsweek* and *Time* ran cover stories blaming Karl Rove for the leak, while grudgingly acknowledging the Twilight

---

*When Novak asked the CIA about Mrs. Wilson, they told him she "was an analyst, not a spy, not a covert operative, and not in charge of undercover operatives. So what is the fuss about, pure Bush-bashing?" he remarked on CNN's *Crossfire* on September 29, 2003.

Zone quality of the allegations. *Time*'s cover package evoked "the long and lively mythology of Karl Rove," whom "Democrats view as the kind of operative who would put a tarantula under an opponent's pillow." *Newsweek*'s Howard Fineman pushed the envelope of rhetorical excess. The Plame story "isn't just about the Facts, it's about what Rove's foes regard as a higher Truth: that he is a one-man epicenter of a narrative of Evil."[8]

The left-wing Veteran Intelligence Professionals for Sanity (VIPS) piled on, led by the ever-intrepid Larry Johnson, who called the Plame affair an "organized plot by White House officials." Using pseudo lawyer-speak, he blasted Rove and Libby "and others not yet revealed" for having "destroyed by their reckless acts her career, a CIA front company, and a network of intelligence assets."

Larry could work himself into high dudgeon when attacking the Bush administration. "The important point is not that a law was broken, but that our country is in the hands of a President who is willing to tolerate people in his Administration who are admitted liars and who played a direct role in compromising our nation's security. President Bush is sending a clear message—it is more important to protect cronies than protect this country," he wrote. To enhance his credibility, Larry Johnson liked to remind people that he was a Republican.[9]

Later, in a particularly puerile rant, he claimed that Vice President Dick Cheney was the real culprit behind the alleged leak, and called on Cheney to resign. "Dick Cheney had a hand in pushing the 'nepotism' charge, you know, Joe Wilson only got the job because his wife hired him. Since Dick got his daughter a sweetheart deal at the State Department he should not be out casting such stones or encouraging others to do so. See Dick. See Dick run. See Dick resign."[10]

Armitage's subsequent admission showed, of course, that all of the them were dead wrong. And besides, the Wilsons' "claims to have been victimized by the Bush White House were destroyed when they agreed to be photographed sitting in their Jaguar for the January 2004 issue of *Vanity Fair*," as author Ronald Kessler pointed out. Wilson might protest that the sunglasses and scarf his wife donned for the glamour shot disguised her, but "anyone she had dealt with overseas could clearly recognize her."[11] And any claim that she had suffered financial damage because of the publicity became a joke after a New York publisher reportedly offered her a $2.5 million book deal.

Former CIA operations officer Bob Baer thought the whole claim that Valerie Plame had been covert was a joke. "You know how long it took me to break down her cover?" he asked me. "Five minutes. And you know why? Because she'd applied for a mortgage in Athens [Greece], using an APO address that was used by the CIA station. So she was under official cover. She was never undercover or covert. Once you have gone out on official cover, you can never go out as a covert officer. Thus, she was not a covert officer."

Similarly, what "covert" officer would give money under her own name to U.S. political candidates, as Plame did, disclosing an allegedly "covert" CIA front company, Brewster-Jennings & Associates, as her employer?

As Robert Novak later found, "There was no Brewster-Jennings & Associates, and there never had been. Brewster Jennings was a famous oil tycoon of the previous generation who had died in 1968." Writing in his recently released memoir, *The Prince of Darkness*, Novak added, "Brewster-Jennings & Associates was no dummy corporation to shield Mrs. Wilson as a covert agent because she was not involved in clandestine activities. Instead, each day she went to CIA headquarters in Langley, where she worked on arms proliferation. Some wag had given her the bogus Brewster-Jennings's corporate name."

In their review of the case, Republicans on the Senate intelligence committee found that intelligence community notes of meetings in which Valerie Plame participated "did not mark her name with a (C) as would be required to indicate that her association with the CIA was classified," as both Plame and her husband have said.[12]

So why did Patrick Fitzgerald pursue his investigation that ultimately led to Libby's conviction in May 2007? One reason has to do with the people involved. On one side were Libby, Rove, and the vice president of the United States. On the other were a pair of Clinton appointees who had burrowed into the Justice Department and vigorously pursued the investigation of the Bush White House, despite what they had already learned about Richard Armitage's role in inadvertently leaking Plame's name.

Before Fitzgerald was appointed, the investigation was being led by John Dion, a career federal prosecutor who was given a political appointment under Clinton. Assisting him was Bruce Swartz, another Clinton political appointee who was a contributor to Democratic party candidates.[13] By a remarkable coincidence, at the same time they were pursuing Scooter Libby mercilessly, these same Justice Department attorneys were heading the stunningly incurious investigation into former national security advisor Sandy Berger for the theft of classified documents from the National Archives, a crime for which he was never even sentenced to jail.[14]

U.S. senator (D-GA) Zell Miller, who bolted his party to support

President Bush's reelection in 2004, called the Valerie Plame affair a "sting operation" by the CIA against the Bush administration.

It had all the hallmarks of a classic spy thriller, where "institutional rivalries and political loyalties have fostered an intelligence officer's resentment against the government." Suddenly, an opportunity comes the CIA officer's way "to undercut the national leadership." Through her official functions, she learns of a vital question of intelligence that "forms the core justification for controversial military actions by the current leaders." If she can insert herself into the middle of the intelligence deliberations, "distort that information and make it public, the agent might foster regime change in the upcoming election," Miller wrote.

Valerie Plame told the Senate Select intelligence committee in 2004 that she thought the whole Niger allegation was just a "crazy report." Despite that, she suggested in a memo that CIA bosses send her husband to Niger to investigate it, noting that he had "good relations with both the PM [prime minister] and the former Minister of Mines *(not to mention lots of French contacts)*."[15] (emphasis mine)

As deputy director of the Counterproliferation Division's Iraq unit, Plame was supposed to be the weapons expert, not her husband. And that was precisely why she needed to send *him* to Niger instead of sending another CIA operative or offering to go herself. Agency rules prohibited employees such as Plame from purposely distorting intelligence, leaking secret information, or using their official position or information they obtained through it to manipulate U.S. elections. But there was no such prohibition on *spouses* of employees.

"Suppose the spouse adds just one more brilliant, well-aimed lie: claim your foremost political opponent put the spouse up to the trip," Miller argued. By suggesting that the vice president's office was behind his trip, as Wilson did in his initial *New York Times* op-ed, he was effectively baiting the trap. "Will your enemy suffer your spouse's lies or take the bait and try to clarify his nonrole? If he tells the press he didn't hire your spouse, the press will demand to know, 'Then who did?' "

And that's when they sprang the trap. "Instead of you violating secrecy laws, it is your victim who is guilty because he tried to set the record straight. Heads, you win; tails, he loses." It sounded incredible, but it was no fiction. "This is the story behind Valerie Plame, Joe Wilson and the Bush administration. And it appears that Plame and Wilson will get away with the biggest sting operation ever," Zell Miller wrote.

Intelligence committee staffers who were following the whole sordid affair agreed with Miller's assessment. "This is the first time the CIA has organized a sting operation not against a foreign enemy, but against the U.S. government," one congressional insider noted. "The CIA has become more concerned with becoming king-makers here at home than pursuing enemies abroad. This is spooks gone wild."

Zell Miller warned that the CIA was becoming a "domestic dirty tricks shop" that allowed its own operatives to conduct a covert operation "to destabilize a U.S. president."

> "Some absurdly claim that Plame had nothing to do with her husband's political activities against President Bush," Miller said. "But let it be clear. Plame could not have done what Wilson did and gotten away with it. Wilson could not have done what he did without Plame giving him a way to do it."

Miller urged Congress to adopt a new "Plame rule" that would impose the same legal obligation of secrecy on the spouses of intelligence officers tapped to help the Agency as on regular Agency employees.[16]

Zell Miller's suggestion made good common sense—and was never enacted.

WHO SENT JOE?

Valerie Plame Wilson went out of her way to dispute the conclusions of the Senate intelligence committee report in a circuslike appearance before a House committee chaired by Democrat bulldog Representative Henry Waxman on March 16, 2007. Under questioning, she insisted that she was *not* the one who recommended her husband for the Niger trip.

"No. I did not recommend him. I did not suggest him. There was no nepotism involved. I didn't have the authority," she said. Instead, she now claimed that the idea of sending him had come from a CIA colleague. She also claimed that the colleague who had testified to the Senate about her role in her husband's junket "came to me almost with tears in his eyes that his words had been twisted and distorted." He had written a memo asking his supervisor "to allow him to be re-interviewed . . . to set the record straight," she said.[17]

He lied once but we should believe him now, seemed to be Plame's message. The committee Democrats just lapped it up.

But the same goes for Valerie Plame herself.

"In February of 2002, a young junior officer who worked for me came to me very concerned, very upset," she told the Waxman Committee. "She had just received a telephone call on her desk from someone, I don't know who, in the Office of the Vice President, asking about this report of this alleged sale of yellowcake uranium from Niger to Iraq." The idea to send her husband to Niger resulted from that call, she insisted.

There's only one problem with her account. It doesn't tally with the evidence presented to Congress previously, or to the federal district court in Washington during the Scooter Libby trial.

Watch the dates.

The original Senate intelligence committee report from July 2004 found that Plame offered up her husband's name in a memorandum to her boss at the CIA's Counterproliferation Division on February 12, 2002.[18] But as *National Review* reporter Byron York, who covered the Scooter Libby trial on a daily basis, found, "it turns out Mrs. Wilson suggested her husband's trip *before* the vice president made his request for information." He explained, "A never-before-seen CIA document entered into evidence at the Libby trial showed that Cheney asked about possible Iraqi uranium purchases on February 13, 2002," the day *after* Plame offered her husband's services.[19]

Here was powerful new evidence supporting Zell Miller's claim of a CIA sting operation. Readers will find that newly declassified CIA document about the vice president's briefing in the appendix to this book.

And there is more. After Valerie Plame's flamboyant testimony before the Waxman committee, Republicans on the Senate Select intelligence committee went back to their original sources at CIA and sought to release documents that previously had been unavailable to the public.

Perhaps Ms. Plame never expected that anyone would challenge her statement, given of her own free will and under oath, that she "did not recommend" or "suggest" her husband for the Niger mission. Perhaps she just assumed that the truth would remain protected by secrecy. But the veil of secrecy was torn asunder on May 25, 2007, when the Senate intelligence committee finally released a facsimile of the entire e-mail from Valerie Plame to her boss at the CIA.

"The Committee did not release the full text of the document [initially], thinking it was unnecessary in light of the other evidence provided in the [original] report, but considering the controversy surrounding this document, making the full text available now seems prudent," Senators Kit Bond, Orin Hatch, and Ron Burr wrote.[20]

The Valerie Plame e-mail shows *without any doubt* that she recommended her husband for the mission in Niger, contrary to her sworn testimony. After recounting an earlier fact-finding mission he had carried out in Niger for the Agency, as well as his good contacts "with both the [prime minister] and the former minister of mines," she concluded by saying that her husband "may be in a position to assist. Therefore, request your thoughts on what, if anything to pursue here."

Either Valerie Plame has the memory of a mouse, or she should be investigated for possible perjury before the Waxman committee. (Readers can read the complete Plame e-mail at www.kentimmerman.com/shadow-warriors.htm).

JOE WILSON'S FRENCH TIES

Valerie Plame and Joe Wilson may have received help in smearing the White House from an unusual source: the government of French president Jacques Chirac.

The Niger uranium case blew wide open when an Italian investigating magistrate, Franco Ionta, summoned intelligence peddler Rocco Martino to give sworn testimony in the forged-documents case. Not only had he provided the fake Niger documents to his French intelligence handler, Martino said, he had acquired the documents at the *request* of the French, who then paid him to launder the forgeries and get them into the system "as part of a sting operation to 'set up' the United States."[21]

Italian diplomats told the *Daily Telegraph* that France "was trying to 'set up' Britain and America in the hope that when the mistake was revealed it would undermine the case for war, which it wanted to prevent."

Through the fog of disinformation, rumors, and outright lies, a pattern of French involvement gradually emerged. And it coincided with the larger French game plan, which I exposed in *The French Betrayal of America*, to undermine the U.S. case for war—not because the French believed it would throw the region into turmoil, as they later claimed, but so the French could benefit from $100 billion in oil contracts they had signed with Saddam that were contingent on Saddam's remaining in power.

The Volcker Commission, which investigated corruption in the UN's flawed oil-for-food program, found that French oil companies engaged willingly in the scheme that kicked back billions of dollars to Saddam. The Banque Nationale de Paris, which was the repository for the oil-for-food funds, made out like gangbusters. Cronies of President Chirac and his former interior minister, Charles Pasqua, were also identified by Volcker's team of forensic accountants as having benefited from Saddam's oil vouchers. Saddam was a cash cow for the French, and they wanted to milk him as long as possible. To achieve that goal they unleashed a bold, coordinated campaign of dirty tricks, disinformation, and outright lies aimed at sabotaging the U.S.-led effort to remove Saddam.

The French instructed Martino to "leak" the forged Niger documents to the Italian media in October 2002, just as French president Chirac was reassuring President Bush in private that France would help the United States if war with Saddam became necessary. (To convince Bush of his sincerity, Chirac sent the French military chief of staff to Tampa, Florida, to work out the operational details of incorporating French troops into the U.S. war plan against Saddam.) "The French forgery was a stink bomb, designed to be exposed in public as soon as Colin Powell publicly accepted it," opined James Lewis, a frequent contributor to the conservative netzine *American Thinker*. Lewis called it a "Watergate-style assault on the American Presidency, fronted by Ambassador Joseph C. Wilson IV."[22]

Wilson, of course, denies having anything but the most noble of motives. "Joe Wilson made the trip out there and reported back because he's a loyal American," he told an audience at the Virginia Military Institute in October 2003. "Joe Wilson did not betray his president."[23]

But Wilson clearly had betrayal on his mind, and joined the Kerry campaign as an advisor in May 2003, well before his initial *New York Times* article accusing the Bush administration of fabricating intelligence appeared.[24] Neither he nor the *New York Times* thought it necessary to disclose his relationship with Kerry, since it could have jeopardized Wilson's credibility as an "objective" observer. Also undisclosed was his previous work on Capitol Hill for Democrats Al Gore and House speaker Tom Foley, as well as any number of vitriolic anti-Bush speeches he gave to antiwar groups. In June 2003, for example, just days after the initial story in the *Washington Post*, Wilson told one such gathering, "I can assure you that that American ambassador to Africa [cited in the *Post* story] is also pissed off and has every intention of ensuring that that story has legs. . . . Because it was absolutely bogus for us to go to war as we did." At another point, he tried humor: "I'm a California boy. I'm moving back to California to run for governor on a secessionist ticket. And my slogan is, We don't want to be part of Texas. We don't want to be part of anything Texas is part of."[25]

Wilson's ties to the French also went way back. His father was a journalist, and when Wilson was a young man his father took him to Paris, where he learned the language and developed "a love of everything French."[26] From an early posting to Niger, Wilson gained a passing familiarity with the Niger uranium industry, which was controlled by

COGEMA, the French nuclear export authority (now known as Areva). He met his second wife, Jacqueline Marylene Giorgi, while stationed in Burundi in 1985. She then served as a "cultural counselor" at the French embassy, a position often used as a cover by French intelligence. In his ironically titled memoir, *The Politics of Truth*, Wilson states that Jacqueline followed him to the Congo, where she worked for the French Ministry of Cooperation, notorious in France for promoting white elephant projects and for funneling huge bribes to the leaders of former French colonies in Africa. Wilson called it "the equivalent of our USAID."[27]

But it was as U.S. ambassador to Gabon that Wilson became a real player for the French.

Gabon was a key French ally in Africa. Once oil was discovered, Gabon became the pearl in France's neo-colonial empire, and French intelligence made sure they kept the country's leaders under control. President Omar Bongo was widely reported to be on the payroll of the DGSE. The country was crawling with French intelligence officers, whose job was to ensure that the Americans didn't encroach on French territory.

When Wilson was ambassador to Gabon from 1992 to 1995, his French counterpart was a DGSE general. While in Gabon, Wilson forged contacts with a number of French personalities of questionable reputation. Among them were Daniel Léandri, a shadowy emissary of former French interior minister Charles Pasqua, and Jean-Christophe Mitterrand, son of President François Mitterrand. Known throughout Africa as "*Papa m'a dit*" (Daddy told me), the younger Mitterrand never hesitated to trade on his name. He was then head of COMUF, the Gabonese mining company controlled by COGEMA. Wilson later boasted that he represented French mining companies in Africa. Mitterrand was subsequently indicted in France for his role in illicit arms deals elsewhere in Africa. It was a small world.

Wilson's French contacts attracted the attention of the CIA even before his third wife, Valerie Plame, cited them as a recommendation. "If Gabon had been a Soviet enclave, the KGB would have claimed him as a confidential contact," a former CIA operations officer said. The French considered Gabon to be "a DGSE fiefdom." It went without saying that French intelligence went to great lengths to co-opt, recruit, or otherwise neutralize any top U.S. official assigned there. A French-speaking U.S. ambassador would be a prime target of DGSE interest.

Before Wilson retired from the foreign service in 1998, he became the senior National Security Council advisor for African affairs in the Clinton White House, and helped steer a major African trade bill through Congress. Gabon's President Bongo was fiercely lobbying in favor of the new bill, known as the Africa Growth and Opportunity Act. Not long after Wilson's divorce went through, Bongo hired Wilson's ex-wife, Jacqueline, and paid her $280,000 in 1998 as his Washington lobbyist. Jacqueline remained on Bongo's payroll until June 30, 2002, right after Joe Wilson's trip to Niger. She received another $250,000 in 1999, $75,000 in 2000, $39,000 in 2001, and $8,000 in 2002, according to her reports to the U.S. Department of Justice under the Foreign Agents Registration Act.[28] Meanwhile, Wilson and his new wife, Valerie Plame, were able to purchase an expensive new house in the Palisades district of Washington in 1998, despite the cost of Wilson's second divorce. Their house at 4612 Charleston Terrace was valued at $1,431,230 in 2007, according to Washington, D.C., property tax records.*

Perhaps Wilson *was* telling the truth when he told the *Washington Post*'s Walter Pincus that he had seen the fake Niger documents the French were peddling. Perhaps he walked back that allegation when talking to Senate intelligence committee investigators because he realized that they were getting too close to the truth. With Wilson, the truth seemed to depend on what day of the week it was. He has told different stories to different people so often that the truth has gotten lost.

At any rate, Wilson shared with French president Chirac a disdain for President Bush and an open distaste for Israel. In a June 2003 lecture, he expressed the view that Bush's policy toward the Middle East was dominated by a cabal of pro-Israeli neo-cons whose "real agenda . . . was to redraw the map of the Middle East" in Israel's favor. The invasion of Iraq had been dictated by the likes of Richard Perle "to provide the Israeli government the wherewithal to impose its terms and conditions on the Palestinian people," he said.[29]

Just as James Baker and Lee Hamilton would claim in the Iraq Study Group report in December 2006, if Iraqi Shiites were killing Iraqi Sunnis, it was all because of the Jews. Like Wilson, they argued that any peace agreement in Iraq had to be linked to progress on Israeli-Palestinian and Israeli-Syrian talks.

Go figure.

---

*Montgomery County voter registration records show that Jacqueline Wilson registered to vote on August 4, 1998, indicating that by the time of her divorce she had become a U.S. citizen.

A FRIEND AT THE PENTAGON

Shahriar Ahy, the Iranian-born media executive, was monitoring the television scene in Baghdad from the safety of Dubai, and what he saw increasingly horrified him. In those early months after the liberation, Baghdad was still under curfew. Law-abiding citizens spent their evenings at home with their families. Those who had generators watched television. The only two stations available were Bremer's public relations channel, run by Saddam University graduates, and the Iranian-produced Al-Alam (The World).

Even to an untrained eye, the two networks were like night and day. But Ahy knew there was much more that distinguished them besides the polished professionalism of the Iranians. The Iranians were using the latest Phillips broadcasting equipment to create the newsroom virtual "screen" and smooth transition effects. "Putting together that quality broadcast took at least nine months of preparation. So that meant that the Iranians had to have started talks with Phillips Broadcasting at least a year earlier. They were so far ahead of us," he said.

In other words, the Iranian regime began planning its campaign to undermine the U.S. liberation of Iraq even before the U.S. government officially began planning for the war. And the media campaign was the most benign part of the Iranian plans.*

Not long after he arrived in Iraq, Bremer visited mass grave sites, to demonstrate his compassion for the victims of Saddam. The CPA propaganda network showed Reuters TV footage of old Shiite women picking through bones and clothes in the dirt, trying to identify the skulls of their murdered relatives. An announcer read stiffly a translation of Bremer's remarks, that Iraqis should be thankful that the United States had gotten rid of Saddam.

"Then you switch to Al-Alam," Ahy said. The Iranian network, with its crisp, state-of-the-art, al Jazeera quality, carried the same footage but with a dramatically different narrative. "The Iranians reminded viewers in Arabic that the victims in those mass graves had been lying there since the

---

*In the Appendix to *Countdown to Crisis: The Coming Nuclear Showdown with Iran,* I published photographs of Iranian Revolutionary Guards officers receiving military training in Tehran before their deployment as "humanitarian aid" workers in Iraq after the liberation. One of the pictures is a group photo of a dozen IRGC officers in civilian clothes, posing for their control officer in front of the Imam Ali shrine in Kerbala.

uprising after the first Gulf War. President Bush 41 got so worried that Iraqi Shiites would join their brethren in Iran that he conspired with Saddam, and this was the consequence."

It was a powerful message, and Ahy knew that it resonated with conspiracy-minded populations of the region. And the United States was doing nothing to counter it.

Ahy phoned an old friend at the Pentagon a few days later and told him the story. "Do you know what this does to people?" he said. "Especially if the Iraqis feel that they are hearing the truth from the Iranis and not from the CPA?"

"What can we do?" his friend asked.

And so Ahy told him. When he had finished, his friend asked if he could put that in writing and bring it by his office in a few days, when Bremer and his new communications guy would be in town.

Ahy's friend was Deputy Defense Secretary Paul Wolfowitz.

Bremer came to the Pentagon on July 21, and sent his new communications advisor, Mark Thatcher, to visit with Wolfowitz. Over the following days, Bremer would hash out a new "strategic plan" for Iraq with top White House advisors. Arabic-language broadcasting was low on the viceroy's list of priorities.

Thatcher came to the CPA from the U.S. government's International Broadcasting Bureau, where he had worked on setting up regional transmitters for Radio Sawa, the Arabic-language "feel good" radio run by Radio Free Europe/Radio Liberty. Short, balding, but with the wired energy of a first-year college professor, Thatcher expressed his frustrations to Wolfowitz. They were having a hard time getting the CPA television station off the ground. The Iraqi broadcasters were not professional, and the only programming they had were the Westwood One soaps, and they were all in English. We could really use some help, he said.

There's somebody in the next room with a proposal, Wolfowitz said. Maybe you should talk to him. That's not an endorsement, but take a look.

Ahy briefed Thatcher on his proposal to train Iraqi broadcasters, and described the extent of the Arabic-language programming that was available from MBC and its Lebanese partner. Thatcher was enthusiastic, and said he would brief Ahy's ideas up the food chain.

Two months went by, and nothing happened.

In the meantime, the insurgency was growing bolder and more successful. In August, they blew up the United Nations compound, killing UN envoy Sérgio de Mello, driving the UN out of Iraq. Car bombings and attacks on oil pipelines became frequent. Toward the end of September, Ahy got an e-mail from Thatcher, asking if he could come to Dubai. Ahy gave him a tour of Media City, and showed him their training facilities. Thatcher told him that the CPA had just received the go-ahead from the White House to revive the Iraq Media Network, and wanted to get the new station up and running by October 19. That gave them just a little more than three weeks.

They signed a deal on the spot. What Ahy had been willing to offer the CPA just three months ago for free now earned him $5 million.

CHAPTER NINE

POLITICIZING INTELLIGENCE

By the fall of 2003, Americans were beginning to realize that the promises of Vice President Cheney and others of a "cakewalk" in Iraq had been wrong. The insurgents were staging dramatic attacks, designed to shock public opinion through their extreme violence. At the same time, the Iraq Survey Group, aimed at finding Saddam's WMD stockpiles, was coming up empty-handed.

A key reason was explained to me by one of the inspectors, who described racing around the country with a three-page, single-spaced list of facilities. "Our mission was to find the first bomb. That was it. Just find one bomb, and we win. That's the approach that gets you home for dinner. That's the approach that shows we were right."

So as the military intelligence officers from the 75th Exploitation Task Force tore through major Iraqi weapons plants during the race toward Baghdad in late March 2003, they never thought to secure the facilities on the list. They never sought to interrogate scientists, or workers from the plants. They never worried about looting, or efforts to conceal sensitive activities. "They figured someone else can come later and secure it, or look through all the papers," the former inspector said. "They were just a handful of guys with gas masks racing through all these facilities, looking for one bomb."

In the best of cases, they would gather every scrap of paper they could find at a facility and dump it into footlockers and send it to the rear. "So you had the system choking with a bolus of paper you simply can't exploit." Even as this book goes to print, four and a half years after the liberation of Baghdad, the overwhelming majority of the documents discovered at this time have still not been translated or analyzed.

"They would interview the big guys out at the airport, the heads of programs, and ask, 'So where's the [nerve gas] VX?' That was the level of it. 'We know you're hiding it—so where is it?' That's not an investigation," the former inspector noted. "There simply wasn't a lot of thought that went into what investigating WMD in Iraq meant."

DAVID KAY'S REPORT

In his interim report to a joint session of the House and Senate intelligence committees on October 2, 2003, David Kay emphasized the breathtaking scope of Saddam's weapons programs. The entire country had been a gigantic weapons plant, he said. There were over a hundred major facilities engaged in various phases of the WMD effort, and hundreds more depots where weapons once had been stored. Sophisticated concealment efforts by the Iraqi Intelligence Service (IIS) had succeeded in keeping the most sensitive aspects of Saddam's WMD programs from international inspectors over the years.

Kay said his team of investigators and intelligence analysts had found extensive evidence of banned programs, including:

- A clandestine network of laboratories and safehouses within the Iraqi Intelligence Service that contained equipment subject to UN monitoring and suitable for continuing CBW research.
- A prison laboratory complex, possibly used in human testing of BW agents, that Iraqi officials working to prepare for UN inspections were explicitly ordered not to declare to the UN.
- Reference strains of biological organisms concealed in a scientist's home, one of which can be used to produce biological weapons.
- New research on BW-applicable agents, Brucella and Congo Crimean Hemorrhagic Fever (CCHF), and continuing work on ricin and aflatoxin were not declared to the UN.
- Documents and equipment, hidden in scientists' homes, that would have been useful in resuming uranium enrichment by centrifuge and electromagnetic isotope separation (EMIS).
- A line of [Unmanned Aerial Vehicles] at an undeclared production facility and an admission that they had tested one of their declared UAVs out to a range of 500 km, 350 km beyond the permissible limit.
- Continuing covert capability to manufacture fuel propellant useful

only for prohibited SCUD variant missiles, a capability that was maintained at least until the end of 2001 and that cooperating Iraqi scientists have said they were told to conceal from the UN.

- Plans and advanced design work for new long-range missiles with ranges up to at least 1000 km—well beyond the 150 km range limit imposed by the UN. Missiles of a 1000 km range would have allowed Iraq to threaten targets throughout the Middle East, including Ankara, Cairo, and Abu Dhabi.
- Clandestine attempts between late 1999 and 2002 to obtain from North Korea technology related to 1,300 km range ballistic missiles—probably the No Dong—300 km range anti-ship cruise missiles, and other prohibited military equipment.[1]

The evidence Kay laid out that Saddam had revived his long-range missile programs in violation of UN Security Council resolutions was extensive. Just before the 2003 war began, Saddam was importing hundreds of liquid-fueled rocket motors from Russia, as well as carbon-fiber technology to make solid-fuel rocket motors. "Where were the missiles?" a top White House advisor commented. "The short answer is, we found them—and no one seems to care." To this day, that remains true.

There was one case where an Iraqi farmer came to U.S. soldiers to complain that a mysterious illness had killed three of his four wives, several of his children, and most of his cows and goats. When he walked the Americans around his farm they found an irradiated uranium fuel rod that had been brought to his farm shortly before the war by Iraqi soldiers. The Iraqis had hidden it near the animal feeding trough in a lead box with no lid, leaving the top exposed. Radiation readings around the box were zero, but over it, the Geiger counter went off the chart.* They all had died from radiation poisoning.

NO STOCKPILES?

But for all the smoke, Kay said, the Iraq Survey Group still hadn't found stockpiles of chemical or biological weapons, and had come to no conclusion

*According to my source, the readings directly over the top of the irradiated fuel rod approached 1,000 rads/hour. "A dose of 1,000 rads per hour would cause radiation sickness in the majority of victims in about 10 minutes and fatal injury in about 45 minutes," according to the International Physicians for the Prevention of Nuclear War. See http://www.ippnw.org/NukeNPTPrepCom2003EPWs.html.

yet as to whether Saddam Hussein had reactivated his nuclear weapons program, as the October 2002 National Intelligence Estimate stated.

When they heard that last part, the Democrats and the elite media suddenly woke up. *What, no weapons stockpiles in Iraq?* Through no intention of his own, Kay's testimony helped fan the spark of the anti-Bush campaign into a bonfire.

Kay responded to one allegation that appeared in a front-page *Washington Post* account on October 26, 2003, under the title "Search in Iraq Fails to Find Nuclear Threat."

In a letter to the *Post* that was printed five days later, Kay protested that the article was "wildly off the mark." Reporter Barton Gellman based his account on statements by an Australian brigadier general who was not involved in the hunt for WMD and "does not report, nor has he ever reported, to me," as the article alleged.

Then Kay tackled the key assertion: that aluminum tubes imported by Iraq, which CIA analysts concluded were intended for a clandestine nuclear weapons program, were really just expensive artillery rockets.

"[T]he tubes were certainly being imported and were being used for rockets," Kay wrote. "The question that continues to occupy us is whether similar tubes, with higher specifications, had other uses, specifically in nuclear centrifuges. . . . Our investigation is focused on whether a nuclear centrifuge program was either under way or in the planning stages, what design and components were being contemplated or used in such a program if it existed and the reason for the constant raising of the specifications of the tubes the Iraqis were importing clandestinely."[2]

The intelligence needed to be gathered, sifted, and evaluated, Kay was saying. But instead, the *Post* and other elite media outlets were rushing to judgment, because their conclusion had been precooked.

Bush lied, people died!

In a June 2003 op-ed in the *Washington Post*, former chief United Nations weapons inspector Rolf Ekéus called the focus on the absence of stockpiles of weaponized chemical and biological warfare agents "a distortion and a trivialization of a major threat to international peace and security." But his voice, like so many others, was being drowned out.

As time went on, the steady assault on Bush's credibility through lying and distorting the hunt for Saddam's WMD was having an impact. The NBC/Wall Street Journal tracking poll taken from November 3 to 10, 2003, showed that 44 percent of respondents now disapproved of the president's job performance.

THE DEMOCRATS' MEMO

On occasion, the leaks helped the administration to make its case.

On Tuesday, November 4, 2003, Fox News rock star Sean Hannity revealed on his nationally syndicated radio show a memo from the Democratic staff of the Senate Select committee on intelligence that laid out in bald terms a strategy for sabotaging the Bush administration. The anonymous author laid out a road map for duping the Republican majority of the committee into serving as a foil for the Democrats' fishing expedition, which was aimed solely at making "major new disclosures regarding improper or questionable conduct by administration officials."

The Democrats had decided to key in on prewar intelligence. They had already compiled public statements on Iraq by senior administration officials and boasted of having sparked "the FBI Niger investigation." Now they intended to "identify the most exaggerated claims and contrast them with the intelligence estimates," which were now declassified. Their goal was to show the American public that Bush lied.

The leaked strategy memo, prepared for the committee vice chairman, Senator Jay Rockefeller, anticipated that the Republicans would wake up at some point to what the Democrats were doing, and would then attempt to limit the scope of their inquiry. At that point, the Democrats would cry foul, claiming they had "exhausted the opportunity to usefully collaborate with the majority."

"The Democrats will then be in a strong position to reopen the question of establishing an independent commission," the memo states. "We can pull the trigger on an independent investigation at any time—but we can only do so once."

And when would be the most appropriate time to "pull the trigger" on a full-blown inquisition focusing on the administration's use of intelligence in justifying the Iraq War? For Senator Rockefeller's aide, that was a no-brainer: just in time for the 2004 presidential elections. "The approach outlined above seems to offer the best prospect for exposing the administration's dubious motives and methods," Rockefeller's aide concluded.

Hannity devoted his entire three-hour broadcast to a discussion of the Democrats' strategy memo, and returned to it repeatedly over the next week. Pundits and editorials picked up on it. Even the White House commented.

The Democrats, not surprisingly, wanted the FBI to investigate who had "hacked" their computers to discover the memo, because the contents were highly embarrassing. Here, in black and white, was proof positive that key Democrats in the United States Senate were not interested in conducting oversight of the intelligence community, as their committee was required to do, but solely in damaging administration officials "who made the case for a unilateral, pre-emptive war."

The leaking of the memo to Sean Hannity did not compromise ongoing intelligence operations, nor did it risk exposing classified sources and methods, as the shadow warriors were wont to do. Instead, the leak exposed the Democrats' plan to politicize the Senate intelligence committee, an act aimed chiefly at undermining the president and the administration, but also the Senate itself.

The Rockefeller memo was a defining moment for the committee chairman, Senator Pat Roberts (R-KS). It was when he realized that the Democrats had no intention of conducting an honest and fair investigation into how the CIA had made such huge errors in judgment about the state of Saddam's WMD program. It was incontrovertible proof that the Democrats intended to use the intelligence committee—and the access to classified documents and protected individuals it afforded them—purely for partisan gain.

When the Democrats briefly held the majority before the 2002 elections, Senator Bob Graham (D-FL) and his staff were no strangers to political grandstanding. But Graham had maintained some semblance of comity, and the traditional respect both parties generally paid to the sensitive, highly classified matters their committee reviewed. When Senator Jay Rockefeller took over as vice chairman in January 2003, all that changed.

"We used to have a single, unified professional staff," a former SSIC staff member said, "with just three Republican and three Democrat staff members on top of the professionals." Professional staffers would specialize in a given area—oversight of the NSA, budget issues, CIA covert operations—and "double-hat" as liaisons for individual committee members. Each staffer was arbitrarily "assigned" a member of the committee, whose needs they were supposed to address. "When Rockefeller took over, he refused the old liaison arrangement," the former staffer said. "Now the staff are the senators' creatures, pure and simple."

Rockefeller brought over from the Pentagon a Clinton holdover, Christopher Mellon, to become his staff director in early 2003. It was Mellon who crafted the Democrats' overall strategy for using intelligence to sabotage the Bush administration. Assisting him was Melvin Dubee, a seasoned partisan, accustomed to the hard-knuckle tactics of his political bosses.

Instead of seeking remedies to the mistakes made by the intelligence community in Iraq and in the years before 9/11, Rockefeller and Levin sought to use intelligence for political purposes. It was the exact same sin they so piously accused the Bush administration of committing.

Intelligence committee members are the cardinals of the Senate. Now Rockefeller and Levin were about to play Rasputin.

DINNER AT MI6

Britain's Secret Intelligence Service, also known as MI6, bears as little resemblance to its fictional representation in the 007 series as the CIA does to *Mission: Impossible.* James Bond would not recognize the sprawling modern headquarters built in the mid-1990s for "M," whose full name is now published. Moneypenny is gone. So is the rabbit warren of dark corridors, the dark oak wainscoting, and the cramped smoky offices. Instead, Britain's spooks now gather in a *Star Wars*–style fortress known as Vauxhall Cross, overlooking the Thames near the old Tate Gallery.

Deputy Undersecretary of Defense John A. Shaw was not a first-time visitor to Vauxhall Cross. His friendship with MI6 director Richard Dearlove (the modern-day "M") went back to graduate school days at Cambridge, England. When he phoned Dearlove from Washington and told him the men he was proposing to bring to the table, the British spy offered to clear his schedule. He suggested they set aside several days for the talks, from February 10 to 12, 2004.

A veteran of several Republican administrations, Shaw was a go-getter. He ran his Pentagon office the way other men run a private intelligence network. He had contacts spread all across the globe, and he used them to open doors in unusual places. In this instance, his entrée was named Ihor Smeshko. A former military attaché in Washington from 1992 to 1995, today he was the head of Ukrainian intelligence, the SBU. Richard Dearlove had never met him. And Lieutenant General James Clapper, the director of the National Geospatial-Intelligence Agency (NGA), had never met Dearlove. It was Jack Shaw's genius to broker a way to bring them all together, and to put himself at the center of the meeting.

Dearlove sent his personal armor-plated BMW sedan to fetch Shaw from the Garrick, his favorite London haunt. Near Covent Garden, the Garrick was a private club frequented by theater folk seeking the aura of its eighteenth-century actor namesake. Luckily for Shaw, it was affiliated with the Metropolitan Club in Washington, where Shaw was a member. Otherwise, he never would have gotten a room.

Shaw's official job as deputy undersecretary of defense for international technology security was to track U.S. high-technology and military exports, something he'd been doing in various positions in government for over thirty years. Once it became clear the United States was going to be searching for Saddam's weapons of mass destruction, however, Shaw started looking for a piece of the action. Relying on a memorandum of understanding he had signed with Pentagon inspector general Joseph E. Schmitz after the 9/11 attacks, he set up an office that combined the investigative powers of the IG with the technical capabilities of his own people, and adopted a new title: director, international armament and technology trade. "That's how I got into the evanescent world of WMD," he told me. "We were the Hardy Boys." As Shaw saw it, their job was to kick over rocks and watch all the strange animals coming out.

Schmitz put him in touch with a Ukrainian-American named Lou D—, who had top-drawer contacts in Kiev and knew General Smeshko personally. At a Christmas party in December 2002, Shaw hooked up with another friend who suggested he hire a British soldier of fortune who had spent a lifetime with the opposition Iraqi Kurds. *Sees himself as Lawrence of Kurdistan*, the friend said. Stephen, the Brit, had also dabbled in the arms trade in the 1980s. Shaw cut him a modest consulting contract and sent him to Syria and Jordan as the U.S. troop buildup against Saddam intensified. "Some of his key buds were generals who were shucking and jiving, and so Stephen's job was to find out who was doing what to whom," Shaw said later. Stephen became a one-man intelligence operation, running a whole network of sources and subsources at the Iraqi border and elsewhere. That was how Shaw first learned of the convoys heading into Syria during the final weeks before the war. "We're talking about eighteen-wheel trucks heading north from Baghdad into Syria packed to the gills with munitions and WMD equipment and coming back empty," he said.

When they finally reached Vauxhall Cross through the evening traffic, it was already dark. Shaw remembers struggling with the armor-plated car door—it was as heavy as an old icebox—until he gave up in embarrassment and the driver freed him from the car. An escort was waiting for him and whisked him into an elevator to the director's private dining room on the top floor. No one even asked to see his identification. That's how you knew you were *somebody*.

Smeshko was already there, along with two deputies, General

Olexander Skipalsky and General Olexander Sarnatsky. So was Dearlove's deputy, Stephen Flaugherty; the British intelligence director of Iraq operations, Michael Shipster; the MI6 station chief from Kiev; and another aide. (Clapper didn't arrive until the next morning.) Shaw's Ukrainian-American partner-in-crime, Lou D—, took him by the arm and introduced him to Smeshko and his deputies. As they took their seats around the large oval dining table, with a panoramic view through floor-to-ceiling windows over the Thames, the Brits made their formal introduction. And then they got down to business.

They looked forward to starting a new relationship with the Ukrainian service, the SBU, and appreciated General Shmesko's willingness to "build bridges" with MI6 and the Americans in this informal setting. They had set aside all day tomorrow for working meetings, "so tonight what we're all about is getting to know each other," Flaugherty said.

Shaw was champing at the bit. Lou had told him that Smeshko knew the secrets of what had happened to Saddam's strategic weapons. *This is the mother lode*, he reported back from Kiev at one point. *This guy is willing to help out with everything he's got. Don't forget, they know everything there is to know about the Russkies.*

Although the broad-faced, nearly bald general spoke no English, he exuded quiet bonhomie, Shaw thought. Perhaps it was the academic in him. (In addition to a lifetime spent in the security services, Smeshko also had a doctorate in science.) Smeshko said he wanted to thank Richard Dearlove for this invitation, and for taking the time to see him privately earlier on. He was looking forward to the next day's meeting with his old friend General Clapper, whose kindness to him while he was military attaché in Washington he would never forget. Military men were straightforward, he said. We understand each other without hidden agendas. *So that's why he didn't want any Agency spooks here*, Shaw thought.

Smeshko was looking forward to creating a new, reciprocal relationship between their services, after years of mistrust during the Soviet era, he said. Since he had taken over as chief of SBU the previous September, a strategic decision had been made "to end the unhelpful relationship with the West" that former KGB elements in his service had pursued. So they had much to discuss, and information to share. Ukraine had been watching what was going on in Iraq, and had been tracking Russian operations in Iran as well, he said. They had recently discovered, for example, the illegal sale to Iran by a former SBU chairman of a Ukrainian nuclear-capable cruise missile system. The sale had been "expedited by suspected organized crime figure Vadim Rabinovich," he said. Smeshko hoped they could cooperate with Western services to shut down this type of thing before any more such systems were delivered.

It was a pretty heady evening, Shaw thought.

Clapper arrived the next morning, and was taken by Dearlove's men from Heathrow Airport directly to elegant meeting rooms in a Regency-style complex above Pall Mall, home of London's most storied private clubs. He was just as frustrated as Shaw was by the lack of progress in the hunt for Saddam's missing WMD. Just three months earlier, Clapper had convened a group of defense correspondents for breakfast at his headquarters in Bethesda, Maryland, to share his concerns. The retired Air Force three-star general, who headed the National Geospatial-Intelligence Agency, had confirmed in public what Shaw already knew through Stephen's private intelligence network: that Saddam appeared to have been evacuating sensitive equipment by truck into Syria during the war. Clapper had speculated that the looting and the chaos that took place after the fall of Baghdad might have included "organized dispersal made to look like looting."[3] In other words, some of the looting could have been the work of regime elements, who were cleaning out sensitive military and intelligence sites.

The problem with overhead imagery was what you couldn't see, Clapper pointed out. You didn't know where the trucks had come from, and you couldn't see inside them to know what they were hauling. "We're just not that good," he said.

Smeshko was Jack Shaw's entry card to the supersecret world of the intelligence elite. Before these meetings, Shaw had never met face-to-face with General Clapper, even though they both worked for the same boss. They had spoken recently by phone to set up the London trip—three times, in fact—but until now they had navigated different circles back in Washington. Clapper had been deputized by CIA Director George Tenet to liaise with Smeshko on the WMD issue. Shaw knew he was going to need General Clapper's support if his outside-the-box search for Saddam's missing WMD was ever going to get traction. Now it was up to Ihor Smeshko to lift the veil.

"We have been pursuing information and leads concerning the wholesale transport of weapons systems into Syria and Iran, before and during the war in Iraq," the Ukrainian intelligence chief said. But every time he had offered his help to the CIA station chief in Kiev, he had gotten the brush-off. That's why he had asked for these meetings in London.

Clapper nodded, but said nothing. He was clearly uncomfortable with the role Smeshko has thrust him into, since it was a throwback to his old job as head of the Defense Intelligence Agency in the early 1990s, when he met the Ukrainian in Washington. Clapper was no longer in the spying business, so to speak. He just processed technical data from spy satellites and turned it into maps for the military. This was messy HUMINT stuff.

What Smeshko said next blew Shaw right off his chair. Ukraine's long involvement as part of the Soviet Union gave them "a unique ability to work with the United States and Great Britain in uncovering Iraq's WMD programs," he said. He knew how the Russians operated, and he personally knew many of the players. He was willing to commit his service to assisting the U.S.-led effort to track Saddam's WMD, as part of Ukraine's decision to participate in the coalition forces.

There it was, Shaw thought. My guy has just put his cards on the table.

They made an informal arrangement over the next two days that the Americans would send Lou D—, the Ukrainian-American who worked with the Defense Department's inspector general, to Kiev for several months to work directly with the SBU. Smeshko said he would like to come to Washington to meet the CIA director at some point in the future. But he wanted nothing more to do with the Kiev station chief.

No wonder. The Kiev station chief, whose name I cannot reveal because he remains under cover, was a close ally of the CIA weasels who had no intention of helping uncover information that would make George W. Bush look good.

Neither Shaw nor Clapper realized it at the time, but the reports they had been hearing of Iraqi convoys heading into Syria loaded with WMD were just the tip of the iceburg. In closed-door testimony before a House international relations committee subcommittee in the fall of 2003, then Undersecretary of State John Bolton cited a half-dozen additional classified cables that provided more details on this WMD ratline into Syria.

The reports Bolton cited had been culled from nearly two dozen citings of the convoys. Many were direct citings by human sources on the ground. "We thought these six or seven reports were credible," a Bolton aide said. "But the U.S. intelligence community tried to discount virtually all of them."

In some cases, the reliability of a human source was questioned by "pro-Syrian elements" at the Defense Intelligence Agency who didn't want to authenticate information that made the Syrian regime look bad. In others, the dissent came from State's Bureau of Intelligence and Research (INR). Both agencies refused to allow Bolton to make more than passing mention of the reports in the public part of his testimony.

It was a problem that went beyond one agency, one official, or one source. There was a systematic effort inside the intelligence community to block the authentication of virtually any information that made the Bush administration look good.

DRAMATIC NEWS FROM AMMAN

King Abdullah II of Jordan had the reputation of being a serious man. Trained at Sandhurst in Great Britain, he pursued a military career in Jordan, with fine-tuning in international affairs at Oxford and at the School of Foreign Service at Georgetown University in Washington, D.C. When he assumed the throne upon his father's death in February 1999, he had been commander of Jordan's elite special forces since 1994.

On April 17, 2004, King Abdullah made a stunning announcement: Jordanian intelligence had just foiled a plot by al Qaeda to launch a deadly attack using chemical weapons in the Jordanian capital that could have killed as many as 20,000 people—seven times the number of casualties in the September 11 attacks. "It was a major, major operation," he said. "It would have decapitated the government."

His intelligence service had intercepted trucks carrying 17.5 tons of explosives and deadly chemical weapons crossing the border into Jordan from Syria, the king said. He took pains not to implicate Syrian president Bashar al-Assad in the al Qaeda plot, saying, "I'm completely confident that Bashar did not know about it."

King Abdullah's statement was picked up by United Press International and Agence France-Presse and was read in newsrooms around the world. An unnamed Jordanian official quoted in the wire service accounts added that the al Qaeda cell they had arrested was also planning to attack the U.S. embassy and the prime minister's office in Amman.[4]

Subsequent reports added that the al Qaeda cell was in possession of twenty tons of Iraqi-made sarin gas. *Twenty tons!*[5]

Here was stunning evidence that Iraq had moved stockpiles of WMD to Syria before the war, and that Saddam Hussein's regime had intimate ties with al Qaeda. And yet, as news editors around the world read the dispatches on their screen, they shrugged. A story that might justify the U.S. "invasion" of Iraq was not a story. Except for the *San Francisco Chronicle*, whose reporter had interviewed King Abdullah in Amman, the elite media simply ignored the news, because it didn't match the politically correct version of the Iraq WMD story they were pushing.

SEVEN MEN WITHOUT A HAND

There were reminders of Saddam's regime everywhere. It wasn't just the fallen statues or the shattered monuments. It was something you could sense when talking to Iraqis. Bob Reilly thought of it as the palpable presence of evil.

Ever since he had come home from Iraq in June 2003, images from Saddam's torture chambers had haunted Reilly. While helping to set up the ill-fated Iraq Media Network that spring, Reilly had spoken to scores of Iraqis for a new radio program he was planning, *At Last, I Speak.* The idea was to give victims of Saddam's regime—those who had survived, or family members of those who had not—the opportunity to tell the stories they had buried deep in their hearts for so many years.

At first, many of the men and women he spoke to just shrugged their shoulders. "It was normal," TV cameraman Farid Putres said of his time in Saddam's jails. But when Reilly finally got him in front of a tape recorder to describe the underground cells, the beatings, and the sound of the executions at night, there was nothing "normal" about it. He choked up, and the normally talkative Iraqi could barely get the words out.

Saddam's thugs routinely charged families for the bullets they used to execute their loved ones. Parents were made to watch as their children were raped, dismembered, or murdered by regime intelligence agents. One father took Reilly aside and swore him to secrecy before telling him the story of his son's genital mutilation.

A hidden thread connected many of these stories, Reilly soon discovered: Saddam ordered his thugs to secretly videotape the murders, the rapes, and the mutilations. Many times, Saddam sent copies of the tapes to the victim's family, after watching them himself.

General Najib Salehi never forgot the day he received one of those tapes in Amman, where he had fled Saddam's reign of terror with his family. It came in the mail, he told Reilly. Without thinking, he popped it into his VCR at a family gathering. To his horror, the film showed his niece being gang-raped by Mukhabarat agents—Saddam's revenge for the general's defection.

Not long after returning to Washington, a former colleague from the Iraq Media Network, Don North, showed Reilly a video he had acquired from an Iraqi journalist in Baghdad. It showed a 30-second "trial" of nine Iraqi merchants in 1995, who had been caught changing money at a time the regime had declared a monopoly on foreign currency transactions. As punishment, the nine men were taken to the notorious Abu Ghraib prison, where their right hands were amputated. To reinforce their humiliation, an X was tattooed into each man's forehead.

Reilly thought he would get sick as the blurred images flickered on the screen. It was like the Nazis, he thought, who had filmed every conceivable act of horror in the twisted conviction that it commemorated their own glory. It was a world beyond our everyday notions of good and evil, a world where nightmares were real.

The former Voice of America chief couldn't shake those images from his mind. For thirty-five years, Iraqis had lived under this tyranny, knowing that at any moment of night or day, without any warning, they could be taken from their homes and brutally tortured, maimed, or murdered. How could anyone doubt the justice of the American-led war of liberation after they had seen images like these?

As the months went by and the media turned increasingly negative toward the administration and the war, Reilly asked around the Pentagon to find out who had been put in charge of collecting the torture videos. After all, they were prima facie evidence of Saddam Hussein's monstrous crimes.

To his surprise, he learned the answer was no one, and that no one was interested in pursuing it. So he called everyone he could think of who might have copies of the torture videos. Finally he reached a friend at the Iraq Survey Group (ISG), the CIA successor to the Army's 75th Exploitation Task Force. He said that during raids of government offices they had seized a number of tapes that might be of interest, and suggested he could send them on to Reilly unofficially.

There was nothing illegal about it. There was nothing classified. And yet both men instinctively knew they had to exercise caution, because this was something their bosses had expressed absolutely zero interest in pursuing.

A few weeks later, the phone rang in Reilly's Pentagon office.

"Are you Bob Reilly?" an unfamiliar voice asked.

Without even thinking, Reilly knew immediately who it was. "Yes," he said. "Who is this?"

The man identified himself as a friend of Reilly's contact at the ISG in Baghdad. "Our mutual friend asked me to bring you a few souvenirs from Baghdad," he said.

They agreed to meet that evening at 7:30 P.M. in the parking lot of

Trader Joe's in suburban Falls Church, Virginia, just a few miles' drive from the Pentagon. The man would recognize Reilly by his height, his graying hair, and his mustache.

For all the cloak-and-dagger preparations, the actual handoff was almost comic. When Reilly saw the unfamiliar man walking toward him with a large paper bag outside the Tysons Station strip mall, he thought he must have used the opportunity to go grocery shopping.

"I think you may be looking for me," Reilly said. He identified himself, the man nodded, and they exchanged cursory greetings. Without further ado, he thrust the shopping bag into Reilly's arms. Instead of groceries, it was packed with videotapes and DVDs.

"This is what our friend in Baghdad asked me to give you," he said. Then he turned away and was gone.

The next day, Reilly took the tapes into an editing studio in the Pentagon, along with two Iraqi translators. When the images flickered onto the screen, the same sensation of horror he had felt when watching the amputation video came over him. There were Baath Party trials; executions by firing squad; amputations; mutilations; scenes of torture and rape. There was also a copy of the footage Don North had shown him of the nine merchants getting their hands cut off. Many of the scenes were shot inside Saddam's notorious prison, Abu Ghraib, known to Iraqis as the "Palace of the End."

Working with the translators over several days, Reilly edited it into a 12-minute DVD, which he called *Victims of Saddam's Regime*. It began with a stark warning that the images it contained were not meant to be viewed by children and contained harsh scenes of violence. He sent copies to every member of Congress, and to major media organizations in Washington.

But there were no one-minute floor speeches by senators and congressmen to express their revulsion at Saddam's practices, and no media inquiries. Just silence.

Don North was equally frustrated by the media silence, and by Bremer's imperious decision to transform the Iraq Media Network into a lapdog of his Coalition Provisional Authority. Unbelievably, Bremer's people were sending Iraqi journalists to be trained by Al Jazeera and Al Arabiya television, even as the Baghdad bureaus of those same Arabic-language TV networks were being closed down for anti-American propaganda and incitement.

After he saw the raw footage of the amputations in Baghdad, North vowed to track down the nine men and make a documentary film about their suffering. Working with Iraqi journalists, he found seven of the Baghdad merchants, who had lived as quiet outcasts ever since Saddam's Dr. Mengele had branded them with Saddam's mark of shame.

One of the seven, Nasaar Jondi, told North about his last night in the Palace of the End. He decided that before Saddam's doctors chopped off his right hand, he would use it one last time for an act of love. "Do not be sad. Hopefully Allah will replace my hand with an even better one," he wrote his wife.

When North was telling Jondi's story to a colleague in a Baghdad coffee shop, an oil engineer from Houston, Roger Brown, overheard him.

You ought to tell that story to Marvin Zindler, he said. Zindler was known in Houston as "the white knight in blue spectacles." A muckraking journalist, he had exposed the scandal that became the 1982 Dolly Parton movie *The Best Little Whorehouse in Texas.* These days, the eighty-two-year-old Zindler paraded about in white trousers and blue glasses and had become a Texas institution. He was the type of person who could mobilize big business backers for a great cause. Maybe he could help that guy get a new hand, Brown suggested.

North took his advice, and over the next eight months he and Zindler raised more than a million dollars in cash and in-kind donations. They convinced businesses and hospitals to contribute their services, and in early April 2004 brought the seven remaining Iraqi merchants (one had died, the ninth had fled to Europe) to Texas to be fitted with state-of-the-art prosthetic devices.*

Reilly followed the progress of the seven men almost daily. Once they had been fitted with their new hands and had learned how to use them, he helped set up a whirlwind tour of Washington for the men.

On May 24, 2004, President Bush welcomed them to the White House. He said he was "honored to shake the hand of a brave Iraqi citizen who had his hand cut off by Saddam Hussein." At a moving ceremony in Arlington National Cemetery three days later, the seven men put their new artificial hands across their hearts as "Taps" sounded from the bugle of Army sergeant major Henry Sgrecci, and they laid a wreath at the

*Bob Reilly convinced the Pentagon to bring the men on a military jet to Germany, and to waive visa requirements so they could come to the United States. Houston-based Continental Airways flew them and their families for free from Germany to Houston. The Methodist Hospital, the Institute for Rehabilitation and Research, and Dynamic Orthotics and Prosthetics in Houston donated doctors and operating rooms. The Marriott and Warwick hotel chains provided free housing, and the U.S. branch of Otto Bock, a German manufacturer of prosthetic devices, provided the artificial hands.

Tomb of the Unknowns. Deputy Defense Secretary Paul Wolfowitz honored them at a dinner with American soldiers who had lost limbs in Iraq and were undergoing physical therapy at Walter Reed Army hospital. It was an incredibly moving evening. "By the time it was over, no one in the room had dry eyes," said Hal Koster, co-owner of Fran O'Brien's Capitol Steakhouse, which regularly hosted dinners for the handicapped vets.

The extraordinary generosity of their American benefactors received wide coverage in the press, but not a single story appeared that focused on Saddam's crimes or that mentioned the stunning video footage Saddam's henchmen had made.

It wasn't because the footage was unavailable. Senate majority leader Bill Frist met publicly with the seven Iraqis at his office in the U.S. Capitol. Senator Rick Santorum (R-PA), Senator Jeff Sessions (R-AL), and Senator Joe Lieberman (D-CT) held a news conference for the seven men and played an excerpt from the tapes. Herman Pirchner, president of the American Foreign Policy Council, also hosted a press conference for the seven Iraqis and played more of the tapes. At all these events, reporters who had questions about the authenticity of the documentary footage were referred back to the Pentagon's public affairs shop.

Reilly later learned what had happened. When reporters called over to the Pentagon, the Public Affairs spokesman disavowed all knowledge of the tapes and would not vouch for their authenticity. It was yet another act of incredible stupidity, if not outright sabotage.

THE HILTON STIFFS THE VETS

There are two codas to this story.

On June 25, 2004, Wolfowitz was back before the Senate Armed Services committee. By this time, Abu Ghraib was in the news—not because new information documented Saddam Hussein's barbaric treatment of his own citizens, but because photographs taken by U.S. military police showed that they had forced Iraqi prisoners to pose in humiliating positions.

The Abu Ghraib prison scandal quickly dwarfed anything else the administration was doing. Human Rights Watch, a group funded in part by left-wing billionaire George Soros, published endless reports on the prison abuse scandal. So did Amnesty International and the International Red Cross. Senator Elizabeth Dole (R-NC) noted that since Abu Ghraib hit the headlines on May 4, the *Washington Post* had run no fewer than 399 stories on the prison abuse scandal, while the *New York Times* had run 437 stories during the same period. However, she noted, the documentary highlighting atrocities under Saddam Hussein in that same prison "received little or no coverage by the mainstream media." So she held up a copy of Don North's DVD and asked Wolfowitz if he had seen the footage of the seven Iraqis who lost their hands to Saddam's torturers.

"I've heard about it," Wolfowitz said. He had met with the seven Iraqis, and he was aware that Senators Lieberman, Sessions, and Santorum had hosted a press conference for the men. "I've read about it—although it's hard to read about it; there's been almost no mention of it anywhere in the press," he added.

"That's right," Dole said.

"It's hideous enough to read it without seeing it," Wolfowitz went on. "But it does seem to me that it introduces a kind of distortion when there's virtually no coverage of that."

Those were the comments Wolfowitz made in public. But in private, he expressed his frustration to Santorum. "Where did you get those tapes?" Wolfowitz asked. "I've been trying to get my hands on them, but nobody over here seems to know anything about them."

Reilly almost fell over when he heard that. The Pentagon public affairs shop knew all about the documentary footage, but when reporters called over to confirm it, Larry DiRita and his aides either dismissed the tapes or pointedly refused to confirm their validity.

The second coda involves Fran O'Brien's restaurant.

For the good deed of hosting dozens of handicapped veterans of Operation Iraqi Freedom to cut-rate dinners every week, the Capital Hilton evicted Fran O'Brien's Steakhouse from the premises on May 1, 2006. These dinners gave an opportunity for soldiers recovering from wounds suffered in Iraq at Walter Reed and other nearby VA hospitals to have a night out on the town with family and friends. The outings were subsidized by the restaurant and by private benefactors, including the Italian aerospace company Finmeccanica, and the Jewish Institute for National Security Affairs, JINSA. Paul Wolfowitz, former deputy secretary of defense, continued to be a regular, way after he left the Pentagon and even after he was forced out as president of the World Bank in June 2007. He never sought publicity by attending the dinners, but felt it was the least he could do to support the wounded vets. The Hilton's decision to stop the dinners was "a disgrace," he told me. The hotel called the termination of Fran O'Brien's lease "a business decision." But many of the older vets who were involved in organizing the weekly dinners believe the

Hilton was embarrassed by having so many men in wheelchairs descend on the hotel, especially since the Hilton had never installed an elevator to reach the basement restaurant, as required by the Americans with Disabilities Act.

"That is totally wrong," the general manager of the Capital Hilton, Brian Kelleher, insisted. Veterans' groups say the hotel chain took millions in dollars in losses from pro-military families, who refused to patronize Hilton establishments nationwide after Fran O'Brien's was shut down. Kelleher acknowledged that the hotel had not found another tenant for the basement restaurant area in the nearly eight months since they had evicted Fran O'Brien's. Although that amounted to staggering losses—the restaurant rented out for $25,000 per month—Kelleher said he had never made an accounting of the losses to the Hilton management. He claimed the hotel had offered repeatedly to host similar events for handicapped veterans, although he admitted that no such events had ever occurred. He hung up angrily when pressed to explain why the Hilton had evicted the restaurant that hosted the vets.

CHAPTER TEN

AIR CIA

British reporter Stephen Grey held his breath when he saw the headline in the *Washington Post* on May 11, 2004. Like any reporter who had invested an immense amount of time, resources, and money to break a major story, he always felt antsy once he had handed over his work to the editors. There was always a dead period between the time you finished a piece and when it came out, and that was when bad things happened. Sources went south. Documents leaked. Government officials panicked and started calling editors, furiously trying to walk back their indiscretions. But when he saw the title to Dana Priest's latest story, "Secret World of U.S. Interrogation," he feared the worst. He had been scooped.

The *Washington Post* had good sources in the U.S. intelligence community, especially the CIA and the State Department's Bureau of Intelligence and Research (INR). For years, *Post* managing editor Bob Woodward, columnist David Ignatius, and reporters Dana Priest and Walter Pincus had been a kind of informal cheering section for their sources, who looked down on the Bush White House as a bunch of neo-con zealots and yahoos in cowboy boots who just didn't understand the complexities of the real world. But would they really compromise the highly classified operations Grey had been investigating for the past two years? And could Dana Priest and the Posties get away with publishing *real* secrets, the kind of secrets that would not only embarrass the Bush administration, as the Abu Ghraib prison scandal that formed the launching pad for their current series had done, but would also embarrass U.S. allies and possibly shame them into changing their secret collaboration?

THE UNEARNED PULITZER

As Stephen Grey sat in his hotel in the southern Iraqi city of Basra and scanned the latest *Washington Post* story on the Internet, phrases from the story he had just filed (but that wouldn't be published for another six days) leapt out at him: "ghost detainees," "rendition," "secret prisons." But by the time he got to the end, he heaved a sigh of relief. The Posties could certainly write breathless prose, but they had missed the real story. It wasn't about Abu Ghraib, or even the nefarious CIA jail outside Kabul known as "The Pit," which Dana Priest described. The real story was much darker, more detailed, and involved the type of secrets the CIA desperately wanted to protect. It was about the little guys with names like Mohamed al-Zery and Maher Arar—men conspicuously absent from the *Washington Post* big blowup of a story that was aimed at smearing George W. Bush, not standing up for real victims of government abuse.

When Stephen Grey first heard about Mohamed al-Zery—an Egyptian asylum-seeker who was handed over by the Swedish government in Stockholm to a CIA snatch team in December 2001—he knew instantly that this was his type of story. It was about democracy gone haywire. It was about governments willing to sacrifice real intelligence for expediency. It was about good men and women who did evil things.

As his article would explain several days later, the CIA system of secret prisons was the Western equivalent of the Gulag Archipelago, the underground network of prison labor camps established by the KGB, described so eloquently by Soviet dissident Aleksandr Solzhenitsyn.[1]

Stephen Grey was an authentic investigative reporter, not a beat journalist like Dana Priest who sucked up to government sources and played to their vanity. He knew the CIA was not about to reveal its secrets; nor were America's partners in British or Swedish intelligence. They had too much to hide and too much at risk. So he went outside the system.

One hook he used with success were boasts by former national security advisor Sandy Berger, who after the September 11 attacks began telling the press how effective the Clinton administration had been at capturing terrorists. When we nabbed them and didn't have a Justice Department indictment, we just turned them over to friendly countries who did, Berger said.

That process, known as "extraordinary rendition," began on a small scale in the mid-1990s, when the United States picked up Egyptians in Bosnia and Albania who were wanted on terrorism charges back in Egypt and handed them over to the Egyptian authorities. "At first, it was just about disappearing people," Grey said, when I asked him how he began investigating this story. Only later, after 9/11, did the real object become intelligence interrogations.

One of the architects of that policy was former CIA officer Michael Scheuer, who became an outspoken opponent of the Bush administration in some areas but remained a strong supporter of the CIA renditions program. His political views made him "quite a funny fish," Grey said. "Basically, he set the whole thing up."

Scheuer told Grey that the Clinton White House ordered the CIA to turn over terrorists to "friendly" third countries such as Egypt or Jordan because the United States at the time had "few options on what to do with terrorists it captured." Rendering them to other countries was just a way of getting them off the streets, and that was fine with him. (The fact that Scheuer's comments directly contradicted Sandy Berger's justification of the renditions—that they involved indicted suspects wanted in third countries—went right past Grey.)

Six days after the *Washington Post* story, the first part of Stephen Grey's investigation appeared in the *New Statesman* in Britain. The story focused on tip-offs from MI5, Britain's domestic intelligence agency, that allowed the CIA to pick up al Qaeda operatives as they were leaving Great Britain and turn them over for interrogation and torture in Syria, Gambia, Jordan, and Egypt.

The same day, an hour-long television documentary that paralleled his own research was broadcast by Sweden's premier investigative news program, *Kalla Fakta* ("Cold Facts"). Unlike Grey's more straightforward magazine piece, Swedish television opted for the huffy indignation only Swedish socialists could adopt without provoking outright laughter.

> "Sweden is known as one of the world´s leading advocates of human rights, swift to condemn torture and summary trials," the Swedish TV documentary began. "But tonight we can reveal that Sweden is itself abusing human rights in the worldwide terrorist hunt that has been going on since the 11th September 2001. Foreign masked agents have been allowed to strip, degrade and arrest suspects in Sweden, at Bromma airport, and take them to a country where they were to be tortured."
>
> The narrator continued, "To expel someone to a country where he or she risks torture or inhuman treatment is incompatible with both international conventions and Swedish law. Yet, that was just what Sweden did when its government in December 2001 expelled Ahmed Agiza and

> Muhammed Al Zery to Egypt—an expulsion that not only was done in a very remarkable manner, but also was based on several incorrect pieces of information."[2]

Over the next two years, Stephen Grey became the quiet, behind-the-scenes "go-to guy" on the CIA "ghost planes." He provided key documents and information to the *New York Times*, *Le Monde Diplomatique*, the *Sunday Times*, the BBC, and countless other publications and TV networks. Dana Priest was awarded a Pulitzer Prize for "breaking" the story of extraordinary renditions and CIA secret prisons in the United States, but it was Stephen Grey who did all the spadework. His involvement in all those stories "was kind of like a trade secret," he acknowledged.

It all began with the tail number of the white, unmarked Gulfstream V aircraft used to carry Mohamed al-Zery from Stockholm to Egypt in December 2001. A Swedish airport official provided the number—N379P—to a Swedish television reporter, who tracked it through the Federal Aviation Administration to a company registered in Dedham, Massachusetts, called Premier Executive Transport Services (PETS). (Dana Priest would later claim that PETS was first identified on the conservative Free Republic website less than six weeks after 9/11.)

The Swedish TV team then decided that one of them would pretend he worked for a Swedish government agency seeking to hire the plane, and phoned Dean Plakias, the Massachusetts-based lawyer who had set up the company. Thinking the reporter really did come from the government, Plakias gave the Swede a phone number in Virginia for the true operator of the aircraft, whom he identified as Mary Ellen McGuiness. And that's when they ran into a brick wall—or rather, smack into a CIA covert operation.[3]

After he returned to Britain from Basra, Stephen Grey says, he was "fired up by the news of the Swedish discovery," and phoned *Kalla Fakta* reporter Fredrik Laurin in Stockholm. "If we teamed up to track his plane across the world, perhaps we could trace the whole pattern of renditions," Grey said.

Grey had a source who probably could get access to the flight logs. If so, many of the pieces of the extraordinary-renditions puzzle would suddenly fall into place. Grey knew that while the U.S. legs of some of the ghost flights might be available, there was nothing on the various websites of the aviation industry or the FAA that would allow them to track the same plane worldwide. "It just wasn't readily available through normal channels," he told me.

That's where Grey's "confidential source" came in, whom he identified to me and to Italian prosecutors as an "ex-CIA agent." After some coaxing, his source agreed to send him complete flight logs for the Gulfstream V luxury jet that had taken al-Zery from Stockholm to Cairo. That information allowed Grey to match flights from Europe to the Middle East with the known disappearances of suspected terrorists. "The flight logs were the key," Grey said.[4]

Grey soon found that former paramilitary officers who had been involved in the renditions "didn't like this kind of thing" and also began to talk. Information provided by plane spotters at airports across Europe allowed him to expand the universe of aircraft and flights involved in the top-secret program, until he had compiled a database of hundreds of flights and a half-dozen CIA planes, each owned by a different CIA proprietary. Each time a former detainee would be released and start to tell his story, Grey would match his claims to the aircraft logs he had obtained from his confidential source. "I've deliberately not published the logs on the Internet or elsewhere because it gives me credibility when I corroborate what the detainees are saying," he said.

Anytime the CIA had wanted to shut down the story, they could have done so, Grey believes. "Although the Agency made a few errors, they made it easier to track this information than it should have been," he told me.

Here he hesitates, because he knows he is getting dangerously close to revealing the source of his information. "It's fair to say, if they had wanted that information to be blocked, it would have been blocked."

While downplaying his own role in Grey's investigation, Bob Baer said that many of the CIA officers involved in the renditions had been "incredibly sloppy," using traceable cellphones, Visa cards, and e-mail. "When you realize that for fifty bucks, I can get anybody's e-mails off of anybody's account I want, you just don't do these things," he said.

Baer pointed to a whole world of private business intelligence companies, staffed mainly with former intelligence officers. "Cellphones? I can get your cellphone bills legally in Northern Ireland. I just send in your name, your number, and $5,000, and it's a done deal. Same thing for plane registrations," he said. "You get the tail number, and you can put it into databases and follow it worldwide. Money. That's all it takes. Money."

The Swedish case began with a tail number and a friendly person in the Swedish police. "They give you the credit card number these guys used to fill the plane with gas, and it's an easy ride to all the other ones. Because a pilot's a pilot. He just knows how to fly the aircraft. He's going to go off and have a massage in Spain, using a private credit card. He's going to keep on charging his meals, charging gas. So the CIA was not professional in the sense of being prepared to do something like this," Baer told me.

"If you've got money, or you're a reporter and you've got favors to trade, everything's for sale," he added.

While Baer is right, penetrating CIA covert operations is not an exercise for the faint of heart. Until recently, it was reserved for hostile foreign intelligence agencies, and traitors.

CHAPTER ELEVEN

THE "CABAL"

On May 8, 2004, the president and his principal advisors met at the White House to discuss the upcoming handover of sovereignty in Iraq. Ambassador Robert Blackwill, who since August 2003 had become Condoleezza Rice's point man on Iraq, made an impassioned argument for sidelining Ahmad Chalabi, a member of the Governing Council who was being touted as a candidate for prime minister.

Chalabi was on the take, he argued. Reliable reporting out of Baghdad indicated that his people were siphoning off billions of dollars from several government ministries where they were advisors. In addition, it now appeared that Chalabi was engaged in massive counterfeiting—fake $100 bills, fake dinars, you name it.

Bremer has been at loggerheads with Chalabi from day one, Blackwill noted. And then Blackwill delivered his blockbuster, aimed squarely at Chalabi's main supporter, Vice President Dick Cheney.

Can anybody explain why Chalabi's intel guy has been meeting with a top Revolutionary Guards official in Iraqi Kurdistan? he said, referring to a memo he had prepared with Rice's approval. The CIA's Counterespionage Group (CEG) had compiled a detailed file on the meetings between the head of Chalabi's intelligence outfit, Aras Karim Habib, and well-known members of the Quds Force, the overseas terrorist branch of Iran's Revolutionary Guards Corps. These were the same people who had blown up the U.S. embassy and murdered 242 U.S. marines in Beirut, hit a U.S. Air Force barracks in Dhahran, Saudi Arabia, and murdered 86 Argentinean Jews at the Buenos Aires Jewish Center in 1994, Blackwill said.

The CIA believed that Chalabi's entire organization was penetrated, and that Chalabi himself was essentially an Iranian government agent.

Part of the CIA dossier on Chalabi had been leaked to *Newsweek* reporter Mark Hosenball, who in a breathless column appearing earlier that week alleged that Chalabi had "provided details of U.S. security operations" to Iran. "According to one U.S. government source, some of the information Chalabi turned over to Iran could 'get people killed,' " Hosenball claimed.

While Cheney had been critical of the CIA for leaking derogatory information on Chalabi to the press, he agreed that the information on these latest alleged meetings between Chalabi's people and the Iranians was troubling. But so was the meeting hosted by the Brits ten days earlier in Basra with a top Iranian Foreign Ministry official, to which Bremer sent his foreign affairs advisor, State Department diplomat Ron Neumann. Certainly no decision was made by this group to talk directly to the Iranians, he pointed out. Did that make Jerry Bremer an Iranian agent?

Undaunted, Blackwill urged the principals as a precaution to terminate the intelligence-collection program with the Iraqi National Congress. Even though DIA director Admiral Lowell Jacoby wanted to continue the program and U.S. field commanders had testified publicly that INC information had saved the lives of U.S. soldiers, the CIA was trying to place the blame on the INC for its own mistakes in analyzing Saddam's WMD programs. "The CIA was pissed with us because we kept coming up with stuff they didn't have," said Chalabi aide Zaab Sethna.

Bush had been a Chalabi fan before and after the liberation of Iraq, and had seated the Iraqi as a guest of honor just behind Laura Bush at the 2004 State of the Union. But he was furious with Chalabi for an offhand remark he'd made to a British reporter in Baghdad in February 2004. When asked if the intelligence the INC had provided the Americans on Saddam's WMD programs had been wrong, Chalabi replied, "We are heroes in error. As far as we're concerned we've been entirely successful. That tyrant Saddam is gone and the Americans are in Baghdad. What was said before is not important."

At Blackwill's insistence, the president agreed to put Chalabi and the INC on probation, while the FBI and the CIA pursued their counterespionage investigation. It was highly unusual for such detailed operational decisions to be made at such a high level.

While Bremer had complained that he didn't want Washington to be micromanaging affairs in Iraq "with an 8,000-mile screwdriver," this was one remote-control order he was happy to implement.

Chalabi later alleged in U.S. court filings that King Abdullah II of Jordan "traveled to the United States and personally delivered to President George Bush a file containing the false accusation that Chalabi had informed the Iranian government that the United States had broken its encryption code and thus could intercept its secret communications."

The Jordanian king met with Bush on May 6, 2004. The two leaders jointly addressed the press from the White House Rose Garden that day. But neither said a word in public about Ahmad Chalabi.

During that same U.S. trip, Chalabi's lawyers alleged, King Abdullah met with other U.S. officials "and with various United States Senators" to repeat the same allegations, "and then caused a detailed summary of these conversations to be sent via wire communications to various newspapers within the United States."[1]

KILL CHALABI

Ending intelligence cooperation and smearing Chalabi as an Iranian agent weren't the only measures the CIA planned to take against the unruly Iraqi. Shortly before dawn on the morning of May 20, 2004, they tried to kill him.

In Baghdad, the bulky Americans wearing Kevlar, camouflage, and driving armored SUVs were known as "OGA"—an acronym commonly used to designate the CIA ("Other Government Agency"). Chalabi woke up that morning to find four armed men pointing guns at him in his bed. "Anybody moves, and we'll shoot!" they said.

Guns drawn and safeties off, the intruders were nervous, shaking their guns at Chalabi for him to get up. Other gunmen broke mirrors, kicked down doors, and overturned furniture, fanning out all over the large house and the gardens. Chalabi was careful to show his hands.

As he stood up in his nightshirt, the portly Chalabi turned to an Iraqi policeman and asked him in Arabic why they were doing this. "We are slaves to the CPA, to Bremer," the man said, averting his eyes.

It was crystal clear to Chalabi and his top aides—three of whom I spoke to later that day—that the American paramilitaries overseeing the raid were deadly serious about shooting anyone who dared offer the least resistance. They were just waiting for someone to pull a gun and they would kill him.

Bremer and the CPA denied all responsibility for having ordered the raid. In his memoirs, Bremer claimed that an "independent" Iraqi judge had issued arrest warrants for six or seven members of Chalabi's staff. (At the time, Iraqi judges were named by Bremer and reported to him.) Bremer grudgingly acknowledged that he had authorized the use of coalition forces, "but only to provide perimeter security for the Iraqi police executing the warrants on the INC."[2] About two dozen armed Americans, none of them in uniform, assisted the Iraqis and left their Humvees parked outside. Some of them worked for the private contractor DynCorp.

Francis Brooke, Chalabi's American political consultant, and accountant Peg Bartell were sleeping in villas across the street. They rushed outside when they heard the commotion. The OGA paramilitaries were shocked to see two Americans, and asked them what they were doing. When Brooke told them that they worked for Chalabi, one of the Americans wrote down their names. Later that day, Brooke learned from a leak to the *Los Angeles Times* that arrest warrants had been issued for both of them.

"I stood for an hour with an American military person pointing a gun at my chest," Brooke said.

Peg Bartell went over to her office, where more armed men in civilian clothes were ripping computers out of the wall and carting out boxes of files. "Are you giving us an inventory of what you're taking out?" she ventured.

"Don't mess with me, lady, or you'll wind up in Abu Ghraib," a burly OGA told her. "You can imagine what they'd do to an American woman there."

Across the street from where he was being held, Francis Brooke noticed a CPA cameraman. "They were hoping to lead out a bunch of guys in handcuffs, but they didn't find anybody they were looking for," he said. Instead, they seized a family Koran, a set of prayer beads, and documents relating to the INC's investigation of the UN oil-for-food scandal. (The INC was instrumental in exposing the massive bribery scheme, and had compiled documents seized in former government ministries that identified hundreds of United Nations and foreign government officials who had taken kickbacks from Saddam Hussein.)

Back in Washington, former Pentagon official Michael Rubin was livid. "This is a huge blow to America's prestige. The message we've just sent is that we do not stand by our allies, that the United States can't be trusted. We've just told Arab liberals and democrats that it's just plain crazy to work with America."

Rubin, who had recently returned from a job with the CPA, spoke by phone with Sunni clerics, Shiite professionals, and independent Kurdish businessmen in Iraq in the hours immediately after the Baghdad raid. "Everyone in Iraq believes that because of U.S. actions, we are now heading for civil war," he said. "We have snatched defeat from the jaws of victory. Basically, Bremer has gone mad," he told me.

The CPA claimed triumphantly that they had seized counterfeit money in Chalabi's house. Later, they spread rumors that Chalabi was running a vast illegal currency operation, and that they had found the printing plates in Chalabi's house during the raid (false). In fact, what they seized were several specimen counterfeit bills, stamped "COUNTERFEIT" in large letters by the Iraqi Central Bank. As chairman of the interim government's Finance committee, Chalabi used them as props to demonstrate how terrorists were counterfeiting Iraqi currency to support murder and mayhem.

Meanwhile, the main person the Americans were hoping to arrest—Chalabi aide Aras Karim Habib, now accused of being an Iranian agent—was watching the whole scene from a nearby building. "We've been fighting Saddam for fifteen years," a colleague of his told me. "You don't think we're going to let these guys catch us!"

LEAKING SLIME

Later that day, back in Washington, a senior U.S. official called CBS's *60 Minutes* and told them the "real" story behind the Chalabi raid.

Chalabi had given incredibly sensitive information to the Iranians. This was the kind of stuff that people die for, the official said. He was going to tell *60 Minutes* the story so they could have a better feel for just how dastardly this Chalabi was. But it was so sensitive, he asked them to broadcast just the main thrust of the story, not the details.

Leslie Stahl's revelations that evening shocked Americans. She said that CBS News voluntarily had agreed to withhold details of Chalabi's treachery because of the incredibly sensitive nature of the secrets he had betrayed. To anyone who didn't know Chalabi and hadn't experienced the deep, personal animosity the CIA continued to harbor toward him, the allegations were stunning. How could America possibly support somebody who was handing our deepest intelligence secrets to the Iranians?

The unnamed "senior administration official" soon called other reporters, and they piled on.

Time reported that the FBI had opened a counterintelligence investigation into Chalabi's relationship with the Iranians. *Newsweek* added that the gumshoes were seeking to determine "who in the U.S. government might have leaked such information to Chalabi or the INC." News of the FBI involvement, and the opening of a U.S.-based investigation, amounted to two additional leaks of highly sensitive classified information. All came from "senior" administration officials and were prima facie violations of the Espionage Act.

As the smear spread, some of Chalabi's most prominent supporters withdrew into their caves. "The press stories would have him as my brother," Undersecretary of Defense Doug Feith said. "I met him a few times. He was very smart, very articulate." But Feith "rejected the idea that he had been Chalabi's tool or dupe," *Newsweek* added. Much later, Chalabi would accuse Feith and Wolfowitz of having betrayed him in his hour of need, by failing to counter the falsified stories about him with the truth.

As details of Chalabi's alleged treachery leaked out, the story became increasingly extravagant. Soon it was reported that Chalabi had learned from a drunken American security officer working at the CPA in Baghdad that the United States had cracked the secret code the Iranian embassy was using to communicate with Tehran. He then blabbed it to the Iranian station chief in Baghdad, who promptly sent a warning message to Tehran, *using the broken code!*

It was so ridiculous that no serious person could possibly fall for it, said Michael Ledeen, a prominent neo-con author and longtime Chalabi supporter. "Basically it assumes, A, that Chalabi is an idiot. And B, that the Iranian station chief in Baghdad is an idiot. And the one thing we know for sure in all of this is that the Iranian intelligence service is very good, and they don't have idiots as station chiefs in places like Baghdad."[3]

Ledeen was right. The story was laughably absurd. Although the Chalabi "scandal" was front-page news all across America, the president managed to put enough distance between himself and Chalabi that his misfortunes did not translate into a significant loss of public confidence in the president or in the war.

But it was just the beginning. The shadow warriors were playing for keeps.

"GUILTY BY FIVE MILES"

At 5 P.M. on June 30, 2004, a team of ten FBI special agents arrived at the Kearneysville, West Virginia, home of a Defense Intelligence Agency analyst named Larry Franklin. As they lined up in front of his door, they said they were hoping to obtain his cooperation in an espionage investigation in which he was currently a target.

Franklin had spoken with the FBI for years about Iran and Hezbollah, and had met with two agents earlier that day at the Pentagon on the same subject. His ex-father-in-law had been an FBI counter-intelligence agent working against the Nazis during World War II, and his best friend in the military had been an FBI arms instructor. It never occurred to him they could be on opposite sides of U.S. national security. So without a thought, he invited the FBI team into his home.

He was a patriot, he said, and didn't need a lawyer. It was the first of many mistakes he made.

Once inside, a twenty-something female FBI Special Agent presented him with a search warrant. If you waive this, we can avoid a lot of unpleasantness, she said. So, Franklin signed a release form consenting to the search. That was his second mistake.

What the FBI didn't tell Franklin was that they had been tailing him for over a year but had nothing solid enough on him to justify an arrest warrant. They knew he had been admonished by the DIA years earlier for keeping classified information at home, and were hoping he had made a similar mistake now. Franklin failed to call their bluff.[4]

Later, reporters quoted FBI sources claiming that Franklin had been the one who had leaked the "information" about Chalabi's ties to the Iranians to *60 Minutes*. This was an utter fabrication, invented to bolster their case. To make it more plausible, the same FBI sources also claimed that Franklin had telephoned prominent neo-cons, including Richard Perle, seeking to "warn" them about Chalabi's Iranian ties. (Franklin made those calls the day *after* CBS broke the Chalabi story, to let them know he had no knowledge of what Chalabi was allegedly doing, and that the whole thing had taken him and his friends at DoD by surprise.)

Larry Franklin was not someone you would picture as a James Bond type. At fifty-seven, he had shaggy brown hair and thick eyebrows streaked with gray, and his inexpensive suits always looked as though they had been left in the backseat of a car. He gave off a dusty, almost bookish air. It was easier to picture him sitting at a cramped back table in some antiquarian shop than operating at the epicenter of Washington intrigue.

But there was another Larry Franklin that lurked beneath his nondescript demeanor. Although he was barely 5'8", Franklin lifted weights and stayed in top shape. And if you met him outdoors in summer, when he often wore short-sleeve Oxford shirts beneath the suit, the weightlifting showed. He was built like a wrestler and slow to anger—but when he got angry, he exploded.

Franklin was concerned the FBI team would disturb his wife, who was confined to a sitting position by several debilitating muscular disorders, so he took them to his study. There they discovered stacks of documents, many of them bearing government classification stamps ranging from "Confidential" to "Top Secret." Franklin offered that he probably shouldn't have left them lying out like that, but he kept them at home in case his bosses called him after hours, as sometimes happened.

That was all his tormenters needed. Catherine M. Hanna, the young Special Agent who signed the affidavit in support of his arrest warrant, told Franklin there was enough right there to put him in jail for a very long time. After all, this was not Franklin's first offense. The DIA had already warned him about taking home classified documents without having a special safe where they could be secured. Larry Franklin had violated the law.

Franklin protested that he had never shared classified documents with anyone outside of government. His lawyer, Plato Cacheris, would later tell the court that he was "guilty by five miles." Because of his job, Franklin had a special permit authorizing him to carry classified documents within the Washington, Maryland, and Virginia area. His West Virginia home was just five miles beyond the Maryland state line.

But police interrogations, especially if a defendant has waived his right to an attorney, are not about the facts. They are about intimidation. And the FBI was intent on pressing its advantage.

We have you on tape, Mr. Franklin, the twenty-something woman said. We know that you have communicated classified defense information to private persons, and that these individuals are in contact with a foreign government. We know all about your involvement with Ahmad Chalabi and his ties with Iran, she added. Our interest is to stop hostile intelligence operations against the United States. If you cooperate with this investigation, we will ask the judge to cut you a break as a cooperating defendant, she said.

The legal talk was over Franklin's head. But as a guilty jumble of meetings and conversations rushed through his mind, he understood that he was in trouble, and that the FBI was offering him a way out. What he didn't understand was that he was about to become the victim of political machinations that had little to do with him.

WITH GHORBANIFAR IN ROME

Franklin was working for a neo-con outpost in the Bush administration. Indeed, the office where he worked—the Pentagon's Office of Special

Plans—had become *the* top target of Bush archenemy, Senator Carl Levin (D-MI). Levin had been trying to shut down the Pentagon's war-planning office ever since he first learned of it in 2002. Larry Franklin was just collateral damage in Levin's assault on the Bush administration.

In the mid-1990s, while working as an analyst at the Defense Intelligence Agency, Franklin had gone back to school at the Foreign Service Institute to learn Persian. During weekends with his reserve unit, he had taken to hanging out with special operators from the 4th Psychological Operations Group at Fort Bragg, North Carolina. They were part of a newly revived Defense human intelligence capability and had been specially trained to deploy into exotic countries. The 4th Psyop Group included regional and language experts who had studied the political, cultural, ethnic, and religious makeup of places such as Iran, Iraq, Pakistan, and Afghanistan. Franklin hoped that one day he could leave behind the analytical world of Bolling Air Force Base and join the 4th Psyop as an Iran operator.

After the September 11 attacks, Franklin got his chance. He was sent by the DIA to work in the policy shop of Undersecretary of Defense Doug Feith, and quickly took part in a series of high-flying (and highly unusual) operations.

In late fall 2001, Michael Ledeen learned from Iran-Contra figure Manucher Ghorbanifar of potential threats to U.S. forces in Afghanistan from Iranian hit squads. He informed Deputy National Security Advisor Stephen Hadley that Ghorbanifar's Iranian sources could come to Rome for further discussions if the U.S. government was interested. Hadley and Zalmay Khalilzhad, then NSC director for Near Eastern affairs, agreed. They asked Ledeen if he had any ideas who should go. Certainly it should be people knowledgeable about Iran and possibly able to speak Farsi, he replied. And so in December 2001, Franklin flew to Rome with Ledeen and Harold Rhode, another Farsi speaker in the Pentagon's policy shop.

Much has been written about the Rome meetings. They have been called a "rogue operation" by a "secret unit" at the Pentagon, part of some dark "cabal" by pro-Israel officials aimed at "drumming up support for war with Iran."[5] But I can reveal here that Hadley briefed Ledeen's offer to CIA Director George Tenet and Deputy Secretary of State Richard Armitage in person, and despite long-standing reservations about Ghorbanifar's credibility, both men agreed that the United States should at least hear what his sources had to say. Far from being some kind of Pentagon "rogue operation," the meetings were sanctioned at very senior levels of the U.S. government. Both Harold Rhode and Larry Franklin were instructed to travel on official red U.S. government passports.

In Rome, the group was hosted by the head of Italian military intelligence, Nicolò Pollari, an old Ledeen acquaintance (they are both avid bridge players). Pollari provided a safe house near the Piazza di Spagna in central Rome, but forgot the caterer. "The place was unheated, it was absolutely freezing, and the food was disappointing," Ledeen recalls. Neither Tenet nor Armitage insisted that representatives from their agencies tag along to monitor the meetings.

For three days, Ledeen, Franklin, and Rhode listened to the Iranians Ghorbanifar introduced to them, including a former senior member of the Revolutionary Guards. The information they provided was later found accurate and saved U.S. lives.

But when Rome station chief Jeff Castelli learned that a U.S. government team was conducting secret meetings on his territory without his involvement, he fired off an angry memo that made it up and down the food chain back in Washington. Before he was finished, hardly anyone in Langley, Foggy Bottom, or the elite media was left in the dark about the "secret" meetings in Rome. The leaks only heightened Ledeen's cynicism about the CIA.

Castelli was a serving CIA clandestine officer. And yet, he made no effort to protect a clandestine operation that had been approved by the CIA director in person. For Castelli and his division chief at the Directorate of Operations, Tyler Drumheller, such behavior was apparently motivated by their utter disdain for Bush administration policies.

When Senator Levin learned of the Rome meetings, he bombarded the Pentagon with long lists of questions and document requests. He wanted to know who had authorized the travel of Pentagon officials Larry Franklin and Harold Rhode. Had they traveled on their own, or on U.S. government passports? Why wasn't the Rome station chief informed of the meetings ahead of time? Why weren't the meetings run through the proper CIA channels and handled by CIA personnel? And on, and on, and on.

"I would love to be subpoenaed by Senator Levin to answer questions on this," a senior administration official involved in coordinating the trip told me. "You are asking if they traveled on official U.S. government passports? Yes, Senator, they did. And you want to know—what? Why these meetings were kept secret? Senator, we were facing people who wanted to kill our servicemen and -women. As the ranking member of this committee, I would think you would be more concerned with the security of U.S. troops, rather than making cheap political points."

Senator Levin got his answers, and of course never demanded that hearings be held. His goal was not to fix the mess the U.S. intelligence community had become from three decades of political correctness, or to protect U.S. troops. His goal was to attack the president and to sabotage his policies.

CRIMINALIZING POLICY

Larry Franklin's involvement in the Rome meetings was the second strike against him. In October 2002, Feith assigned him to the newly created Office of Special Plans, the infamous "secret office in the basement" run by Deputy Undersecretary of Defense Bill Luti. While there, Franklin continued to work on Iran, and got to know people at the American Israel Public Affairs Committee (AIPAC), the semiofficial Israeli government lobby in Washington. Those ties were the third and fourth strikes that ultimately doomed Franklin's career, as fiercely anti-Israel elements within the U.S. counterintelligence community sought to prove the anti-Semitic smear that Israel was guiding Bush administration policy like a hidden puppeteer.

Larry Franklin believed he was fighting the good fight. He believed that America truly was the "City Upon a Hill" of Matthew 5:14 that the Puritans, John F. Kennedy, and Ronald Reagan had evoked, a beacon of freedom and a light to the world. He believed the war against Saddam Hussein was just and that America had a moral imperative to help the Iranian people in their struggle against the fundamentalist regime in Tehran. Both efforts were key to defeating the Islamofascists who had declared war on America in 1979 when Khomeini's student-soldiers took their first Americans hostages during the assault on the U.S. embassy in Tehran, he believed.

In the summer of 2002, National Security Council official Flynt Leverett, a Clinton holdover, drafted a National Security Presidential Directive on Iran that called on the United States to support Iranian president Mohammad Khatami, a "reformist" cleric who was seeking to make the Islamic regime more palatable to the West. Feith and others at the Pentagon believed the Leverett draft was gravely mistaken, and amounted to legitimating Iran's clerical regime. They tapped Luti deputy

Michael Rubin to write a competing draft and circulate it within the administration. Franklin contributed to the Pentagon draft.

This was politics as it has always been played in Washington. Two competing groups within the administration were vying to get the president of the United States to adopt their position. To win the president's attention, each side sought allies willing to lobby the White House in favor of their respective positions.

Leverett and his supporters reached out to the foreign policy and intelligence establishment. They promoted their point of view with the *Washington Post*, the *New York Times*, and establishment think tanks. The Council on Foreign Relations issued a major study, coauthored by Robert M. Gates and Zbigniew Brzezinski, that championed the accommodationists' line.

When the Michael Rubin draft of the Iran policy document began circulating in February 2003, Franklin's bosses were excited. This draft openly discussed options for regime change in Iran, instead of muddling forward or acquiescing to Tehran's demand that the United States recognize the legitimacy of the clerical dictatorship.

Both draft documents were classified. But the ideas and the policy options were well known and widely discussed in Washington—and indeed, in foreign capitals monitoring the U.S. policy debate.

On February 12, 2003, Franklin met AIPAC's director of foreign policy issues, Steve Rosen, for breakfast in Arlington, Virginia. Rosen had been instrumental in AIPAC's successful campaign the year before to get the Bush administration to change its position toward Israel's retaliatory attacks on Palestinian terrorists. Until then, U.S. presidents had always urged Israel to "restrain" itself whenever the bombers murdered the innocent. Israeli prime minister Ariel Sharon argued that Israel had the same right to respond to unprovoked attacks against civilians as the United States had after the September 11 attacks. After much lobbying by AIPAC and friends in Congress, Bush agreed. From now on, when the Israelis launched a full-scale invasion of the West Bank in retaliation for the murder of twenty-nine Israelis at a Passover seder, or carried out targeted killings of terrorist leaders, the White House kept silent, and at times publicly supported Israel's right to retaliation.

Joining Rosen was his top Iran expert, Keith Weissman, a rumpled, overweight scholar, who had lived in Iran before the revolution that ousted the shah. On the way over, Rosen phoned a colleague and said he was looking forward to meeting with the "Pentagon guy" because he was a "real insider." All three of them were excited about the meeting.

Franklin asked if they had heard about the new Iran policy draft. Rosen said he was aware that it was in the works. He ran through the outlines of the competing proposals, as they were then being debated in public.

Finally the Pentagon was pushing back, Franklin said. But they still faced a lot of opposition. It would really help if AIPAC could use its influence with top officials at the National Security Council in support of the Pentagon draft.

They spoke again two days later, and Rosen said he would "put in a good word" for him with friends at the White House. "I'll do what I can," Rosen said.*

None of the three men realized that the FBI was listening. They had intercepted Rosen's cellphone call on the way to the restaurant, and had learned of his interest in the draft Pentagon Iran policy paper from bugs placed in his office. They also had agents physically present in the restaurant, who managed to catch snippets of their conversation on tape.[6]

Franklin had never shown Rosen or Weissman an actual document, nor had he offered to. Their meetings involved the type of policy discussions and insider gossip that took place hundreds of times every day around Washington. Indeed, that was why the FBI had never made a move on Larry Franklin until now.

But Franklin's culpability was not the issue. This was not about Larry Franklin. This was about AIPAC, which the FBI had been shadowing for years, without success. Finally someone had fallen into their net who had committed enough of an offense to convince a judge to issue a search warrant. FBI Special Agent Catherine M. Hanna's job was to scare the nonsense out of Larry Franklin and squeeze him for all he was worth.

Larry Franklin was going to be used as bait to entrap the Jews.

TAKING DOWN THE "CABAL"

The FBI agents who carried out the search of Franklin's residence may not have been aware of the intense politics and personal animosity that had motivated the investigation into Franklin, but their boss was.

---

*There was another reason Franklin wanted to move to the White House, conveniently absent from the prosecution case: to avoid harrassment from Senator Levin and the Senate intelligence committee. Franklin wasn't the first person in the Pentagon policy shop to seek a transfer to the White House, beyond the reach of Congress. Bill Luti himself, the director of the "secret office in the basement," transferred over to the vice president's office in 2005.

David Szady returned to FBI headquarters in March 2002 as assistant director in charge of the counterintelligence division, after several years on loan to the CIA. While at the Agency, he headed the Counter Espionage Group (CEG), part of a "fusion" center within the Directorate of Operations, formed to help the Agency recover from the devastation wrought by longtime Soviet spy Aldrich Ames.

Szady had a checkered record. Well after Ames was uncovered in 1994, the CIA continued to lose top-level agents in Russia and began to suspect they had a second mole. As the hunt progressed under Szady's direction, the Counter Espionage Group hounded the CIA's top spy-catcher, Brian Kelley, ultimately destroying Kelley's career without ever turning up evidence that he was spying for the Russians, as Szady believed.[7]

All the indices pointed to a man who frequented strip joints, visited Internet porn sites, and asked his Russian spymasters to pay him in diamonds. That profile was correct. The problem was, it didn't fit Brian Kelley. It fit Robert Hanssen, a senior FBI agent who for years had worked right down the hall from Szady. But Szady never suspected his co-worker, who was only uncovered once Szady was taken off the case.

"Szady was an idiot," two former colleagues at the FBI told me. "He spent two days of every week working out, prepping for his fitness tests. He never went after the tough Soviet spies, only ham and eggs." That meant, the easy cases. The cases that everyone had signed off on.

While at the CIA, Szady hounded an entry-level Jewish lawyer named Adam Ciralsky, apparently on no other grounds than his religion. Just days after Ciralsky joined the CIA, Agency security officers opened a special file on his Jewish background. They circulated a classified four-page "Jewish résumé" of Ciralsky that identified teenage trips to Israel and work as a Jewish camp counselor as indicators of possible disloyalty.

As soon as Szady took over as CEG chief in May 1997, the investigation of Ciralsky accelerated. A June 12, 1997, memo entitled "Spot Report—Next Steps in the Adam Ciralsky Case" outlined a strategy for forcing Ciralsky to leave the Agency. Routing slips showed that C/CEG/CIC—the bureaucratic acronym for Szady's position as chief of the Counter Espionage Group—had initialed the report. So had CIA director George Tenet. The document's classification was unusual, since it was marked "eyes only/no registries," a notation aimed at ensuring no trace of it would show up if someone tried to search the classified archives.

When challenged later about the investigation, Tenet agreed with Ciralsky's attorneys that the "no registries" notation was probably illegal, since the CIA was required by law to maintain its classified holdings in such a way as to be accessible to lawmakers for purposes of oversight. He also acknowledged that the behavior of Szady's CEG had been "insensitive, unprofessional and highly inappropriate," and ordered Szady and his subordinates to undergo a "sensitivity training" course with the Anti-Defamation League. The clearly anti-Semitic documents Szady and his people had generated were an embarrassment.

There was a straight line from the Ciralsky case to the AIPAC/Larry Franklin investigation. "David Szady made assumptions about Jewish loyalties," a source with detailed knowledge of both cases said. "He wouldn't trust Jews with secrets."

Like many of his former colleagues at CIA and in Division 5 of the FBI, the counterintelligence section, David Szady believed that Israel had a high-placed intelligence asset in the U.S. government, whom they sometimes referred to as "Mr. X."

"It's no longer just our traditional adversaries who want to steal our secrets, but sometimes even our allies," Szady said. "The threat is incredibly serious." It was Szady who fired up the AIPAC investigation, soon after he was called back from a forced retirement by FBI director Robert Mueller in early 2002.

In a sharply anti-Bush account that appeared in the left-wing monthly *Rolling Stone*, James Bamford described Szady's efforts to find the traitorous Jews. "To locate the spy sometimes referred to as Mr. X, agents working for Szady began focusing on a small group of neo-conservatives in the Pentagon—including Feith, Ledeen and Rhode."

Tracking the Jewish neo-cons led Szady to Larry Franklin, who worked in Feith's office. When Franklin led them to AIPAC, everything clicked, all the ties were there. Once again, the Jews and the neo-cons were hatching a new war. "Even before the bombs fell on Baghdad, a group of senior Pentagon officials were plotting to invade another country," Bamford's article begins. "Their covert campaign once again relied on false intelligence and shady allies. But this time, the target was Iran."[8]

To Szady, to the LaRouches, and to reporters who saw Israeli agents lurking behind every policy decision they rejected, it all made sense. Right-wing American Jews were pulling the strings in the White House and the Pentagon, and taking the nation to war after war on Israel's behalf. "Wolfowitz-Feith-Ledeen-Rhode!" they screamed, as if Jewish names alone could make a conspiracy.

When I asked Richard Perle his opinion of David Szady and his reported hunt for traitorous Jews, he just shrugged. "David Szady is a nutcase," Perle said. "He brought in as a consultant this guy Stephen Green from Vermont, who believes there's a Jonathan Pollard under every bed. It's like bringing in a Holocaust denier. It's just not serious."

Green, sixty-four, a former United Nations official, claimed to be an "investigator" of secret Israeli networks in the United States. He had just penned a vicious article in a left-wing webzine that dredged up well-known accusations against top neo-cons in the Bush administration and accused them of "dual loyalty" to Israel.[9] It was that article that apparently caught David Szady's attention and prompted him to use Green as an "expert" on AIPAC.

Perle compared Szady to his dog, Reagan, who loved to chase squirrels. "I don't think Reagan has ever caught a squirrel and never will. But that doesn't stop him from chasing them. David Szady is obsessed with Jews."

When questioned about Szady's motivation, an FBI spokesman denied that Szady ever had been driven by anti-Semitism.

THE STING

Once they had entrapped Larry Franklin and gotten him to admit he had mishandled classified documents, the FBI counterintelligence squad decided to use Franklin in a sting operation against the Jews. They started by asking him to call Richard Perle and other prominent neo-cons in Washington, offering classified intelligence. When that didn't work (one recipient of his calls found them "bizarre"), they tried to entrap Chalabi's Washington spokesman, Francis Brooke. "They figured if they could get Perle and Francis Brooke, they could knock out the main backers of the Iraq war," a source with intimate knowledge of the case told me. "They were hoping to shut down the neo-con cabal."

Only after all those attempts failed did they send Larry Franklin to entrap Keith Weissman at AIPAC.

Seymour Hersh, another anti-Bush reporter who wrote for *The New Yorker*, alleged darkly in a June 2004 article that Israel had top-secret operatives on the ground in northern Iraq, gathering intelligence in preparation for war with Iran.

It was part of the general theme the anti-Bush and anti-Israel crowd was pumping. The Jews pushed Bush to war in Iraq, and now they were trying to get America to fight another war on their behalf with Iran.

Szady had Franklin phone Weissman out of the blue in July 2004, nearly a full year after their last contact. When they got together for lunch at the Tivoli restaurant near the Pentagon, Franklin talked about the Sy Hersh article alleging that "Israeli agents" were on the ground in northern Iraq and were being targeted by Iranian intelligence officers, and said it was true. But he had nothing new and nothing specific. Weissman thanked him for the insights, and did nothing.

When Szady saw that Weissman wasn't taking the bait, he decided to up the ante. Two weeks later, the FBI mole-hunter instructed Franklin to try again.

This time, Franklin called Weissman and said they had to meet "urgently." Something had come up, he said. He had now been "cleared" to give Weissman more details than the last time they had met. On edge, Weissman joined Franklin at the Patisserie, an upscale coffeehouse on the third floor of the Pentagon City shopping mall.

Franklin said the Pentagon had "ticking time bomb" intelligence that the Iranians were planning to move in the next few days against the Israelis in northern Iraq. I've been cleared to give this information to you, he said. But my bosses won't lift a finger to alert Israel officially.

You've got to warn the Israelis before their people get killed, he added.

Weissman found that information alarming. Trusting Franklin because of their earlier contacts—and because he stated explicitly that he had been "cleared"—Weissman phoned a friend at the Israeli embassy and passed on the information. All he could think of was bumping into someone in the future whose child was dead because he had done nothing.

Instead, he and Rosen fell into the FBI's trap. Franklin had been wearing an FBI wire, and so every word of his pitch to Weissman made its way to federal prosecutors. Similarly, Weissman's calls to his Israeli embassy friend were also intercepted by an FBI team sitting a few miles away at the FBI Language Services Section.

It took the FBI almost another full year to arrest Weissman and Rosen. But when they did, it became the highest-profile case of so-called "espionage" on behalf of a foreign power in many years.

And yet, no secrets were passed to any foreign power, and no U.S. secrets were compromised. Instead, it was part of an effort by enemies of the Bush administration to settle personal scores and destroy political enemies.

It was all about taking down the "cabal."

CHAPTER TWELVE

CIA INSURGENCY

CIA Director Porter Goss knew from the start that his days in the seventh-floor suite at CIA headquarters in Langley, Virginia, were going to be numbered.

When President Bush picked him for the CIA spot in July 2004, it was unclear that Bush would even be reelected that November. And if he was, the CIA was likely to be subsumed in some new umbrella organization, once the 9/11 Commission issued its recommendations for how the intelligence community should be restructured and Congress applied its brickbat. Porter Goss knew he was intended to be a transitional leader, and in one way that suited him perfectly. He had been telling associates in Congress for years that he was ready to retire. Now, at sixty-five, he was embarking on a final mission, one that the president personally had entrusted him to carry out.

Put simply, he was supposed to "clean house," a former CIA officer explained in one of many off-the-record conversations. That meant getting rid of the dead wood of CIA analysts and operations officers who couldn't adapt to the post–Cold War world, and those who—for ideological reasons, ineptness, or personal animosity toward President Bush—refused to prosecute the war on terror aggressively, or worse, actively undermined it.

But Goss's mission was not political—at least, that's not how he, his staff, or his supporters saw it. It was nothing less than transformational, remaking the CIA so it could meet the challenges of the post–Cold War world, where a bunch of often-hapless terrorists, armed with nothing more than airline tickets and box cutters, could wreak devastating havoc upon America, as they had on 9/11.

AN AGENCY IN TURMOIL

For the past seven years, Goss had chaired the House Permanent Select Committee on Intelligence (HPSCI), one of just two congressional committees that oversee the work of the CIA and the fourteen other agencies that constitute the vast U.S. intelligence community. Members of these two committees have access to the nation's greatest—and sometimes darkest—secrets. A close-knit community, they had remained remarkably nonpartisan until recently, when the American public clamored for them to apportion responsibility between the administrations of Bill Clinton and George W. Bush for the September 11 attacks.

The first warnings that Goss was headed for trouble emerged well before Bush sent his nomination to the Senate on August 10, 2004, when CNN reported that outgoing CIA director George Tenet had fired off an angry letter to Goss following the release of a report by the House intelligence committee that sharply criticized Tenet's management of the Agency.

The CNN account quoted just one word from the entire 75-page report: "dysfunctional." That was how Goss's committee described CIA management of human intelligence-gathering operations. Tenet was furious, complaining to Goss that his criticism was "ill-informed" and "absurd."[1] Anyone reading the press accounts would have concluded that Goss had committed an outrageous slander of the patriotic men and women of the CIA, who were risking their lives to keep America safe during the war on terror. Tenet was a master of spin.

In fact, Goss's committee had been warning of problems with CIA management for several years, and actually supported giving greater responsibility to case officers in the field and to intelligence analysts back at headquarters—the two Great Orders of CIA lore. The committee specifically blamed the CIA's skewed judgments on Iraq on "inadequate or insufficient HUMINT collection" and said that "senior DI [Directorate of Intelligence] managers still do not have the ability to drive collection priorities, despite past Committee exhortations about the urgency of fixing this problem."[2]

Until then, Goss had reserved his most scathing criticism for the classified annex to the annual intelligence authorization bill, where Tenet felt he could safely ignore it. For eight years, Tenet had been telling Congress and the media that he was hard at work rebuilding the CIA's capabilities, after budgets had been slashed and operatives had rushed for the doors during the first Clinton administration. Goss felt it was time to get it all out into the open. Two and a half years after the September 11 attacks, the picture the report painted was dire:

> "All is not well in the world of clandestine human intelligence collection (HUMINT). The DCI himself has stated that five more years will be needed to build a viable HUMINT capability. The Committee, in the strongest possible terms, asserts that the Directorate of Operations (DO) needs fixing. For too long the CIA has been ignoring its core mission activities. There is a dysfunctional denial of any need for corrective action."[3]

The committee warned that the "damage to the HUMINT mission through its misallocation and redirection of resources, poor prioritization of objectives, micromanagement of field operations, and a continued political aversion to operational risk" was "significant and could likely be long-lasting."

> "If the CIA continues to ignore the experience of many of its best, brightest, and most experienced officers . . . the DO will become nothing more than a stilted bureaucracy incapable of even the slightest bit of success."

Goss was throwing down the gauntlet. The classified annex to the report spelled out in excruciating detail a "comprehensive analysis" of how overseas spying operations were being mismanaged, details Goss and his staff had gathered from dozens of overseas trips where they met discreetly with CIA officers in the field.

The DO had become an old boys' club, a closed network that sought to protect itself before it protected the country, Goss believed. The James Bonds of America in reality were more like the Keystone Kops. Officers covered up the mistakes of their fellows, whether they involved sexual harassment, missing expense account funds, or graver deeds. Sometimes, to meet what many in the DO considered to be a counterproductive system of grading them on the number—rather than the quality—of the foreign agents they recruited, they would invent sources, invent contacts, and invent intelligence out of whole cloth. It was Graham Greene's *Our Man in Havana* on a grand scale. And then there were allegations that DO officers were taking kickbacks from Agency contractors, and steering contracts to companies in which they themselves were silent partners or investors.

One such company that was partially owned by a top CIA manager benefited from billions of dollars in secret contracts from the war in Iraq just before the CIA manager retired. If the president agreed to give him a chance, Porter Goss was going to change all that.

And the problems weren't just at the DO. Goss also skewered the community of intelligence analysts and their managers, faulting them for "the culture of analytic risk aversion." It had begun long before 9/11, he wrote, and was "fostered through the continued perception on the part of the rank-and-file that senior DI managers do not want risk taking—however calculated, caveated, and warranted—and that they will not stand by an analyst who has made the wrong prediction."

Ironically, the much disputed October 2002 National Intelligence Estimate on Iraqi Weapons of Mass Destruction was just such a product. It erred not because it stretched the intelligence, as administration critics argued, but because it was too cautious. In Goss's view, "analysts should be encouraged to be more forward leaning and to push the analytic envelope whenever possible, lest consumers turn more and more—as they have in recent years—to uncorroborated single-source HUMINT or SIGINT [signals intelligence] reports to inform their decisions."

Those would turn out to be prophetic words. In this and other statements in the HPSCI report, Goss was laying out in explicit terms the change agenda he wanted to bring to the CIA should the president choose to nominate him as the next director.

Across the river at Langley, Tenet and his top aides took those statements as a declaration of war, because they had deep dark secrets to protect. Goss's report revealed an Agency that had run amok.

"MY NAME IS PORTER . . ."

Porter Goss knew he would face opposition, and spent much of his initial pep talk with Agency employees on September 24, 2004, on the CIA campus in an attempt to set them at ease. An old hand at the Agency, where he served as a case officer in Latin America in the 1960s, he still referred to the Directorate of Operations by its earlier name, the Directorate of Plans. He told the staff gathered in the dome-shaped amphitheater that he still remembered the thrill of walking through the back doors of the temporary CIA headquarters in a disused Navy building down on the National Mall as a lowly GS-7 employee. Back then, it was all about freedom and liberty, he said. Today was no different.

"It is good to be back. And my name is Porter. That's enough to know," he said.

Of course, it wasn't. All the bonhomie in the world could scarcely disguise the deep hostility bubbling away just beneath the surface. Even Goss understood he had to say more, and tried to address the Agency skeptics.

"Now, before making any more judgments about me, sit back, relax, and I will tell you who I am, what I believe, and where I plan to take the intelligence community," he said.

America was at war, Goss said, a different type of war from anything they had fought before. They had to "collapse bureaucratic layers" and get rid of the "stovepipes" that kept intelligence collectors from sharing information with analysts. They needed to place greater emphasis on developing languages—not the French, German, and Russian that most DO officers spoke, but the languages of today's targets in places that were dangerous and unpleasant and difficult to penetrate. They had to allow case officers greater freedom to do what they did best: taking calculated risks to recruit spies. It was all about Mission, Capabilities, and Success, he said. The intelligence community was the "pointy end of the spear."[4]

Goss used all the buzzwords, but it wasn't going well. Much of what he said boiled down to one simple message: we need to work harder, do better, and take more risks. The era of day care centers and "diversity quilts" at CIA headquarters was about to be replaced with hard work. The old-boy networks of the DO, where failure had protected failure for a generation, had to change.

"Porter clearly started off at CIA knowing that the intelligence community needed to be shaken up," Pete Hoekstra, who succeeded Goss as the top Republican on the House Permanent Select intelligence committee, told me. "He was breaking the china and he was getting results when he was summarily fired by the president."

Goss was recruited into the CIA during his junior year at Yale, where he had majored in Ancient Greek and learned Spanish and French. He was a member of the Psi Upsilon fraternity (known to rival frat houses as Pee-You), where he first got to know Yale classmate John Negroponte.

Goss has rarely spoken about his years in the Agency, giving rise to speculation that he was involved in recruiting Cuban immigrants for the failed Bay of Pigs invasion in 1961. As one online biography of him notes in crediting these rumors, he told the *Washington Post* in 2002 he had done some "small-boat handling" and had "some very interesting moments in the Florida Straits" at the time.

He retired from the Agency in the early 1970s, after he collapsed in 1970 from a massive infection of the heart and kidneys in a London hotel room.

Goss then returned to Florida, starting a local newspaper with two former CIA colleagues, and in 1974 was elected to the city council of his hometown of Sanibel, Florida, eventually becoming mayor. Elected to Congress in 1988, he returned to Washington the following January.

Goss was never known as a flashy member of Congress, preferring to work quietly on substantive issues behind the scenes. Over the years, he became a trusted advisor on national security to Illinois Republican Dennis Hastert, who named him chairman of the House Permanent Select Committee on Intelligence in 1997. So he was already a key power broker when the president selected him to replace George Tenet, who announced his resignation on June 2, 2004. Tenet had led the agency into the worst intelligence failure in its history by failing to "connect the dots" of the many pre–September 11 warnings. Most congressional Republicans thought Bush should have fired him much sooner.

The reasons for Tenet's failures were many, Goss knew. Part of it was Tenet's management style. Known for his locker room personality, "Slam Dunk" Tenet was so eager to please his consumer—the president—that he often exaggerated the Agency's real capabilities, even as they were shrinking before his eyes.

"Porter didn't want to nourish false expectations, and found himself in the uncomfortable position of telling the president that he couldn't provide all the things George [Tenet] had promised him," a source close to the former director told me. "It wasn't a very popular message."

Under Tenet, a "take-no-risk culture" had seized top Agency leaders and field officers. Risk was like oil, the field operatives knew. It made the machine function efficiently. Without it, the wheels ground to a halt.

"When we saw under Tenet that the head of the Operations Directorate and his deputy—the nation's top spies—had never been posted overseas, everyone understood this whole thing was headed south," one retired, highly decorated covert operator told me. "Tenet allowed non-operational types to rise to the CIA equivalent of three-star general."

It's an article of faith among former case officers that if you want your field officers to take risks, to penetrate hard "targets," then they need to be supported by management back in Langley that understands the obstacles and the risks they face. It helps if those managers themselves have faced similar risks in their own careers.

But with some notable exceptions, that wasn't the case before September 11. James Pavitt, who retired from the agency as deputy director for operations (DDO) just before Goss came in, had only one overseas posting in his career. He had been running the Operations Directorate since 1999. His predecessor, David Cohen, had none—same for his deputy, David Edger.

Under their direction, avoiding risks became the Agency's standard operating procedure. A field officer who had been in charge of the Agency's efforts to support an Iranian opposition radio station based in Paris in the 1990s gave me a stunning example. "My case officers were being tracked by Iranian agents, right in the streets of Paris," he told me. Iran's spy agency, the Ministry of Information and Security, "had a reputation for thuggishness, and we respected them."

Several members of the Iranian Flag of Freedom Organization had been assassinated by regime agents in Paris, Dubai, and Istanbul in the early and mid-1990s. "In the end," the case officer recalled, "we were told to stand down and cut off all contact with the opposition group. The message from headquarters was crystal clear: No risk is too small to avoid."[5]

Tenet made a halfhearted attempt to reform the CIA's clandestine service in 1997, replacing Edger with decorated operator Jack G. Downing, who had just retired at the end of a long career when Tenet called him back. A Harvard-educated Marine who won the Silver Star as a Green Beret in Vietnam, Downing was the only CIA officer during the Cold War to serve as station chief in both Moscow and Beijing.

Downing's solution to the DO's problems was to reinstate jump training—paramilitary style, at 1,200 feet—for new recruits. "Ordinary people are not inclined to jump out of an airplane," Downing told reporters, "and we are not looking for ordinary people."[6]

While recruitment numbers went up during Downing's two-year tenure, Tenet undid any benefit by taking the unprecedented step of promoting case officers while they were back at headquarters, not out in the field. "This sent just the wrong message to the DO," the highly decorated Agency veteran said. After all, it wasn't the managers who were taking the risks. "We got to the point where the only thing that distinguished the CIA from the Department of Agriculture was that we recruited and ran sources in hard places," he added.

Curing the risk-avoidance culture would take time, Goss knew. He had to send a clear message to the rank and file, and the standard pep talk of an incoming director wasn't enough. He had to fire people. That's where the rubber hits the road in any bureaucracy.

THE DEMOCRATS' MOLE

Democrats on Capitol Hill got wind of Goss's prospective nomination in late June 2004, and successfully delayed his confirmation hearing for three months so they could secretly organize the opposition. They called on an unusual network of sources planted deep within the CIA itself to spy on the nominee and spread rumors about a dark past.

It was a job for the shadow warriors.

Key to their effort was an individual who amounted to a mole-in-place: a CIA detailee who headed intelligence programs at the National Security Council (Tenet's old job), and who went on to become a top deputy to Director of National Intelligence John Negroponte.

Because of his NSC position, the Democrats' mole had access to the "murder boards" organized to vet the candidate and prepare him for his nomination hearing. Frequently used in political campaigns and in corporate America, murder boards prepare the most hostile, insulting, and insinuating questions they could assemble from close scrutiny of a candidate's background, to prepare him in the event of a hostile hearing. "Because [the CIA detailee] leaked all the information used by the murder board to the Democrats, we had to organize our own briefings of Porter in a classified area within the Capitol building," a former Goss staffer told me.

The Senate Select intelligence committee had a field day. They requested document after document, pored through Goss's financial holdings and those of his wife, who came from old money, in addition to combing through his CIA past. In the meantime the 2004 presidential elections were approaching, key positions at CIA were unfilled, and every agency in the U.S. government was on heightened alert for the massive terrorist attack Osama bin Laden and his henchmen were warning they would carry out before the elections.

Think of it: America had been attacked on September 11, was at war in Iraq, and was in desperate need of an effective secret intelligence organization that could penetrate the enemy and steal his secrets to save American lives. And yet, instead of encouraging the president to take every possible step to strengthen the CIA and to get rid of the dead wood, the Democrats—aided by a coterie of rogue CIA officers—tried to prevent the president's pick as CIA director from ever getting to sit in the captain's chair.

It was sabotage. But delaying Goss's confirmation was just the beginning. The Democrats had an election to win. They intended to use sympathetic elements within the CIA to leak classified information—arguably aiding and encouraging the enemy—in order to undermine Goss, sidetrack the CIA from the important work it had to do, and especially, smear the president of the United States of America.

During the three-month hiatus between Tenet's June 2 resignation and Goss's confirmation on September 24, acting CIA director John McLaughlin, whom Tenet had promoted to become his top deputy, worked with Tenet to stack the decks, appointing dedicated Goss opponents and enemies of change to senior management positions. (McLaughlin took over the reins fully on July 11, when Tenet left.)

McLaughlin's motive appeared to be simple: If he could stall the nomination of Tenet's replacement until after the November election and the Democrats won, he felt confident that a President Kerry would keep him on as CIA director.

Failing that, he intended to make life so difficult that Goss would abandon his attempts to reform the Agency and allow McLaughlin and his clique to run the place.

McLaughlin denies his role in the CIA insurgency against the Bush administration and Porter Goss, and says he "sought to help Porter" as DCI. (He also claims that Tenet made the last-minute hiring decisions, a highly unusual practice for an outgoing agency chief.) But multiple interviews with other eyewitnesses, and more than two dozen former CIA officers who were tracking these events closely through their own old-boy network, lend credibility to those who asserted that McLaughlin had thrown in his lot with the shadow warriors at the CIA.

The inside story of their insurgency is told here for the first time.

CHAPTER THIRTEEN

"ROGUE WEASELS"

Bush lied, people died!

That was the Democrats' slogan going into the November 2004 elections, and they hammered it home at every opportunity.

"He misled every one of us," said Senator John Kerry.

"He lied about weapons of mass destruction, and he lied about the war," added Representative Maxine Waters (D-CA).

"We cannot lead if our leaders mislead," former president Jimmy Carter admonished in a speech at the 2004 Democratic National Convention.

Once he officially became the Democratic Party nominee, Kerry accused the president of "refusing to come clean with the American people" on the Iraq War, which by September 2004 had cost the lives of more than 1,000 U.S. soldiers and civilians.

It's one thing for a political candidate and his surrogates to chip away at his opponent's credibility, and Kerry was certainly not the first presidential hopeful to stretch the facts to fit his case.

It's quite another, however, for active-duty U.S. intelligence officers to clandestinely join a U.S. election campaign, leak classified documents to the press, and spin them in such a way as to inflict maximum damage on the president whose administration they are constitutionally bound to serve.

The shadow warriors felt that their actions—and their leaks—might actually determine the outcome of the 2004 presidential race. It gave them a tremendous incentive to make sure the president's new choice to head their agency failed and failed miserably.

Porter Goss inherited a Central Intelligence Agency that was in open revolt against the Bush administration and that rejected the very notion of a global war on terrorism. "We hope he appreciates that he now has two insurgencies to defeat: the one that the CIA is struggling to help put down in Iraq, and the other inside Langley against the Bush Administration," the *Wall Street Journal* wrote shortly after his confirmation.[1]

"The CIA has been at war with the Bush administration since the beginning," said Richard Perle, the prominent neo-conservative defense strategist. "What is astounding is the CIA campaign to discredit this administration."

Perle cited to me numerous examples where the CIA had dropped the ball—failing to warn about the threats from Islamic extremism, missing Iran's nuclear weapons program, reinterpreting intelligence on Saddam's weapons programs after the 2003 war. "The CIA has a lot of explaining to do" for its past failures, he argued. Instead of cleaning house, the career bureaucrats found it "easier to attack the president than own up to their own deficiencies."

During the first three years of the Bush administration, the CIA's Counterterrorism Center (CTC) spent more than $15 million funding studies, reports, and conferences produced by former Democratic administration officials and critics of the Bush administration, *Washington Times* reporter Bill Gertz revealed.

These included a $300,000 grant by the CIA to the Atlantic Council to fund a study coauthored by Richard A. Clarke, the former National Security Council official who wrote a bestselling book accusing the Bush administration of failing to take the threat of al Qaeda seriously before 9/11. Clarke's allegations were used by Kerry throughout the campaign, even though many of them were demonstrably false.

The CTC also funded studies by the Brookings Institution and the Carnegie Endowment for International Peace, both liberal think tanks, and provided assistance to a Muslim scholar known for public statements supporting jihad against the United States. Gertz found that the academic outreach program "has not funded any studies or conferences at conservative organizations."[2]

As the presidential race heated up, the CIA authorized the longtime head of its bin Laden desk, Michael Scheuer, to anonymously publish a book that has been portrayed by the media as a frontal assault on the Bush administration's war on terror from an all-knowing insider. In *Imperial Hubris*, which hit the stores in July 2004, Scheuer not only called the Iraq War "a Christmas present to Bin Laden," but accused Israel of controlling U.S. foreign policy. The Agency expedited the normal prepublication vetting process for Scheuer's book, a process that can take many months and sometimes years, and has caused some former CIA officers to break publishing contracts. But as Scheuer himself told the *Washington Post* after the election, "As long as the book was being used to bash the president, [the CIA honchos] gave me carte blanche to talk to the media."

Scheuer and the Counterterrorism Center were not alone in the Bush-bashing. Intelligence community insider Jack Wheeler asserted that a band of "rogue weasels" led by top Near East analyst Paul R. Pillar were driving a CIA "war . . . to secure Bush's defeat."[3]

"JUST GUESSING"

Tensions between the CIA and the administration escalated dramatically on September 15, 2004, when a recent National Intelligence Council estimate on the growing violence in Iraq wound up in the *New York Times*.

The classified National Intelligence Estimate spelled out "a dark assessment of Iraq," with civil war as the "worst case," the source who leaked the document told the *Times*. The Kerry campaign jumped all over it, citing the leaked document as damning new evidence that Bush had ignored clear warnings from the intelligence community about his "failed policy" in Iraq.

White House spokesman Scott McClellan dismissed the August 2004 NIE as written by "pessimists" and "hand-wringers." But the president weighed in personally one week later, upping the ante.

Bush said that the NIE on Iraq laid out "several scenarios that said life could be lousy, life could be okay, or life could be better, and they were just guessing as to what the conditions might be like."

Just guessing: that drove Pillar and the shadow warriors nuts.

Pillar immediately launched his counterattack. Now that the document was out, he was immunized and could describe it openly, to correct misconceptions generated by the press accounts. (This was a strategy frequently used by high-level leakers, and not only at CIA.) The venue he chose was a CIA-sponsored "outreach" event before a group of private individuals on the West Coast. It was the type of event that had to be approved at the highest level of the Agency—acting director John McLaughlin or his top deputies.*

These outreach events were nothing less than "a license to leak," one

*An Agency spokesman said that Pillar's presentation had been approved by his "management team," which was in fact the top management of the Agency.

former Agency staffer told me. They were the brainchild of top CIA operations officers allied with McLaughlin, as I will describe later in this book.

Pillar revealed to the group that he was indeed the author of the gloomy August 2004 NIE on Iraq, but strenuously denied that he was the source of the leak. And anyway, the document was only the latest in a series of "secret, unheeded warnings" from the CIA that war in Iraq would have disastrous consequences for the United States throughout the Middle East, he added.

Those comments constituted yet another leak, this time in person. Pillar and those who authorized him to make this disclosure were never reprimanded for their actions.

Syndicated columnist Robert Novak was the first to report Pillar's presentation. The CIA analyst "was not talking off the cuff," Novak explained. "Relying on a multipaged, single-spaced memorandum, Pillar said he and his colleagues concluded early in the Bush administration that military intervention in Iraq would intensify anti-American hostility throughout Islam."

Asked why he had never passed on those warnings to President Bush, Pillar replied that nobody asked—not even DCI George Tenet.

"This exchange leads to the unavoidable conclusion that the president of the United States and the Central Intelligence Agency are at war with each other," Novak concluded. "For President Bush to publicly write off a CIA paper as just guessing is without precedent. For the agency to go semi-public is not only unprecedented but shocking."[4]

Pillar was a career analyst, not an undercover operator. He rose during his twenty-five years at Langley to become the Agency's top analyst for the Near East and South Asia, a region that covered everything from Egypt, the Palestinian territories, Iraq, Iran and the Arabian Peninsula to Pakistan and Afghanistan.

Just four months before the 9/11 attacks, he penned a book of essays, *Terrorism and U.S. Foreign Policy*, published by the liberal Brookings Institution while he was on leave from the Agency. In the book, Pillar set out the "concept" he had elaborated earlier in a 1995 National Intelligence Estimate that abolished the notion of state-sponsored terrorism.

Pillar called it "a new terrorist phenomenon." The old leviathans of the Cold War were gone, including the state sponsors of terror. The United States could not be "at war" with small, isolated terrorist groups such as al Qaeda, because they were amorphous, nonstate actors. Instead, he argued, "a better analogy" for U.S. efforts to defeat the terrorists was "the effort by public health authorities to control communicable diseases."

From now on, he argued, terrorism was small, it was limited, and it was easily brought under control.[5] It was like the flu—or perhaps, gonorrhea.

If anyone had missed the stupendous growth of al Qaeda, it was Paul Pillar. He failed to warn about growing contacts between al Qaeda and Saddam Hussein, which have been widely documented by the Senate Select intelligence committee and, increasingly by documents seized in Iraq by U.S. forces as they progressively get translated and incorporated into the HARMONY database.[6] Nor did he warn of al Qaeda's secret relationship to the Iranian regime, which he insisted could not exist because the two came from opposing sects of Islam.*

Pillar never grasped the fact that Osama bin Laden and his jihad organization were serious about their threats to attack America. The Democrats and the *New York Times* thirsted for his wisdom for one simple reason: he was willing to openly criticize the Bush White House.

POLITICALLY TIMED LEAKS

Never before had a director of Central Intelligence been confirmed just five weeks before a presidential election. And never before had intelligence become so politicized.

By its very nature, intelligence information lends itself to political manipulation. The layers of secrecy give almost oracular weight to the whisperings of the Langley bird, who can never be trapped and never be grilled to determine the veracity of his claims.

On Tuesday, September 28, 2004, just four days after Goss was sworn in as CIA director, the shadow warriors leaked yet another classified intelligence assessment on Iraq to the *New York Times.* The leak couldn't have been timed more strategically, given that Bush and Kerry were scheduled to debate the Iraq War that Thursday evening.

The *Times* announced breathlessly that this latest leaked report, penned in January 2003, "warned the Bush administration about the potential costly consequences of an American-led invasion two months before the war began," and predicted "a possible insurgency against the new Iraqi government or American-led forces."[7]

---

*The al Qaeda–Iran connection was discovered by accident by the 9/11 Commission when an alert staffer stumbled upon a top-secret document the CIA had hoped the commissioners would never find. I discuss this incident in detail in *Coundown to Crisis: The Coming Nuclear Showdown with Iran*, pp. 268–71.

They added this stunning prescience to the growing list of wise pronouncements by the Agency that the Bush administration had refused to heed in its single-minded obsession with toppling Saddam Hussein. Democratic nominee John Kerry jumped all over it, and made Bush's "failed" Iraq policy the central focus of a new 60-second campaign spot that aired in sixteen major markets across the country just before the debate.

In fact, the warning of a possible insurgency was an afterthought, thrown in the very last sentence of the 38-page document in typical CYA fashion, just to make sure the Agency analysts had covered all their bases. (After all, if you predict that tomorrow could be sunny, partly cloudy, or raining, you've got a better chance of appearing prescient than if you actually chose the most likely outcome based on the facts.) That was what Bush had meant when he said the Agency was "just guessing" about future trends in Iraq.

The January 2003 document was little more than a compendium of everything that could possibly go wrong in Iraq. It predicted sectarian violence (which didn't occur until Iran started directing its proxies to fuel it). It warned that Kurds in the north and Shias in the south were planning to seize the oil fields (never happened). It predicted that Saddam's forces were likely to use chemical or biological weapons against coalition forces (which assumed, of course, that Saddam had stockpiles of WMD). The analysis also reassured the president that the Iraqi police and regular armed forces would remain intact, and could be counted on to maintain security after the war. American soldiers and Iraqis are still paying with their lives for that monumental misjudgment today. It was vintage Pillar—all things to all people. It was precisely the type of "mush" that Porter Goss and his team had come in to correct.

But the leaker of the report didn't dwell on those errors. Instead, he steered the *New York Times* to the last sentence, which in hindsight appeared to provide a stunning foretaste of things to come: "In addition, rogue ex-regime elements could forge an alliance with existing terrorist organizations or act independently to wage guerrilla warfare against the new government or coalition forces."

The message of the leakers was clear: don't blame us, blame Bush.

Nowhere did the document mention the "Party of Return," the clandestine Baath Party structure already put in place by Saddam's intelligence agencies to fight a guerrilla war against U.S. forces. Nor did it mention Abu Musab al-Zarqawi, the al Qaeda terrorist who was already in Iraq. "I'll take a bet that not a single analyst or Iraq task-force case officer foresaw, in a written report, the all-important role of Grand Ayatollah Ali al-Sistani and the senior Shiite clergy; the power of the Salafi fundamentalist movement among the Sunnis; or the speed and nature of the Sunni insurgency before the insurgency actually developed," says former CIA case officer Reuel Marc Gerecht, now a policy analyst at the American Enterprise Institute.[8] In other words, the CIA completely missed the most important developments inside Iraq, and yet was now claiming uncanny foreknowledge of the insurgency.

Richard Perle contested Pillar's claim that he and the Agency had warned the administration of dire things to come in Iraq. Perle was in a position to know, since he then was chairman of the Defense Policy Board, which advised the secretary of defense.

"Paul Pillar briefed senior policymakers before the start of the Iraq War in 2003," Perle told me. "If he had reservations about the war, he could have voiced them. He was in a very serious position and was able to make his views known, if that is what he believed."[9]

But as Pillar told his West Coast audience when he leaked the existence of the January 2003 NIE and all the other supposed "warnings" about the consequences of any invasion of Iraq, he never said anything because he was "never asked." It makes you wonder just who Pillar thought he was working for, or as Richard Perle hinted, whether the strong conclusions he later claimed were unanimous within the intelligence community had ever existed at all.

Perle also told me that an official who received Pillar's prewar briefing in January 2003 told him "it was the worst briefing he'd had in twenty-five years. Pillar couldn't answer questions, he didn't speak the language. He was clueless" to what was actually going on in Iraq.

"Congratulations to Porter Goss for being confirmed last week as the new Director of Central Intelligence," the *Wall Street Journal* wrote in a tongue-in-cheek editorial. The *Journal* called the leak "the latest improvised explosive political device" hurled at the president by an openly "insurgent" CIA, and warned that "at senior rungs of the agency there is a culture that has deep policy attachments that have been offended by Mr. Bush, and these officials want him defeated. American voters need to understand this amid this election season. As for Mr. Goss, his task is to tell the Pillars of Langley to shut up—or quit and run for office themselves."[10]

THE GREEN BADGERS

Pillar was by no means the only vehicle for leaking the content of highly classified CIA documents, and as noted above, he was careful to wrap himself with approvals from top management.

There were several other conduits the shadow warriors used to funnel potentially embarrassing intelligence information from Agency files to the media and, ultimately, to the Kerry for President campaign.

Foremost among them were the Green Badgers. I learned about this unusual Langley fauna from former CIA managers, career officers, and congressional sources.

The Green Badgers were former Agency employees, hired by private contractors after leaving the Agency to do work that required Top Secret and above clearances. (Full-time CIA staff used a blue badge to enter CIA headquarters. Green badges were given to contractors with security clearances.)

There were many inducements for CIA officers to leave government service and hook up with a private contractor. For starters, there was the money. "A Top Secret clearance is worth around $130,000 per year right off the bat," a former clandestine service officer familiar with the system told me. "Everyone knows you can walk out of the Agency and walk into the office of some Beltway bandit the next day and essentially double your government salary."

But some Green Badgers also had a political ax to grind. "People who felt threatened or who disagreed with what we were doing would leave their blue badge at the door on Friday, and come back on Monday with a green badge," a former top Agency manager told me. And suddenly, as if by magic, Agency secrets would wind up on the front pages of the *New York Times*. The shadow warriors had struck again.

Goss had made clear as chairman of the House intelligence committee that he found the hiring back of recent CIA retirees to be a deeply flawed management decision. Not only were they expensive; they were given sensitive tasks that Goss felt should be handled by full-time officers in the clandestine service, who were directly accountable to Agency management.

But above all, in the political context of the 2004 elections, the Green Badgers gave disgruntled officers inside the Agency a safe conduit to smear Bush and make known their loyalty to a future Kerry administration.

Because they were no longer CIA employees, the Green Badgers were never held accountable for leaks of Agency products. "There was nothing to stop a DO officer from sitting down in the CIA cafeteria with a Green Badger who was a former colleague and talking about classified material," a former Agency official told me.

It was not only legal, it was expected. "So even if they were polygraphed, the blue badges had done nothing wrong," he said.

In addition to the Green Badgers, there were the congressional intelligence committees. Prior to 2002, both the Senate and the House committees had been run on a fairly collegial basis, with a single staff not divided along party lines.

But that all changed during the buildup to the Iraq War, with Democrats in both the Senate and the House appointing partisan operatives to committee staff, who were given access by statute to the nation's most highly classified intelligence information.

The Kerry campaign set up a war room to exploit leaks from the intelligence community. It was run by Rand Beers, a Clinton administration appointee who burrowed into the National Security Council under Bush, thanks to Richard Clarke. Beers reportedly tried to get his security clearances renewed after he left government with help from Clarke, who had remained at the White House. "We thought this was the Kerry people trying to get a direct line to classified information during a presidential campaign," a Bush loyalist said. "It was a bit like the Clinton passport files case in 1992."

Beers knew the value of the CIA leaks, and had the political savvy to understand how they could be exploited to political benefit in the highly charged atmosphere of the presidential election campaign.

In August 2004, he made a key hire for the campaign, recruiting the former Democratic minority counsel of the House intelligence committee, Suzanne Spaulding. A former lawyer with the CIA Office of General Counsel, Spaulding was known for her partisan zeal when she worked under Representative Jane Harman, the Democratic co-chair of the House intelligence committee.

Spaulding had Top Secret clearances and took part in committee oversight hearings that put her in direct personal contact with the rogue weasels. Few were better placed than she was to lend a sympathetic ear to the grievances of friends and former colleagues inside the Agency.

It's long been a dirty secret of inside-the-Beltway Washington that friends leak to friends. But the extent of the hemorrhage of Top Secret documents and information from the CIA and other agencies to the Kerry campaign was unprecedented.

Never in the history of the United States has intelligence information, often gathered by risking the lives of agents working in the field, been put to such raw political use.

THE GOSLINGS

On September 30, 2004, six days after Goss was finally sworn in, he announced at the morning staff meeting of top CIA management that he was replacing four top deputies.

Goss understood Ronald Reagan's famous maxim of good government: people are policy. He knew that if he was going to seize control of the *Titanic* that the CIA had become, he had to do more than just rearrange the deck chairs. He had to get his own people into the engine room and post his own guards at the wheelhouse door, if he was ever going to grab the wheel to turn the ship around.

First to go was Tenet's executive director, A. B. "Buzzy" Krongard, an investment banker Tenet had brought on in 1999. Executive director was the third-ranking position at CIA, the guy in the engine room who transformed the captain's orders into actions. When Krongard agreed to announce his resignation, Goss introduced his replacement, Mike Kostiw.

Like Goss, Kostiw was a former CIA case officer. Goss had come to respect his knowledge of the Agency subculture when Kostiw had worked with him as staff director of the House intelligence subcommittee on terrorism, a position that put him in daily contact with Agency management and field officers.

Kostiw was one of four House intelligence committee staffers Goss brought with him to Langley. On the very first day they arrived at CIA headquarters, the agency rogue weasels whispered to reporters that everyone was referring to them as "the Hitler Youth." That was just one of many lies that would be told about Goss's aides.* When they realized that was over-the-top, the rogue weasels settled on a more humorous monikor, "the Goslings." The term soon appeared with remarkable regularity in anti-Bush articles in *The Nation*, the *New York Times*, the *Washington Post*, and elsewhere.

"So which were we? Hitler Youth or baby geese?" said one of Goss's staff. "They couldn't make up their minds." Later, the director of Euro-

*No one I have spoken to who worked at the Agency at the time had heard the term until it appeared in an article in *U.S. News & World Report.*

pean operations, Tyler Drumheller, boasted that his staff had come up with the geese reference. (He also acknowledged that both he and his wife, who also worked at the CIA, had become active in the Kerry campaign, and that she "captained the Democratic effort at a local precinct to take Virginia back for the Democrats."[11])

Walter Pincus, a *Washington Post* reporter who covered the intelligence community, led the media cheering section for the shadow warriors' assault on Porter Goss. The Friday afternoon staff meeting where Goss introduced his top aides "sent a tremor through CIA headquarters in Langley," he wrote. "It looks as though [Goss] is installing people known to be partisan politicos," he quoted one unnamed former intelligence officer as saying. "When you parachute in with a whole raft of people right away, it doesn't bode well."

"There is great concern about the migration of Hill staffers to the Agency because it creates a clash of cultures," another unnamed former CIA official said.

Howard Hart, who retired from the clandestine service in 1991 but still didn't shy from revealing Agency secrets (such as divulging fairly precise estimates of the current size of the clandestine service—one of the CIA's most-prized secrets[12]), unleashed the Democrats' standard ad-hominem attack. Goss's aides "will have no credibility in the agency because of their past performance on the House intelligence committee staff," he said.

James Pavitt, the outgoing deputy director of operations (the one with virtually no overseas operational experience), piled on. "My hope is they don't come in and do a wholesale change," he told Pincus. "Does it make a lot of sense to set the place on its head at a time when the nation is under a multitude of threats? They need to listen and learn first."[13]

But every director of Central Intelligence has brought his closest aides with him from earlier jobs. This was true with Bill Casey in the 1980s, and with George Tenet in the 1990s. During his brief tenure in 1995–1996, John Deutch brought on board Nora Slatkin as CIA executive director. She infamously required CIA officers to contribute to a gigantic "diversity quilt" on display at the headquarters building, and made crystal clear that political correctness was more important than recruiting spies within terrorist organizations for those who wanted to keep their jobs. Deutch also brought in Tenet, whose only experience with the spy world was as a Democratic political staffer—first with the Senate intelligence committee, later at the Clinton White House. But that never bothered Pincus or anyone else at the *Post*.

"The reason the CIA hated Kostiw and the Goslings was that they knew where the bodies were buried," a former CIA analyst who went to work for the Bush administration told me.

In addition to Kostiw, Goss brought over Patrick Murray to be his chief of staff. Murray had been a federal prosecutor in Chicago before coming to Washington and was Goss's chief counsel on the House intelligence committee beginning in 1997. In 2001, President Bush appointed him an associate deputy attorney general, where he worked under Larry Thompson. In 2003, Murray returned to HPSCI as staff director, where he reported directly to Goss and managed the committee's oversight inquiries and investigations, as well as the implementation of the "improvements" made to the intelligence community in the wake of the 9/11 intelligence failures. At HPSCI, he was directly involved in examining the CIA's lack of HUMINT, and the failure of the Directorate of Intelligence in preparing the Iraq WMD estimate. If anyone understood the complex relationship of spies to prosecutors, and the pre-9/11 "Wall" between the two that caused both agencies to refuse to share vital information that could have prevented the hijackings, it was Pat Murray.

Goss tapped two additional top committee staffers, Merrell Moorhead and Dr. Jay Jakub, as senior advisors. Moorhead had worked with Goss for eight years, ultimately as deputy chief of staff for the House intelligence committee. He had done much of the spadework on intelligence reorganization that made its way into the huge classified appendix to the intelligence authorization bill. He became Goss's big thinker, his main advisor on strategic programs.

Jakub, whom Goss asked to advise him on improving CIA operations and analysis, spent seven years as a CIA analyst before training to become an operations officer, giving him unique insight into the complex rivalries between the two Grand Orders of spookdom. Jakub resigned from the agency in 1995 when John Deutch came in as director and massacred the clandestine service, and went to Oxford to do a doctorate in the history of intelligence. When he returned to the Hill, he worked for the Cox Commission in 1998, investigating Chinese high-technology networks in the United States, then did a stint with Senator Saxby Chambliss, a Georgia Republican on the Senate Select intelligence committee, before going to work for Goss.

Such were the "Goslings." Not only did they know where the bodies were buried, they knew which corpses were still breathing. Because of that extraordinary depth of experience, they had to be discredited, smeared, and neutralized, to prevent them from launching the much-needed purge of Agency dead wood that Goss had been ordered to carry out.

Pillar and the rogue weasels at the Directorate of Operations struck back immediately, displaying a war room organization one would have thought the CIA reserved for destroying enemies of the United States of America.

They did a run on the Agency's most secret personnel files, and leaked them to Pincus and the *Post*.

"Dredging up an old shoplifting charge from 1982, the CIA rogue weasels gave the Posties all the private files of the investigation which—even though Kostiw was exonerated—they managed to twist into character assassination," wrote Jack Wheeler. "The hit piece appeared in the October 3 edition and Kostiw resigned the next day. It had taken the lefties five short days to knock Kostiw off."[14]

OPEN REVOLT

Emboldened by their success, a group of senior CIA officers—led by the former acting director, John McLaughlin—decided they could put an end to Goss's rule once and for all.

The plan drew on all the tradecraft of the CIA's clandestine service: manipulation, disinformation, destabilization, and provocation. The key actors were the Agency's top spies, the men McLaughlin made sure got promoted to the highest positions in the Agency's clandestine service just as Tenet left in June: Deputy Director for Operations Stephen R. Kappes and his assistant, Michael J. Sulick.*

"The Directorate of Operations lords it over everyone at the Agency," a former CIA officer said. "If they tell the Office of Security to get the dirt on someone, they do it. That's just the way this place works."

Kappes, fifty-two, was a former Marine who came to the CIA in 1981. Like McLaughlin, he came out of the Soviet Division and had been

*McLaughlin claims that Tenet actually signed the promotions, and that there was "nothing unusual" about them. But as several sources pointed out to me, would an incoming secretary of defense, or secretary of state, expect his predecessor to stack the deck with hostile, senior-level appointees just as he was heading out the door? "It's something that just isn't done in government, especially once the president has identified his nominee," one Washington insider said. In his May 2007 memoir, Tenet says nothing about this episode, apparently devastated by having to leave the CIA.

posted to Moscow, Islamabad, Beijing, and Kuwait. In the late 1990s, Tenet promoted him to head the Near East division, replacing Steven Richter, whose ouster was demanded publicly by Richard Perle. (Among other misdeeds, Perle accused Richter of having compromised an entire network of agents inside Iran in 1999 by doubling their reporting requirements without upgrading their covert communications.) As Near East chief, Kappes closed the books on recruiting spies inside Iran as too dangerous, and refused several opportunities to recruit defectors from Iranian intelligence agencies. To this day, the CIA has no spies in Iran, numerous Agency insiders and other sources say.

Despite his poor performance, Tenet promoted Kappes again in 2000 to head the Counterintelligence Center, the internal police of the Directorate of Operations. It was here that he first clashed with Porter Goss and his top aides, by failing to report in a timely fashion the compromise of the CIA station in Belgrade following the bombing of the Chinese embassy the year before. Goss's aides suspected at the time that Kappes was covering up for a careless operations officer, who had left classified documents lying around when the embassy was hastily evacuated and abandoned. But some sources believed the CIA leaks in Belgrade were far more serious, and may have been the deliberate act of a mole.[15] To this day, it has never been revealed what intelligence documents were compromised in Belgrade. Kappes continues to insist that nothing serious happened, but I am told by sources who were involved in the investigation that extensive photographic evidence proved "beyond any doubt" that the most highly sensitive documents any CIA station held had been compromised.

Despite this record, which was well known to Goss and his staff, Kappes felt he had a strong hand to play. As associate deputy director for operations under Pavitt in 2003, Kappes had headed a CIA team that successfully convinced Libya's Colonel Muammar Qaddafi to give up his previously clandestine nuclear weapons program. While the CIA's role in the Libyan negotiations has been known for some time, Kappes has not been shy about promoting it as a personal success. (Despite his claims to reporters to the contrary, he knew no more Arabic—or Farsi for that matter—than he knew Russian, and spoke to Qaddafi through an interpreter.) In her account of the negotiations, former *New York Times* reporter Judith Miller emphasized that Kappes reported on his dealings with Qaddafi "personally" to President Bush, "to prevent leaks and sabotage by neo-conservatives and other officials opposed to normalizing relations with Tripoli."[16] Kappes clearly believed that his relationship with

Bush gave him a trump card he could play in the power struggle with Porter Goss.

His deputy, Michael Sulick, was two years his senior and had moved up the ladder with him. McLaughlin installed them as a team in late June 2004 to ensure that he had a lock on the DO.

Whenever a new director comes in, he gets briefed every morning by the head of the clandestine service. "They normally do it one-on-one, so they can woo and seduce the new director with all the incredible stuff they do—and they really do some incredible stuff," a former CIA official who had served under several directors told me.

"Their goal is quite simple. They want the director to stop asking questions on what they've got, how they got it, and what they don't have," he added.

Within the DO, it's known as "capture the flag." That's how the DO, led by Kappes, viewed Porter Goss, the presidentially appointed director of the CIA: as an enemy standard-bearer they had to capture—or, at the very least, captivate so he would leave them alone to run their own show.

When Goss came to the Agency as DCI, he and his top staff were not newcomers. Over many years, they had established their own network of contacts deep inside the DO, who were feeding them information that showed a far less rosy picture than the one Kappes tried to paint during those early briefings.

Goss understood well that Kappes, as DDO, could pick and choose the operations he briefed to the director. He instructed his staff to get access to the raw cable traffic from the CIA stations worldwide, so they could help him to understand what Kappes *wasn't* telling him.

For nearly six weeks, Kappes balked. Not only did he refuse to grant Goss's top managers access to the DO database, he told members of Congress that Goss's chief of staff, Pat Murray, was being "obstructive" by demanding the information. Working together with his deputy, Mike Sulick, and their patron, John McLaughlin, he engineered a series of confrontations with Goss and his personal staff aimed at embarrassing Goss, undermining his status with the president, and creating pressure on him from Congress through the press to fire his top staff and leave the Agency to them.

"It was all about Steve," a former Kappes colleague told me. "This was his dream job to head the clandestine service, and he felt he was owed it. So anyone who he saw getting in his way he treated as the enemy."

Before Goss ever came to Langley as director, Kappes and Sulick told Vice Admiral Albert "Bert" M. Calland III, the head of the CIA Military

Office, that they would never work under Goss. They intended to remain true to their word. This has never been reported before and goes a long way toward explaining the ferocity of their confrontation with Goss's aides.

Kappes didn't just bide his time. He worked actively to subvert Goss and the president of the United States, even if it meant feeding them false information. Like many of the shadow warriors, he was not just praying for a Kerry victory in November as a private citizen, he was actively working to achieve it from inside the CIA.

LYING TO THE WHITE HOUSE

In October 2004, the White House learned that an Arabic-language television network had recently acquired a tape that provided dramatic proof that Bush's approach to the war on terror was working. It showed that the terrorists were still bent on attacking America but that administration policies had stymied them. White House officials were seeking a way of getting the network to air the tape.

Kappes knew that the material was a home run for Bush, and was determined to prevent the White House from exploiting the tape. During one of his morning sessions with Goss in his seventh-floor office, Kappes warned that the CIA had a source working for the Arab TV station who would be compromised and possibly killed if the tape ever became public.

You've got to tell them they can't use that tape unless they want to answer to me for getting one of my guys killed, Kappes said.

Goss took that information to the White House and asked the president and his top advisors to back off. Reluctantly, they did.

Soon afterward, one of Goss's aides learned from an operations officer who worked under Kappes that the whole story was a lie. We have no source at that Arab TV station, he said. The whole thing was Steve's invention. He just wants to keep the president from looking good.

When Goss learned that, he insisted on going back to the White House to correct the information he had provided them earlier.

The whole incident gave the White House the impression that Goss was clueless as to what was going on inside his own agency, and that was exactly what Kappes and the shadow warriors wanted. It was all part of their long-term plan to destabilize Goss and undermine the president of the United States.

Also joining the revolt against Goss and his top aides was the chief of counterintelligence, Mary Margaret Graham, who had just returned in August 2004 from New York, where she had headed the CIA's largest domestic spy station. In her new job, she reported directly to Sulick, and had access to the darkest secrets buried in the Agency's personnel files—things such as the twenty-two-year-old shoplifting allegation against Mike Kostiw.

Goss and his aides were thrown off-balance by the sudden withdrawal of Kostiw from the Agency's number-three slot, and didn't have another candidate. It took some time before Murray, Jakub, and Moorhead came up with a replacement, Kyle "Dusty" Foggo, a twenty-six-year Agency veteran who was then running a mission support station overseas.

They had met Foggo during a fact-finding mission to Germany, where he had run logistics for the war in Afghanistan, and felt he shared their vision for reforming the Agency. But after the Kostiw fiasco, Goss and his aides wanted to make sure they knew every jot and tittle from his personnel file. A single check mark from the Office of Security, the counterintelligence chief, the inspector general, the general counsel, or the director of operations would doom his appointment. They didn't want to wake up one morning and read about it in the *Washington Post.*

According to sources familiar with the events, Murray was in his seventh-floor office when Pat M—, the deputy director of the CIA's Office of Security, whose full name I have agreed to withhold—came in, waving a single sheet of paper. (Pat M—and his immediate boss, Robert F. Grimsland, were among the many top CIA managers who had been put in place by McLaughlin over the summer.)

You need to take a look at this, he told Murray. It was the Office of Counterintelligence report on Dusty Foggo, and it wasn't good.

The unsourced, half-page document contained two allegations. It claimed that while he was posted in Vienna in the late 1980s, Foggo had dated the girlfriend of Felix Bloch, the deputy chief of mission at the U.S. embassy in Vienna. Bloch was widely believed within the intelligence community to have been an East German spy and was stripped of his pension in 1993 despite thirty-three years of government service but was never prosecuted. It also claimed that when Foggo was assigned to Mexico City, he had been "targeted" by Philip Agee, "a known Cuban intelligence source."

Both allegations were extremely serious. As one person put it, Foggo had just been accused of the Fat Man and Little Boy of Espionage, a reference to the two nuclear weapons the U.S. detonated over Japan in 1945. Consorting with a Soviet-bloc spy and an Agency traitor were considered cardinal sins.

The deputy security chief said there was widespread agreement among McLaughlin, Kappes, Sulick, Mary Margaret Graham, and Bob Grimsland that they should go with the alternative candidate, Alan C. Wade, a computer expert who was the intelligence community chief information officer.*

Murray smelled a rat. Clearly the McLaughlin crowd was terrified of Dusty Foggo coming to the seventh floor, and he thought he knew why. As a veteran support officer, Foggo had worked very closely with the DO over the years. He knew whose operations had worked, and whose hadn't, and how to get things done. McLaughlin and Kappes knew they couldn't crush him.

So the former prosecutor began to dig. He called the Counterintelligence office and had them send up Foggo's personnel file, then called Foggo into his office to go over the half-page report line by line. It was only the third time they had met, and it wasn't a pleasant encounter.

Yes, Foggo said, he had stolen the girlfriend of another embassy official when he was posted in Vienna, but it wasn't Felix Bloch. The disgruntled boyfriend had gone to the FBI when he returned to the United States, claiming Foggo was tied to Felix Bloch, who by that time was the target of an FBI espionage investigation.

That must have raised a flag when you came back to headquarters after Vienna, Murray remarked.

You're damned right it did. I was polygraphed on it before I was sent back out. And I cleared, Foggo said.

The Mexico City allegation was even more risible. The alleged "contact" with Philip Agee had occurred after Foggo had been assigned to the Mexico City station, but *before* he actually moved down there—hence the careful language on the half-page CIA scandal sheet.

Agee had come to Mexico City claiming he was from the CIA office of inspector general, and became friendly with the secretary of the CIA station. He said he had been ordered to get a list of all CIA employees at the station, which she gave him. Even though Foggo was still in the United States, his name was on the list.

So much for the contact with Cuban intelligence. The whole thing was

---

*Wade retired after thirty-five years at the CIA in October 2005 and went to work for Unisys Systems.

a piece of trash, Murray said. It had been concocted for no other reason than to prevent the director of Central Intelligence from naming his choice to a key Agency position.

After clearing the decks with Foggo, Murray asked the CI chief, Mary Margaret Graham, to come to his office. It was a Friday. He held up the single sheet of paper with the unsourced allegations.

Are you aware of this? he said.

I sure am, she said. She gave him a grim look, pleased that her strategy had worked. It's pretty bad, isn't it.

It sure is, Murray agreed. Are you aware that he never dated Felix Bloch's girlfriend?

No-o-o, she said.

Are you aware that the complaint against him to the FBI came from the disgruntled ex-boyfriend of the girl he dated?

No, she said, quieter this time.

Are you aware that he passed his polygraph on this?

I guess he'd have had to, before he went back out, the Counterintelligence chief admitted. Otherwise, they wouldn't have cleared him for Mexico City.

Yeah, but did he? Murray insisted. You're the professional CI officer here. You're accusing him of serious lapses and you don't even know for a fact that this whole thing was put to rest in his polygraph?

Murray was fuming by this point.

In a small voice, Graham said she'd double-check with her office and get back to him on Monday.

On Tuesday, she returned, accompanied by the chief investigator who had compiled the scurrilous half-page against Foggo, and by Bob Grimsland, head of Security. They agreed that there was nothing of substance to the allegations.

So why did you give it to me in the first place? Murray asked.

We thought you needed to see it after the Kostiw debacle, Grimsland said.

But it was false and misleading! Murray said. Unless you've got something else you haven't shown me, I see nothing in his personnel file that disqualifies him for this position.

After a pause, the chief investigator cleared his throat. He, er, does have a reputation for being a womanizer. It's his reputation in the hallway.

His reputation *in the hallway*? Murray repeated, unable to disguise his incredulity. Do you have any documents to back this up? Have there been any harassment charges? Complaints?

They agreed there was nothing.

Murray had had enough. This is incredibly unprofessional, he said. I am well aware of what happened to Mike Kostiw.

Mary Margaret Graham interrupted at that point. Pat, I understand, she said. If this leaks, you have every right to march my ass out of the Agency.

There it was. While it wasn't quite an admission to having leaked the information on Kostiw, it was a backhanded acknowledgment. There was nothing more to say, so the meeting ended.

Later, the shadow warriors would repeat those words in breathless whispers to sympathetic Washington reporters. But they attributed them to Pat Murray and accused *him* of verbally abusing his CI chief by threatening to "march her ass out" of the Agency.

Both Patrick Murray and John McLaughlin refused to confirm or to deny this account.

CHAPTER FOURTEEN

OCTOBER SURPRISE

On Monday, October 25, 2004—just one week before the presidential election—the *New York Times* published a front-page story alleging that a huge cache of military explosives, used in nuclear weapons, had "gone missing from one of Iraq's most sensitive former military installations."

Some 377 tons of powerful HMX, RDX, and PETN explosives* placed under International Atomic Energy Agency seal at the al Qaqaa plant had been looted under the eyes of U.S. soldiers, despite repeated warnings from the IAEA to safeguard the site, the *Times* reported.

To illustrate the seriousness of the loss, which the *Times* blamed squarely on the Bush administration, the newspaper reminded readers that "the bomb that brought down Pan Am Flight 103 over Lockerbie, Scotland, in 1988 used less than a pound of the same type of material." And nearly 380 *tons* of the same material was missing—*380 tons!*

These shocking revelations came after the IAEA's Mohamed ElBaradei "put public pressure on the interim Iraqi government to start the process of accounting for nuclear-related materials still ostensibly under IAEA supervision, including the Qaqaa stockpile," the *Times* wrote. It wasn't the first time ElBaradei had attempted to insert himself into domestic U.S. politics with statements aimed at embarrassing President Bush, but coming just before the presidential election it was the most blatant and, potentially, the most damaging.

The *Times* had conducted its investigation into the missing explosives jointly with CBS's *60 Minutes,* and was originally planning to release the

*HMX = high melting-point explosive, RDX = rapid detonation explosive, PETN = pentaerythritol tetranitrate.

story on Thursday, after *60 Minutes* aired its version on Wednesday evening. But the reaction they had gotten from Pentagon officials in last-minute interviews in Washington convinced both organizations to rush the news into print, before the White House could do damage control.

Senator John Kerry issued a scathing statement the morning the story came out, condemning the administration's "unbelievable incompetence." Less than twenty-four hours after the *Times* hit the newsstands, the Kerry campaign bought time for a 30-second spot slamming President Bush for having "failed to secure 380 tons of deadly explosives" and started airing it on television stations across America. Either the Kerry media team had changed into their Superman costumes and could defy the laws of physics (not to mention network advertising execs), or they had been tipped off ahead of time by one of Dan Rather's friendly producers. (A 24-hour turnaround in the final days of a presidential campaign is virtually unheard of, besides the fact that advertising slots are booked and paid for way in advance.) But the Democrats were desperate. Bush had begun to pull ahead in the tracking polls, and they were looking for any hook they could use to trip him up.

Pentagon spokesman Larry DiRita pushed back weakly, telling reporters that the explosives had probably been moved before U.S. troops overran the al Qaqaa facility south of Baghdad. At any rate, he added, extensive searches of the 1,100 buildings at the site had turned up no equipment or materials that were under IAEA seal. Fox News was the only news outlet that aired a Pentagon press conference laying out the facts of the six-day search by the 3rd Infantry Division when U.S. troops first entered the facility on April 4, 2003.

Lieutenant General Tom McInerny, a Fox News senior military analyst, remembers talking to top Wolfowitz aide Dave Patterson the day the IAEA leak broke. "You've got all the answers to what happened to those explosives right here in this building," he said. "You need to get Jack Shaw out there leading the charge."

Deputy Undersecretary of Defense John A. Shaw had briefed McInerny on his contacts with the Brits and the Ukrainians, and had asked the retired three-star to accompany him to Iraq in December 2003 for a field investigation. "It's Monday morning, and Rome is burning," McInerny added. But Patterson brushed him off.

EMERGENCY EXIT

Two days went by, and Bush was getting creamed in the press. It looked as though the Kerry campaign had pulled off their October Surprise after all, with a little help from Dan Rather, the *New York Times*, and Mohamed ElBaradei. When no one from the E-Ring called asking Shaw to brief reporters on what he had discovered about the "theft" of high explosives and WMD materials in Iraq, he figured he had to act on his own. "I wasn't going to play Mother May I," Shaw said later. His arrangement with the inspector general's office did not require him to go through the Pentagon's public affairs shop as long as the information he revealed did not come from U.S. sources.

Shaw called two reporters he knew personally and offered to brief them on what his office had uncovered during an investigation spanning nearly three years. It was quite a tale, he said.

"The short answer to the question of where the WMDs went that Saddam bought from the Russians is Syria and Lebanon," he said. "They were moved by Russian Spetsnaz [special forces] units out of uniform, that were specifically sent to Iraq to move the weaponry and eradicate any evidence of its existence."

Shaw had dealt with weapons-related issues and export controls for the U.S. government for over thirty years, so his allegations carried weight with Bill Gertz of the *Washington Times* and Guy Dinmore of the *Financial Times*. Their articles, based on separate interviews, appeared on Thursday, October 28, 2004, the fourth day of what the Left was now calling "Qaqaa-gate."

Shaw described in detail a Russian operation, apparently run off the books, that involved "a whole series of military units" posing as civilian contractors and consultants. "Their main job was to shred all evidence of any of the contractual arrangements they had with the Iraqis," he told Gertz. "The others were transportation units." He believed they were responsible for hauling away the 380 tons of explosives from al Qaqaa.

The Russian cleanup operation was entrusted to a combination of GRU (Russian military intelligence) and Spetsnaz troops and to Russian military and civilian personnel in Iraq under the command of two experienced former Soviet generals, Colonel-General Vladislav Achatov and Colonel-General Igor Maltsev. Both men had retired from the Russian military and were posing as civilian commercial consultants.

Shaw suggested that Gertz might want to pull up Gazeta.ru, the Russian newspaper that had published photographs of the two generals receiving medals from Iraqi defense minister Sultan Hashim Ahmed in early March 2003, in a Baghdad building destroyed by U.S. cruise missiles just days later in the first air strikes of the campaign. While the Russian website didn't explain in its April 2, 2003, report why the two generals were in Iraq, General Achatov said that he "didn't fly to Baghdad to drink coffee."

When Shaw got into his office on Thursday morning, he had two messages waiting on his machine from Pentagon spokesman Larry DiRita. *Mother's worried*, he thought. As he was deleting them, Wolfowitz aide Dave Patterson called. "He didn't ask me where I'd gotten the information," Shaw recalled. "He didn't want to know more about it. He just said, Don't talk to the press about it." *Incredible*, he thought.

Later that morning, Shaw's boss, the undersecretary of defense for acquisition, technology, and logistics, Michael W. Wynne, showed up, brandishing a medieval battle mace that his predecessor, Dave Oliver (a Clinton holdover), had left him. It was pretty brutal-looking—a stout baton wrapped in leather, with a spiked lead ball attached to it by a metal chain. It was the type of thing Braveheart had used to rip the smile off the face of his English overlords.

Shaw turned to his deputy, Ed Timperlake. "I guess they're ready to shoot me today," he said.

"You got that right," Timperlake said.

A few days after the initial Gertz article appeared, the Pentagon released overhead imagery that appeared to support Shaw's claim, showing civilians loading barrels of explosives into a convoy of 10-ton trucks at a facility initially identified as al Qaqaa, the former Iraqi nuclear plant. The immediate controversy died down when it became apparent that U.S. troops had found no equipment at al Qaqaa under IAEA seal, contrary to ElBaradei's outraged assertions to the elite media.

But what Shaw couldn't tell Gertz and Dinmore was even more astonishing than what he could tell them. He gave me the full story later, as I was preparing this book.

His new friend General Ihor Smeshko, head of Ukrainian intelligence, had given him the names of dozens of Spetsnaz officers who helped to evacuate Saddam's WMD, as well as their units and their commanding officers. The whole operation to clean up Saddam's WMD sites was organized by Yevgeny Primakov—a KGB general and the former head of Russian intelligence, who had long-standing ties to Saddam Hussein.

Primakov went to Iraq in December 2002 and stayed until just before the war began in March 2003. In public, he said he was trying to find a negotiated solution to avoid war. But Smeshko said that his real job was to supervise the execution of secret agreements, signed between Iraqi intelligence and the GRU, that provided for cleanup operations to be conducted by Russian and Iraqi military personnel to remove strategic weapons, production materials, and technical documentation, so Saddam could announce that Iraq was "WMD-free."

The Russians call it *Sarandar*, Smeshko said. It means "Emergency Exit."

Shaw learned more about *Sarandar* operations from Ion Pacepa, the former head of Romanian intelligence who defected to the United States in the 1970s and still gave advice on occasion to the U.S. government. The GRU had been doing *Sarandar* operations for years, whenever they felt the Americans getting close, Pacepa said.

Smeshko provided Shaw with photographs and documents from a conference in Baku, Azerbaijan, where Primakov and the retired Russian generals planned the evacuation of Saddam's WMD before coming to Iraq in December 2002. The Baku conference, chaired by the Russian minister of emergency situations, Sergei Shoigu, "laid out the plans for the *Sarandar* cleanup effort so that Shoigu could leave, after the keynote speech, for Baghdad to orchestrate the planning for the disposal of the WMD," Shaw said later.

Subsequent intelligence reports showed that Russian Spetsnaz operatives "were now changing to civilian clothes from military/GRU garb," Shaw said. "The Russian denial of my revelations in late October 2004 included the statement that 'only Russian civilians remained in Baghdad.' That was the only true statement the Russians made," Shaw deadpanned.

From Stephen, the British self-styled "Lawrence of Arabia" who was on the ground, Shaw received detailed reports on the Russian evacuation convoys. In some cases, Stephen was able to track a convoy to a specific building in a specific village on the Syrian side of the border, where the trucks were unloaded. In another case, he tracked steel drums with painted warnings that had been moved to the cellar of a hospital in Beirut. He not only had the name of the hospital, but also the name of the doctor who received the drums, which were painted with a yellow skull and crossbones indicating that the contents were "some kind of poison gas," Shaw said.

In addition to the truck convoys that carried Russian-supplied weapons and technology to Syria and Lebanon, Shaw learned that two Russian ships had set sail from the Iraqi port of Umm Qasr just before the war and headed out to the Indian Ocean, where they emptied hundreds of drums of chemical weapons agents into the sea—quite possibly, the famous "stockpiles" of Iraqi weapons that neither coalition troops or the CIA's Iraq Survey Group ever found.

The evacuation of Saddam's WMD stockpiles was "a well-orchestrated campaign using two neighboring client states with which the Russian leadership had a longtime security relationship," Shaw said later.

Shaw tried to get his information into intelligence channels, but when he approached the Defense Intelligence Agency they dismissed his initial reports on the convoys as "Israeli disinformation." It took him a while to realize they weren't joking. "I was stunned," he said.

A month after that initial contact, Shaw learned that the DIA general counsel complained to his own superiors that Shaw had eaten from the DIA "rice bowl." It was a Washington euphemism that meant he had committed the unpardonable sin of violating another agency's turf.

The CIA responded in even more diabolical fashion. "They trashed one of my Brits and tried to declare him persona non grata to the intelligence community," Shaw said. "We got constant indicators that Langley also was aggressively trying to discredit both my Ukrainian-American and me in Kiev," he added.

The shadow warriors were at work.

For reasons Shaw has never fully understood, the Pentagon would rather take a hit from a hostile media than follow through on hard intelligence that implicated high-ranking Russian officials in aiding Saddam.

"Larry DiRita made sure that this story would never grow legs," Shaw said. "He whispered *sotto voce* to journalists that there was no substance to my information and that it was the product of an unbalanced mind."

Lieutenant General Thomas McInerney thought the reason was Iran. "With Iran moving faster than anyone thought in its nuclear programs," he said, "the administration needed the Russians, the Chinese and the French, and was not interested in information that would make them look bad."

OFFICE SHOWDOWN

At the CIA, the revolt against Porter Goss was coming to a head. In addition to blocking access to DO cables to Goss's staff, both Kappes and his deputy, Mike Sulick, had refused a direct order from Goss to send Mary Margaret Graham back to fill her previous post as chief of a New York station, a position that was temporarily empty. Kappes had been telling

DO officers that if he caught them cooperating with Goss and his deputies, they could kiss their careers goodbye, and he had specifically told Graham not to accept the posting. It was an act of direct insubordination.

But the final spark was a secret program to establish a separate channel of communication between the DO and Democrats in Congress that bypassed the CIA director's office. The existence of this program and the treachery it involved are revealed here for the first time.

Kappes called it his special project. Goss and his aides called it a license to leak. Deputy Director John McLaughlin said he knew nothing about it, even though Kappes said he had launched the program while McLaughlin was acting director. McLaughlin's denials "made it even worse," one source who was knowledgeable about these exchanges said. "That made it a rogue operation."

There was no reason the Agency should keep getting beaten up on the Hill when the FBI came up smelling like roses, Kappes told Goss's staff once they learned of the program. We have good stories to tell. So why not engage Members of Congress in their districts, conduct outreach events with Agency personnel, and suggest plans for Members to visit overseas Agency outposts with a DO nanny along for the ride?

It sounded great, Murray said. The only problem was, it was completely illegal. Members of Congress aren't stupid. They know when they are being manipulated. Besides, approaching members who did not sit on the intelligence committees—as Kappes and Sulick were suggesting—was a clear violation of the National Security Act, which established the oversight committees as the sole channel for communications between the Agency and Congress.

We don't need some Madison Avenue marketing scheme, he added. What worked with the Hill was truth, integrity, and timeliness—the same tools the FBI was using—not just good-news stories. Murray ordered them to stop all such efforts immediately. This shows the bankruptcy of respect you have for the intelligence oversight process, he told them.

Things came to a head on Friday, November 5, 2004, when Kappes and Sulick marched into the seventh-floor office suite of CIA Director Porter Goss. With Bush's reelection as president earlier that week, they figured they had to play their cards now or never. At stake was not just the issue of the DO "Special Project," but who was going to be running the Agency: Goss and his staff, or McLaughlin, Kappes, and a clique of DO operatives who had utter disdain for the director and for the president of the United States.

By all accounts, it was an epic confrontation. Goss was stunned when

Kappes demanded that he ask Murray to leave the room. He held his ground, and watched, dumbfounded, as Sulick and Kappes shouted across the table at his top aide. It was like something out of a movie, Goss thought. Maybe if he just closed his eyes, they would all go away. Twice during the meeting Sulick angrily crumpled up pieces of paper and tossed them at Murray, including a copy of his e-mail outlining the congressional outreach program Murray told him was illegal. After Goss and other staff members excused themselves to attend another meeting, Kappes went to the door and physically blocked Murray from leaving. He and Sulick apparantly had rehearsed what they would do next. Now they made their move.

At fifty-six, Mike Sulick was no wet-behind-the-ears junior operative. He had been assigned to operational posts in Eurasia, Latin America, and East Asia, and spoke Polish, Russian, and Spanish. He was also a large man, and he physically crowded Murray. "You can't treat me like some f—ing Democratic Hill puke," he screamed, finger wagging, spittle flying, chest bumping into Murray's own. With that, he stormed out of the room.

Murray was stunned by the violent outburst. Turning to Kappes, he said, Either Mike is completely out of control, or he's working for you. If he's working for you, then you'd better bring him under control. Otherwise, we'd better think about reassigning him.

Kappes seemed to have rehearsed his reply. I have complete control of Mike's actions, he said. Then he turned to leave.

Goss had gone to a nearby conference room for a meeting of top management, and now they all joined him. When Deputy Director John McLaughlin saw them come in, he gestured for Kappes to join him. Without saying a word, he raised his eyebrows expressively, as if to say, "Well?"

The look on Kappes's face was unmistakable, said several people who were in the room. "He could barely keep from laughing. He looked like the cat that had swallowed the canary," one participant said.

By all appearances, the whole thing had been a put-up job, with John McLaughlin, Kappes, Sulick, Mary Margaret Graham, and NSC detailee David Shedd working it from the start.

PORTER'S PURGE

Like many of his peers, Mike Sulick was a product of the East Coast liberal establishment. He had received a B.A. and an M.A. from Fordham

University in Russian Language, and completed his Ph.D. in 1977 at the City University of New York in Comparative Literature. As unlikely as that might seem to some, Comp Lit was not bad training for someone whose job was to penetrate hostile intelligence services. "It helps you to imagine what the other side is up to," one veteran intelligence professional said.

Increasingly that establishment—and the CIA officers who had been bred and trained by it—had come to detest George W. Bush for taking the war on terror into the heartland of the Muslim world. They believed, as Paul Pillar had written, that terrorism had been a containable threat until George W. Bush invaded Iraq. They maintained close contacts with "allied" intelligence services in Egypt, Jordan, and Saudi Arabia, who were keeping tabs on al Qaeda; even Syria was willing to help, they claimed. But Arab cooperation was in jeopardy because U.S. foreign policy under George W. Bush had become subordinated to the interests of the state of Israel, as Michael Scheuer alleged in *Imperial Hubris.*

To these CIA officers, America had more in common with Arab Muslim dictators, who could freely torture al Qaeda detainees with nothing leaking to the press, than we did with the only democracy in the Middle East, since it was run by Jews.

Over the weekend, Kappes sounded out colleagues inside the Agency and recent retirees, and came to the conclusion that he and Sulick had the upper hand. After all, he was the man who had gotten Colonel Qaddafi to give up his nuclear weapons program. And he had run that as a personal operation for the president of the United States! He and Sulick represented the elite of America's premier spy agency. If they walked out, half the Operations Directorate would follow. Porter Goss and the Goslings were attempting to dismantle the cushy empire of the covert operators. It was unthinkable, unacceptable, and Steve Kappes and his colleagues were determined to prevent it from happening.

Early the following week, Kappes marched into Murray's office and said that he and Sulick would hand in their resignations if Murray didn't back off, and that they would tell the intelligence committees exactly why they were leaving. (Jane Harman, Democratic cochair of the House committee, parroted those reasons to the news media later.) Murray suggested he get Sulick to apologize for his outburst and they all get back to business. And if he wouldn't, then why not assign Sulick to Mary Margaret Graham's domestic station—which was still vacant—to cool off? After all, he said, Sulick had been telling colleagues for some time that he wanted to return to his hometown as the final assignment in his career.

Kappes then went to Goss and announced that he and Sulick would resign if Goss didn't get rid of Murray and the Goslings. It's us or them, he said.

Fine, Goss said. To Kappes's utter astonishment, Goss expressed his regrets, and said he wanted their letters of resignation on his desk on Monday morning.

"Kappes was convinced that Goss would be so nonplussed at his threat to resign that he would back off," a former Agency officer who closely followed these events told me. "He was stunned when Goss accepted it on the spot."

Said another, "They bet everything on a single hand of poker. Porter called their bluff, and they lost."

Down in the parking lot that evening, Sulick turned to Kappes in shock. I can't believe what has just happened to me, he said.

MSM TO THE RESCUE

Realizing they had lost the game, McLaughlin bumped up the announcement of his own resignation—planned for the following month—to Friday, November 12.* Although he claims today that he "wanted to help Porter Goss," the thirty-year Agency veteran timed his resignation to inflict the maximum damage. Rumors that he was not alone in leaving bubbled away over the weekend, and by Monday, November 15, the news was out. "We're told this represents something of a revolt against the new management style of the new director Porter Goss, and specifically of the management team he brought with him," National Public Radio reporter Mary Louise Kelly revealed cattily.

Her reporting was typical of the treatment accorded Goss by the liberal media. She said that "several former top intelligence officials" had told her that Goss staff "have been abrasive, and downright disrespectful" to long-term intelligence officials. No mystery who her sources were.

Asked what kind of reputation Sulick and Kappes had at the Agency, she didn't miss a beat. "They had very good reputations. Both were senior spies, and had only been in their jobs a few months. . . . They were seen by

---

*McLaughlin went to the Paul Nitze School of Advanced International Studies at Johns Hopkins University, and consults often with the Center for American Progress, a left-wing think tank set up by former Clinton administration officials, and for CNN. In May 2006, he was a nonresident fellow at the Brookings Institution, another well-established Democratic think tank.

many within the agency as the future, and a pretty bright future," she added. Noting that Kappes was "a former Moscow station chief," she then said that he was "widely credited with being the key negotiator" with Muammar Qaddafi to convince him to give up his nuclear weapons program.[1] Both items from his Agency career as an operations officer were classified.

Time magazine and other media organizations quickly took the defense of Sulick and Kappes, calling them "two pragmatic and tough-minded officers who were regarded almost universally as mission oriented, apolitical and aggressive—exactly the traits Goss was supposedly looking for."[2]

Michael Scheuer followed Sulick and Kappes out the door, as did Jami Miscik, the deputy director of intelligence (the agency's top analyst), and her deputy, Scott White, as well as the European operations chief, Tyler Drumheller, and his colleague for East Asia. "I've never experienced this much anxiety and controversy," Scheuer told reporters afterward. "Suddenly political affiliation matters to some degree. The talk is that they're out to clean out Democrats and liberals. The administration doesn't seem to be able to come to grips with the reality that it was a stupid thing to do to invade Iraq."[3]

As more and more top CIA officers turned in their resignations, *Time* quipped that Langley "was changing its name to Fallujah," seat of the Iraqi insurgency. "[T]he question wasn't whether the place was eventually going to be cleared of rebels, but how many would be killed in the process."[4]

Ironically, one person who didn't leave was Mary Margaret Graham, the counterintelligence chief Goss's staff suspected of being at the center of personnel leaks. She stayed another six months, joining the staff of John Negroponte at the newly formed Office of the Director of National Intelligence in April 2005. Despite the fact that she had little overseas experience, Negroponte put her in charge of collection activities by the fifteen other agencies of the U.S. intelligence community, making her the nation's top spy. It was a staggering appointment for someone who had barely cut her teeth in the clandestine service at the CIA.

As the shake-up continued, Goss felt he needed to remind Agency staff that their job was not to speak out in public against the administration they were supposed to serve, but to steal secrets from the enemy and present them to U.S. policymakers. In an internal memo distributed by e-mail on November 15, Goss laid out what he called "the rules of the road."

"We support the Administration and its policies in our work," he wrote. "As Agency employees we do not identify with, support or champion opposition to the Administration or its policies. We provide the intelligence as we see it—and let the facts alone speak to the policymaker."[5]

If Goss had intended the memo to remain within the Agency, he underestimated the fierce opposition and the skill of his own employees. "Within a few hours of the e-mail, much of the agency's clandestine arm was on war footing, e-mailing friends, dialing up agency veterans and generally lighting fires all over town," *Time* reported. The shadow warriors had become apoplectic. They claimed that Goss was imposing a "loyalty oath" on them.

No amount of explaining by CIA spokesmen that Goss was not talking about *partisan* support for the administration, but *intelligence* support aimed at helping policymakers, could calm the waters. Vincent Cannistraro, who left the Agency in the 1990s for still unexplained reasons, told London's *Guardian* newspaper that the memo could "only be interpreted one way—there will be no more dissenting opinions."[6]

Washington Post columnist David Ignatius signed on almost immediately as a champion of the disgruntled spooks.

"It's crazy for a nation at war to be purging its spies," he wrote in a column that appeared shortly after the Goss memo leaked. He blamed Goss "and a phalanx of conservative congressional aides" for carrying out a "putsch . . . that could do real damage to the nation's security."[7]

While grudgingly admitting that the Agency "could improve its performance," and had become "too risk-averse, too prone to groupthink, too mired in mediocrity," Ignatius exonerated the very officers whose poor performance was in question. Instead, he placed the blame for the Agency's poor performance on Goss and his closest aides, "a team of ideologues from Capitol Hill" who had been sent "to drive out the agency's most experienced intelligence officers."

The intelligence officers whose "cause" Ignatius was championing had been trained to use every dirty trick of the trade to undermine the enemy. Now they were using their expertise to undermine the head of their own agency and, through him, the president of the United States. If anyone was attempting a "putsch"—a forceful takeover of a legally elected government—it was the CIA dissidents and their supporters at the *Washington Post*, the *New York Times*, *Time* magazine, and the congressional intelligence committees.

The ranking Democrat on the House intelligence committee, Representative Jane Harman, acknowledged that Goss "has every right as the president's nominee to make changes to his agency, and I think changes are needed. But those changes should be made with a scalpel, not a sledgehammer," she told *USA Today*. Later, she would whine that Goss had purged operatives with "[m]ore than 300 years of experience" and that his actions had sent the agency into a "free fall."[8]

Assuming that Harman was actually doing the math, that amounted to around ten career employees who left the Agency as a result of Goss's new policies—hardly a "putsch." As CIA spokesman Paul Gimigliano pointed out, when George Tenet took over at CIA in July 1997, he announced the appointment of ten officers to senior posts *in a single day*. "Each director builds his own leadership team," he said.[9]

Congressman Pete Hoekstra (R-MI) who succeeded Goss as House Intelligence Committee chairman, was a key ally. "This was not about staff but about getting results. And Porter was getting results," he told me. "He had plans to increase HUMINT by 50 percent. But the entrenched bureaucracy pushed back." They hated Goss's efforts to reform the CIA, and especially to change its risk-averse, East Coast establishment culture.

Hoekstra, a former vice president of a Fortune 500 company, compared the unwillingness of intelligence community managers to change after the end of the Cold War to old-time business managers who refused to adapt to new business practices, such as just-in-time inventory.

"There's always someone who's going to tell you, it can't work. The truck is going to break down, something's going to happen. There are people who fight change like crazy," Hoekstra said. "Porter said we need a new paradigm for HUMINT, new capability, new staff who do new things."

But Goss never got the chance to see his reforms bear fruit. Alarmed at the leaks, and at Goss's apparent inability to run a tight ship, National Security Advisor Condoleezza Rice and her top deputy, Stephen Hadley, "told Goss to stop firing people" just months after he took the helm at the CIA, "because they didn't want any more bad press," several former Agency managers told me.

Unable to dominate the bureaucracy, Rice and Hadley chose to appease the bureaucracy—with predictable results.

CHAPTER FIFTEEN

PEOPLE ARE POLICY

Carl Levin understood that no president could govern effectively without putting his own highly skilled political appointees into key government positions. Although their numbers were small—the congressional "Plum Book" that was published every time a new president came into office listed just 7,000 in the year 2000—they were critical. These were the men and women who gave direction to the unwieldy federal bureaucracy. Effective political appointees were essential for any president to transform his political vision into action. Without them, a president was like a cork bobbing in the ocean, swept by the wind and the currents.

Levin and other top Democrats in the U.S. Senate were determined to prevent George W. Bush from getting the people he wanted into positions of power. Since all top nominees had to be confirmed by the U.S. Senate, that gave the Democrats—who held a 50-49-1 majority once Vermont Republican James Jeffords quit the Republican party unexpectedly in May 2001—powerful tools.

Senate confirmation has always been a contentious process. Since the Nixon years, Senators Edward Kennedy and Joseph Biden have held conservative judges hostage to a litmus test on abortion and other left-wing causes. But at the start of the Bush administration, the Democrats took aim not at judges (that would come later) but at the president's counterterrorism and national security team.

For nearly seven months, Levin and his Democratic teammates prevented confirmation hearings of Defense Secretary Donald Rumsfeld's top advisors—Undersecretary of Defense for Policy Douglas J. Feith, Assistant Secretary of Defense for International Security Programs J. D. Crouch, and Assistant Secretary of Defense for International Security

Affairs Peter W. Rodman. "While Levin was holding up their appointments, the incoming Pentagon policy team had no legal or political authority to do their vital jobs—a fact that helps explain why it took eight months for the Bush administration to draw up a strategic operational plan to destroy al Qaeda," wrote J. Michael Waller, a defense and intelligence policy specialist at the Institute of World Politics.

The joke around the building was that with Rumsfeld and Wolfowitz the only political appointees who had cleared the Senate, "it was *Home Alone 3*," one appointee said.

The sabotage continued via Clinton "holdovers," people such as Peter F. Verga, Clinton's deputy undersecretary of defense for policy integration, a major intelligence post. While "Verga made himself useful to the Rumsfeld team, he beavered to curry favor at the top, in part by sniping and playing bureaucratic games to make life difficult for the incoming defense policy team," Waller wrote.[1]

Ken deGraffenreid was the administration's pick to replace Verga. A former White House hand from the Nixon days, he had been writing about intelligence reform for years, so Rumsfeld decided to give him an opportunity to put his theories to work. By the time his appointment finally cleared the Senate, it was already July. But even then, the bureaucratic fencing continued.

"Verga just stayed in place," deGraffenreid recalls. "I arrived—I had put my company out of business—and this guy wouldn't leave the job. He had the big office and I was put in the back room, next to the refrigerator, the copying machine, and the coffee-maker."

That wasn't the worst, deGraffenreid said. "I'm an old Navy pilot. I've lived in a hangar, so that part didn't bother me. But then I went to Doug [Feith], and to use an old Navy term, I said, 'What the f—?' " Verga had used the six months he was alone in his office with only Rumsfeld and Wolfowitz above him to ingratiate himself with his new bosses. "He made them feel they owed him something, so they kept him in place," deGraffenreid said.

It reminded him of Cook County, Illinois, where he had grown up. "If you wanted your street paved, you went to Mayor Daley. The Pentagon in July 2001 was like Cook County in 1962. The Clintonistas were the Mayor Daley who ran the place. It took me six months to get rid of the son of a bitch," he said of Verga. "I'm not sure that Rumsfeld and his undersecretaries ever recovered from that situation."

Feith's reputation as someone who refused to confront the partisan Democrats in the bureaucracy who were undercutting his own employees became legendary over the next five years. "They asked us to stick out our necks for this president," another appointee who worked with Feith told me in confidence. "And then they chopped them off."

While any new administration needs the benefit of experience of career diplomats, military officers, and intelligence experts, since the September 11 attacks these positions became critical in a way that only happens in times of war.

Richard Clarke was just the sort of person a new administration would want to have around as it crafted its approach to the terrorist threat from al Qaeda. As counterterrorism "czar" during most of the eight Clinton years, he arguably knew more about al Qaeda than any other American official.

But as Clarke's strident and highly personal denunciation of the president and his top advisors during his March 2004 testimony before the 9/11 Commission showed, that experience could become a double-edged sword. Clarke's self-serving account of how the Bush team failed to grapple with the al Qaeda threat during their first eight months in office conveniently left out the failures of eight years of the Clinton administration, when the United States was attacked five times by al Qaeda and did almost nothing in response. Clarke also neglected to mention in his public testimony that until just two months before the September 11 attacks, "nearly all the senior counterterrorism and intelligence officials on duty at the time were holdovers from the Clinton administration," Waller noted.

"We were really quite taken aback by Clarke's public testimony," 9/11 Commissioner John Lehman told me the day after Clarke appeared before the commission. "It differed dramatically with the fifteen hours of detailed, dispassionate testimony he gave in closed session, which was much more of an indictment of the eight Clinton years than the eight months of Bush. There was just a lot more policy to criticize. There wasn't a lot of policy to criticize under Bush because the administration didn't have its people in place for most of the eight months. Hell hath no fury like a bureaucrat scorned." Lehman believed Clarke was bitter because the Bush White House hadn't recognized his talents and given him the same powers he had under Clinton, when he was treated as a member of the cabinet.

But Richard Clarke didn't always use those talents and that power wisely. In February 1999, several months after al Qaeda blew up two U.S. embassies in Africa, the United States had overhead imagery that showed bin Laden and his top deputies at a royal falconry camp outside Kandahar, Afghanistan, where for several weeks they had been hunting bustard with Arab royals. They were perfect targets, and intelligence suggested they were likely to stay in the area for several more days at least. The CIA and the Pentagon requested the authority to take them out, but Clarke, Secretary of State Madeleine Albright, and National Security Advisor Samuel "Sandy" Berger turned down the request, ostensibly because of the presence in the hunting party of UAE foreign minister Sheikh Hamdan bin Zayed. At the time, Clarke was personally engaged in negotiations with Sheikh Hamdan and the UAE royal family to sell them eighty F-16 fighter jets, a contract worth $6.4 billion to U.S. defense contractors.[2]

According to Alan Parrot of the Union for the Conservation of Raptors, which tracks the illicit trade in falcons through sources in the region, "not a cockroach can come into these camps without the sheikh's approval." Parrot has hunted with Sheikh Hamdan and other top UAE princes in these royal hunting camps, and they have boasted to him of their relationship to bin Laden. Sheikh Hamdan "personally invited UBL to the Sheikh Ali camp, and spent more than three weeks hunting with him," Parrot says. He believes Clarke should have allowed the bombing, instead of protecting Sheikh Hamdan.

At the end of the hunting season, it became customary for Sheikh Hamdan to give bin Laden as a present the four-wheel-drive vehicles he transported to the camp on UAE government C-130 aircraft—sometimes as many as 400 specially outfiitted Nissan Patrols and Toyota Land Cruisers. After his return to Afghanistan in 1996, bin Laden was on the outs with the Taliban and gave them a bunch of these cars as a bribe, Parrot says. "Mullah Omar learned about it and asked where they came from. It was those gifts, which originally came from the UAE, that cemented bin Laden's friendship with Mullah Omar," Parrot says.[3]

Clarke has steadfastly refused any further comment on why he recommended against bombing the Sheikh Ali camp beyond the testimony he provided to the 9/11 Commission. "That's all I have to say about the matter," he told me.

THE BURROWERS

Richard Clarke was just one of many career bureaucrats who knew how to fight in the shadows against their own elected government.

Rand Beers was a well-known Clinton-era appointee at State. Shortly after the Bush team took over in January 2001, White House political aides wanted to fire him as a "Clinton holdover." Not so, retorted Deputy

Secretary of State Richard Armitage. "He's a public servant." Armitage, like Doug Feith at the Pentagon, was extremely protective of the partisan Democrats who worked beneath him. Perhaps unknown to Armitage was the fact that Beers had set up a veritable "Fort Clinton" within his State Department office suite, where he was joined by at least two other Clinton holdovers, Ed Rindler and David M. Luna, political appointees who had "burrowed" into the system.

"These are people who were dedicated to a political agenda, not to their job," says a former colleague who was appointed by Bush. "They and others peppered throughout the bureaucracy made life miserable for Bush political appointees, gumming up the works, even accusing them of malfeasance—anything to keep them from pursuing the Bush agenda."

David Luna successfully reinvented himself as a "career" bureaucrat, even though he appeared in the 2000 edition of the *Plumbook*, the congressionally mandated listing of all political jobs in government, as a Clinton political appointee. He became director for anticorruption and governance initiatives in the State Department's bureau of international narcotics and law enforcement affairs, and remained in the executive branch well into Bush's second term. So did Ed Rindler. Their State Department office issued regular reports on drug eradication programs that blamed the U.S.-backed government in Afghanistan for continued opium production, while praising the anti-American government of Iran, which Iranian exiles say encourages drug addiction among the young as a means of controlling antiregime protest.

Beers was eventually replaced as assistant secretary for counter-narcotics in 2002. But instead of leaving the administration, he was hired by Richard Clarke at the National Security Council, where he remained until he resigned in protest over the Iraq War in April 2003. Just weeks later, Beers joined the Kerry campaign and Clarke—still working at NSC—tried to get his security clearances renewed. "We thought this was the Kerry people trying to get a direct line to classified information during a presidential campaign," a Bush loyalist said. "It's a bit like the Clinton passport files case in 1992."

"What's so shocking about Beers and others at State is that it's so open," the Bush loyalist said. "They believe they are the permanent government, and that it's their duty to oppose a Republican president."

"They see Republicans as a temporary setback," said another. "They view us as Neanderthals."

When former Republican congressman Bob Barr was asked to brief Undersecretary of State Bob Joseph in late 2005 on a new UN treaty to impose worldwide controls on individual gun owners, the permanent bureaucracy went haywire. "They said, 'We need to bring in someone from the other side,' " an aide to Joseph confided. "I kind of looked at them and said, 'You mean, someone who opposes the administration's policies?' "

Of more than 22,000 employees at the Pentagon complex in Washington, just 270 are political appointees. More than five years into the administration, many were partisan Democrats who had "burrowed" into the bureaucracy and had managed to snatch plum political jobs. "There are 240 political appointees at the Department of Agriculture, for crying out loud!" a Bush administration political operative at the Pentagon told me. "We have just the faintest veneer of political control in this building. It's stunning."

In late 2005, as the president tried to fight off sagging opinion polls pegged to the war in Iraq, Feith's replacement, Eric Edelman, decided to hire a career bureaucrat from State named Deborah Kagan to run the critical "Coalitions for the War" office.

"This is a woman who openly boasts to her colleagues that she would *never* vote for a Republican, and that she voted against Bush twice," a Bush administration loyalist complained. "And we put her in charge of building coalitions in support of a war that she says is wrong? It's insane!" Kagan worked on the Democratic staff of the Senate Foreign Relations committee during the Clinton administration, and boasted of close ties to Sandy Berger and Deputy Secretary of State Strobe Talbot, who helped her to burrow into a career position at the State Department.

Condoleezza Rice was also singled out by administration loyalists for her willingness to appoint partisan Democrats to political positions where they were responsible for carrying out the very policies they so vigorously opposed. "The president trusted Condi to pick his people, and she has picked people who are not loyal to the president," one Republican political operative said.

"Richard Clarke and Rand Beers—who worked under Condi—did real damage before the 2004 election. After their defection, she should have paid more attention to people, but she didn't." Instead, she placed Scowcroft protégés, Democrats, and milquetoast Republicans in senior positions.

While she was at NSC, Rice refused to discipline David Shedd, the CIA detailee in charge of intelligence programs, when he was accused of trying to derail the nomination of Porter Goss as CIA director. She also promoted Meghan O'Sullivan, a former staffer for Democratic senator Daniel Patrick Moynihan and a top aide to Jerry Bremer in Iraq. (O'Sullivan was promoted again in October 2005 to become an NSC division chief in charge of Iraq and Afghanistan, a position she held until leaving government in April 2007.)

At the State Department, John Kerry protégé Suzanne Maloney, a junior member of the policy planning staff, was "blocking the expenditure of $3 million to promote pro-Western democratic forces in Iran," despite strong support for the program from the White House and in Congress.[4] Maloney and her husband, Council on Foreign Relations analyst Ray Takeyh, staffed a 2004 CFR study, authored by Robert Gates and Zbigniew Brzezinski, urging the United States to open direct talks with Iran's Islamic government and to provide security guarantees to Tehran, including a pledge to not support Iranian opposition groups. Dialogue with Tehran's clerics was a policy favored by Kerry and other Democrats, such as 2008 presidential candidate Senator Joe Biden.

In an August 28, 2007, op-ed in the *Financial Times*, Takeyh opposed administration plans to designate the Iranian Revolutionary Guards Corps as a "global terrorist" organization, calling them "yet another example of Washington's incoherent Iran policy." He warned that any U.S. efforts to sanction the Guards Corps would "trigger its antagonism towards further dealings with the U.S." His abject willingness to appease the Iranian regime was reminiscent of British Prime Minister Neville Chamberlain, who made a similar argument after caving in to Hitler's demand that the Western powers abandon Czechoslovakia in 1938. Chamberlain called it "Peace in Our Time."

Once Maloney's role in blocking the Iran pro-democracy projects was revealed, top aides to Secretary Rice engaged in a "witch hunt"—not against Maloney, but against the source who revealed her role in undermining the Bush policy, Institute of World Politics scholar J. Michael Waller revealed. "Instead of trying to root out who blew the whistle on the sabotage of administration policy, the State Department should be asking this question: How did someone with documented credentials against presidential policy and a possible conflict of interest with an oil company ever get appointed to the Iran policy planning job? And why are some of its officials rallying around the saboteur when they should be carrying out the president's policy?"[5] According to Maloney's official bio, she had been a consultant for Exxon Mobil, then became an Exxon Mobil fellow at CFR, before coming to State as a CFR fellow.

In April 2007, when the next round of "democracy-support funds" for Iran was announced, Maloney continued to be instrumental in steering grants to groups that promoted "reform" in Iran, rather than groups that sought a nonclerical alternative to the current regine. Pro-democracy leaders such as Roozbeh Farahanipour, who was jailed and tortured by the regime for over a year for his role in the July 1999 student uprising in Tehran, have warned the administration that the reform movement was a "hoax" perpetrated by the regime to trick the West.[6]

The State Department shadow warriors also did their best to block efforts by the U.S. Treasury to ban Iranian banks from the international financial system, a former Treasury Department official told me. "We should have designated [banned] many more banks and other Iranian companies by now," the official said. "But State has consistently held up our efforts—at times, by up to eight months—hoping we would back off."

One example: In September 2006, the Treasury Department announced it was cutting Iran's Bank Saderat off from the U.S. financial system. "Bank Saderat facilitates Iran's transfer of hundreds of millions of dollars to Hizballah and other terrorist organizations each year," said Stuart Levey, Undersecretary for Terrorism and Financial Intelligence (TFI). "We will no longer allow a bank like Saderat to do business in the American financial system, even indirectly."[7]

And yet, the former Treasury Department official said that Levey was ready to blacklist Saderat more than eight months earlier, but was blocked by Undersecretary of State R. Nicholas Burns. Why the State Department would want to allow Iranian banks to continue using the international banking system to fund international terrorism is anybody's guess.

THE ROCKEFELLER LEAK

Porter Goss hadn't been at the helm for three full months when the leaks began in earnest. At first, all indications led him and his top aides to suspect they originated with Democrats on Capitol Hill, where a handful of powerful senators and their top aides had access to the family jewels of the U.S. intelligence community. Senator Jay Rockefeller of West Virginia, cochair of the Senate intelligence committee, became the prime suspect.

In what Rockefeller himself called a "somewhat unprecedented action," he took the floor of the Senate on December 9, 2004, to announce that he planned to vote against intelligence authorizations for 2005, because of wasteful spending on a classified program.

"Because of the highly classified nature of the programs contained in the national intelligence budget, I cannot talk about them on the floor," he began. Then he proceeded to do just that, giving a series of clues that spelled "big-budget surveillance satellite" to anyone who was paying attention.

The program he was referring to was a "major funding acquisition program" that he felt was "totally unjustified and very wasteful and dangerous to national security." For the past two years, he said, the Senate intelligence committee had voted to terminate the program but was repeatedly overruled by the appropriators. Despite his efforts, full funding for "this unjustified and stunningly expensive acquisition" was included in the 2005 intelligence authorization bill. "I simply cannot overlook that," he said.

If the Senate refused to follow his advice and insisted on funding the program, "I will seriously consider and probably will ask the Senate to go into closed session so the senators can understand, fully debate, become informed upon, and then vote on termination of this very wasteful acquisition program."[8] In other words, Rockefeller was claiming for himself a license to leak, since everyone knew there was no way that secrets would be kept secret once they were aired during a meeting of the full Senate. The *Desperate Housewives* on Wisteria Lane had tighter lips.

Senator Ron Wyden (D-OR) jumped up to second Rockefeller's objections, and provided a whole series of additional clues.

The program was "unnecessary, ineffective, over budget, and too expensive," he said. He added that the Senate intelligence committee first raised "concerns" over the program in 2000. "This has not been a political issue, a Democratic or Republican issue, nor should it be," he said. Now it was clear that this wasn't a new program, but had started under Clinton.

"Numerous independent reviews have concluded that the program does not fulfill a major intelligence gap or shortfall, and the original justification for developing this technology has eroded in importance due to the changed practices and capabilities of our adversaries," Wyden said. "There are a number of other programs in existence and in development whose capabilities can match those envisioned for this program at far less cost and technological risk."

Now for the kicker: The Senate intelligence committee had raised questions on how the original contract had been put out to bid, he said. (Hint hint: What major U.S. defense contractor who worked on satellite programs had been assessed huge fines for cost overruns and contracting irregularities?)

Porter Goss was furious when he read the senators' remarks in the *Washington Post* the next morning during the predawn limousine ride to Langley. From what Rockefeller and Wyden had said in public, it was a no-brainer to conclude that the highly classified program in question was the newest-generation surveillance satellite, as the AP story clearly stated.[9]

As chairman of the House intelligence committee, he had argued with the senators only the year before about the same program, and had insisted that it contained key new capabilities the United States needed for the future. At the time, they had agreed to disagree, and said nothing in public. This was a clear breach of the Senate ethics rules, Goss believed.

But it wasn't until Monday that Goss got fully engaged and had his aides call the Senate Ethics committee and the Justice Department to launch a criminal probe. Far worse than the transparent hints that Rockefeller and Wyden had made on the Senate floor were the leaks someone with access to the most highly classified details of the program had made to *Washington Post* reporter Dana Priest in a front-page story that appeared over the weekend.

You could have legitimate policy debates over classified programs, but when you lose you don't go to the newspapers. That was a basic rule of conduct Goss believed strongly.

The leakers had revealed, for the first time ever, that the United States was working on a new generation of spy satellites "designed to orbit undetected." It was a hugely costly effort, and the price tag had already doubled from $5 billion to nearly $9.5 billion, the *Post* said, citing unnamed U.S. officials.

The National Reconnaissance Office, the top-secret agency that managed all U.S. spy satellite programs, "has already spent hundreds of millions of dollars on the program," the article reported, and that amount was expected to rise steeply once the new stealth satellite was launched sometime "in the next five years."

Priest then quoted several unnamed sources who asserted that a stealth satellite was useless against terrorists and nations such as Iran and North Korea, "which are believed to have placed their nuclear weapons programs underground and inside buildings specifically to avoid detection from spy satellites and aircraft."

Every single line of it was highly classified, and potentially tremendously damaging to national security, Goss knew. The *Post* claimed that Lockheed Martin Corporation was the main contractor for the project, and that it was "the third and final version in a series of spacecraft funded under a classified program once known as Misty."[10]

By divulging the code name of the program, whoever had leaked had provided a key so intrepid reporters could comb through public reports from various congressional committees that tracked spending on classified programs by code name, without further identification. By analyzing the spending patterns, a hostile intelligence service could piece together the program's history, its current status, and its probable launch date.

The leaks got even worse in Sunday's *New York Times*. This time opponents of the program had decided to provide additional details, in an effort to derail it completely.

The leakers told reporter Douglas Jehl that the new satellite system "could take photographs only in daylight hours and in clear weather," and had become "the single biggest item in the intelligence budget."

Jehl claimed to quote "a former government official with direct knowledge of the program," who provided perspective but no details that in themselves were classified.

"These satellites would be irrelevant to current threats, and this money could be much better spent on the kind of human intelligence needed to penetrate closed regimes and terrorist networks," Jehl's source said. "There are already so many satellites in orbit that our adversaries already assume that just about anything done in plain sight is watched, so it's hard to believe a new satellite, even a stealthy one, could make much of a difference."

The most damaging revelation came near the end of Jehl's piece, where he too appeared to have reached the same government official who had leaked the information on Misty to the *Post*.

"Officials have suggested that new technologies may also be able to detect the presence of objects underground," Jehl wrote. This was a critical new capability, since many future threats the United States was likely to face came from nations such as North Korea and Iran, who had built extensive networks of underground nuclear weapons plants and missile storage bunkers, whose location and content the United States could only guess. Jehl then revealed to our enemies that the new satellites under discussion "generally operate successfully only during the day and in sunny weather."[11]

As concern among Democrats mounted that they may have overstepped the bounds in their revelations to the press, Senator Dick Durbin (D-IL) appeared on the Sunday talk shows to applaud the leakers as the true patriots.

"Eventually some information will come out," Durbin told ABC's *This Week*. But leaks didn't mean the congressional oversight process was flawed, he insisted. "It takes a leak to understand that billions of taxpayers' dollars are being wasted that could be spent to make America safer."

It was an argument the Democrats would use increasingly. It was their way not only of covering their backs but also of encouraging dissidents within the intelligence community to step forward.

THE BATTLE OVER BOLTON

By 2005, the Senate confirmation process had become a battleground where the Democrats were determined to punish an administration they felt had led the nation into a "rush to war" with Iraq.

Even though Democrats were now in the minority, the arcane parliamentary rules that have governed the U.S. Senate for generations allowed a single senator to place a "hold" on a political appointee. That effectively prevented the president's choices for top positions from ever getting a hearing, let alone a floor vote. The anonymity of the process meant that senators rarely paid a political price. There was no legal step the president could take to compel the anonymous senator to lift his hold or to declare himself, even though his identity was usually known to his colleagues. It was backroom politics, pure and simple.

Levin placed "holds" on top national security appointees in 2005 and 2006 with astonishing regularity. At a time when the administration was eager to work out a new legal basis for detaining and questioning al Qaeda detainees, Levin held up for over six months the confirmation hearing of Benjamin Powell as chief counsel to the director of national intelligence, the man who was supposed to draw up the new guidelines. After Deputy Secretary of Defense Paul Wolfowitz left office at the end of March 2005 to become president of the World Bank, Levin placed a hold on his successor, Gordon England, leaving the Pentagon's number-two spot vacant until January 4, 2006. Bush eventually gave England a recess appointment.

Other top Pentagon nominees placed on hold for months by Levin were Feith's replacement as undersecretary for policy, Eric Edelman, and Peter Flory, for assistant secretary of defense for international security affairs. At Justice, Levin placed a hold on the nomination of Alice Fisher to become head of the Criminal Division. "These are crucial jobs for fighting the war on terror," an administration lawyer told me. "Levin held all of them."

Everyone in Congress knew that Levin was responsible for the holds, and yet the White House was never willing to use the one weapon at its disposal to force Levin's hand: the shame factor. Instead, Bush eventually gave all three officials recess appointments.

But the big kahuna was John Bolton. By the time Bush nominated him to become the U.S. ambassador to the United Nations in March 2005, he had become the personification of everything the Left loved to hate, a lightning rod for the anti-Bush elites. If any man other than George W. Bush had to be stopped, it was John Bolton. He was a neo-con; worse, he was articulate, he had a sense of humor, and he didn't hesitate to shout from the rooftops that the emperor had no clothes (as in his oft-quoted remark that you could lop ten floors off UN headquarters in New York and no one would notice any difference). And so, in confirmation hearings dominated by Democratic senators Joseph Biden, Christopher Dodd, and John F. Kerry, the Left launched an all-out assault. This was one battle they were willing to fight out in the open, because there was much more at stake than just one man's career. Whoever won this game would be able to exert control over the course of U.S. foreign policy for the rest of Bush's second term, they believed.

If Bolton was confirmed to the UN post, the Democrats knew that he wouldn't tolerate UN intervention in Iraq, unless carefully crafted to meet U.S. national interests. And the Democrats—as exemplified by John Kerry's call during the 2004 presidential campaign to subject American foreign military action to a UN vote—were hoping to use the UN as an extraconstitutional check against what they now were calling "Bush's war."

Bolton also sought to put the United Nations, especially the Security Council, on notice that it had to step up to the plate in confronting the security challenges the world now faced from the nuclear weapons programs of North Korea and Iran. In 2002, he traveled to Vienna in an effort to force the resignation of International Atomic Energy Agency director general Mohamed ElBaradei, because of the Egyptian lawyer's utter failure in eight years to deal with either problem. If the UN continued to tread water on Iran and North Korea, it would become irrelevant, Bolton argued. Bolton's determination on this score terrified Democrats, who had no doubt that the UN would fail, and thus remove an important fig leaf from their bankrupt internationalist policies.

THE "CONTROVERSIAL" NOMINEE

The Bolton confirmation hearings that began on April 11, 2005, exposed the Left's agenda, their supporters within the bureaucracy, and their secret ties to major media organizations and a supposed apolitical think tank.

Among those who provided testimony against John Bolton to the Senate Foreign Relations committee staff were current and former CIA officers, analysts and managers at the State Department Bureau of Intelligence and Research (INR), and none other than the chief of staff of Secretary of State Colin Powell, who had recently resigned.

Piling on through leaks and public statements to the press was Powell's former deputy, Richard Armitage.

The *Detroit Free Press* called Bolton "controversial" and opined (in a news article) that his nomination was "odd in light of Bush's second-term efforts at mending fences with allies alienated by the unilateralist foreign policy that Bolton advocated."[12]

The *New York Times* led the charge with a lead editorial on April 8, 2005, titled "The Worst of the Bad Nominees," and published every leak they could get their hands on from the Senate Foreign Relations committee Democratic staff and their surrogates. On at least one occasion, they claimed that Bolton actually *shook his finger* at an analyst from the State Department's Bureau of Intelligence and Research! (That was after the analyst, Christian Westermann, attempted to change the wording of a speech Bolton planned to deliver without his knowledge.) On another, Bolton allegedly told the man's superior, Tom Fingar, that he "wasn't going to be told what he could say by a mid-level INR munchkin analyst."

"Did he actually use those terms?" a staffer for Senator Richard Lugar, the Republican committee chairman asked in shock.

"That's my recollection," Fingar replied. "He said that, one way or another, several times." Transcripts of those interviews were released by the committee—but only after they had been leaked to left-wing blogger Steve Clemons.

Clemons wore two hats, as many in Washington do. He ran the New America Foundation in Washington, a respectable if left-leaning think tank that Clemons tried to pass off as apolitical. At the same time, he was a dedicated left-wing activist, whose anti-Bush blog (TheWashington-Note.com) was read by the elite media and by the MoveOn.org crowd. Unlike his counterparts on the right, he seldom saw the need to take one hat off before donning the other. It was all one happy, well-funded Trekkie continuum.

The Democrats did their best to spin the hearings in support of their trumped-up assault on Bolton's character, his alleged "abuse" of intelligence-community staffers, and his skepticism of the United Nations itself. And while they succeeded in derailing his confirmation, thanks to the last-minute defection of Republican turncoat George Voinovich of Ohio, they did not sully Bolton's motives and intentions as much as they revealed their own.

The first victory was never announced. It took place when Senator Lugar failed to conduct the Bolton hearing before the Easter recess, as he (and the administration) had originally planned. "We placed 3,000 calls to Lugar's office that Friday," Clemons the left-wing activist boasted to me proudly, during a pause in a foreign policy event sponsored by his "apolitical" think tank. The extra time he bought his Democrat allies allowed them to rake more thoroughly through Bolton's past and conduct additional interviews, he said.

As soon as Clemons got the raw transcripts, he worked up talking points "to make it all digestible." In addition to feeding the press, he focused on Republican "weak links" Lisa Murkowski of Alaska, George Voinovich of Ohio, Lincoln Chafee of Rhode Island, and Chuck Hagel of Nebraska.

Clemons realized early on that foreign relations committee chairman Richard Lugar wasn't solidly behind Bolton and was not supporting his own members with talking points, so he stepped in to fill the void. "I knew from the start that Voinovich would switch," he told me. "But I thought Hagel or Murkowski would be first."

The "gotcha" nature of the Democrats' assault on Bolton can be seen in this exchange between the nominee and Senator Joe Biden, the ranking Democrat on the committee. Biden had asked Bolton if he had ever tried to get Christian Westermann "removed" from working on proliferation-related issues, Bolton's portfolio at State.

> MR. BOLTON: I think, as the interviews that your staff conducted show—and that's one reason why I want to get them all out in public—we believe Mr. Westermann had behaved in an underhanded fashion. And I think I—as my assistant mentioned to your staff, I said to him at the time, "I don't care if you disagree with me, just don't do it behind my back." I mentioned it—
>
> SENATOR BIDEN: Well, that's not my question. I only have ten minutes, so I don't want you to be a Senator and filibuster me. Did you attempt to have him removed from your portfolio?
>
> MR. BOLTON: I mentioned it to Mr. Fingar. I may have mentioned it to one or two other people. But then I shrugged my shoulders, and I moved on. He was—
>
> SENATOR BIDEN: So the answer is, yes, you did.
>
> MR. BOLTON: And he was not moved, and I did not—
>
> SENATOR BIDEN: Okay, and that's all I wanted—I just wanted to make sure we're talking about the same thing.

And so the headlines screamed: PRESSURE ON C.I.A. ANALYST CAUSED ANGER (Douglas Jehl, *New York Times*, April 16, 2005). The *Washington Post* upped the ante (while replicating Westermann into the plural): BOLTON FACES ALLEGATIONS THAT HE TRIED TO FIRE ANALYSTS (Dafna Linzer, *Washington Post*, April 15, 2005).

Imagine career intelligence officers getting intimidated by a political appointee. It was just shocking, shocking.

FOR THE LOVE OF CASTRO

But Bolton's managerial style was not the real issue. Fueling the Left's zealous hatred of Bolton was a speech he gave as undersecretary of state for arms control and international security affairs to the Heritage Foundation on May 6, 2002. Entitled "Beyond the Axis of Evil," it shone a spotlight on nations in the early stages of developing weapons of mass destruction that potentially could become serious threats to U.S. security.

As Bolton described it, the germ for the speech began "just a few months after September the 11th, when I think we all conclude that, however horrible September the 11th was, it could have been far worse had the terrorists had access to chemical, biological, or nuclear weapons. And it was our feeling in the Administration that we wanted to talk seriously to the American public about these kinds of threats."[13]

Among those he singled out for developing an offensive biological weapons capability was Castro's Cuba.

He might as well have been screaming "God is Dead!" in front of the Spanish Inquisition, for if there was one thing that united the Left, it was Fidel Castro. From Michael Moore and Barbra Streisand to Senator Christopher Dodd of Connecticut, the Left idolized Fidel Castro as a hero-martyr who had been unfairly targeted by the American Right. And Castro continued to return the Left's favors. In 2004, Castro showed *Fahreinheit 9/11*, the anti-Bush propaganda film of "that outstanding American," as Castro called Michael Moore, in every movie theater in Cuba, later even airing it on state-run television.[14]

"Here is what we now know," Bolton said in the speech. "The United States believes that Cuba has at least a limited offensive biological warfare research and development effort. Cuba has provided dual-use biotechnology to other rogue states. We are concerned that such technology could support BW programs in those states."[15]

Even those three sparse sentences were too much for some U.S. intelligence analysts. The State Department's Christian Westermann worked behind the scenes to prevent Bolton from getting the language cleared, even though it was taken from existing intelligence reports. Bolton's top aide, Frederick Fleitz (a CIA weapons analyst on loan to his office), eventually uncovered the scheme. This prompted Bolton to confront Westermann, asking him why he had attempted to block the Cuba language through stealth, instead of approaching him directly. Westermann then alleged to the committee that Bolton tried to get him fired.

Why would anyone get so upset over three skimpy sentences describing a biological weapons program that had failed to excite the U.S. government for years? The reason was simple: Many of the finished analytical pieces coming out of the intelligence community on Cuba had been written by Ana Belen Montes, a woman subsequently convicted as a Cuban spy. Despite that, those products—and her pro-Castro analysis—had never been pulled back. Bolton wanted to find out what the CIA actually knew before Montes applied the pro-Castro spin. To the Left and their supporters in the United States Senate, Bolton's refusal to be duped was a capital crime. To make matters worse, by confronting Westermann and others over the issue, he had flushed many of the shadow warriors into the light.

In his May 2002 speech, Bolton made a point of explaining why "Cuba's threat to our security often has been underplayed." He cited a 1998 report from the Defense Intelligence Agency that concluded, "Castro poses no significant threat to the United States or any of its Hemispheric neighbors." In fact, the 1998 report went even further, broadly asserting that "no evidence exists that Cuba is trying to foment any instability in the Western Hemisphere."

Why was U.S. intelligence reporting skewed so favorably toward Castro? Bolton asked. "A major reason is Cuba's aggressive intelligence operations against the United States, which included recruiting the Defense Intelligence Agency's senior Cuba analyst, Ana Belen Montes, to spy for Cuba," Bolton explained. "Montes not only had a hand in drafting the 1998 Cuba report, but also passed some of our most sensitive information about Cuba back to Havana. Montes was arrested last fall and pleaded guilty to espionage on March 19."[16]

If anything, Bolton understated the importance of Castro's star intelligence agent. In the mid-1990s, Montes was promoted to become the top Cuba analyst *for the entire U.S. intelligence community.* In that capacity, she influenced every product on Cuba that came out of the National Intelligence Council as well as her home agency, the DIA. Indeed, just one year after the 1998 report Bolton cited, the NIC produced a National Intelligence Estimate on Cuba that parroted her claims of a benign Castro. "Ana Montes had been spying for the Cubans for approximately sixteen years, her entire career with DIA—from day one," wrote Scott Carmichael, the DIA counterintelligence officer who ultimately exposed her and turned her case over to the FBI.[17]

When the 1999 NIE on Cuba was issued, it was heralded by Castro himself as "an objective report by serious people," Humberto Fontova wrote in his book on the Cuban dictator.[18] Small wonder. Those "serious people" were Castro's people.

Montes was arrested by the FBI just nine days after the September 11 attacks and charged under the Espionage Act—the same charge that led to the execution of Soviet spies Ethel and Julius Rosenberg. She escaped a potential death sentence through a plea bargain, in which she agreed to serve a twenty-five-year prison sentence in exchange for her cooperation.

Even though the Montes story had received coverage in the news media, senior intelligence officers tried to block Bolton from referring to it. They dropped this demand when Bolton's staff demanded justification, if only to avoid further embarrassment. Bolton's reference to the story of Ana Montes in his speech infuriated the pro-Castro Clinton holdovers, who continued to use the intelligence products she had written or influenced as if nothing had happened. Indeed, when I asked Scott Carmichael, he said that "the entire intelligence community must review its judgments" about Cuba because of Montes's treachery. But as recently as June 2007, neither the DIA nor the NIC had formally withdrawn her work or issued a warning to intelligence consumers.

"She was not just reporting information," Representative Ileana Ros-Lehtinen, a Cuban-born Republican from South Florida, told me. "She was *creating* information that was widely distributed by the intelligence community for sixteen years."

Carmichael put it even more bluntly: "She compromised every source and method, every judgment ever made on Cuba, and possibly, on all of Latin America," he told me.

Carmichael said he believed Montes was to blame for the death of Army sergeant Gregory A. Fronius, a Green Beret who was killed while on a training mission to El Salvador on March 31, 1987, because she had visited his camp and reviewed its security procedures just weeks before it was overrun by Cuban-backed guerrillas. But beyond his death, the damage she caused was enormous.

By compromising U.S. sources and methods, "she allowed the Cubans to manipulate us," he said. "They could manipulate the message we'd be getting. They could have shared that knowledge of those sources and methods with others, so they too could manipulate the information the U.S. intelligence community was getting.

"This is called perception management," he added.

Castro continues to have a chorus of sympathizers in Congress and among congressional staff even today. It will be interesting to see if any of them turn out to have been on the Cuban payroll, congressional sources speculated.

FULTON WHO?

Jimmy Carter got wind of the Bolton speech at Heritage, and demanded to be briefed on what the CIA knew of Castro's biological weapons programs. As a former president, he had every right to demand a classified briefing, and so the Agency dispatched Fulton Armstrong, the national intelligence officer for Latin America, and a team of briefers to Atlanta.[19]

Armstrong had recently returned to CIA with a promotion from the Clinton White House, where he had been on loan to the National Security Council. He told Carter that Bolton's speech was full of lies, and that he personally had tried to prevent Bolton from embarrassing himself by contradicting published intelligence products on Cuba. There was nothing to it, he said. No evidence whatsoever behind Bolton's claims. The community consensus had been expressed in the 1999 NIE on Cuba, which concluded that Castro had no offensive biological weapons program and did not pose a threat to the United States.

Armed with that classified (but erroneous) information, Carter flew to Havana and appeared publicly with Fidel on May 13, 2002, to refute Bolton's charges as "lies."

Cuba had no biological weapons program and was not helping Iran, the two men said. The Cubans insisted that their biotechnology and genetic-engineering program—reputedly the most advanced in Latin America—was "dedicated only to peaceful purposes and to making medicines and vaccines, including generic versions of four AIDS drugs."

But as the *Washington Times* reported ominously, "since 1996, Cuba and Iran have been building a pharmaceutical research and production facility in Karaj, outside the Iranian capital of Tehran."[20] Carter and Castro insisted that this was all for peaceful purposes.

Armstrong's involvement came as a surprise to Bolton and to Fred Fleitz, his top aide. Before Bolton's Heritage Foundation speech, they had never heard of him. "He was not someone we even knew about, but after the speech he called me and said the speech had not been IC cleared," Fleitz said under hostile questioning from Democratic staff.

After that exchange with Armstrong, Fleitz says he learned that the CIA analyst "campaigned against the speech, telling people within the policy community, Congress, and we believe, in the media, that the speech was not cleared, and misrepresented the Intelligence Community. These statements were false. This caused Mr. Bolton to be concerned that there was an Intelligence Officer . . . making policy statements that a person in an Intelligence Analyst position should not have been making."[21]

Bolton then consulted with the assistant secretary of state for Western Hemisphere affairs, Otto Reich, who said he had already compiled a three-page letter for Armstrong's superiors at the CIA, citing numerous examples that demonstrated "the consistent unacceptable quality of his work." Reich said they should demand that Armstrong be removed from his current portfolio. Bolton agreed.

That sent the Democrats into hissy fits. Bolton and Otto Reich dared—*dared!*—suggest that a career intelligence officer be reassigned from Latin America just because he continued to parrot the views of a self-avowed Cuban intelligence officer who had just copped a twenty-five-year sentence!

But it was one more thing Bolton never acted upon. He never sent any letter to the CIA about Armstrong, and never went to Tenet asking that he be removed from his position. Never happened.[22]

Bolton did pay a brief visit to Armstrong's superiors, Alan Foley and NIC Chairman Stuart Cohen, in July 2002, but it was described as a "courtesy call" by State Department lawyer Patricia McNerney.[23] That distinction was lost on the Democrats, just as it was on Colin Powell's chief of staff, Larry Wilkerson.

Senator Dodd's chief staffer, Janice O'Connell, asked if he was "aware that John Bolton went out to the CIA to try to have the NIO for Latin America removed."

> MR. WILKERSON: I heard about it. Didn't know that it happened. I mean, I had no other way to know about it, other than—

MS. O'CONNELL: Was that in a—
MR. WILKERSON: —people telling me.
MS. O'CONNELL: —was that something he should have done on his own time?
MR. WILKERSON: I wouldn't have done it. There were a number of analysts at the CIA I would love to have relieved.
[Laughter.]
MS. O'CONNELL: But you would not have thought it appropriate for you to go—
MR. WILKERSON: No.
MS. O'CONNELL: —out there and speak to their superiors—
MR. WILKERSON: No.
MS. O'CONNELL: —to have them removed?
MR. WILKERSON: Do what I did. I would talk to John McLaughlin or—and DCI Tenet, in one case. And this simply had to do with professionalism; and not remove them or throw them out, but counsel them.[24]

You almost wondered if these people listened to themselves talk. Here was Larry Wilkerson saying how awful John Bolton was for not doing something he was accused wrongfully by the Democrats of having done, then turning around and saying he would have done exactly the same thing! It was typical of the hearings, of Bolton's enemies, and of the career bureaucrats who served the Bush administration while they detested the president and tried to derail his policies and his top aides.[25]

There appeared to be much more behind the three sentences Bolton's staff eventually got cleared on Cuba's biological weapons program and its ties to Iran.

Shortly after the May 2002 speech, Bolton tried to get intelligence community clearance to give congressional testimony on Cuba's program. According to Martin Arostegui, a reporter with *Insight* magazine, the CIA had source reports from Cuban scientists who had defected to the United States that Castro was seeking to weaponize some of the world's deadliest toxins, including anthrax, smallpox, and West Nile virus. There was circumstantial evidence suggesting that a small number of birds may have been infected at a Cuban bioweapons facility and smuggled into the United States, including a crow later found dead on the White House lawn. There also was the official visit to Iran in 2000 by Castro's vice president, Carlos Lage, where he inaugurated a Cuban-built biotechnology research plant; he told the press the plant was intended to produce hepatitis B vaccine. The equipment in such plants is inherently dual-use, and can be used to produce vaccines or to cultivate biological warfare agents.[26]

Larry Wilkerson tried to claim that Colin Powell issued a "gag order" on Bolton after the Heritage Foundation speech. While it is true that Powell and Armitage asked to personally review Bolton's speech drafts, this didn't appreciably slow the process used to clear them. From the start, Bolton's staff cleared his speeches and testimonies throughout State, with other government agencies, with the intelligence community, and with the White House. Powell and Armitage were always in the loop but tended to defer to comments from staff.

After the Senate failed to vote on Bolton's nomination, Bush gave him a recess appointment in August 2005 and he served with great distinction at the United Nations through the end of December 2006. Thanks to John Bolton, the United States for the first time succeeded in convincing a reluctant Security Council to gradually ratchet up the pressure on Iran over its nuclear weapons program, by issuing first a presidential statement, then a Security Council resolution giving Iran one month to come clean and open all its nuclear sites to inspection. When Iran ignored both, Bolton worked with council members to get UN Security Council Resolution 1737, which finally passed, in weaker form than he would have liked, on December 23, 2006.

For his work on Iran, a former deputy prime minister of Sweden, Per Ahlmark, nominated John Bolton for the Nobel Peace Prize for 2006. "Let us focus on the good guys. The fools of the Iranian nuclear tragedy we already know," he wrote in the *Wall Street Journal.* Needless to say, the Nobel Prize committee did not act on his nomination. (Full disclosure: Ahlmark jointly nominated me, whom he cited for having exposed Iran's nuclear program "for 20 years.")[27]

The wonder is not that President Bush frequently failed to achieve his policy goals. The true miracle was that he had any success at all.

When those successes happened, they depended on the willingness of individuals such as John Bolton to sacrifice their careers, knowing they would not last long in the highly charged political atmosphere of Washington where not only the Democrats but the permanent government as well was constantly seeking their demise.

THE DISPUTE CONTINUES

The dispute over Ana Montes, Cuban influence on the U.S. intelligence community, and Castro's biological weapons program continues even as this book goes to press.

On February 28, 2007, the *Miami Herald* reported that a former top Cuban military official was calling for international weapons inspections of a secret underground lab near Havana, where he said Castro's government was conducting research in offensive biological weapons.

Despite this, the director of national intelligence fired his office's top Cuba/Venezuela analyst, Norman Bailey, a few days later, because Bailey was "asking the wrong questions" and had developed "independent sources of information" that rankled his boss, Thomas Fingar, according to congressional sources.

This is the same Fingar who was head of the State Department's Bureau of Intelligence and Research during the confrontation between Bolton and analyst Christian Westermann over Cuba.

Bailey also clashed with Thomas A. Shannon, a former Clinton administration National Security Council director for inter-American affairs, who was appointed by the Bush administration as assistant secretary of state for Western Hemisphere affairs in October 2005 to replace Roger Noriega, a hardline neo-con who used to work for Senator Jesse Helms.

Applauding Bailey's departure from the ODNI, the Cuban government news service Granma derided him as "a patent relic of the Reagan regime."

"It's almost as if Cuba has become the third rail of the American intelligence community," a former colleague of Bailey's told me.

It took Scott Carmichael, the DIA counterintelligence officer, two and a half years to get his book on Ana Montes cleared for publication by the intelligence community. Even so, what he revealed in *True Believer* was a vast penetration by Castro's spies that went well beyond Ana Montes.

"I believe that the Cuban Intelligence Service has penetrated the United States government to the same extent that the old East German intellignce service, the Stasi, once penetrated the West German government during the Cold War," he said. "I believe that Ana was not the exception, but the rule."

DEMS LOVE PONTY

The one top appointee whose confirmation no one placed on hold was John Negroponte, who breezed through hearings at the Senate Select Committee on Intelligence for the newly created post of director of national intelligence on the very same day that Bolton was getting torpedoed.

The Democrats, Rice, and Hadley saw Negroponte as an effective counter to Porter Goss, who they felt was riding roughshod over the CIA. Like Bolton, Porter Goss was actually having some success, and so he needed to be stopped. Unlike Bolton, Goss—to his peril—paid little heed to the scheming taking place all around him.

As Goss was settling in as CIA director in the fall of 2004, the congressional intelligence committees crafted legislation to create a new intelligence czar, as recommended by the 9/11 Commission.

Under the existing system, the director of Central Intelligence performed two key functions: He ran the CIA, and he culled the jewels from another fourteen agencies and presented a daily summary of the hottest items to the president of the United States. His job was to manage the entire intelligence community, and to be the president's chief intelligence analyst—in other words, to "connect the dots." And that was where George Tenet had fallen down, as a CIA inspector general report on the intelligence failures leading up to the 9/11 attacks would soon determine.[28]

Once he had completed the initial wave of purges at the CIA and began restructuring the DO, Goss was convinced he would be tapped as the new intelligence czar. So were his allies on Capitol Hill. In a nod to Goss, the original House version of the Intelligence Reform and Terrorism Prevention Act of 2004 specified that if the current DCI were selected for the newly created position of director of national intelligence, then Senate confirmation would not be required. That provision lasted about a New York minute once the bill went over to the Senate, since there is nothing a United States senator treasures more dearly than his constitutional prerogative to question the abilities and acumen of presidential appointees, especially if live TV cameras are present. So the new DNI would require Senate confirmation, something the shadow warriors believed was now beyond Goss's reach because of the public controversy they had jinned up surrounding his management of the CIA. The president signed the final bill into law on December 17, 2004.

Despite that setback, Goss was convinced he had the inside track. So when the president announced that Negroponte was his choice for the new position on February 17, 2005, Goss was stunned. He felt personally betrayed.

Friends, associates, and others who met with him over the ensuing months said he appeared "demoralized" and "distracted" as he watched career diplomat John Negroponte brazenly grab assets from the CIA and expand his turf as the new DNI. (Whenever Congress tried to do intelligence reform, joked Senator Pat Roberts, chairman of the Senate intelligence committee, "You heard the bulldozers late at night scraping turf up against the doors.")[29] Most galling of all to Goss was losing responsibility for preparing and delivering the President's Daily Brief.

Sitting with the president of the United States every morning in the Oval Office, going over the most secret intelligence the government possessed, was the ultimate power trip. And unlike President Clinton, who shunned the CIA director, President Bush was an avid consumer of intelligence. He thrived on the personal relationship with his intelligence chief; indeed, that is why George Tenet, for all his failings, survived for so long. A born courtier, who learned how to please his political masters as a congressional staffer and as a deputy national security advisor for intelligence affairs under Clinton, Tenet cultivated Bush even before he took office. He traveled to Crawford, Texas, in the days following the disputed November 2000 election to brief Bush personally on the most secret affairs of state while much of the nation thought of little other than hanging chad.

Goss lost that privilege to Negroponte, who had just come back to Washington from his latest posting as ambassador to Iraq, where he had been in regular contact with Bush in what arguably was the most politically sensitive position in the entire administration.

THE GREEK IMMIGRANT'S SON

"Ponty," as Goss called him, had a résumé a mile long. Born in 1939, John Dimitri Negroponte graduated from Yale at the age of twenty-one, after spending a junior year abroad in France. That youthful dalliance gave him an affection for things Gallic that never left him, despite the clashes with French president Jacques Chirac over war with Iraq.

Unbeknownst to Goss, Negroponte still remembered the slights he had suffered at the hands of his more socially adjusted peers at the Psi Upsilon frat house at Yale, including Porter Goss. "Negroponte nursed a deep personal animosity for Porter that went back to their college days," one source who knew both men said. "Porter never realized it."

Goss came from affluence. Well-adjusted, outgoing, sociable, he became a natural case officer, the recruiter. Negroponte was the Greek immigrant's son. Shy, introverted, and brilliant, he was determined to claw his way to the top, which he felt was unfairly dominated by WASPs like Porter Goss.

Whereas Goss joined the CIA fresh out of Yale, Ponty found the State Department suited him better. He was given his first posting abroad, as a vice consul to Hong Kong, under President Kennedy.

Negroponte served as a political officer in Vietnam from 1964 to 1968 when the CIA was running Operation Phoenix, whose goal was to identify and assassinate South Vietnamese civilians working with the Vietcong. A series of leaks exposed the Top Secret program to the point that it became widely known in the embassy, to the press, and ultimately to the enemy.[30]

While he was in Saigon, Negroponte made the acquaintance of a fresh graduate from the U.S. Naval Academy named Richard Armitage, who was on his first tour in Vietnam, and of a young officer named Colin Powell. Years later, when Powell became secretary of state and Armitage his deputy, those friendships would serve Negroponte well.

Negroponte thrived under both Republican and Democrat administrations. After three years as director for Indochina at the National Security Council under President Nixon, he was promoted to become a deputy assistant secretary of state with the rank of ambassador under President Carter.

During the Reagan administration, he was appointed ambassador to Honduras, and he played an instrumental role in supporting the Nicaraguan Contras, an activity that rankles the Left even today. (The Honduras job gave him the reputation in some circles of being a conservative stalwart. He was not.)[31]

Sent to Mexico as U.S. ambassador by President Bush in 1989, he was allowed to finish out his term by President Clinton, who named him ambassador to the Philippines in October 1993. By the time he left government in September 1997, he had been confirmed by the Senate five times. He was a mandarin of the permanent government, not someone who was about to "break the china," as Goss was doing.

As Negroponte told members of the Senate Select intelligence committee, his main qualification to become director of national intelligence was having "served in foreign policy and national security related positions for more than forty years." He hadn't spent all those years in government without learning the three basic rules of the successful bureaucrat:

1. Identify your enemies, and undermine them
2. Identify your friends, and keep them happy
3. Grab as much turf as you can

During his confirmation hearing, he pointedly refused to say how he intended to structure his brand-new government department (the *sixteenth* U.S. intelligence agency), and for good reason: he planned a massive expansion of the DNI beyond the roughly 250 positions he had been allotted by the loosey-goosey authorization bill passed by Congress.

But he minced no words when asked by Senator Rockefeller how he intended to deal with Porter Goss and the CIA. "What is the relationship of the DNI to the CIA on these issues? Well, of course, the Director of the CIA will report to me, as the law states and as the President also reaffirmed."[32]

That was what the Democrats wanted to hear. They wanted a director of national intelligence who was going to listen to them, not to Goss, and who would keep neo-cons like John Bolton from sounding the alarm on Iran. They wanted to ensure that no new threats were revealed to the American public until every analyst in the intelligence community was on the same page.[33]

From the minute he entered his temporary headquarters in the Defense Intelligence Agency complex at Bolling Air Force Base, directly across the Potomac from Reagan National Airport, Negroponte began creating a parallel CIA that sat on top of the CIA—precisely what the 9/11 Commission had sought to avoid in its recommendations.

"Most of the new hires who have come to Bolling have been brought on by Negroponte through cronyism," a senior manager who left CIA to work under Negroponte told me in January 2006. "The newcomers aren't without talent, but they don't know the ropes. They don't know the organization or how the intelligence community works."

While this manager was being diplomatic, what he described was Negroponte's preference for selecting former colleagues from the State Department to run a host of new departments he had created, giving them broad responsibilities over the entire intelligence community and empowering them to hire as many people as they could—all with the intention of diminishing the CIA as the lead U.S. intelligence agency.

Negroponte gave two of the most sensitive top jobs at the ODNI to career State Department officers of dubious talent.

Thomas Fingar was a State Department intelligence analyst with no known overseas experience who briefly headed the State Department's Bureau of Intelligence and Research (INR). Fingar became Negroponte's deputy for analysis. In his new job, Fingar was not only responsible for pulling together the President's Daily Brief, he also chaired the National Intelligence Council, the elite group that produced National Intelligence Estimates.

Fingar had recently made headlines for his vigorous opposition to John Bolton during his May 2005 confirmation hearing. Although Fingar was considered unreliable (even disloyal) by Republican political operatives, Negroponte had no qualms about installing him as his personal overseer over the analytical products of the entire U.S. intelligence community. It was a huge promotion that sent a clear message to congressional Democrats and to the president's enemies within the intelligence establishment that Negroponte was siding with INR in a whole series of ongoing disputes on Iran, North Korea, and Iraq—all of them potentially issues of war and peace.

Fingar's first product was a National Intelligence Estimate concluding that Iran would not acquire enough fissile material to make a bomb until "early to mid-next decade." In other words, America, *Don't worry, be happy.*

That good news was promptly leaked to a friendly reporter at the *Washington Post,* who contrasted it to the more "forceful public statements" about Iran's nuclear weapons coming from the White House. "Administration officials have asserted, *but have not offered proof,* that Tehran is moving determinedly toward a nuclear arsenal," the Postie scolded (emphasis mine).[34] To reach his more serendipitous conclusion, however, Fingar had to ignore a mountain of proof, including the fact that Iran was known to be modifying the warheads of deployed Shahab-3 ballistic missiles so they could carry a nuclear payload to hit Israel. Just a detail, folks.[35]

The most damning evidence, including Iran's own timetable for nuclear development, was publicly available in IAEA reports. No wonder that Fingar's shop and Democrats on the House intelligence committee leaked furiously to discredit the August 2006 publication of a competing study on Iran's nuclear weapons program by HPSCI Republicans, which relied exclusively on the public evidence. The HPSCI report concluded that Iran could have the capability to produce a nuclear weapon by 2008 if it maintained its current level of progress, and it cited "significant information gaps" in the knowledge of U.S. intelligence agencies. In addition to calling on reporters at the *Washington Post* and the *New York Times* to debunk the report, Fingar and his colleagues successfully weighed in with IAEA Director General Mohamed ElBaradei, who had a deputy write a scathing letter to the committee, dismissing the report as "erroneous and misleading."

The second official, who was a key contributor to the gun-shy intelligence community assessment of Iran's progress toward nuclear weapons, was Kenneth Brill, a former U.S. ambassador to the International Atomic Energy Agency in Vienna. He came on board in June 2005 to head the newly created National Counterproliferation Center.

While in Vienna, Brill consistently failed to confront Iran once its clandestine nuclear weapons program was exposed in February 2003, and had to be woken up with the bureaucratic equivalent of a cattle prod to deliver a single speech condemning Iran's eighteen-year history of nuclear cheating. (The cattle prod was a special envoy from John Bolton's Washington office, who wrote the speech and handed it to Brill for delivery to the closed IAEA council chamber in March 2004.)[36] Brill, who was hopelessly incompetent, was ultimately removed and sent home to retire, although the State Department bureaucrats pushed hard to get him appointed to John Bolton's former position as undersecretary of state for arms control (T).

Once Fingar and Brill joined Negroponte's staff, they tapped careerists from the State Department's Bureau of Nonproliferation for virtually all the top positions. Some of their new hires had downplayed Soviet violations of arms control treaties in the 1980s and 1990s. Others had pooh-poohed nuclear weapons development by Iraq and Iran. "These are the folks who wouldn't see a nuclear weapon if they tripped over it," a former colleague told me. Among them was Vann H. Van Diepen, a Clinton holdover who became NIO for Weapons of Mass Destruction and Proliferation. "Van Diepen was an enormous problem at State," a former colleague and Bush loyalist told me. "He was insubordinate, hated WMD sanctions, and strived not to implement them," even though that was his specific responsibility. He clashed frequently with Bolton when he worked under him and asked to be transferred to the ODNI with "return rights," meaning he could sit out the rest of the Bush administration working for Brill and then return to the State Department, presumably after a Democrat won the White House in 2008.

Also among the careerists Fingar and Brill tapped was the now infamous Christian Westerman. After failing to recognize the signs of biological weapons development in Cuba and Cuba's cooperation with Iran, Westermann was promoted to become national intelligence officer for biological weapons. Let's hope a walk-in defector from Iranian intelligence doesn't tell us that Iran has given biological weapons to terrorists to attack New York or Chicago, because Westermann will certainly object that the source of that information was not reliable—at least, until Americans start dying.

Negroponte brought on board two more State Department careerists as deputies:

- Thomas E. "Ted" McNamara, a former ambassador to Colombia and counterterrorism official. He was put in charge of information sharing.
- Patrick F. Kennedy, assistant secretary of state for administration from 1993 to 2001. He was tapped by L. Paul Bremer in 2003 to become his top administrative assistant in Iraq (there's a sign of success!). Negroponte made him the deputy director of National Intelligence for Management, the guy whose job was to knock the heads of the nation's fifteen other intelligence agencies to apportion budgets and resources.

Negroponte also brought on board Mary Margaret Graham, the CIA counterintelligence chief whom Goss had suspected of leaking the personnel file of a prospective employee to the press, to become his deputy for intelligence collection. Of all the bad appointments, hers was arguably the worst of all. Here was a woman whose job was to coordinate HUMINT activity across the intelligence community who had "virtually no overseas experience with the Directorate of Operations," a former colleague told me. But that was okay in Negroponte's book. Her real job was to diminish Porter Goss's role in reforming the Directorate of Operations (now renamed the National Clandestine Service), and to keep the DIA out of the HUMINT business. Negroponte had gotten to know her when he was the U.S. ambassador to the UN and she headed the CIA domestic station in New York.

Finally, as his chief of staff, Negroponte picked none other than David R. Shedd, the same former CIA operations officer who had been detailed to the National Security Council in February 2001 to work on intelligence programs and who was suspected of leaking to Democrats in Congress in an effort to derail the Goss nomination in September 2004.

Negroponte's new shop wasn't just a mini State Department. "The

NDIO has become a refugee camp for those who have not been happy with this administration," a former colleague who was tracking Negroponte's operation said.

No wonder the Democrats loved Ponty.

Goss watched helplessly as Negroponte expanded his agency fivefold. Many top CIA officers resigned—not because of any political witch hunt but because the price of staying had become too high. They were second-guessed, undermined, demoralized. Everyone was getting lawyered up—because congressmen such as Christopher Van Hollen (D-MD) were warning them that they could be prosecuted if they didn't report "illegal" intelligence operations. (He included in that category presidentially approved activities, including the NSA's terrorist surveillance program, which I will examine in the next chapter.)[37]

It would be only a matter of time before Ponty got Goss's scalp as well.

CHAPTER SIXTEEN

THE DAILY LEAK

There were days when Porter Goss felt the bottom had dropped out of his universe. The leaks were absolutely killing them. Every day, it seemed, some Top Secret intelligence program suddenly appeared on the front pages of the *New York Times* or the *Washington Post.* And now CIA officers were being indicted in a foreign country.

The action by Judge Chiara Nobili in Milan, Italy, announced on June 22, 2005, risked opening the whole can of worms that the extraordinary rendition program had become. She issued arrest warrants for thirteen current and former CIA officers in connection with the kidnapping of a radical Egyptian cleric named Hassan Mustapha Osama Nasser, known more commonly as Abu Omar.* Chief among them was Robert Seldon Lady, fifty-one, the recently retired CIA station chief in Milan.

Most of the CIA officers mentioned in the warrant had used assumed names, but not Bob Lady. He was out there and exposed, left to dangle in the wind. Even worse, he had purchased a farmhouse for his retirement in the Piedmont north of Milan. And now the Italians had put out a warrant for his arrest!

Abu Omar was seized in broad daylight off a street in Milan on February 17, 2003, by a special CIA rendition team. Two men speaking perfect Italian asked him for his papers. Once they were certain of his identity, they sprayed an incapacitant into his nose and mouth and threw him into a white van, where they told him to keep quiet or he would be dead.

After sealing his mouth with duct tape, they drove for nearly five hours

*Later, the number of Americans indicted was expanded to twenty-two and ultimately to twenty-six.

until they reached the U.S. air base at Aviano. His captors turned him over to a larger team of men and women, some of whom spoke only English. They used an Arabic-language interpreter to interrogate him.

According to a confidant of Abu Omar, who was in constant contact with the cleric's wife, "the Italian and English speakers, whom Abu Omar believed to be Americans, asked him questions repeatedly, accompanied with outbursts of violence, on three specific issues: his dealings with al Qaeda, his activities related with the war in Iraq, if he was sending volunteers to fight the U.S. in there, and his relationship with Albanian Islamic groups."[1]

Flight records obtained by the prosecutors showed that the questioning at Aviano—if it occurred at all—didn't last very long. Thanks to information provided by the Italian base commander, Colonel Rosario Scarpolini, who came forward voluntarily after reading newspaper accounts about the case, they were able to determine that Abu Omar was loaded onto a U.S. Air Force Learjet 35, registration number SPAR 92, that took off from Aviano at 6:20 P.M. that same afternoon.

By cross-indexing that information with flight logs obtained from EUROCONTROL in Brussels (the European equivalent of the FAA), they discovered that the plane "arrived certainly, after a flight of about one hour, in Ramstein [Germany], the biggest American base in Europe."[2] From there, the Egyptian was transferred onto a waiting Gulfstream IV, tail number N85VM, registered to Richmor Aviation of Hudson, New York, that took off almost immediately for Cairo.

The prosecutors believed that CIA Milan station chief Bob Lady accompanied Abu Omar on that flight and stayed with him for the next few weeks, while he was tortured by the Egyptian security forces on the basis of an outstanding arrest warrant.

For crying out loud, it wasn't as if the guy sold soda pop and coached Little League, Goss thought. He'd been through the al Qaeda terrorist training camps in Afghanistan, and had deployed with al Qaeda units to Albania to fight for the liberation of Kosovo, where he was captured by U.S. forces as a terrorist. Somehow, he had managed to escape to Germany, where he claimed political asylum, ultimately making his way to Milan. The Viale Jenner Milan mosque where Abu Omar preached had become a known recruitment hub for would-be jihadis hoping to join Osama bin Laden and al Qaeda.[3]

And the Egyptians had a file on the guy a mile long, which is why they had asked the CIA to facilitate his return to Egypt. They were hoping they could "turn" him and use him as an informer in Europe against the radical wing of the Gama'a al-Islamiya, arguably the most vicious al Qaeda component.

Abu Omar, it turned out, was a disciple of GI founder Ahmed Taha Rifa'i, better known to his followers as Abu Yasser. Rifa'i was one of the original signers of bin Laden's famous 1998 fatwa that announced a worldwide jihad against Americans, both civilian and military, by his newly formed International Islamic Front Against Jews and Crusaders.[4]

Even British journalist Stephen Grey, who was sympathetic to the plight of the kidnapping victims, pointed out that Abu Omar was "suspected . . . of being part of a cell of militants that had been in contact by satellite phone with militants based in Herat, Afghanistan, who had moved after 9/11 to northern Iraq." Among the "militants" Abu Omar was chatting with by satellite phone was the infamous Abu Musab al-Zarqawi, Grey noted—the same Zarqawi who boasted of beheading Americans in Iraq and who was killed in a U.S. air strike on June 7, 2006.[5]

If they were being polite, most normal Americans would refer to Zarqawi and to Abu Omar's other friends as "terrorists."

To Goss, it all smacked of a leak. But by whom?

FIND THE LEAKER

Normally this type of operation would be run in the field by a special renditions team sent by the Counterterrorism Center (CTC). They would parachute in for the operation and coordinate with CIA officers on the ground. That meant that Bob Lady in Milan would have operational control, and would report back to Langley either directly or through the Rome station chief, Jeff Castelli.

At headquarters, their field reports would be channeled through Tyler Drumheller, the Operations Directorate chief for Europe, to the head of the CTC. At the time, the chief of the CTC was Jose Rodriguez, the man Goss eventually picked to become his deputy director for operations.

But because the potential for political blowback was so high, Goss knew that his predecessor, George Tenet, would have wanted to run chops at the highest level in Washington. That meant for starters that Drumheller's immediate boss, the associate deputy director for operations (ADDO), would have been required to sign off on the operation.

At the time of Abu Omar's rendition, the ADDO was Stephen Kappes, the same Kappes who led the "insurrection" against Goss when he first arrived. (Jose was his protégé.) Kappes had gone to London shortly after leaving the Agency to take up a rainmaker's job with ArmorGuard, a private security contractor making out like gangbusters with the Pentagon in Iraq.

London—where muckraking journalist Stephen Grey was based.

Kappes's boss at the time, the deputy director for operations, was Jim Pavitt, who was now retired. Was either one speaking to the press on the q.t.? Grey told the Italian prosecutors that "ex-CIA agents" were his sources. It was hard to know—and hard to ask without pulling the Justice Department into it, which Goss was reluctant to do at this point, since literally hundreds of top-level Agency management had been briefed into the program. A DoJ investigation would shut down operations in the war on terror. It was unthinkable—at least, for now.

On this particular abduction, the National Security Council liaison for intelligence matters had also been advised. At the time, that was David Shedd—the same David Shedd who became a de facto Democratic Party mole during Goss's long-delayed confirmation. (Goss had tried to get him recalled to the Agency from the White House, without success.) And because of the political sensitivity, both Tenet and his deputy, John McLaughlin, were in the loop and had to approve the operation before it could come down. Not to mention the Agency's top lawyers, who would have had to sign off on the operation as well.

So there it was: the whole Gang of Weasels. Castelli, Drumheller, Kappes, Pavitt, Shedd, McLaughlin—the very people Goss had fired because they were unwilling to change the go-along, get-along culture of the Agency. This was an operation run by the Old Guard.

The day after the Italian arrest warrant was issued, police investigator Bruno Megale showed up with seven detectives at the farmhouse in the tiny village of Penango where Robert Seldon Lady had planned to retire.

Lady was gone, but his wife was there, and so was Lady's computer, which the Italians seized. They were able to trace back through the cache of his Internet browser the MapQuest search he had done to find the shortest driving route from Milan to Aviano. They also found a surveillance photograph his team had taken of Abu Omar shortly before he was snatched walking down the same street to the mosque. (In the photograph, Abu Omar wore a long beard, jihadi style, and looked as if he could have stepped right out of Afghanistan.) And they found an e-mail from Susan Czaska, a CIA colleague in Rome, sent on Christmas Eve. The message carried the subject line "Merry Christmas."

"Dear Bob," she began. "I am so glad to hear from you. Since I got your last note, I suddenly got an email through work which was entitled 'Italy, Don't go there. . . .' "[6]

Lady had been warned—get out of the country. He was able to take refuge in Geneva, several hours' drive away. But it was one of the most miserable bits of tradecraft Porter Goss had ever seen.

THE ITALIAN PROSECUTOR

There were many things Goss didn't know.

Among them was the fact that the CIA inspector general, John L. Helgerson, had opened his own investigation into the Milan rendition. This latest move by the controversial Helgerson came in the wake of a spring 2004 report he had circulated to top Agency managers and to congressional lawmakers that raised questions about CIA interrogation methods of al Qaeda prisoners. As chairman of the House intelligence panel at the time, Goss had swept aside the Helgerson report, convinced that a series of presidential findings had put the administration on sound legal ground.[7]

Helgerson was discovering a great deal of resentment bubbling away beneath the surface among the Old Guard at the DO. Officers were volunteering information about renditions they considered to have been unethical. They came to Helgerson seeking advice. They were worried about getting indicted.

"This is not what we do," one former clandestine officer told me. "Rendition and torture are simply bad business. The vast majority of our guys are opposed to torture. It's not who we are. It's bad business."

Lots of these al Qaeda prisoners were really just "big babies who are ready to cooperate," this career veteran ventured. "Our greatest successes were gotten by offering benefits. You say to them, We can do this the hard way, or the easy way. Over time, they think it over and cooperate.

"It's the old Mary Poppins thing," he added. "A spoonful of sugar . . ."

When I suggested that the Old Guard was hopping mad with Porter Goss and with the Bush administration over the war in Iraq, he agreed. But he insisted that from there to leaking highly classified information about CIA proprietaries and flight logs to the press was a huge stretch that none of them was willing to make. "It is beyond my ken that a senior officer would blow a proprietary," he said. "These cost us a fortune to set up. And now it's going to cost us a fortune to replace them."

He and many other of the Old Guard pointed fingers at the Democratic staff on the Senate intelligence committee. But again, without a Justice Department investigation, there was no proof.

The other key piece of information Goss didn't know at first was the character of the Italian prosecutor, Armando Spataro.

Italy's justice minister, Roberto Castelli, accused Spataro of being a "left-wing militant" who was deliberately seeking to undermine Italy's good relations with the United States. Castelli flew to Washington in early November and met with U.S. attorney general Alberto R. Gonzales in Washington in an attempt to halt the proceedings. "The interests of the State are on the line," he said.[8]

Spataro denied the charge, pointing out that he had prosecuted the hard-left Red Brigade terrorists in the 1980s. "Under the law, if a crime is reported, we are obliged to open an investigation," he said.[9]

But the facts of the case and the way Spataro handled it lend credence to Castelli's charge. Prosecutors in Italy operate independently from the political authority of the state, much as investigative magistrates in France. They have almost total discretion over the cases they choose to pursue or to drop. When Spataro took over the case in April 2004, he dropped everything else he was working on, including open terrorism-related cases. Because now it looked like the CIA was involved.

Just three days after Abu Omar disappeared, his wife walked into a local police station to report him missing. The police opened an investigation, and assigned young police inspector Bruno Megale to the case.

Almost immediately, they discovered an eyewitness, a twenty-three-year-old Egyptian woman, Merfat Rezk. She had been returning to the mosque where she had left her two daughters so she could run some errands when she was forced to cross the street by a light-colored van blocking the sidewalk. She told police that she noticed "a bearded Arab-looking man wearing a traditional tunic walking down the left-hand side of the street, and another man, Western-looking and wearing sunglasses, who was talking into a mobile phone resting between his head and shoulder."[10] It later transpired that the man with the cellphone was reading out the details from Abu Omar's passport, to make sure they had the right man before seizing him.

The prosecutor at the time who was in charge of terrorism cases in Milan, Stefano Dambruoso, took advantage of the lead to order records on every cellphone that was switched on in the vicinity of Abu Omar's disappearance at that time. (This was possible because cellphones automatically log onto the network when they are turned on, so that network operators can monitor traffic at each base station.) He also began to identify and interview other witnesses who knew Abu Omar. Despite these steps, "No significant progress was made in the investigation for over one year after the abduction," the arrest warrant states. "Indeed, investigators had almost disregarded the matter after a communication forwarded in March 2003 by 'American authorities' to the Direzione Centrale della Polizia di Prevenzione in Rome, stating that Abu Omar had relocated to an unknown Balkan location."[11]

That "communication" was a memo, stamped "Secret//Release to Italy Only," sent by Rome station chief Jeff Castelli to Italy's central police intelligence unit, the DCPP, dated March 3, 2003.[12] It was Castelli's crude way of steering Italian investigators away from the case. But it worked—until Spataro took over in April 2004.

On April 20, 2004, the Italian police intercepted a telephone call from Abu Omar, who was now in Cairo, to his friend Mohamed Elbadry in Milan. In the call, Abu Omar alluded to the fact that he had been thrown in jail by the Egyptians and tortured—and that the Americans were involved.

When the police finally translated the call and presented the transcript to Spataro on May 9, he suddenly shifted gears. "His attention was now completely engaged" on the case, because of the American involvement.[13]

And Spataro was a thorough investigator. He put the cellphone records ordered by his predecessor—all 10,718 calls!—into a computer database, cross-checking to see who was calling whom. As patterns emerged, he focused on the connections between those numbers. When he found calls made to hotels, he pulled the guest records. (That's how he found, for example, that two of the women in the snatch team had been shacking up in five-star hotel rooms with men twenty years their senior.) In the end, he managed to name nineteen alleged CIA operatives and published full lists of their identities, cellphone records, hotel records, rental car agencies, and credit card receipts for all the world to see. It was an extraordinary performance that went way beyond anything attributable to even prosecutorial zeal. At fifty-eight, Spataro was no novice, nor did he need to prove his stripes. He was out to get the CIA and to get Bush.

Why was the tradecraft of Lady and the CIA rendition team so bad? Why did they leave so much evidence behind? The simple answer is, Because they knew that their operation had been sanctioned at the highest levels of government in both the United States and Italy. Their goal was to be invisible to their target—and they succeeded. But they had never built an operation aimed at remaining impenetrable to a full court press from an Italian prosecutor who would choose to use the extensive powers of his office to the hilt.

HOEKSTRA COMES TO BAT

If news of the Milan arrest warrants left Goss stunned and dispirited, when his team started circulating a complete copy of the Italian legal file translated into English, key Goss allies on the Hill got hopping mad. Chief among them was Representative Pete Hoekstra, the chairman of the House intelligence committee.

On July 29, 2005, Hoekstra gave a speech at the Heritage Foundation that sent tremors throughout the intelligence community and won him no friends among the press. He said the unthinkable: leaks of classified information got people killed.

He told his listeners that he had ordered his staff to install framed posters from World War II to remind them every day of the dangers. "LOOSE LIPS SINK SHIPS," the most famous of the posters said. Another one showed a ship in flames, its crew bobbing in the water and on lifeboats, with the statement, "A CARELESS WORD . . . A NEEDLESS SINKING." Hoekstra scolded, "The ghosts of leaks past serve as potent reminders for us of the dangers of leaks today."

Hoekstra knew he had to show a little leg if he was to have any hope of making news, so he quoted from a June 2002 memo from the CIA that discussed the damage that leaks to the media had caused. It read in part:

> "Information obtained from captured detainees has revealed that al Qaeda operatives are extremely security-conscious and have altered their practices in response to what they have learned form the press about our capabilities. A growing body of reporting indicates that al Qaeda planners have learned much about our counter-terrorist capabilities from U.S. and foreign media."

Turning to the Milan case, Hoekstra continued his scolding. "We also know that unauthorized leaks put strains on our relationships with foreign intelligence services," he said. "The reality is, many foreign leaders and their governments provide us with valuable help in the war on terror, but they do so at tremendous political peril. If the United States can't promise to protect classified information and where we got it from, why should we expect these leaders, or even our overt allies, to be willing to share their information?"

Then he mentioned a by-now-infamous case, that of the Iraqi defector code-named CURVEBALL, whom the Democrats cited frequently as prima facie evidence that Vice President Cheney and his neo-cons were cherry-picking fake intelligence to justify the "rush to war."

In fact, Hoekstra revealed, "the primary reason" the intelligence community misjudged the status of Iraqi's biological weapons program in the 2002 National Intelligence Estimate and elsewhere was their "heavy reliance" on CURVEBALL—a source that no American had ever met or debriefed.

Why had CURVEBALL been kept away from the CIA? Simple. The foreign government that had introduced him to the United States "refused to provide us direct access to CURVEBALL because of past leaks from within our government."[14]

By that time, it had been widely reported that CURVEBALL was being run by the German intelligence service, although Hoekstra refused to name them. As I will show below, the CURVEBALL fiasco is yet another intelligence failure that falls squarely on the shoulders of the CIA's inept—some say, disloyal—European Division chief, Tyler Drumheller.

AN INSIDE JOB

Goss's nightmares were just beginning. No one person—not ten, even—had enough fingers to plug the leaky dike the CIA and its sister agencies had become. As for federal prosecutors, until now, they had focused all their attention on prosecuting the Office of the Vice President of the United States ("Plamegate") and neo-con supporters of Israel (the AIPAC/Larry Franklin case).

Sometimes the leaks were so blatant, the press couldn't quite believe they were happening. Take Mary Margaret Graham, the overseer of all covert operations throughout the community who reported to John Negroponte. Speaking at a public conference in San Antonio, Texas, in early November 2005, she revealed the precise amount the United States was spending on intelligence—one of the best-kept secrets until then. Democrats had been clamoring for years for the CIA to release the budget figures; during Negroponte's confirmation hearing, they again made their case, but to no avail. When the *New York Times* got wind of Graham's leak, they called it "an apparent slip."[15] Graham was never reprimanded for divulging classified information, let alone fed to the FBI.

On November 2, 2005, *Washington Post* reporter Dana Priest published another installment in her ongoing assault on the Bush administration, listing eight foreign countries that were hosting "secret prisons" used by the CIA for terrorist detainees. It was a huge blow to one of the U.S. government's most sensitive operations, as Priest herself made clear. "The existence and locations of the facilities—referred to as 'black sites' in classified White House, CIA, and Justice Department documents—are known to only a handful of officials in the United States and, usually, only to the president and a few top intelligence officers in each host country," she wrote.[16]

Clues to the existence of the secret prisons, where al Qaeda captives were allegedly being tortured, had been seeping out as some of the former captives were released. But Priest based her account primarily on a different source: one or several "dissenters" within the CIA itself.

"The secret detention system . . . has been increasingly debated within the CIA, where considerable concern lingers about the legality, morality and practicality of holding even unrepentant terrorists in such isolation and secrecy, perhaps for the duration of their lives," she wrote. "Mid-level and senior CIA officers began arguing two years ago that the system was unsustainable and diverted the agency from its unique espionage mission."

Even the leakers were aware of the sensitivity of the information they were providing to Priest. The Agency had never acknowledged the existence of the "black sites," they said, because to do so "could open the U.S. government to legal challenges, particularly in foreign courts, and increase the risk of political condemnation at home and abroad."

As conservative commentator John Hinderaker pointed out, "Recent events indicate that the CIA might even be willing to compromise the effectiveness of its own covert operations, if by doing so it can damage the Bush administration."[17]

Speaking to Diane Rehm on National Public Radio the day after her "scoop" appeared, Dana Priest speculated that her story was likely to cause "political embarrassment" for the administration, in particular with European allies. She hastened to add that her sources wanted people to know it was not a CIA "rogue operation" but a White House operation, and hinted that they had talked about it because they were afraid the

Agency would be hung out to dry.* For her "courage," Dana Priest was awarded a Pulitzer Prize a few weeks later.

Porter Goss was furious. He knew how close-hold this information was. This was clearly an inside job. He couldn't continue to allow the leakers to roam freely through the bowels of the Agency, so he phoned Bob Grimsland, who headed the Office of Security, and told him he was pulling the trigger on an internal investigation. It was time to identify the leakers and put a stop to this.

Six days after the *Washington Post* exposé, Senate majority leader Bill Frist (R-TN) and House speaker Dennis Hastert (R-IL) sent a letter to the chairmen of the congressional intelligence committees requesting an immediate joint investigation to determine the source of the leaks. "Democrats immediately responded by calling for Republicans to begin a congressional investigation of the alleged manipulation of intelligence leading up to the war in Iraq and how White House officials allegedly released CIA officer Valerie Plame's identity to the media in retaliation for her husband's criticism of the war," the *Atlanta Journal-Constitution* noted.[18]

For the top Democrats on the Senate intelligence committee, Rockefeller and Levin, it was all about politics, not national security.

SACRIFICIAL VICTIM

By this point, all hell was breaking loose in Europe. The leaks on the CIA's network of "secret prisons" and on Air CIA were having precisely the impact that Dana Priest and her editors at the *Post* had predicted (and some believe, actively sought). Human rights groups and left-wing politicians were demanding explanations and clamoring to "shut down" CIA operations in their countries. European Union officials wanted to know which East European countries were hosting the CIA's "black sites." Goss hastily ordered the European sites to be closed down and their few inmates transferred elsewhere, reportedly to new sites in North Africa.[19]

Sweden's Left Party leader Lars Ohly said the latest reports on secret

*This is exactly the same language and arguments used by the "father" of the rendition program, Michael Scheuer, in congressional testimony he gave on April 17, 2007, to the House Foreign Affairs Subcommittee on Human Rights, International Organizations, and Oversight. Scheuer blasted Dana Priest repeatedly during the hearing, but also made clear his resentment for the way the Agency had been used by the White House, both under Clinton and under Bush.

prisons were "proof that we are cooperating too intimately with the CIA and the American government in the so-called war on terror." In Norway, the Foreign Ministry summoned U.S. diplomats "to explain the activities of a specific aircraft that was at Oslo Airport for about 12 hours in July."[20]

In Spain, Interior Minister José Antonio Alonso revealed that a judge was investigating reports that at least ten flights landed in Mallorca as part of the CIA's program, following a complaint by authorities in the Canary Islands. And in Portugal, the Communist Party and the Left Bloc were demanding an explanation from the government after the newsweekly *Focus* reported that CIA planes had been photographed at international airports in Porto and at Tires, near Lisbon.[21]

Online databases listing the previously secret CIA flights were being expanded daily, as "plane spotters" snapped pictures of suspected prisoner convoys on runways from Shannon, Ireland, to remote Afghanistan.[22]

A Phoenix, Arizona, webzine revealed that the CIA's deputy director for operations, Jose Rodriguez, was running the CIA's secret airlines, and had been involved in Iran-Contra as the division chief for Latin America:

> The US media—*NY Times*, *Washington Post*, CBS—are only showing how CONTROLLED they really are by calling the CIA's latest (appointed Nov. 2004) Deputy Director of Operations just "Jose." Google his predecessor as DDO, Stephen Kappes (Google this: "stephen kappes" cia) and you get about 515 results. Google the DDO before that—"james pavitt" cia—and you get 23,000 results. Google this—"Jose Rodriguez" cia—and you get three or four results (*The Nation*, *Asian Times*, and a couple others). The DDO is under cover? Give me a break.

But most damaging was the list they published of CIA proprietaries that had been used to operate the aircraft needed for the extraordinary renditions. The article provided names, addresses, and known commercial agents for ten CIA mailbox companies. While some of the names had appeared before in the press, others hadn't. And there it was, assembled neatly in a package, all in one place—very helpful to anyone looking for political ammo against the CIA and the Bush administration.[23]

In Italy, a lawyer for former CIA officer Robert Seldon Lady filed a motion at the Palace of Justice in Milan, requesting that charges against him be dropped because he was covered by diplomatic immunity.

While not admitting the kidnapping or any knowledge of it, the lawyer argued that "any such activity would have been carried out under the orders of the U.S. government and with the knowledge and permission of Italian officials." Italian state security law granted immunity for such activities, she argued.

Since Italian justice minister Roberto Castelli had returned from Washington in early November 2005, he had been fighting a losing battle with the prosecutors, who were eager to see the CIA and the Bush administration dragged through the mud. They had already sent him a formal request that he enforce an expanded arrest warrant against Lady and twenty-six others and demand their extradition from the United States. Now Spataro ally Judge Enrico Manzi went further and swept aside Lady's request for immunity, arguing that he had lost immunity when he retired from the U.S. government in July 2004. To counter the objection that the acts in question took place when Lady still worked for CIA, Manzi said that the laws governing immunity "need not always apply if the alleged crimes are sufficiently serious."[24] Law? What law?

Bob Lady was about to become the sacrificial victim on whom the Italians—and through them, the entire European Left—would heap their hatred of the Bush administration.

CONDI'S ROAD TOUR

On December 5, 2005, Condoleezza Rice stepped up to the plate and made a detailed public defense of extraordinary renditions. "For decades, the United States and other countries have used 'renditions' to transport terrorist suspects from the country where they were captured to their home country *or to other countries* where they can be questioned, held, or brought to justice," Rice said. Citing former CIA director George Tenet, she added that "earlier counterterrorism successes included 'the rendition of many dozens of terrorists *prior to* September 11, 2001' " (emphasis mine).

Probably the best-known case was that of Carlos the Jackal, the nom-de-guerre for Venezuelan-born terrorist Illich Ramirez Sanchez, who was wanted in France for the murder of two French policemen in the 1990s. The United States captured him in Khartoum, Sudan, and flew him to France in 1997, where he stood trial that December. The only one to protest the U.S. action was Carlos himself.[25]

Rice took her defense on a European road trip later that week. "One of the things she will be saying is, 'Look, we are all threatened by terror. We need to cooperate in its solution,' " National Security Advisor Stephen

Hadley told *Fox News Sunday*. "As part of that cooperation for our part, we comply with U.S. law," he added. "We respect the sovereignty of the countries with which we deal. And we do not move people around the world so that they can be tortured."[26]

Parliamentary investigations had begun in Scotland, Britain, Germany, Ireland, Spain, Portugal, Austria, and Greece into the alleged use by the CIA of their nation's airports for the rendition flights. A full-scale revolt of America's European allies was under way, which would take all of Rice's diplomatic skills to quell.

HUMAN RIGHTS, OR ANTI-BUSH?

The relentless assault on the administration during the Bolton hearings, followed by the revelations of the CIA extraordinary renditions, contributed to the erosion of the president's popularity. By November 2005, the NBC News/Wall Street Journal poll found, 57 percent of Americans surveyed disapproved of the way the president was handling his job. Bush's negatives reached 60 percent in the ABC News/Washington Post poll, and 61 percent in the Zogby America poll, both of which consistently found high negatives.

Fanning the flames were a number of "human rights" groups that provided investigative assistance to reporters and members of Parliament who wanted to track the secret CIA flights. In the United States, Human Rights Watch had assigned experienced investigator John Sifton to the case, working with a network of plane spotters and activists around the world. They published several reports that told the stories of "ghost detainees" held by the United States in "secret prisons" around the world. "Human Rights Watch is more concerned with the rights of terrorists than with the rights of victims," said J. Michael Waller, professor at the Institute of World Politics. The group's October 2004 report on "ghost detainees" focused on eleven top al Qaeda terrorists, starting with Khaled Sheikh Mohammed, planner of the 9/11 attacks—not exactly the type of individual most Americans believe should be put up in a five-star hotel at government expense.

Founded by former Random House publisher Robert Bernstein in the 1970s as "Helsinki Watch," the organization had a venerable past of helping victims of the Soviet gulag, including Aleksandr Solzhnitsyn. But over the past decade, it had changed its name and "veered sharply to the left," says Gerald Steinberg, a researcher at Israel's Bar Ilan University, who tracks Human Rights Watch and other nongovernment organizations at www.ngomonitor.org.

The Human Rights Watch website has 13 full pages of links to reports it has published on U.S. "crimes" in Iraq since the 2003 war began. These cover such topics as the Abu Ghraib prison abuse scandal, alleged "collateral damage" during U.S military operations, and numerous allegations of U.S. "massacres" of Iraqi civilians, sometimes fueled by "sources" in Iraq later shown to have ties to the insurgents. There are over two hundred reports in all.

One might conclude that Human Rights Watch had a sincere concern for the sufferings of the Iraqi people. And yet for the entire decade following the end of the first Gulf war in 1991, HRW did just over a dozen reports on Saddam's crimes, few of them as voluminous as its anti-U.S. propaganda and lawsuits. Its main villains are not dictators such as Saddam or Bashar al-Assad of Syria or Iran's clerics, but Western democracies, especially the United States.

Funding for the group has doubled from around $26 million per year to over $50 million per year since the war in Iraq began. Not surprising, they have received significant financial support from the Open Society Institute, which is funded by left-wing billionaire George Soros, and the Tides Foundation, a network of nonprofits backed by Teresa Heinz Kerry, the billionaire wife of Senator John Kerry.[27]

In her November 2, 2005, exposé, Dana Priest said that after speaking to White House lawyers her editors had agreed not to name the two East European countries that were hosting "secret prisons" for the United States. Human Rights Watch felt no obligation to respect such restraints. In a report they released later that day, they identified Poland and Romania as the culprits. (Whether they had provided the information to Dana Priest initially or obtained it from her remains unclear.)

The group openly championed the cause of suspected terrorists who had been "abducted" by CIA snatch teams and who claimed after they were released months and sometimes years later that they had been brutally tortured.[28] These were the stories being told by the likes of Stephen Grey, Jane Mayer of *The New Yorker*, and increasingly by beat reporters at the *Washington Post* and the *New York Times*. Amnesty International and the World Organization for Human Rights USA contributed their resources, lobbying on behalf of the CIA's alleged victims.

The American Civil Liberties Union was also trawling for victims, and eventually convinced Khaled El-Masri, a German citizen of Lebanese descent, to become party to a lawsuit filed in Alexandria, Virginia, on

December 6, 2005, against George Tenet and three CIA contractors for kidnapping and sequestration. El-Masri was picked up in Macedonia and flown by a CIA contractor to the "Salt Pit" prison in Afghanistan "long after his innocence was known," the ACLU claimed.

Another group targeting the Bush administration from the left was the Center for International Policy, run by William Goodfellow. The CIP traced its roots to the antiwar movement of the 1970s and was "created with the assistance of the Marxist Chilean diplomat and suspected Cuban spy Orlando Letelier, who was assassinated in Washington, DC," according to Accuracy in Media, a conservative watchdog group.

In October 2003, Goodfellow's CIP hosted a congressional conference titled "Cowboy Diplomacy," focusing on the war in Iraq. Heading one panel was CIP's national security director, Melvin Goodman, a retired CIA analyst who happily appeared at a field "hearing" sponsored by Representative Cynthia McKinney, where the Georgia Democrat reiterated her view that George W. Bush was behind the September 11 attacks. ("I hope some day her views will be considered conventional wisdom," opined Goodman.)[29]

Joining Goodman on the CIP panel to blast the Bush administration's "rush to war" was Dana Priest, who apparently felt it was entirely appropriate for her as a reporter to participate in a rank partisan event. As it turned out, she was also the wife of CIP executive director William Goodfellow, an affiliation neither she nor her employers were wont to publicize. Once, when cornered, she described her husband blandly as a "human rights activist."[30]

Just as Rice was leaving for Europe, the *Mail on Sunday* reported in London that the British government had granted the CIA "full access" to use British military airfields as refueling stops for the rendition flights. The reception she received was like walking into a buzz saw.

During her trip, she ignited a firestorm by stating that in certain circumstances, the local government can make the sovereign choice to cooperate in "the transfer of a terror suspect to a third country." But Rice had come armed with a secret weapon: a copy of the minutes of the confidential talks held in Athens on January 22, 2003, between the United States and European Union officials. These minutes showed that she had been telling the truth, and that European governments not only knew about the rendition flights but had approved them.

"The minutes were prepared by Greek officials—who at the time held the rotating EU presidency," the London *Sunday Telegraph* reported. The document, entitled "New Translatlantic Agenda, EU-US meeting on

Justice and Home Affairs," showed that ministers focused on the fight against terrorism, drug trafficking, and extradition agreements. According to the minutes, "EU officials agreed to give the United States access to facilities—presumably airports," the paper added. "Both sides agreed on areas where cooperation could be improved [including] . . . increased use of European transit facilities to support the return of criminal/inadmissible aliens," the minutes of the meeting stated.[31]

For Claudio Fava, a former journalist who was now a left-wing member of the European Parliament, the revelation that European governments were witting partners to the CIA's "crimes" presented a momentous opportunity. Here was a chance to strike a blow at the CIA and undermine right-wing governments in Europe, all rolled up in one. Working quietly with like-minded colleagues, he convinced the European Parliament to authorize a full-blown investigation into CIA "dirty tricks." It would be several months before the fruit of their efforts became public. But when it did, it would do lasting damage to the war on terror.

THE NSA LEAKS

New York Times reporter James Risen watched the lionization of his *Washington Post* competitor Dana Priest with chagrin. Risen had been sitting helplessly for over a year on what could turn out to be the biggest scoop of his career. Initially, he had planned to break the outrageous scandal that the Bush administration was using the National Security Agency to listen in on the private conversations of ordinary Americans in October 2004, just before the presidential elections. But sharp administration lawyers kept challenging him on factual details and convinced his editors to put the story on ice. *Times* executive editor Bill Keller explained laconically that he ordered "more reporting" before giving the go-ahead to publish.[32]

Still, when the story finally appeared on December 16, 2005, it understandably caused an immediate sensation. The story started out with a bang: "Months after the Sept. 11 attacks, President Bush secretly authorized the National Security Agency to eavesdrop on Americans and others inside the United States to search for evidence of terrorist activity without the court-approved warrants ordinarily required for domestic spying, according to government officials," Risen and Eric Lichtblau wrote.[33]

The pair had torn the wraps off a previously unknown and unsuspected secret program that allegedly violated the civil liberties of Americans and lent credence to fears that President Bush was seeking broad powers that went way beyond the constitutional limits on presidential authority. "There is no doubt that this is inappropriate," commented Senator Arlen Specter (R-PA), before even picking up the phone to ask the White House what was going on.

It was a huge story, and the *Times* played it big, rolling out all the huffing and puffery they reserved for Pulitzer Prize material. With nothing more than a secret order signed by the president, the National Security Agency had "monitored the international telephone calls and international e-mail messages of hundreds, perhaps thousands, of people inside the United States." It was a massive expansion of government power that marked "a sea change" in how the executive branch could operate, they wrote.

The reception the Left gave this exposure of highly sensitive national security secrets was clear from the start. "Bush Authorized Domestic Spying," the *Washington Post* headlined that same day, citing its rival. News of the NSA program, quickly dubbed "warrantless wiretapping," was "the most significant thing I have heard in my twelve years" said California Democratic senator Dianne Feinstein. "This is Big Brother run amok," intoned Senator Edward Kennedy (D-MA). Senator Russell Feingold (D-WI) called it a "shocking revelation" that "ought to send a chill down the spine of every senator and every American."[34]

As congressional aides rushed to brief their bosses, it became clear that the *New York Times* had scheduled the release of the scoop to coincide with the upcoming vote to reauthorize the U.S.A. Patriot Act. Thanks to these latest revelations, the vote was shelved later that day.

That evening, Senator John Kerry addressed a gathering of "veterans" from his 2004 presidential campaign at Finn McCool's bar in Washington. After praising the activists who had gone on to volunteer for Senate and House campaigns, Kerry said, "If we take back the House [in 2006], there's a solid case to bring articles of impeachment against this president" on the basis of the NSA wiretapping of U.S. citizens. When the press picked up on it, Kerry's communications director, David Wade, insisted that Kerry was just "joking."[35]

The timing of the front-page blockbuster also happened to correspond with the publication of Risen's book on Bush's use of the CIA in the war on terror, an extra perk that the *Times* failed to mention when it released the story. " 'I think it's a crying shame," said Senator John Cornyn (R-TX), "that we find that America's safety is endangered by the potential expiration of the Patriot Act in part because a newspaper has seen fit to release [this story] on the night before the vote on the floor on the reauthorization of the Patriot Act as part of a marketing campaign for selling a book."[36]

Executive Editor Bill Keller was still nervous because of the fierce arguments and veiled threats of prosecution administration lawyers had used in their effort to keep the *Times* from publishing the story. In a statement released simultaneously, Keller revealed that the administration "argued strongly that writing about this eavesdropping program would give terrorists clues about the vulnerability of their communications and would deprive the government of an effective tool for the protection of the country's security." Based on those concerns, the *Times* "agreed not to publish at that time."

What had changed over the ensuing year to convince him to go ahead with publication? On that count, Keller was less clear. "Before running the story we gave long and sober consideration to the administration's contention that disclosing the program would damage the country's counterterrorism efforts," Keller said. "We were not convinced then, and have not been convinced since, that our reporting compromised national security."

There you have it. The *New York Times* decided that exposing a top-secret program to eavesdrop on al Qaeda terrorists as they phone and send e-mails to contacts in the United States has had no negative impact whatsoever on national security. We can all sleep more soundly now.

PUSH BACK

Bush began to push back that same night, telling Jim Lehrer on PBS's *NewsHour* that he would not discuss ongoing intelligence operations. "The reason why is that there's an enemy that lurks, that would like to know exactly what we're trying to do to stop them."

In his weekly radio address the next day, Bush became more explicit, acknowledging for the first time that he had ordered the National Security Agency to conduct an electronic surveillance program in the United States without first obtaining warrants. He said he would continue the highly classified program because it was "a vital tool in our war against the terrorists," and noted that information on the program had been "improperly provided to news organizations."

On Monday, *Newsweek* columnist Jonathan Alter revealed that the

White House had "summoned" *New York Times* publisher Arthur "Punch" Sulzberger and executive editor Bill Keller to the Oval Office on December 6, in a "futile attempt" to talk them out of running the NSA story.

In a column dripping with venom, Alter claimed that Bush was not motivated by national security concerns. "No, Bush was desperate to keep the *Times* from running this important story—which the paper had already inexplicably held for a year—because he knew that it would reveal him as a law-breaker."[37]

That morning, the president walked into the White House East Room and answered questions from a hostile White House press corps for 56 minutes in a nationally televised press conference.

"People are changing phone numbers and phone calls, and they're moving quick," he said. "And we've got to be able to detect and prevent. I keep saying that, but this . . . requires quick action."

To critics who said he had gone beyond his constitutional powers, he reasserted that he had the "legal authority" to approve the intercepts, which he called the Terrorist Surveillance Program.

He revealed that congressional leaders had been briefed on the program and that his administration reviewed it periodically to determine if the ongoing threats to America warranted continuing it. "That's what's important for the American people to understand. I am doing what you expect me to do, and at the same time safeguarding civil liberties of the country."

To a *Washington Post* reporter who asked if these new, "unchecked" powers violated the constitution, Bush replied curtly, "To say 'unchecked power' basically is ascribing some kind of dictatorial position to the president, which I strongly reject." *Post* reporters noted that Senator Barbara Boxer (D-CA) had sent an inquiry to presidential scholars to see if they agreed with the notion that the NSA program was "an impeachable offense."[38]

Much of the media coverage glossed over or omitted key statements by Bush. The *Washington Times* was a notable exception. "Bush Calls Leak 'Shameful,' " they headlined their report on the Bush press conference. Reporter Joseph Curl included a key quote that had been omitted by other news outlets; it explained for the first time the rationale for the program. It also put the Democrats on notice that Bush was going to hold their feet to the fire, because they had been briefed and had signed off on the program.

"We know that a two-minute phone conversation between somebody linked to al Qaeda here and an operative overseas could lead directly to the loss of thousands of lives," Bush said. "I've reauthorized this program more than thirty times since the September the 11th attacks, and I intend to do so . . . for so long as the nation faces the continuing threat of an enemy that wants to kill American citizens."[39]

For all the threats—and despite Alter's claim that Bush had broken the law—not even the Party of Surrender would raise that issue once they took control of Congress in January 2007.

As I can reveal here for the first time, they had good reason for such unusual reserve: A senior member of the Senate intelligence committee is under investigation by the FBI in connection with the leak. "Usually a leak of that magnitude happens at the member level, not from staff," a knowledgeable source told me as this book went to press. Whereas members of Congress would normally not be prosecuted for revealing classified information in speeches on the floor of the House or Senate, "behind-the-scenes leaking would not be protected," said Victoria Toensing, who helped craft the 1982 Intelligence Identities Protection Act.

In July 2007, federal agents armed with a classified search warrant raided the suburban Maryland home of Thomas M. Tamm, a lawyer who had worked at the Justice Department Office of Intelligence Policy and Review (OIPR) in 2004, at the time when Justice Department officials were calling into question the legality of the Terrorist Surveillance Program. Under normal procedures in such an investigation, the Justice Department will question executive branch witnesses before it takes the highly politicized step of seeking to interview a sitting member of Congress. Neither the Justice Department nor the FBI would comment on any potential linkage between Tamm and the senator, or on the status of the Washington, D.C., grand jury hearing evidence in the case.

THREE CHEERS FOR THE PERMANENT GOVERNMENT

As soon as his book hit the stores, James Risen took to the airwaves to defend the leakers who had broken the law by divulging classified information to him on the NSA's Terrorist Surveillance Program.

His sources were "truly American patriots," he told Katie Couric on NBC's *Today Show* on January 3, 2006. They were just the opposite of the White House officials who (allegedly) had leaked Valerie Plame's identity to Robert Novak, because his people had come forward "for the best reasons." They leaked "because they thought you have to follow the rules and you have to follow the law."

Katie Couric wanted to know why the *New York Times* had held his story for nearly a year. Gosh, if only editors had published it when you were ready to go in October 2004, James, why today we would all be saluting president John Kerry!

Risen didn't take the bait, saying it "wasn't my decision" and refusing to "discuss the internal deliberations" at the *Times.*

That got conservative blogger Michelle Malkin's juices flowing. "In other words: Keeping secrets to protect counterterrorism operations is an impeachable offense, but keeping secrets to protect the Gray Lady's fanny is an elite media prerogative," she wrote. (The "Gray Lady" is media jargon for that most venerable of institutions, the *New York Times.*)[40]

Risen then gave a tortured exposition of how he believed government should be run (at least, as long as Republicans held the White House).

> Well, I—I think that during a period from about 2000—from 9/11 through the beginning of the Gulf—the war in Iraq, I think what happened was you—we—the checks and balances that normally keep American foreign policy and national security policy towards the center kind of broke down. And you had more of a radicalization of American foreign policy in which the—the—the career professionals were not really given a chance to kind of forge a consensus within the administration. And so you had the—the—the principals—Rumsfeld, Cheney and Tenet and Rice and many others—who were meeting constantly, setting policy and really never allowed the people who understand—the experts who understand the region to have much of a say.

Risen made a similar comment, phrased slightly more coherently, to National Public Radio two days later.

> [A]fter 9/11, I think there was a breakdown in the normal checks and balances in the U.S. foreign policy community. Principals in the Bush administration, the top people, kept meeting every single day. And they kept setting policy in these meetings so rapidly that the career professionals in the interagency reviews that tended to moderate things couldn't catch up.

U.S. News & World Report columnist Michael Barone, arguably the best-informed analyst of the U.S. political system alive today, is not known for his sarcasm. But after listening to Risen, he couldn't resist. "What a scandal! Presidential appointees like Donald Rumsfeld, George Tenet, and

Condoleezza Rice and an elected official like Dick Cheney were meeting together! How dare they? And they were setting policy! Astonishing! What will such people dare to do next?" he wrote.[41]

Bit by bit, more government officials were willing to show that they had discussed the highly classified Terrorist Surveillance Program with the media. Two unnamed judges from the ultrasecret Foreign Intelligence Surveillance Act court, which previously had been responsible for authorizing national security wiretaps on a case-by-case basis, told the *Washington Post* they were concerned and "want to know whether warrants they signed were tainted by the NSA program. Depending on the answers, the judges said they could demand some proof that wiretap applications were not improperly obtained."[42]

Former federal prosecutor Andrew C. McCarthy, now a commentator at *National Review Online*, found the revelation that FISA court judges would discuss their cases with reporters "inexplicable judicial misconduct."

"To find federal FISA court judges leaking to the *Washington Post* about an upcoming closed meeting with administration officials about the highest classified matters of national security in the middle of a war is simply shocking," he wrote. "Even more mind-blowing, though, is to find them discussing what they see as the merits of the issue. . . . If a judge pulled a stunt like this in a run-of-the-mill criminal case, it would be grounds for his removal."[43]

Russell Tice had worked on Special Access Programs at the National Security Agency, but was fired for unexplained reasons by his employer in May 2005. Now that the *New York Times* had exposed the Terrorist Surveillance Program, he was seeking whistleblower protection from Congress. "I intend to report to Congress probably unlawful and unconstitutional acts conducted while I was an intelligence officer with the National Security Agency and with the Defense Intelligence Agency," he wrote to the House and Senate intelligence committees.[44]

Wisely, both committees referred Tice's letter back to the NSA for legal review. On January 9, Renee Seymour, head of NSA Special Access Programs, informed Tice that he had "every right" to speak to Congress and that NSA has "no intent to infringe your rights." The programs he had worked on were so secret, however, that "neither the staff nor the members of the [commitees] are cleared to receive the information covered by the special access programs, or SAPs."

Apparently, Seymour's warning did not deter Tice from speaking to the press. He told ABC News the next day that he was a source for the *New York Times*. "As far as I'm concerned, as long as I don't say anything that's classified, I'm not worried," he said. "We need to clean up the intelligence community. We've had abuses, and they need to be addressed."[45]

The leaks were coming from all sides, and increasingly, they were being coordinated and shared among left-wing reporters. Former Pentagon official Michael Rubin noted that *New York Times* reporters who had called him to verify an allegation that he had taken money from the Lincoln Group to advise them on a Pentagon contract were using "a private Internet listserv in which they discuss targets with left-wing bloggers."[46]

One thing the Left conveniently forgot was that the Clinton administration also conducted "warrantless" wiretapping of domestic targets. But instead of suspected terrorists, they were listening in on the private conversations of Republican politicians, including the likes of Senator Strom Thurmond of South Carolina.[47]

As far as the elite media was concerned, wiretaps by Democrats of their political enemies were okay. But wiretaps by Republicans of suspected terrorists were not.

"Unless you're holding conversations with al Qaeda, you have nothing to worry about with this program," said House intelligence committee chairman, Representative Pete Hoekstra.[48]

In his preview of the president's January 31, 2006, State of the Union Address, White House advisor Karl Rove told conservative activists that Bush planned to make a "passionate defense" of the NSA Terrorist Surveillance Program. "We're in a war," Rove said. "You'll hear the president say clearly tomorrow night that in a time of war, if Osama bin Laden picks up his cellphone in his cave and calls someone in the United States, we shouldn't consider it someone calling for pizza."

Buried deep in the elite media's coverage was a stark reminder of why the administration had ordered the NSA program to begin with. Former NSA director General Michael Hayden, then serving as deputy director of national intelligence under Negroponte, told reporters that if the NSA Terrorist Surveillance Program had been up and running in early 2001, "it is my professional judgment that we would have detected some of the 9/11 al Qaeda operatives in the United States."

You would think that would be an important piece of news. Sources tell me that among the facts Hayden was referring to were calls from an al Qaeda cell in Yemen to 9/11 hijacker Khalid al-Mihdhar in 1999–2000, which the NSA didn't pick up because they were made to a U.S.-based number. But instead of meriting front-page coverage, Hayden's comment was buried three paragraphs from the end of a twenty-paragraph *Washing-*

ton Post story that examined Karl Rove's strategy for "making the controversial eavesdropping program a political winner for the White House in a midterm election year."[49]

It was yet another reminder that for the shadow warriors, the Democrats and their cheering section in the elite media, this was all about politics, not national security.

CHAPTER SEVENTEEN

THE MISSING WMDs

Bill Tierney was a former military intelligence officer and Arabic linguist with extensive experience in Iraq and the war on terror. From 1996 to 1998, he was detailed to the UN Special Commission for the Disarmament of Iraq (UNSCOM) and witnessed at first hand the "denial and deception" operations run by Saddam's Special Security Organization to keep UNSCOM from discovering ongoing WMD programs.

That experience left him with a gut conviction that Saddam Hussein was not merely continuing his WMD programs but was laughing at the inability of the UN inspectors and especially the United States to do anything about it.

After President Clinton ordered the four-day Desert Fox bombing raids on Iraqi military facilities in December 1998, Saddam concluded the United States just wasn't serious. "Who would be so stupid as to start a bombing campaign and just stop?" Tierney said. To the Iraqis, it showed a lack of U.S. resolve.

It was after Desert Fox that Saddam realized that "the doors were wide open for him to continue his weapons programs" with no real opposition from the United States. This also is when Tariq Aziz, Saddam's right-hand man, succeeded in changing the meaning of the phrase "smoking gun," Tierney said.

Until then, the phrase was used in Iraq to describe circumstantial evidence—the smoke trail that would lead investigators to conclude that a bullet had just been fired. A smoking gun document discovered by nuclear inspector David Kay in 1993, for example, provided a situation report on PC-3, Iraq's secret procurement-and-development program to build a nuclear weapon. Another "smoking gun" was found when UN inspectors discovered eighteen-wheel trucks hauling uranium-enrichment calutrons out the rear gate of a military base. The inspectors never found the weapons-grade material or the weapon itself, and through most of the 1990s, no one ever expected that they would. Saddam was too clever for that.

Bit by bit, Tariq Aziz succeeded in transforming "smoking gun" to mean the actual bullet—the physical stockpiles of WMD—"knowing that as long as there were armed guards between us and the weapons, we would never be able to 'find,' as in 'put our hands on,' the weapons of mass destruction," Tierney says.[1]

It was a brilliant shift of perception, not just words—an extreme makeover that today has become the implacable standard adopted by Bush foes for judging the evidence the administration used to determine the threat posed by Saddam Hussein.

PROJECT HARMONY

In 2004, after spending time in Guantánamo Bay as an interpreter for the interrogation of al Qaeda prisoners, Tierney was sent back to Iraq as part of a counterinfiltration team. He was there as the Iraq Survey Group (ISG) completed its investigation into Saddam's weapons programs, and he spoke to ISG officers frequently.

"During my eight months of counterinfiltration duty, we had fifty local Iraqis working on our post who were murdered for collaborating," Tierney said "This was just one post, yet the DIA believes no one was afraid to talk, even though scientists who were cooperating with ISG were murdered."

Tierney's experience led him to conclude that "the arrogance and hubris of the intelligence community is such that they can't entertain the possibility that they just failed to find the weapons because the Iraqis did a good job cleaning up prior to their arrival."

During their initial triage of documents, computer disks, hard drives, audiotapes, CDs, and other materials seized at hundreds of sites as the fighting waned in April 2003, the Defense Intelligence Agency translated only what appeared immediately relevant to the work of the Iraq Study Group. Forty-two pages of those documents, which were not U.S. government classified, were made available to Cybercast News Service, a conservative website, in October 2004. They included purchase orders for anthrax vials (apparently for use by terrorists), decontamination equipment, and large quantities of gas masks and chemical weapons protection gear, all dating from 1999 and 2000. The ISG (and the elite media) treated this as just an average day in Saddam's Iraq.

Another document, dated January 18, 1993, transmitted Saddam Hussein's order, delivered through his personal secretary, "to hunt the Americans that are in Arab lands, especially in Somalia, by using Arab elements or Asian [Muslims] or friends."

In response, the head of the Iraqi Intelligence Service informed Hussein that Iraq already had ties with a large number of international terrorist groups, including "the Islamist Arab elements that were fighting in Afghanistan and [currently] have no place to base and are physically present in Somalia, Sudan, and Egypt." *In other words, al Qaeda.*[2]

Was nobody awake when that story ran? Because there was little pickup, no blaring headlines saying the United States now had proof that Saddam had been working with al Qaeda before the September 11 attacks—indeed, right at the time of the Mogadishu debacle portrayed in *Black Hawk Down.* (Remember, bin Laden says the Mogadishu attacks, which now are recognized as the first anti-U.S. strike by al Qaeda, convinced him that his men could beat the Americans just as the Afghan mujahideen had beaten the Soviets in Afghanistan.)

Besides the willingness of the elite media to dismiss any story that might reflect favorably on the Bush administration, especially right before the presidential elections, the conventional wisdom still prevailing within the U.S. intelligence community when CNS first published these documents was that Saddam's secular Baathist regime was bitterly opposed to bin Laden and the Islamists. That continued even as the CIA was forced to face facts on the ground in Iraq of intimate cooperation between the Baathist "stay-behind" networks and the Islamist insurgent groups, both Sunni and Shiite.

"It is almost an article of religious faith among opponents of the Iraq War that Iraq became a terrorist destination only after the U.S. toppled Saddam Hussein," the *Wall Street Journal* opined in a lead editorial fifteen months later. "But what if that's false, and documents from Saddam's own regime show that his government trained thousands of Islamic terrorists at camps inside Iraq before the war?"[3]

The new documents becoming available made Tierney see his pre-9/11 experience as an Iraq intelligence analyst at CENTCOM Headquarters in Tampa, Florida, in a new light. Back then, the Iraq "shop" was focused on detecting signs of another Iraqi invasion of Kuwait, the no-fly zones, and WMD. "Like many others, I bought into the idea that UBL was too devout to have a relationship with a *mushrik*, idolator, like Saddam," Tierney said. "I had made an unwarranted projection that the more devout the jihadists were, the more principled they were."

Tierney recalls bringing a report on terrorist training being conducted at a facility just off Canal Sreet in Baghdad to the terrorism section at CENTCOM. "They treated me like I was from another planet," he said. "The terrorism shop was joined at the hip with the Iranian section, but there was no synergy with the Iraq intelligence section." And they were dead wrong, he now realized.

Bit by bit, more documents were finding their way to conservative publications, including a report that "elite Iraqi military units" had trained some 8,000 terrorists, mainly from other Arab countries, before Operation Iraqi Freedom. These documents were drawn from the HARMONY database, where everything exploitable that had been collected in Afghanistan and Iraq was now being catalogued and centralized.

It was a vast treasure trove of information. Representative Pete Hoekstra told reporters there were more than 35,000 boxes of HARMONY documents that the U.S. government hadn't translated or analyzed that should be examined—several million pages in all. He had been trying for months to get Director of National Intelligence John Negroponte to release just forty documents, whose titles and HARMONY record identifier he had obtained from officials with access to the system. The titles were consistent with the 42 pages released in October 2004 and clearly suggested ongoing WMD programs in Iraq, as well as extensive ties between Iraqi intelligence and al Qaeda. But it was impossible to know how much hard information they contained without seeing them.[4]

DIA analyst Michael Tanji, who had managed the captured-document project before leaving government service in 2005, was bemused at the way the press, Congress, and even some within the intelligence community were politicizing the whole question of standards of evidence. "Critics of the war often complain about the lack of 'proof'—a term that I had never heard used in the intelligence lexicon until we ousted Saddam—for going to war. There is really only one way to obtain 'proof' and that is to carry out a thorough and detailed examination of what we've captured," he said.

But that didn't seem to be the goal of his former bosses. Work was progressing at such a slow pace that unless something radical was done and more resources were committed to the task, "our great-grandchildren will still be sorting through this stuff," Tanji said.[5]

THE SADDAM TAPES

In late 2005, Tierney was asked by an outside translation service to examine twelve hours of audiotapes that had been discovered at Saddam's main presidential palace in Baghdad and set aside as part of Project HARMONY for future review. The tapes were all unclassified.

When Tierney popped the first tape into his cassette recorder, he couldn't believe what he was hearing. It was the distinctive reedlike voice of the Iraqi dictator himself. Saddam was alternately ebullient, sarcastic, commanding, disdaining, or magnanimous as he listened to subordinates report on their confrontations with UN inspectors or as he discussed strategy with his top deputies.

It was like Richard Nixon and the White House tapes. "Saddam had a special librarian in charge of taping all of his meetings and keeping track of them, so Saddam could ask him who he talked to about a particular subject three months earlier and find that particular tape. It completely floored me,"* Tierney said.

Among the revelations that immediately leapt out: details of a secret uranium-enrichment program that Iraqi scientists told Charles Duelfer and his CIA-sponsored Iraq Survey Group had been shut down in 1988.

That revelation was contained on a tape Tierney examined dating from 2000, two years *after* Iraq expelled UN arms inspectors. Saddam had summoned two top nuclear scientists to the presidential palace in Baghdad to brief him on their progress in enriching uranium using plasma separation. It was clear that Saddam had great expectations. It was equally clear that the scientists were nervous, Tierney said. If successful, their efforts could have given Saddam the fissile material he was seeking to make a bomb.

"One of them is telling Saddam all these wonderful things they can do with the plasma process, which they had developed in the 1980s for the nuclear weapons program," Tierney said.

---

*"Mr. Tierney may very well be the first person to listen to the entire tapes and recognize the value of them," said former ISG analyst Ray Robison. "I know it is hard to conceive, but without going into details, the linguists were generally not intelligence experts but were hired merely because they spoke Arabic. One linguist I worked with worked at a liquor store before coming to ISG and had no military or even State Department experience. This is not to disparage them; they were great Americans for the most part." Ray Robison, "The Saddam tapes (2)," *The American Thinker*, Feb. 18, 2006, http://www.americanthinker.com/blog/2006/02/the_saddam_tapes_2.html, accessed Jan. 21, 2007.

The scientist tried to convince Saddam to use the technology for other, purely peaceful purposes, but the Iraqi dictator just listened politely. "You can imagine him nodding his head as you listen to the tape," Tierney said.

The plasma-enrichment program was so well protected that its very existence remained a secret until after the fall of Saddam's regime. "This not only shows the capabilities the Iraqis had, but also the weakness of international arms inspection," Tierney believes. "There were never any defectors with knowledge of this program, so neither UNSCOM, UNMOVIC, or the ISG learned about it. Arms inspection regimes just don't work."

Iraq's plasma research got a brief mention in the 2004 final report of CIA arms inspector Charles Duelfer, but only as a legacy program the Iraqis claimed they had abandoned in 1988.[6] Saddam's secret presidential palace tapes were the first concrete evidence that Iraq had continued clandestine uranium plasma-enrichment work at least until 2000, right under the noses of UN inspectors.

Another exchange that revealed Saddam's continued efforts to conceal his WMD programs took place in April or May 1995. Saddam's son-in-law, Hussein Kamil al-Majid, came to brief the Iraqi dictator and his top advisors on his sparring with UN inspectors.

"We did not reveal all that we have. . . . [T]hey don't know about our work in the domain of missiles. Sir, this is my work and I know it very well. I started it a long time ago, and it is not easy," Hussein Kamil said on the tape.

None of the information Iraq had provided the UNSCOM inspectors was accurate or complete, Saddam's top weapons' advisor said. "Not the type of the weapons, not the volume of the materials we imported, not the volume of the production we told them about, not the volume of use. None of this was correct. They don't know any of this," he said.

But as far as the president's critics were concerned, the UN inspectors were on the verge of completely disarming Iraq in March 2003, when George W. Bush led the nation in a "rush to war."

Other tapes Tierney translated dealt with Saddam's support for international terrorist groups, and specifically his desire to give terrorists chemical or biological weapons to attack the United States.

One terror tape was so dramatic that ABC News producer Rhonda Schwartz convinced her editors to use a 20-second sound bite in Arabic with English subtitles, in a piece that aired on February 15, 2006, on *World News Tonight* and on ABC's *Nightline*.

"Terrorism is coming," Saddam tells Tariq Aziz on the tape, which dated from 1996.

The idea appealed to the Iraqi dictator, and he began to toy with the possibilities. "In the future, what would prevent a booby-trapped car, or causing a nuclear explosion in Washington or a germ or a chemical one?" He let the thought dangle. They had been talking about getting revenge against the United States ever since the Gulf War. Then he added, "But Iraq would not be involved. This story is coming, but not from Iraq."

As Tierney told the ABC news producers, Saddam frequently used irony in this way when talking with his subordinates. No one in his inner circle doubted his meaning: he was planning to use his intelligence services to hand off a chemical or biological weapon to terrorist groups, while instructing them to keep it free of Iraqi fingerprints.

But that is not how ABC decided to spin it. Instead, they took Saddam's words literally and portrayed the Iraqi dictator as some kind of clairvoyant, who foresaw the day when unknown terrorists would attack the United States.

"The biological is very easy to make. . . . An American living near the White House could do it," Tariq Aziz said. Saddam agreed. For ABC, however, these statements proved that Iraq no longer had biological weapons, not that they still had them and were looking for ways they could use them.*

NEGROPONTE'S RAVEN

Tierney may not have realized it, but he had stumbled into a minefield. The discovery of the Saddam tapes was a tremendous embarrassment to the intelligence community, and specifically to the Director of National Intelligence, John Negroponte.

The twelve hours of audiotapes Tierney translated were only a fraction of hundreds of similar tapes in the vast HARMONY database. Up until that point, barely 50,000 items from Project HARMONY had been rendered into English. According to *Weekly Standard* reporter Stephen F.

---

*ABC News reporter Brian Ross also called the former deputy chief of the Iraqi air force, General Georges Sada, to authenticate the tape. Sada immediately recognized Saddam's voice. "They interviewed me for forty minutes, but didn't run a single quote," Sada told me. "After listening to the tape, Ross asked me if I still believed the Iraqis had WMD, and I said, 'YES.' I don't think they liked my answer."

Hayes, "[f]ew of those translated documents have been circulated to policymakers in the Bush administration."[7]

Why hadn't the documents been circulated? Because the Defense Intelligence Agency, which now took orders from Negroponte, was sitting on them, Hayes said. Even worse, the DIA wanted to shut down its translation warehouse, based in Doha, Qatar, where 700 Arabic linguists were working in three shifts on Document Exploitation (DOCEX) for Project HARMONY. "The Bush administration seems remarkably uninterested in discovering, now that we have reams of material from Saddam's regime, what the actual terror-related and WMD-related activities of that regime were," Hayes wrote.

It was to get around the DIA/DNI logjam that the twelve hours of audiotapes wound up in Bill Tierney's cassette player. And why, once they had been translated and checked by other UNSCOM inspectors, they ultimately found their way to former federal prosecutor John Loftus.

Tierney had gone on to other assignments after he translated the tapes, gratified that finally the truth would come out on Iraq's programs. But two months later, when he heard National Security Advisor Stephen Hadley state publicly that the administration had been wrong in their WMD assessments, he went to Loftus.

If anyone could get the story out, it was John Loftus. A pugnacious investigator with a nose for the sensational, Loftus had broken stories based on hard-to-acquire information and witnesses, and had a track record with the media. More important, as far as the elite media was concerned, he had gone after Republicans as well as Democrats.

In the 1980s, he had investigated the Reagan administration's arms-for-hostages deal with Iran, tracking down travel voucher and expense account claims of participants to show that they had met with international arms dealers a full year before the official account. In 2002, he filed a civil lawsuit in South Florida that accused the Saudi government of backing Islamic charities in Virginia and Florida that he alleged were laundering money for Palestinian Islamic Jihad. As part of his claim, Loftus revealed that the Clinton administration had shut down a federal grand jury looking at Islamic charities in 1995, "concerned that a public probe would expose Saudi Arabia's suspected ties to a global money-laundering operation that raised millions for anti-Israel terrorists," federal officials said.[8]

Loftus told the press that he planned to release the Saddam tapes at the upcoming Intelligence Summit he was organizing in Arlington, Virginia, on February 18, 2006. Tierney would play segments of the tapes, present his translations, and provide extensive commentary and context at a special "pre-briefing" for the press.

As the date of the "Summit" approached, Tierney was putting the finishing touches on a 160-page PowerPoint presentation he planned to use as a backdrop for his talk. There was a great deal of nuance he wanted to present—he called it "granularity"—things like Saddam's speech habits, his sense of humor, the inside jokes that were familiar to fellow clansmen from Tikrit. These were things that didn't come across easily in a straightforward English rendering and that allowed reporters and intelligence analysts seeking a benign explanation for Saddam's behavior to misconstrue his true meaning.

As Tierney was preparing, John Negroponte was desperately fishing for a way to shut down the conference. At the very least, he sought to prevent the appearance of heavyweights such as former CIA director R. James Woolsey, who was a scheduled speaker. Beyond that, he wanted to curtail the participation of active-duty law-enforcement and intelligence-community personnel, paying participants who were Loftus's bread and butter.

Working through an outside consultant, Negroponte spread the rumor that "the" financial backer of the Loftus summit was a Jewish Russian "mobster" who was about to be indicted in Israel. The file on this man, Michael Cherney, was so thick that he couldn't come to the United States for fear of being arrested, Negroponte's graveyard-whisperer told me in a hush-hush telephone call. As a scheduled speaker at the conference, I was curious and mildly concerned. I had never heard of Cherney, let alone had dealings with him. But neither did I want to have any association with the Russian mob. "Jim Woolsey has already announced that he's pulling out. So is everybody else," the Raven croaked, mentioning the names of several friends. "If you take part in this conference, Ken, you will be tainted forever. But please, don't tell anyone that I told you this."

That last bit was the tip-off. I found the Raven's assertions a bit too intense, a bit too last-minute, a bit too deniable to be credible. I called the Justice Department to see if they were aware of the allegations about Cherney. They refused to comment. I phoned other participants, who confirmed that they had received similar phone calls. Some took the allegations seriously; others dismissed them as fabricated.

As it turned out, Cherney was being slandered by a rival in the Israeli police, who himself was later indicted. But Negroponte's strategy worked up to a point. Thanks to the lies spread by the Raven, a number of prominent speakers, including Woolsey, withdrew from the conference at the last minute. So did many paying participants from government, who were simply ordered to stay away.*

Instead of addressing a standing-room-only crowd in the huge ballroom at the Hyatt Regency in Crystal City, Virginia, that Saturday morning, Loftus and Tierney spoke to rows and rows of empty seats.

"They had a plasma program," Tierney said, summing up the tapes he had just presented. "We've seen that they rebuilt an electrical power station in Basra so they could divert the energy for uranium enrichment. How long is it going to take them to get nuclear material, folks? Simply because we don't have the evidence sitting in our face? That's pathetic! We've got to have a little more respect for our enemies."

Press coverage of Tierney's presentation of the Saddam tapes was minimal. But Negroponte's Raven didn't stop there. He apparently had access to Tierney's personnel file, and told a reporter from a network news channel that Tierney was psychologically unstable. "Ask him why he was fired by the DIA," the Raven suggested.

And so the reporter did. He had no interest in doing a story on Tierney or on Saddam's WMD programs, and had not come with a camera crew. But when Roger Simon of the upstart Pajamas Media was interviewing Tierney in the hallway outside the ballroom shortly after his presentation, he popped the Raven's question.

Bingo! Tierney almost did a double take. After a pause, he launched into the story. He wasn't fired, he said. He had resigned.

"I resigned in protest because I was interviewing somebody who was a Christian, and I prayed with him. He was wrapped up tight, so I prayed with him to calm him down. The government tried to say that I was proselytizing a Muslim, when they knew very well and it was on record that he was a Christian. I couldn't let that be a precedent. I had to stay true to what I believed"—Tierney choked up at this point, and Roger Simon's camera closed in on his face—"when I took my oath to defend the Constitution of this country. So I resigned rather than let it be a precedent. I had to stand up for what I believe. . . . I am *so* glad you asked that question."

There it was. Tierney was unstable, breaking down on camera. He was a kook, a fanatic. Not only was he a patriot, who believed in his oath to the Constitution. He was a Christian!

---

*I did not withdraw from speaking at the conference, and presented information on the history of Iran's ties to al Qaeda.

Also revealing his story for the first time at the Intelligence Summit that weekend was former deputy undersecretary of defense Jack Shaw. He provided the outline of how Russian Spetsnaz units, working for several months before the war began, cleaned out WMD materials from Iraqi factories and warehouses and shipped usable material to Syria (see Chapter 9).

Like Tierney, he too was now the subject of a smear campaign, in his case aimed at showing that he was somehow corrupt, and helping private contractors to win cellphone contracts in Iraq.[9]

It was part of the old Washington playbook that John Negroponte knew well: If you can't kill the story, kill the messenger.

GENERAL SADA'S STORY

General Georges Sada had been deputy commander of the Iraqi air force when Saddam Hussein threw him in jail during the Gulf War in 1991. Although Sada, an Assyrian Christian, was known for speaking truth even to Saddam, his crime was not lèse-majesté. It was far worse.

"Qusay came to me during the war," he said, referring to Saddam's younger son, who had begun to play a major role in the intelligence apparatus of the regime. "He gave me orders to kill the six British and thirty American pilots who had been shot down [during Operation Desert Storm]. I told him I wasn't going to do that, that we had to treat them as POWs in accordance with the Geneva conventions. I told him, 'If you kill them, the Americans will declare another war—on you and your family. And none of you will survive.' "

The next day, Republican Guards soldiers arrested him at his office and threw him in jail. "I was waiting to be hanged," Sada says. "But Saddam knew I was right and finally gave the orders to release me two weeks later."

For the next eleven years, Georges Sada lay low. Retired from the air force, he remained in Iraq but stayed away from politics. He never revealed his confrontation with Qusay until much later.

In 2002, he left Iraq and went to work for the International Centre for Reconciliation, an Anglican group working out of Coventry Cathedral in Britain. As international pressure on Iraq grew, Sada sought to use his contacts within Saddam Hussein's inner circle to convince the Iraqi dictator to find a peaceful way out of the impasse with the UN inspectors and the United States. "I took a delegation from the International Centre for Reconciliation to Baghdad, where we met for hours with Tariq Aziz," he told me. "We asked him to allow international inspectors back into Iraq by October 1. The Brits who were with us told him, 'If you don't do this, Iraq will be flattened.' "

To Sada's surprise, Tariq Aziz agreed to the demand—but insisted that inspectors not return to Iraq until after November 1. "Later, I learned why," Sada says. "They needed the extra time to transfer WMD stockpiles and materials to Syria."

After the liberation of Iraq, Sada returned to Iraq and spoke to a number of former colleagues from the Iraqi air force, some of whom had gone to work for Iraqi Airways. The story they began to tell him was extraordinary, and yet it fit entirely with everything Georges Sada knew about Saddam Hussein and his method of operating.

"These were people I had known for thirty years. They were my friends. They knew my connection to Saddam Hussein and to the Americans, and were worried that the weapons would fall into terrorist hands."

The pilots told him that they'd been ordered to fly the weapons to Damascus on board two Iraqi Airways passenger planes—a Boeing 747 and a Boeing 727—that had been converted to freighters. "They were surprised the first time when they got to the planes and found the cabins stripped and set up to haul cargo," Sada says. "Republican Guards troops were loading the planes with yellow drums stamped with the skull and crossbones. These were sarin 1, sarin 2, and tabun"—deadly nerve gases Saddam had produced in German-built factories.

Also on board the flights were stockpiles of biological weapons, the pilots told him. (The UN inspection teams that eventually came to Iraq in December 2002 confirmed that Iraq had produced more than 8,000 liters of deadly anthrax but could not account for why or how they had gone "missing." The whereabouts of Saddam's bioweapon stockpiles remains a mystery to this day.)

All together, the pilots flew fifty-six sorties from Baghdad to Damascus. "The cover story was that the flights were bringing humanitarian aid to Syria after the collapse of a dam in June 2002," Sada says. Iraq used a front company, SES, for the transfers, he added. The pilots told him they were aware that additional material was being sent to Syria in convoys of eighteen-wheel trucks.

Sada kept silent on what he had learned until April 17, 2004. That was when King Abdullah II of Jordan announced that Jordanian intelligence had just arrested an al Qaeda cell that was planning a massive terrorist attack using chemical weapons in Amman. "The Jordanians intercepted twenty *tons* of sarin gas coming into the country from Syria," Sada says. "These were Iraqi weapons."

Here were some of the weapons the pilots had been telling him about, Sada realized. And now their worst fear had been realized and they had fallen into the hand of terrorists.

General Sada knew that the former Baathist networks were working hand in glove with the al Qaeda–backed insurgent groups, and was worried of reprisals if he went public with the story precipitately. "My family was still in Iraq, my children, my grandchildren," he says. After talking it over with them and with a newfound friend in Phoenix, Arizona—Dr. Terry Law—Sada decided in February 2005 to inform the chairman of the House Permanent Select Committee on Intelliegnce, Representative Pete Hoekstra, and to write a book about what he had learned.[10]

THE CONGRESSMAN

Hoekstra sat with General Sada for over two hours and made sure his staff from the intelligence committee took careful notes. He planned to send them to Iraq to interview the pilots. He wanted as much detail as the retired general could provide.

The evidence was all pointing in one direction, Hoekstra believed. General Sada was only the latest in a series of witnesses who had provided verifiable information that revealed bits and pieces of Saddam's plan to evacuate his WMD stockpiles and key materials to Syria before the war.

Just two months earlier, Lieutenant General Moshe Yaalon, chief of staff of the Israel Defense Forces from July 2002 until June 2005, had gone public with what he knew. Saddam Hussein "transferred the chemical agents from Iraq to Syria," Yaalon said. "No one went to Syria to find it."[11] And there were plenty of other credible witnesses—Jack Shaw; Lieutenant General James Clapper; Lieutenant General Michael DeLong, deputy CENTCOM commander during Operation Iraqi Freedom; and a host of others. In Paris, a Syrian dissident named Nizar Nayouf had even produced a map indicating three burial sites in Syria that he alleged were controlled by Major General Al-Shaleesh, a relative of the Syrian president.[12] Both David Kay and Charles Duelfer, his successor at the Iraq Survey Group, concluded in their reports that there was strong but inconclusive evidence that WMD materials had been evacuated to Syria.

"ISG analysts believed there was enough evidence to merit further investigation," Duelfer wrote.[13]

Hoekstra had also been meeting with former U.S. Air Force investigator David Gaubatz, who said that when he accompanied combat units during the initial thrust into southern Iraq in March 2003, they had come across a number of flooded bunkers, which local sources told him contained artillery rockets filled with poison gas. Neither the Pentagon nor the Iraq Survey Group had shown an interest in investigating the sites, despite his repeated offers to lead a team to the area. Gaubatz was looking for funding to return to those sites and excavate them. Medical records for Gaubatz and his team showed that they had been exposed to high levels of radiation when initially inspecting the sites.

Hoekstra was increasingly frustrated with the way the intelligence community was handling the documents captured in Iraq. Negroponte was stonewalling. Despite promise after promise, he continued to hold back key documents from Project HARMONY—probably because the evidence all tended to implicate Syria in the scheme to hide Saddam's weapons, Hoekstra believed. For reasons that were beyond him, the State Department continued its decades-long love affair with Syria, and wanted nothing out on the public record that would embarrass the new leader, Bashar al-Assad. And Negroponte was a pure product of Foggy Bottom.

The most intriguing evidence of hidden Iraqi WMD stockpiles, however, did not come from any of these sources. It came from a source that Hoekstra had developed all on his own: a former top CIA operations officer, who had returned to Iraq after the war and stumbled onto information pointing to a vast and previously unknown site, buried deep beneath a hillside north of Baghdad, where former Iraqi officials alleged Saddam had pursued nuclear weapons work in the utmost secrecy.

THE DISCOVERIES OF COMPANY X

After a business trip to Iraq in February 2004, the former operations officer was contacted by an engineer, working for a company in a former Eastern European country, who had worked on infrastructure projects under Saddam. The engineer and his company were hoping to win new contracts in Iraq, and had also traveled to Baghdad. On their way back to Turkey, one of the Eastern Europeans pointed to a hilltop east of the Baghdad-Mosul highway, on the far side of the Jebel Makhoul, along the

Tigris. He had always been told that the hilltop disguised an underground weapons plant, he said.

Some of the engineers traveling with them offered that they had worked on a nearby infrastructure project. As they got to talking, they mentioned that they had always whispered among themselves that the underground site housed a secret centrifuge uranium-enrichment plant.

When he first heard this story, the former operations officer felt it had the ring of authenticity. "These guys had been there for thirteen or fourteen years," he told me. "They would get drunk with the Iraqis and learn things about the WMD programs they were not supposed to know."

Along with a business partner, he began tracking down the Eastern European engineers who had worked in Iraq and interviewing them. "We found five or six independent sources who all noted that they had seen eighteen-wheel trucks pass through an entrance into the hill area we were looking at," the former operations officer said. What the trucks did once they entered the hillside, nobody knew. The entire area was a military zone, ringed with several rows of barbed wire.

In his reports to Hoekstra, the former operations officer referred to himself and his partners as "Company X of McLean, Virginia" (where the CIA was located), and encrypted the names of sources in CIA-style diagraphs. He and his associates interviewed thirty-one engineers and workers from a former Soviet-bloc country who had never been debriefed by any U.S. or UN agency before. One of the engineers, identified as LYHUNT/103, had been in Iraq from September 1984 until April 1994 "with a short interruption for the Gulf War." He returned to Iraq several times a year after that until 2000.

LYHUNT/103 and his colleagues worked directly with TECO, the Technical Corps for Special Projects, project manager for "Iraq's highest priority weapons projects." TECO was headquartered within the Ministry of Industry and Military Industrialization, and "reported directly to Saddam's household," the former operations officer said. Among TECO's responsibilities were Iraq's clandestine nuclear weapons, its long-range ballistic missile programs, and the Super Gun that was being built by the former American ballistics genius Gerald Bull. LYHUNT/103 and other colleagues agreed to talk to the former CIA operations officer on condition that they not be identified in any way. They were well aware that their activities in Iraq after 1991 were in violation of international sanctions, U.S. law, and the laws of their own country. They risked serious jail time if they were identified. But they said they were willing to share their knowledge, because they now understood the full import of the highly compartmented project where they had worked, and it scared them. They referred to it as Site 555.

Site 555, also known as the al-Fajr facility, was "intended to be an electromagnetic isotope separation (EMIS) uranium-enrichment facility," the former CIA operative told Hoekstra. Bombed and partially destroyed during the Gulf War, it was leveled in accordance with UN Security Council Resolution 687 in 1991. According to Iraq's declarations to the UN, the al-Fajr facility was a "duplicate" of an EMIS plant in Tarmiya, but uranium-enrichment equipment was never installed. Once the buildings were leveled, the site was no longer inspected.

But there was much more at the site than the UN inspectors ever saw, the Eastern European engineers said. Hidden beneath a nearby hill was an underground structure about 600 meters deep not related to any mineral quarry. Another East European source, LYHUNT/101, commented that it would have taken only minimal effort to level the entry to the shaft and cover it with sand, leaving the deep underground installations hidden, the former CIA operative told Hoekstra.

In April 2004, the Eastern European engineers drove together down from Mosul to Baghdad, and LYHUNT/103 pointed to a series of low hills beyond the road. "That's where the shaft is," he said. But upon further questioning, the former agency officer realized that neither LYHUNT/103 or his colleagues had ever seen the actual opening or visited the underground site itself. They had worked on a water-purification plant and other engineering works on the surface.

Bit by bit, as Company X debriefed more of the Eastern Europeans who had worked in the area, they got a better idea of where to look for the underground site.

"The debriefings indicated that the underground facilities had been dug by 2,500 Vietnamese laborers during the mid-1980s, who toiled for $4 per month," the former CIA officer said. "They dug at night to avoid infrared signatures. It was all done by drill and blast, without heavy machinery." To the trained eye, these were all telltale signs of Iraq's intent to camouflage the work from satellite surveillance.

The former operative informed Hoekstra of information he had learned from another of the East European engineers:

> Per LYHUNT/105's knowledge and his recollection of documentation that had been available to him, the factories at Site 555 were installations for the enrichment of uranium and nuclear chemistry, with one produc-

> tion building having a large internal movable horizontal crane for some kind of assembly, and a single airstrip runway at the bottom of the hill near the cave. The cave represented the entry to a major underground structure, with horizontal elements (tunnels or pathways), but LYHUNT/105 did not know how many tunnels or how deep the structure was. The location of the entry to the underground structure was by the end of the airstrip towards the bottom of the hill.

The man running the site was an Iraqi general, identified in the Company X report as PEAIR/13. According to the Eastern Europeans who had worked with him, he was "not young, but looked younger than he was." He wore a military uniform "with no indication of rank on it; he was also a senior member of the Baath party who often traveled by helicopter." Later, the Eastern European project manager identified him as "Saddam's cousin."

By early June 2004, they were ready to make a foray to the area. Traveling with LYHUNT/101, they drove in through Turkey to Mosul, where they were met by another Company X associate, a number of Iraqi shooters from Baghdad, and a contingent of Kurdish peshmergas. By now, security had become an issue throughout Iraq.

The first surprise when they reached the site was the chemical plant in the valley on the far side of the Jebel Makhoul. It didn't fit with the description of the facilities they had heard from other engineers who had worked in the area in the 1980s, until they realized it had been built later. After the 2003 war, it had been looted right down to the rebar.

When they reached the hillside overlooking the Tigris, they found what appeared to be a large cistern. "It had some interesting features," the former CIA officer said. "It was fed by a 24-inch pipe that drew water from five miles up the river."

They thought the cistern might be camouflaging the entry to the underground site, but they had no excavation equipment to test their hypothesis. It was serviced by a double-paved macadam road—the only paved road in the area—thick enough to accommodate 20-ton trucks. Nearby they found a Soviet-designed power station large enough to provide power to a town of 30,000 people, although there was no town of that size nearby. But uranium enrichment required huge amounts of power, and large supplies of fresh water as coolant, to disguise the plant from heat-sensing satellites. The power station had also been looted.

That was when they saw the spoils from the digging. "They weren't piled, but spread over a very wide area, so satellites wouldn't pick up signs of excavation," the former CIA officer said. They later estimated the Vietnamese had hauled up the equivalent of 5,000 truckloads of dirt and ground rock from below the surface. Whatever they had built, it was enormous.

After that unsuccessful attempt to find the entry shaft to the underground site, the former operations officer reported his findings to U.S. military intelligence and to a top-ranking officer at CIA. The CIA was "not responsive," he said. But the military intelligence officer jumped at the information—at first. He sent representatives to debrief one of the former Eastern European engineers, but then let it drop. When asked, he said he had "no command authority" to pursue the investigation.

The former operations officer had a long-established relationship with Lieutenant General William "Jerry" Boykin, a legendary figure in the special operations community who was now deputy undersecretary of defense for intelligence. Boykin also jumped at the information at first, and gave the order to send in a SEAL team specialized in WMD sites to hunt for the hidden access shaft. "Then we got a call from Jacoby"—that would be Admiral Jacoby, the head of the Defense Intelligence Agency. "He said, 'Don't go to Baghdad, it's too dangerous.' "

This was the same Jacoby who, other Pentagon sources told me, "was too busy working on his third star" through politicking in Washington to take an active interest in what was going on in Iraq.

Finding the entry shaft to a suspected WMD site hidden in a ten square mile area that was covered with rubble and ruined buildings was no mean feat. It was going to require significant excavation work. But before that, they had to narrow down the area to search, and the DIA made it clear they were not going to help.

Not long after this, a left-wing think tank, the Center for Public Integrity, released an "investigation" alleging that the wife of a top Company X executive involved in tracking down Site 555 had improperly used her position as a deputy assistant secretary of defense to steer Iraq reconstruction contracts his way. "She stayed clear of this," the former operations officer said, referring to their investigation and other operations in Iraq. "This was just a smear aimed at sabotaging our efforts."

Returning to Baghdad on his own dime in September 2004, the former operations officer decided to brief U.S. Ambassador John Negroponte, whom he had known from Iran-Contra days in Honduras. "His people said we were full of shit," he told me. "But remember, this was when the

ISG was coming out with their final report. They wanted no waves, no loose ends."

The Iraq Survey Group "inspectors" rarely left their compound near the Baghdad international airport because of the danger of IEDs and insurgent attacks. Their rare sorties mainly involved trips to the airport stockade, where top officials from Saddam's regime were being held. "The big shots knew about the programs, but they didn't know the details," the former operations officer said. Details such as the precise grid coordinates of the underground facility beneath Site 555.

The more Hoekstra learned about Site 555, the angrier he got. He had encouraged the former operations officer to return to Iraq several times in 2005, and again in early 2006. By now, they had narrowed down the area to search for the hidden entry tunnel, and believed they had located what appeared to be ventilation shafts for the underground production halls. But still the DIA refused to help.

Hoekstra pounded on the table, and sent House intelligence committee staff members repeatedly to DIA headquarters. He wanted them to send in a team with handheld underground anomaly detectors, but the DIA refused. So did General Boykin's boss, Undersecretary of Defense for Intelligence Stephen A. Cambone.

Finally, Hoekstra went to the White House and met with Vice President Dick Cheney's chief of staff, David Addington, and suggested that he request a copy of the Company X report from General Boykin's office at the Pentagon. Boykin eventually sent it over—minus the pictures, site diagrams, and key pages. What you guys are doing is history, one of Boykin's aides said. We're not interested in history.

Didn't anybody get it? If they could locate an underground nuclear weapons site that had eluded the UN investigators and where uranium-enrichment work had continued undetected for years, it would provide dramatic proof that Saddam Hussein had never abandoned his WMD programs, as the CIA, the Democrats, and the United Nations claimed.

Sometimes Hoekstra felt he was the only one who cared any longer to learn the truth about Saddam's weapons programs.

CHAPTER EIGHTEEN

SINKING THE SHIP

As more information from the Saddam tapes, Project HARMONY, and General Sada's story became public, it was time for the shadow warriors to leak again, to steer public opinion back their way. They couldn't allow the White House to spin Iraq in its favor when the "real" story line was "wrong war, wrong place, wrong time."

This time they turned to Lisa Myers of NBC News. They had a great spy story to tell that "raises new questions about prewar intelligence."

Just before the Iraq War, when the CIA and the Bush administration "erroneously believed that Saddam Hussein was hiding major programs of weapons of mass destruction," both actually knew better but had lied to cover it up. "Now NBC has learned that for a short time the CIA had contact with a secret source at the highest levels within Saddam Hussein's government, who gave them information far more accurate than what they believed," Myers reported on March 20, 2006.

The source was none other than Saddam's foreign minister, Naji Sabri, the shadow warriors told NBC. During a trip to New York for the UN General Assembly in September 2002, the CIA established a "secret contact" with Sabri that was "brokered by the French intelligence service."

Sabri gave the French and the Americans the lowdown on Saddam's WMD programs. His information was "closer to reality than the CIA's estimates, as spelled out in its October 2002 intelligence estimate." But the Bush White House was not interested in hearing the truth, the weasels said.

Myers also quoted former CIA director George Tenet, who had alluded to Sabri in a February 5, 2004, speech at Georgetown University, where he gave the first detailed public justification of the CIA's prewar intelligence estimates on Iraqi WMD programs.

Tenet spoke of a source "who had direct access to Saddam and his inner circle," who told the Agency that "Iraq was stockpiling chemical weapons and that equipment to produce insecticides . . . had been diverted to covert chemical weapons production." Both pieces of information, Myers noted (to the chagrin of her secret source), were correct. She hastened to point out, however, that Tenet also noted Sabri's revelation that Iraq had no active biological weapons program, and that "Saddam wanted nuclear weapons but had none."[1]

Lisa Myers had been far too balanced in her reporting, so the shadow warriors tried again. This time they went to their old standby, Walter Pincus of the *Washington Post*.

Citing "a former intelligence officer" as his source (we'll find out who that was shortly), Pincus said that Sabri told the United States that Saddam "had ambitions for a nuclear program but that it was not active, and that no biological weapons were being produced or stockpiled, although research was under way." As for chemical weapons, "Sabri told his handler that some existed but they were not under military control." The weasels' message was clear: NO WMD IN IRAQ!

And that wasn't all. The source told Pincus that when the White House learned Sabri wasn't leaning their way, they simply brushed aside his information. "The White House was far more interested in trying to get Sabri to defect than in the information he was providing on Iraq's weapons programs," Pincus wrote.[2]

All the public opinion polls showed that the Democrats were making deep inroads into the president's popularity by sounding these themes. With the news from Iraq uniformly bad, and no dramatic WMD finds to announce, the Bush administration appeared to be on the defensive. The Democrats became increasingly convinced they had a winning theme for the November 2006 elections: Bring the troops home.

A March 19, 2006, story in *Time* by reporter Tim McGirk provided additional fodder. It alleged that U.S. Marines had "massacred" innocent Iraqis after their convoy had been hit by a roadside bomb in the Sunni town of Haditha on November 19, 2005. Although military field commanders had found nothing unusual in the initial after-action reports, Representative Jack Murtha, a Marine himself, said Bush had turned U.S. troops into "cold-blooded killers."

Time subsequently revealed that McGirk had based his report in part on video footage, showing large numbers of corpses piled up in a bloodstained house, that had been shot by a former Baath party member more than 24 hours after the alleged massacre took place. Well before the military began a court-martial inquiry, individuals with access to internal reports on the incident were leaking them to McGirk and to Murtha as part of a campaign to turn the U.S. public against the military and the war.

HUNTING WEASELS

Leaks have consequences, Porter Goss knew. Not only was one of his agents at risk of being arrested anywhere he set foot in Europe because of the "secret prisons" leak, but U.S. allies were refusing to cooperate in the war on terror because they couldn't trust the U.S. to keep a secret.

Goss felt the sting at first hand during a December 12, 2005, trip to Turkey, where he sought approval from the Turkish general staff for U.S. overflights in the event it became necessary to conduct air strikes against Iran's nuclear facilities. The Turks had just held secret talks on the same subject with Israeli prime minister Ariel Sharon, Goss knew. But to his utter astonishment they rebuffed his request, because they feared someone in the CIA would leak the information. "You Americans can't keep secrets," one general told Goss. If the news leaked out that the Turkish military had approved a U.S. air strike on Iran, it would cause a revolt in Turkey and only strengthen the Islamist government, he added.

When he returned to Washington, Goss checked in with his internal security chief, Bob Grimsland. He wanted to step up the pace of the leak investigation, he said. To kick it into higher gear, he asked Grimsland to start polygraphing everyone who had access to the information that wound up in Dana Priest's secret prisons article, starting with himself, his personal staff, and all the deputies. He made one exception: director for operations Jose Rodriguez, and his new deputy (Rob Richer had retired in September 2005), in hopes that the leak investigation would not cripple the Agency totally.

There is an old Washington adage: No good deed goes unpunished. Goss's solicitude only angered the Agency weasels the more, and word of the leak investigation and the "special issue polygraphs" soon leaked out. Former operations officers began whispering to friends on Capitol Hill that Goss was "obsessed," and was personally leading the leak investigation, something that was "unheard of" in the Agency's sixty-year history. "This is eating them up," one former operations officer said.

While Goss was *not* personally leading the investigation, he had initiated it, and he and his staff met several times a week with Grimsland to track its progress and hold Grimsland's feet to the fire. On February 2, 2006, Goss told the Senate intelligence committee that the Justice Department should empanel a federal grand jury to prosecute the leakers—something the Agency had never requested after Valerie Plame's name appeared in Bob Novak's now-famous column.

"The damage has been very severe to our capabilities to carry out our mission," Goss told the senators in a testy, four-hour public session. "I use the words 'very severe' intentionally. And I think the evidence will show that," he added.

Goss said the leaks had caused a "disruption to our plans, things that we have under way." Because of the public exposure, a number of CIA sources had dried up. Assets such as the proprietary companies used by the Agency were "no longer viable or usable, or less effective by a large degree."

During his trips overseas, Goss said he was finding that America's foreign partners no longer trusted him. "I'm stunned to the quick when I get questions from my professional counterparts saying, 'Mr. Goss, can't you Americans keep a secret?' " he said.

The lead Democrat on the panel, Senator Jay Rockefeller IV, brushed Goss's complaint aside. "The president has not only confirmed the existence of the [rendition] program, he has spoken at length about it repeatedly." The leaks probably "came from the executive branch" of the government, Rockefeller said—meaning, of course, the Bush White House.

After that hearing, Goss intensified the mole hunt. His top staffers had never seen him so exercised. He'd call Grimsland repeatedly, pressing him for news. "I want this done. Don't let it drop," Goss urged him.

He also wrote an op-ed that the *New York Times* published eight days later. In that piece, "Loose Lips Sink Spies," Goss reminded readers that the Robb-Silberman Commission had determined that unauthorized leaks of critical intelligence assets had cost America "hundreds of millions of dollars; in security terms, of course, the cost has been much higher."

Part of the problem was leakers who tried to elevate their treachery by claiming they were "whistleblowers."

"As a member of Congress in 1998, I sponsored the Intelligence Community Whistleblower Protection Act to ensure that current or former employees could petition Congress, after raising concerns within their respective agency, consistent with the need to protect classified information," Goss wrote.

But that wasn't what was happening here. Rather than exercising their rights by going to Congress (or to the Agency's own Office of the Inspector General), the leakers had chosen to "bypass the law and go straight to the press." Such individuals "are not noble, honorable or patriotic. Nor are they whistleblowers. Instead, they are committing a criminal act, that potentially places American lives at risk."

Goss also revealed that he had filed several criminal reports with the Department of Justice over security breaches and willful compromises of classified information. "Our enemies cannot match the creativity, expertise, technical genius, and tradecraft that the CIA brings to bear in this war," he concluded. But leaks were erasing much of that advantage. "The terrorists gain an edge when they keep their secrets and we don't keep ours."[3]

By early April 2006, Grimsland was still investigating several dozen potential suspects. But they were starting to get repeat indications from a single Agency element: the Office of the Inspector General (OIG).

Like the General Counsel's office, the Inspector General's office had access to every secret that was worth knowing. As a check on executive branch power, Congress had made the OIG independent from the director, and given the office the authority to conduct investigations into any form of potential wrongdoing by Agency officers, including the director and his personal staff. If officers felt that they had been the victim of sexual harassment, or racism, or religious discrimination, they could file a complaint and the OIG would investigate. Or if field officers were concerned that an operation they had been ordered to execute might be illegal, or that the behavior of their colleagues might have crossed the boundaries into torture or other crimes, they could go to the OIG.

Inspector General John L. Helgerson had been investigating the extraordinary-rendition program for the past two years, and he didn't like what he was seeing. But neither did he like the insinuations from Bob Grimsland's polygrapher that he was disloyal. In an internal investigation of this sort, Agency employees are required to sign a release form saying that they voluntarily agreed to be polygraphed. Helgerson checked the box, but then drew an insertion mark and a line to the margin, where he scrawled "DEFINITELY NOT" voluntary.

PRIME SUSPECT

Helgerson's deputy, Mary O. McCarthy, never suspected that Grimsland and his polygraphers were closing in on her. After all, at sixty-one, she was scheduled to retire at the end of April after twenty-two years in the

Agency. Sure, she knew *Washington Post* reporter Dana Priest. She was a social acquaintance, that was all. They saw each other over lunches, and occasional dinners, but she never gave Dana an interview. No way.

The night before Mary McCarthy was frog-marched out of CIA headquarters on April 20, 2006, and her dismissal revealed to the press, she e-mailed a former colleague about doing lunch when she retired at the end of the month. That's how unsuspecting she was.

The press release announcing the dismissal of an Agency officer for unauthorized contacts with the media didn't name her or Dana Priest. It did say that the officer in question had failed "more than one" polygraph examination and had "knowingly and willfully shared classified intelligence, including operational information," with reporters. NBC News identified Mary McCarthy as the alleged leaker almost immediately. (McCarthy denied the allegations through her attorney, Ty Cobb, and was not indicted or accused of any crime.)

Within hours a concert of weasels came to her defense. Senator John Kerry told George Stephanopoulos on ABC's *This Week* that he was "glad she told the truth." Because under Bush, secrecy and classification had become "a tool that is used to hide the truth from the American people." He then went on to compare the courageous truth-telling of Mary McCarthy with the "lies" of former deputy national security advisor Scooter Libby, charged with perjury in the Valerie Plame case.

"Here's my fundamental view of this," Kerry said. "You have somebody being fired from the CIA for allegedly telling the truth, and you have no one fired from the White House for revealing a CIA agent in order to support a lie. That underscores what's really wrong in Washington, D.C."

Kerry was repeating almost word for word a comment by one-time Agency officer Larry Johnson, who opined that the firing of McCarthy "smells a little fishy." Noting that "she may have been fired for ensuring that the truth about an abuse was told to the American people," Johnson went on to comment, "There is something potentially honorable in that action, particularly when you consider that George Bush authorized Scooter Libby to leak misleading information for the purpose of deceiving the American people about the grounds for going to war in Iraq."[4]

Conservative bloggers soon discovered that Mary McCarthy was not your run-of-the-mill CIA lawyer. She had been named to the all-important National Security Council position in charge of intelligence programs by President Clinton, and was kept at that post for some time by President Bush. While at the NSC, she overlapped briefly with Joe Wilson, who now liked to identify himself as the "husband of Valerie Plame."

She also had worked with Rand Beers, who went on to become John Kerry's top national security advisor during the 2004 presidential campaign.

In 2004, back at CIA, she maxed out the legal contributions to Kerry's presidential campaign ($2,000 each for her and her husband) and to the Ohio Democratic party, to whom she gave $5,000—not a trifle on a bureaucrat's salary.

She also joined a team of former Clinton administration national security officials in financially supporting the campaign of Vice Admiral Joseph Sestak, who ousted incumbent Representative Curt Weldon of Pennsylvania in the 2006 elections. Weldon had long been a thorn in the Democrats' side, first for doggedly going after the Clinton administration for selling off military technology to Communist China, and more recently for investigating the cover-up of an Army Special Operations data-mining effort known as Able Danger, which he said had identified 9/11 hijackers early in the year 2000.[5]

Mary McCarthy's supporters began spoon-feeeding other Posties with the reasons why she felt compelled to leak to the press. It all began at a closed-door briefing to the Senate intelligence committee in June 2005, when she listened to a senior CIA official tell lawmakers that the Agency was not torturing terrorism suspects in secret prisons, they claimed. According to this new leak, she was "startled to hear what she considered an outright falsehood." Mary McCarthy became convinced that the CIA had lied to lawmakers about policies "she considered cruel, inhumane or degrading," and so took it upon herself to play Deep Throat.[6]

Representative Pete Hoekstra believed the attempts to justify her actions were an outrage. She had plenty of alternatives to leaking to the press. For starters, if she had questions about the legality of some program or some action by the CIA, she should have come to the congressional intelligence committees. "That's where you go to make sure what's being done is legal and within the law," he said.

Hoekstra knew that the Mary McCarthy case was just the beginning. "What we are seeing is a systematic breakdown in the intelligence community," he told me. "Most of these leaks are politically driven." Mary McCarthy clearly represented "the entrenched bureaucracy" and "wasn't the only one who was leaking to the media, not by a long shot."

I asked Hoekstra to comment on the theory I had heard from several Agency contacts. They believed that instead of talking to the press directly, the leakers would discuss highly classified matters with former colleagues with known media connections, and encourage *them* to reveal the secrets to the press. "That's the way it is done," he agreed.

Hoekstra had no respect for active-duty intelligence officers who took matters into their own hands. "Someone who goes to the press is no better than a common thief. Nobody's given you that authorization to determine what information should be made freely available to the public. Nobody's given you the authorization to determine what should or should not be classified, or to make those decisions for the American people," he said.

Hoekstra hoped she would be prosecuted, along with others. As this book goes to press, however, the only government official to be indicted for unlawfully divulging classified information was Larry Franklin.

Just days after Mary McCarthy was forced to resign, President Bush made a much-remarked-upon appearance at the White House Correspondents Association Dinner, a black-tie affair with a cast of thousands, where reporters and their sources schmoozed and boozed. In a side-by-side performance with impersonator Stephen Bridges, the president made fun of his recent troubles. "I'm feeling chipper tonight," he said toward the end of their routine. "I survived the White House shake-up."

Some of the president's friends walked out during a tasteless routine by Comedy Central's Stephen Colbert. But the White House staff stayed for the entire evening. As they surveyed the tables reserved by the *Washington Post*, one attendee piqued their curiosity. Newly crowned Pulitzer Prize winner Dana Priest Goodfellow had invited as her guest the former head of the CIA's Middle East operations, Robert Richer.

When he announced he was quitting the Agency in September 2005, Richer told reporters that he had "lost confidence" in the leadership of CIA Director Porter Goss.[7]

A close confidant of ousted Deputy Director of Operations Stephen Kappes, Richer was promoted to become the associate deputy director for operations after Kappes left, the number-two slot in the clandestine service. Like Kappes, upon leaving the Agency he took a lucrative position with a private security contractor, Blackwater USA, that had extensive contracts with the Pentagon. CIA insiders say that before he left the Agency, King Abdullah II of Jordan offered him a fully loaded SUV as a gift for his daughter's sixteenth birthday. To his disappointment (and hers!), Agency lawyers told Richer he couldn't accept it.

As he watched Richer and Dana Priest, one former Hill staffer wondered whether the CIA leaks would stop now that Mary McCarthy was gone, or whether the investigation would have to cut harder and deeper.

CHAPTER NINETEEN

THE EMPIRE STRIKES BACK

Just two days after Porter Goss and his weasel hunters forced Mary McCarthy to resign, CBS's *60 Minutes* aired an explosive interview with the former European division chief of the CIA's Directorate of Operations.

"Tyler Drumheller, a twenty-six-year veteran of the Agency, has decided to do something CIA officials at his level almost never do: speak out," intoned correspondent Ed Bradley, with all the gravitas he could muster.

Clearly undeterred by the CIA's internal investigation, Drumheller was an angry man. Despite all his best efforts, the story line on prewar intelligence had shifted once again from White House lies to CIA incompetence, or even perfidy. "It just sticks in my craw every time I hear them say it's an intelligence failure. It's an intelligence failure? This was a *policy* failure!" he sputtered, his thick jowls shaking righteously.

JABBA THE HUT

Drumheller had decided to reveal details of two classified operations: the recruitment of Iraqi foreign minister Naji Sabri, and the debriefing of the Iraqi defector known as CURVEBALL. Along the way, he told a series of outright lies that left his former colleagues just shaking their heads.

According to Drumheller, who ran both operations, CIA director George Tenet delivered Sabri's information to the president, the vice president, and then–national security advisor Condoleezza Rice at the White House. "They were excited that we had a high-level penetration of Iraqis," Drumheller said.

And what did this high-level source tell them? Bradley wanted to know.

"He told us that they had no active weapons of mass destruction program," Drumheller said. *Bush lied, people died!*

Ed Bradley wanted to make sure his viewers understood the full import of what Drumheller had just revealed. "So in the fall of 2002, before going to war, we had it on good authority from a source within Saddam's inner circle that he didn't have an active program for weapons of mass destruction?"

"Yes," Drumheller replied. "He says there was no doubt in his mind at all."

How could that be so, Bradley wondered. "It directly contradicts what the president and his staff were telling us."

No one at the White House cared about the facts, Drumheller said. "The policy was set. The war in Iraq was coming. And they were looking for intelligence to fit into the policy, to justify the policy."

Bradley also asked him about the Niger uranium scam. Drumheller claimed he understood immediately that the whole thing was a fake and tried to put the kibosh on the story, but the White House politicos overruled him. This, too, was patently false. Drumheller passed on three glowing reports from Rome station chief Jeff Castelli without any such comment. The Robb-Silberman Commission concluded that the "failure to undertake a real review of the documents—even though their validity was the subject of serious doubts—was a major failure of the intelligence system."[1] In the coded, impersonal language of government reports, those words constituted a serious rebuke.

The same went for CURVEBALL, the Iraqi defector in Germany who provided false intelligence on mobile biological weapons labs—labs the CIA later said did not exist. Drumheller claimed that he had seen right through the fraud, but nobody—nobody!—would listen to him, because the fix was in at the White House.[2]

In CIA circles, Tyler Drumheller was known as Jabba the Hut, after the grotesque *Star Wars* character whose toadlike face disappears into a blubbering mass of fat. After watching him on *60 Minutes,* conservative talk show host Laura Ingraham quipped that he was the only person who could make Web Hubbell look like Arnold Schwarzenegger.

"I thought he was pathetic and the entire episode degrading," a former colleague of Drumheller's told me. "Don't ask me how he ever got to be European division chief. I never heard about him until late last year with all the hoohaw about CURVEBALL."

Then there was Drumheller's claim that he had recruited the Iraqi foreign minister, when in fact he was a French source.

One of Drumheller's superiors, who asked not to be quoted by name, said he was struck when he watched the *60 Minutes* piece because he knew that Drumheller's claims were just flat-out wrong. "Drumheller never told *me* that CURVEBALL was a fabricator. Didn't happen."

But apparently Drumheller had no intention of letting the truth get in the way of a good story, especially now that he had a book contract. He repeated his allegations that the Bush White House ignored information "proving" that Saddam had no WMD on MSNBC's *Hardball* with Chris Matthews, on CNN's *Lou Dobb's Tonight*, and other shows. Then, in June, he told the *Washington Post* that "he personally crossed out a reference to the [mobile biological weapons] labs from a classified draft of a UN speech by Secretary of State Powell because he recognized the source as a defector, code-named CURVEBALL, who was suspected to be mentally unstable and a liar."

Those statements finally attracted the attention of Senator Pat Roberts (R-KS). In a stunning and unprecedented rebuke from the chairman of a congressional intelligence committee, Roberts cited Drumheller's media appearances and said it was necessary to correct the record. His staff had gone back to review the original source reports and other operational documents relating to Iraqi foreign minister Naji Sabri. They even called back for renewed questioning CIA officers who were involved in the operation. "We can say that there is not a single document related to this case which indicates that the source said Iraq had no WMD programs. On the contrary, all of the information about this case so far indicates that the information from this source was that Iraq *did* have WMD programs," Roberts said.

"Both the operations cable and the intelligence report prepared for high-level policymakers said that while Saddam Hussein did not have a nuclear weapon, '*he was aggressively and covertly developing such a weapon.*' Both documents said '*Iraq was producing and stockpiling chemical weapons*' and they both said Iraq's weapon of last resort was mobile launched chemical weapons, which would be fired at enemy forces and Israel."

Rather than contradicting the conclusions presented in the October 2002 National Intelligence Estimate, the information from Naji Sabri was totally consistent with it, Roberts concluded. "The only program not described as fully active [by Sabri] was the biological weapons program, which the source described as 'amateur,' and not constituting a real weapons program."

And Roberts wasn't speaking just for himself. In July 2006, he revealed,

Tenet told a closed meeting of the Senate intelligence committee that Drumheller "had mischaracterized [Sabri's] information." Going after Drumheller by name, Tenet said that the former Chief/EUR "never expressed a view to him, as the former Chief/EUR has claimed publicly, that the source's information meant Iraq did not have WMD programs." Roberts concluded, "The committee is still exploring why the former Chief/EUR's public remarks differ so markedly from the documentation."[3]

It was a stunning disavowal that got absolutely no attention in the elite media. Besides myself, the only reporter to pick up on this remarkable airing of the CIA's dirty laundry was my colleague at NewsMax.com, Ronald Kessler.[4]

In his self-serving memoir, George Tenet devotes seven pages to debunking Drumheller's account. He says that he could find no trace of the warnings Drumheller claimed to have disseminated about CURVEBALL, and insists that the issue was never brought to his attention. "In fact, I've been told that subsequent investigations have produced not a single piece of paper anywhere at the CIA documenting Drumheller's meeting" with the German intelligence officer he claims warned him over lunch that CURVEBALL was unreliable. "Drumheller insisted that the news of the German lunch hit Langley like a small bombshell," Tenet writes. But when CIA officers went back to the German intelligence officer to ask him about the lunch with Drumheller, "[h]e denied ever having called CURVEBALL a 'fabricator,' " as Drumheller alleged.

If Drumheller had been so concerned about CURVEBALL or the Sabri story he "had dozens of opportunities before and after the Powell speech [at the UN] to raise the alarm with me, yet he failed to do so." A search of his records showed that Drumheller "was in my office twenty-two times" during that period, Tenet added.

Tenet left the most damning piece of evidence for last. Far from having sought to warn the CIA about CURVEBALL, Drumheller drafted and signed a memo to prepare Tenet for a May 27, 2003, meeting with the head of German intelligence, Dr. August Hanning. The third of five items in the memo was all in bold. It suggested that Tenet, "Thank Dr. Hanning for the Iraqi WMD information provided by the [German intelligence] asset 'Curve Ball.' "

Tenet concluded: "If the chief of the European division believed that it was a mistake for us to use the Curve Ball material and knew that the Germans had warned us off it, why was he asking me to thank the Germans?"[5]

THE FIRING OF PORTER GOSS

George W. Bush didn't know that he was going to fire Porter Goss when he came down from the White House residence for his morning briefing at 7:30 A.M. on Friday, May 5, 2006.

The president liked the former Florida congressman. He thought Goss was making progress in transforming the Agency to more aggressively pursue the hard targets confronting America. He was expanding the clandestine service and had recruited a whole new generation of young, diverse Americans. These were long-term strides, performed quietly out of the limelight. That was the type of progress this president liked.

Bush was certainly aware of the growing flap over Goss's executive director, Kyle "Dusty" Foggo, now the target of a Justice Department investigation for alleged bribery in relation to disgraced Republican congressman Randy "Duke" Cunningham. Lurid stories in the drive-by media described mysterious late-night poker games with hookers at a suite in the Watergate Hotel attended by Foggo, Cunningham, and a shadowy defense contractor named Brent Wilkes. But so far, no one was reporting that Goss had any knowledge of Foggo's moonlighting. Until such information emerged, Bush felt confident Goss could weather the storm.

But there are many things the president of the United States doesn't know. For one, he has little awareness of the petty scheming carried out behind his back by rival members of his own administration—until they erupt into public disputes, as did Colin Powell's disagreements with Donald Rumsfeld over Iraq.

For months, Director of National Intelligence John Negroponte had been sharpening his knives, looking for a way to get rid of his old rival from Psi Upsilon at Yale. In December 2005, he had argued inside the administration that Goss was "not a team player" because he was cooperating with Senator John McCain and congressional Democrats in their effort to impose new legal guidelines on CIA interrogators.

Goss's reasoning for working with McCain was simple: he saw his operations guys and paramilitaries "lawyering up," because they felt they had entered a legal no-man's-land as a result of the rendition program. How many of them were going to suffer the same indignity as Bob Lady, who had been forced to abandon his retirement plans (including his house) in northern Italy, in order to avoid arrest? "We knew we were going to get hung out to dry," former Agency officer Michael Scheuer said later.[6] Goss agreed with McCain that they needed clear legal guidelines that defined torture (and banned it), so he suspended the interrogations quietly in December 2005 until the Justice Department could draw them up.

When he heard what Goss had done, Negroponte told his own supporters in Congress and at the White House that the CIA director was "disloyal." Once, he even used the word "unpatriotic." They were strong terms and they didn't go unnoticed. It was just a matter of time before the DNI found his opening.

That spring, Washington was awash in rumors of a "malaise" that had gripped the Bush White House. Bush's staff were dispirited with the lack of progress in Iraq, racked by internal policy disputes, and destabilized by the ongoing investigation by Special Counsel Patrick Fitzgerald. Just days after Mary McCarthy was forced to resign at CIA, Karl Rove was hauled in for the fifth time by Fitzgerald to give sworn grand jury testimony about when he first learned that CIA analyst Valerie Plame had recommended her husband, Joe Wilson, for the Niger trip. Left-wing bloggers, including former CIA analyst Larry Johnson, were cackling that Fitzgerald had sent Rove's lawyer a "target letter," saying that Rove could soon be indicted.

Sally Quinn, a glorified gossip columnist for the *Washington Post* (and wife of former *Post* executive editor Ben Bradlee), published a catty Style piece on Bush's woes that called on his wife to use her influence to prevent the wholesale collapse of her husband's second term. "Dear Laura," it began. "It's time for you to act. Nancy Reagan did it. You can too. Things are falling apart. . . ." Quinn described a White House that was closed to outside advice, "incompetent, unrealistic, and insincere." They weren't listening to anybody, not even to Papa Bush. It was time for a major shake-up, she urged.[7]

In Washington, there is rarely smoke without a hidden fire, and Quinn was right that Chief of Staff Andy Card looked wan and exhausted. He'd been in the saddle for six years, running himself ragged with sixteen-hour and even twenty-hour days. So when Bush announced a staff shake-up just four days later, bringing in former budget director Josh Bolten to replace Card, no one was really surprised. The shift had been in the works for some time.

Bush gave Bolten carte blanche to make whatever staff changes he felt were necessary, but he wanted them done right away. He didn't want people drifting out of his administration in the last year or eighteen months. If anyone was thinking of leaving, say, after the midterm elections that November, the time for them to walk through that door was now.

"Porter had always said he would stay at the Agency for two years, then retire," a close advisor told me. "He was always talking about retirement. It was not a secret." But he made the mistake of talking about it with Negroponte, perhaps during a shared weekend when the two saw each other on Fisher's Island in Florida, where they both had vacation property. If we lose the elections, I'll go longer, Goss said. But otherwise, he was ready to head home after November.

When Negroponte heard that, he knew he had his hook. Coupled to the growing flap over Dusty Foggo, it was enough to hang Porter Goss.

BACK TO THE FUTURE

On the afternoon of Thursday, May 4, 2006, Goss picked up the message as he returned from a meeting to his seventh-floor office suite overlooking the old-growth forest on the CIA campus in Langley, Virginia. It said, Bolten—WH—tomorrow 9 AM w/DNI. He inquired if the caller had left any additional details. Was there a particular file the president wanted to discuss? His secretary said no, that was it.

Goss mentioned the White House summons when he met with his staff late that afternoon. He wasn't even sure which Bolten it was—John Bolton, or Josh?

Probably Josh, they told him. (Bolten had officially assumed his new duties, replacing Card, just two weeks earlier.) And if he didn't give you a subject, it can only be one of two things. Either they're going to tell you that you're leaving, or they're going to ask you how much longer you intend to stay. As a precaution, Goss's staff suggested he draft a statement and have it ready for the next afternoon.

The following morning when Goss arrived at the White House, he was surprised to find that Negroponte had already arrived.

Porter has indicated to me that he was intending to leave by the end of the year, the DNI began, formally addressing the president's new chief of staff.

Goss nearly fell off his chair. What are we talking about here? he said. Are you saying you want me to leave now?

Bolten nodded. Yes, he said. He repeated what he had been telling the press, that the president wanted any personnel changes that were going to take place to happen now.

Okay, Goss said. Then let's do it today. I'll have a statement ready by 3 P.M. this afternoon.

Now it was the turn of Negroponte and Bolten to show their surprise. They hadn't expected Goss to take it like this, to move so precipitately. Bolten realized that he hadn't prepared the president for Goss's resignation, so he tried to stall for time, but Goss remained adamant. He would announce his departure that afternoon.

Twenty minutes later, he was back in the Langely woods, drafting his resignation letter. He knew all too well how Washington worked. If he allowed them to let it drag out over the weekend, the news would leak out in dribs and drabs and he would be made to look like a liability to the president. This way, he would go out the door with his head high.

Bolten phoned back at 11 A.M., and asked him to come to the Oval Office to meet with the president at 1:15 P.M. The president wanted to give him a proper send-off from the Oval. It was the least he could do to show his appreciation for Goss's loyalty and his service.

Both men were awkward as they made small talk in front of the television cameras that Friday afternoon. The reason was simple: neither one was prepared for the kabuki dance they now had to act out for the public. Neither Bush nor Goss gave any reason for his departure. Their meeting appeared to be unscripted and unplanned because it was.

In the meantime, sources from Negroponte's office were calling the ranking minority member on the House intelligence committee, California Democrat Jane Harman, to bring her up to speed. Within minutes of the public announcement, Harman released a statement blasting Goss for his stewardship of the Agency. "In the last year and a half, more than 300 years of experience has either been pushed out or walked out the door in frustration," she said. "This has left the Agency in free fall."

For John Negroponte, it was sweet revenge. He and Josh Bolten had already decided that General Michael Hayden, then serving as Negroponte's deputy, would move over to replace Goss at the CIA. But they also had another surprise up their sleeve. As deputy director, they were bringing back Stephen Kappes, whose noisy resignation in November 2004 had provoked the insurrection at the Agency by the DO old-timers.

Representative Pete Hoekstra thought Goss's firing was outrageous. "Here's someone who went in when you asked him, knowing that it was going to be hard, and then you cut him off at the knees," he said. All the flap about Dusty Foggo and the alleged bribery scandal was a distraction. "This was not about staff, but about getting results. And Porter was getting results."

He had no doubt that Goss had ruffled feathers during his tenure at the CIA. "But when you ask someone to do a tough job like this, you can't expect him to be Mr. Nice Guy."

While Hoekstra had been closely following Negroponte's efforts to grab as much turf from the CIA as possible, he saw something equally important at work. "This was pushback," he told me. "Bringing back Steve Kappes is a huge win for the CIA bureaucracy. They felt they were bringing back one of their own, and that they had succeeded in purging the foreign object in the blood—that they had purged the body of the intelligence community of the infection caused by the agent of change, Porter Goss."

Kappes's appointment was "back to the future. This is a vindication of all those people who didn't want to change," he said. "The person Porter saw as the primary obstacle to change is now in charge."

Hoekstra just shook his head. This was no way to run a railroad.

The night he was fired, Goss received a call from Governor Jeb Bush in Florida, who pressed him to run for the U.S. Senate. Florida Republicans weren't happy with Katherine Harris, he said. She didn't have a chance of winning in November. But everyone thinks you do, Bush said.

Goss thought about it long and hard overnight, then turned it down. But at least that phone call told him that he hadn't been fired in disgrace.

He had been sabotaged, yet one more casualty of the shadow warriors.

TREES FALLING IN THE FOREST

When I spoke to Representative Pete Hoekstra about Goss's removal in June 2006, he ended the interview by asking if I believed that the discovery of WMDs in Iraq would still be news. I said it all depended on what they found.

The congressman was clearly excited about something, and wanted to do a little test marketing without revealing the full details of what he knew. He had been hearing a number of stories about unexplored Iraqi weapons storage depots, hidden bunkers, and underground sites he felt should be investigated. Remember that the Iraq Survey Group concluded that they could not say with any high degree of certainty that Saddam's weapons had *not* been moved before the war, he said. "I suggest you take another look at WMD."

Then he popped the question: "What would happen if we found a bunker with hundreds of shells filled with sarin?"

We got the answer a few days later, after the Pentagon released the declassified overview of a report produced by the National Ground Intelligence Center, which took over the search for Saddam Hussein's WMDs where the Iraq Survey Group left off in November 2004. It revealed—*ta-da!*—that there were WMD stockpiles in Iraq after all.

Since 2003, the report revealed, coalition forces had been finding hundreds of munitions containing degraded mustard or sarin nerve gas in locations all over Iraq. In addition, they were finding stockpiles of specially designed chemical munitions—warheads designed to be filled with chemical weapon agents just before they were used on the battlefield.

This was significant, Hoekstra told reporters when he and Senator Rick Santorum (R-PA) released the report, because "the impression that the Iraqi Survey Group left with the American people was they didn't find anything."

Coalition forces recently had discovered a bunker with several hundred warheads still filled with sarin, the report revealed. This was in addition to the hundreds of tons of "agricultural chemicals" labeled as pesticides found by coalition troops during the initial phase of the war. These chemicals were, in fact, what remained of the "stockpiles" of chemical weapon agent everyone had been seeking, says former military intelligence officer Douglas Hanson, who worked for an operations intelligence unit in Iraq just after the liberation. The earlier reports were dismissed by the press even though a CNN cameraman, a Knight Ridder reporter, more than a dozen soldiers, and two Iraqi POWs were hastily decontaminated after approaching a storage bunker near Karbara where the first drums of CW agent were found.[8]

The National Ground Intelligence Center report was released just as the Senate was debating an early Democratic proposal to set a timetable for the withdrawal of U.S. troops from Iraq. "This is an incredibly significant finding," Santorum said. "The idea that, as my colleagues have repeatedly said in this debate on the other side of the aisle, that there are no weapons of mass destruction is in fact false."

But the report's findings were dismissed by both Democrats and the press. The *New York Times,* which had devoted hundreds of articles to debunking administration claims about Saddam's WMD programs, didn't report it at all. The *Boston Globe* devoted two paragraphs to the report, and the *Washington Post* just five.[9] For the Left, finding WMDs in Iraq just wasn't news, because it risked making them look like the petty, foolish partisans that they were.

The left-wing Daily Kos website featured the headline "PA-Sen:

Santorum Makes Shit Up." As proof, it cited the UN inspectors who had failed to find the hidden WMD depots before the war. That prompted a conservative website to comment that it was "rather like the defense calling witnesses who had not seen the accused commit the murder."[10]

Former *New York Times* executive editor Howell Raines, who had been forced to resign over made-up news stories, leveled that same charge against Fox News, which was the only one to devote significant coverage to the Pentagon report. "The key to understanding Fox News is to grasp the anomalous fact that its consumers know its 'news' is made up," he wrote.[11]

Encouraging that view was an unnamed "senior Pentagon official," who inexplicably dismissed the report's findings in a background briefing right after the Hoekstra and Santorum press conference.

"This does not reflect a capacity that was built up after 1991," the official said. These latest finds "are not the WMDs this country and the rest of the world believed Iraq had, and not the WMDs for which this country went to war." Then he added that the "report does suggest that some of the weapons were likely put on the black market and may have been used outside Iraq. . . . It turned out the whole country was an ammo dump."[12]

And that wasn't news?

The philosopher Wittgenstein once posed this famous conundrum: If a tree falls in a forest and nobody is around to hear, does it make any noise? These latest revelations were like trees falling in the forest but with plenty of people around to hear. They just had their fingers in their ears.

EUROPE'S PHILIP AGEE

By mid-June 2006, Claudio Fava had wound up his research and was ready to drop a thick file on the press. His document, titled modestly "Research on the Planes Used by the CIA," was a bombshell. It exposed the involvement of twenty-one companies and one bank—Wells Fargo—in Air CIA.*

Fava was a leading member of Italy's left-wing Socialist alliance, and he was following a long-standing tradition of the Left. He was naming names, just as former CIA renegade Philip Agee had before him. Agee had exposed the names of hundreds of CIA undercover operatives in the 1970s

*Wells Fargo reportedly co-owned a Raytheon Hawker 800 XP Fava, tail number N168BF, with a company that owned other aircraft identified as part of the CIA operation, Fava said.

and 1980s, some of whom were assassinated by left-wing terrorist groups not long afterward. Fava was now naming their operations.

Five of the entities he named were identified as "CIA Operating Companies." Their role was to manage the aircraft, provide flight crews, and file flight plans with the appropriate authorities. They might or might not have other legitimate commercial activities. Thirteen more were "shell companies"—proprietaries—set up by the CIA to disguise CIA ownership of an entire fleet of aircraft, most of them executive jets. Fava had less information on the other three, but he named them nonetheless. Crystal Jet Aviation owned a Gulfstream III, tail number N50BH, "used in the past for prisoner transports and flights to Guantánamo." Premier Aircraft Management, incorporated in North Las Vegas, Nevada, owned a Boeing 737-300 that appeared to be used mainly by the U.S. military. United States Aviation Co., of Tulsa, Oklahoma, was an air charter company "working with CIA as with any other private client," Fava wrote.

Some of the CIA fronts were typical inside jokes. There was Premier Executive Transport Service (PETS), Rapid Air Trans (RAT), and Devon Holding and Leasing (DHL). These were among the "assets" Porter Goss was alluding to when he said the leaks had compromised ongoing CIA operations. Fava supplied abundant footnotes (especially websites) with the report, but remained mum on his actual sources of information.

As a former journalist, Fava knew that most reporters were lazy, and didn't have the time or the inclination to do this type of research themselves. The 75-page document he released on June 13, 2006, was a huge data dump. In addition to information on the companies themselves, he provided reporters with the tail number and registration history of twenty-five "CIA aircraft," extensive flight logs he had compiled with help from EUROCONTROL in Brussels, and photographs of the planes taken by a network of plane spotters and other sources around the world. It was an investigative reporter's wet dream, all the more so because it was an official document, released by the European Parliament. Here was the first hard evidence, provided by a legal authority, of what some journalists were now calling the CIA "torture taxis."

Fava and his colleagues from the EP investigative committee were traveling extensively to gather information. Before they filed their final report, they had visited Macedonia, Germany, Britain, Romania, Poland, and Portugal in their quest to expose CIA covert operations.

On May 9 to 12, 2006, they made a much-publicized trip to Washington, but were given the cold shoulder by the newly designated CIA director, General Michael Hayden, who was not yet confirmed, and by DNI

Negroponte. Former CIA director R. James Woolsey agreed to meet with them—with reporters present—but told them he would not discuss CIA interrogation techniques, special prisons, or related issues. "I refused to talk to them at all on these subjects and would only discuss public intelligence issues," he said.

Secretary of State Condoleezza Rice sent legal advisor John Bellinger (a former Agency lawyer) to meet with the European parliamentarians, who were seeking confirmation that the CIA had set up "secret prisons" in prospective European Union members Poland and Romania, as had been bruited in the press. While he disappointed them on that score, Bellinger acknowledged that some of the 1,254 "secret" flights Fava and his colleagues had exposed *could* have involved renditions. "Bellinger didn't deny there were a large number of CIA flights," Fava's Portuguese colleague, Carlos Coelho, told reporters. "That is a positive development and a sign of increased cooperation," he added. Bellinger's "admission" of the secret flights was widely reported by U.S. and European media the next day.

If the Bush administration stonewalled the Europeans, congressional Democrats and others did not. The Europeans shared notes with lawyers from the American Civil Liberties Union, Human Rights Watch, Amnesty International, and Human Rights First, all of whom were either suing the Bush administration on behalf of former detainees or were otherwise involved in exposing the extraordinary rendition program.

They also acknowledged they had "an extremely useful meeting" with Representative Ed Markey (D-MA), who told them he planned to criticize the Bush administration "for the rendition of his constituent, Mr. Arar," Fava said.

Maher Arar, a Canadian software engineer born in Syria, was arrested in New York on September 26, 2002, by U.S. immigration officials and sent back to Syria, where he claimed he was tortured for several months before being released. When I pointed out to Fava and Coelho that Arar was a Canadian citizen, they were perplexed, and could not explain why Markey would have called him a "constituent." (Presumably, Markey considered any "victim" of the Bush administration his constituent.)

Bellinger told the commissioners that Arar's expulsion was not a rendition but was a decision taken by a U.S. immigration court. Since that fact was inconvenient, the Europeans and their supporters among the Party of Surrender in Washington promptly swept it aside. Arar continues to be held up by Democrats such as Representative Jerrold Nadler of New York as "the most famous case" of rendition, even though it is now widely understood that renditions began in the late 1990s under Clinton.[13]

Similarly, Fava and Coelho took a pass when asked about press reports that they had met with a U.S. reporter who claimed to have received information on the extraordinary renditions and the secret prisons from "active-duty CIA officers" disturbed by the practice. "Commission members have their own contacts with former agents" of various intelligence agencies, Coelho said. "Just as you won't share your sources, I won't share mine," he told me.

President Bush and the CIA could see the writing on the wall. As a precaution, the White House announced on September 6, 2006, that it had ordered the transfer of all remaining "high-value detainees" currently in CIA custody to Guantánamo Bay, Cuba, where they would face eventual prosecution in military tribunals. There were just fourteen of them—not "scores" or "hundreds," as the Europeans and the drive-by media asserted. Fourteen. Among them was Khaled Sheikh Mohammed, the mastermind of the September 11 attacks.

In his statement before a military tribunal at Guantánamo on March 10, 2007, Khaled Sheikh Mohammed not only confessed that he was "responsible for the 9/11 operation from A to Z," but boasted that he also had been planning a "second wave" of attacks aimed at destroying the Sears Tower in Chicago, the Library Tower in Los Angeles, the Plaza Bank building in Seattle, and the Empire State Building in New York. He also claimed that he was "responsible for planning, surveying, and financing" a whole series of other attacks, including plans to blow up Heathrow Airport, Canary Wharf, and Big Ben in London, the Israeli city of Eilat, and U.S. embassies in Indonesia, Australia, and Japan.

There were no apologies, no regrets—just a bloodcurdling glorification of murder. "I decapitated with my blessed right hand the head of the American Jew, Daniel Pearl, in the city of Karachi, Pakistan," he boasted. "For those who would like to confirm, there are pictures of me on the Internet holding his head."[14]

Such were the men the Europeans apparently sought to protect.

TREASON AT THE <u>TIMES</u>

Like the Europeans and congressional Democrats, the *New York Times* apparently believed that the United States should return to the Clinton era and send lawyers knocking on terrorists' doors with subpoenas rather than use more forceful tactics. The relentless efforts of the *Times* to expose highly classified U.S. intelligence programs aimed at diminishing the ability of the terrorists to harm America were not matched by a similar effort to expose the tactics and the networks actively being used by the terrorists to strike us. One might forgive the likes of a Claudio Fava or a Stephen Grey; after all, they weren't Americans. It was much harder to forgive the *New York Times*, which apparently had yet to discover a secret U.S. intelligence program it felt should *not* be revealed to our enemies.

On Thursday, June 23, 2006, James Risen and his reporting partner Eric Lichtblau lifted the veil on yet another secret U.S. intelligence effort. This time, their target was an obscure financial clearinghouse in Belgium.

The privately owned Society for Worldwide Interbank Financial Telecommunication was certainly not a household name in America or indeed anywhere else. Known by the acronym SWIFT, it kept a record of every electronic transfer of funds that occurred among banks around the world. If the government of Germany made a payment to a weapons supplier in Great Britain, chances were the money was wired and tracked by SWIFT. If a retiree in Italy wanted to send money to his daughter in Venezuela, his bank instructions at some point would be handled by the SWIFT network. And if a terrorist planner, such as Ramzi bin al-Shibh or KSM's nephew in the UAE, wanted to transfer money to the hijackers in the United States, they used the traditional banking system, as the 9/11 Commission report revealed. SWIFT kept a trace on all such transfers.

Not long after the September 11 attacks, the White House authorized the U.S. Department of Treasury to negotiate an arrangement with SWIFT, so the United States could gain access to the entire SWIFT wire transfer system, to monitor it for potential terrorist funds.

It was a highly classified program, very close hold. Information from the SWIFT program helped the United States to thwart several terrorist attacks, administration officials told the *Times* once it became clear they were going to publish the article. The information also led to the capture in 2003 of the Indonesian Riduan Isamuddin, aka Hambali, believed to be the mastermind of the 2002 al Qaeda bombing of a Bali resort.*

U.S. Treasury Secretary John Snow personally met with *New York Times* editors and reporters in an effort to dissuade them from running the story. But *Times* editor Bill Keller ruled that exposing the secret program was a matter of "public interest."

The *Times* was well aware of the sensitivity of the program, and noted

---

*In the transcript of his hearing before a special military tribunal in Guantánamo released in April 2007, Hambali denied involvement in the Bali bombing.

in the story that "nearly twenty current and former government officials and industry executives" would only discuss it "on condition of anonymity because the program remains classified."

Stuart Levey, undersecretary of the treasury for terrorism and financial intelligence, noted, "Until today, we have not discussed this program in public for an obvious reason: the value of the program came from the fact that terrorists didn't know it existed. They may have heard us talking about 'following the money,' but they didn't know that we were obtaining terrorist-related data from SWIFT. Many may not have even known what SWIFT was. With today's revelations, this is unfortunately no longer true. This is a grave loss."

At his noon briefing on Friday, June 23, 2006, the day the story appeared in print, White House press secretary Tony Snow asked reporters, "When did you know about SWIFT before [the *Times* story appeared]?"

Democrats in Congress said little after this latest exposure of classified national security programs. But New York Republican Representative Peter King called on the Justice Department to prosecute the newspaper. "We're at war, and for the *Times* to release information about secret operations and methods is treasonous," he said. Predictably, the *Times* buried King's comments.[15] Former attorney general Ed Meese agreed. He told Rush Limbaugh that the *Times* was "giving aid and comfort to the enemy"—the classic definition of treason—and pointed out that exposing the terrorist finance tracking operation was the newspaper's "third offense."[16]

Treasury Secretary John Snow wrote to *Times* executive editor Bill Keller on June 26, 2006, reminding him of "repeated pleas from high-level officials on both sides of the aisle, including myself," to keep the SWIFT program secret. Among them were the cochairmen of the bipartisan 9/11 Commission, Governor Tom Kean and former Representative Lee Hamilton, he revealed. The *Times*'s decision to publish was "irresponsible and harmful to the security of Americans and freedom-loving people worldwide," Secretary Snow said. The *Times* "undermined a highly successful counterterrorism program and alerted terrorists to the methods and sources used to track their money trails."

"You have defended your decision to compromise this program by asserting that 'terror financiers know' our methods for tracking their funds and have already moved to other methods to send money," Snow wrote. "The fact that your editors believe themselves to be qualified to assess how terrorists are moving money betrays a breathtaking arrogance and a deep misunderstanding of this program and how it works. While terrorists are relying more heavily than before on cumbersome methods to move money, such as cash couriers, we have continued to see them using the formal financial system, which has made this particular program incredibly valuable."[17]

Thanks to the *New York Times*, the United States now had lost that window into the shadowy world of terrorist financing.

President Bush called the disclosure "disgraceful" and said it "makes it harder to win this war on terror." But he did not join the calls to prosecute the *Times*.

CHAPTER TWENTY

LAME DUCK NATION

With the polls overwhelmingly in their favor, the Democrats had one final order of business to clear up before the November 2006 elections. They had to finish rewriting the history of the war in Iraq.

On September 8, 2006, the Senate Select Committee on Intelligence released a remarkable pair of reports that reexamined for the umpteenth time the prewar intelligence on Iraqi WMD programs and Saddam's ties to al Qaeda. They were produced at the demand of committee Democrats as part of the vast fishing expedition they had launched in the fall of 2002. Their goal, now that the 2006 elections approached, was to ram home the message that the Bush administration had cherry-picked intelligence and exaggerated the threat from Saddam Hussein in a despicable "rush to war." *Bush lied, people died!*

The truth mattered little to their assertions of Bush administration perfidy. Nobody was going to read the fine print anyway, Senators Rockefeller, Levin, and Durbin knew. All the press would look at would be the Executive Summaries and eventually the conclusions they had sprinkled throughout the main body of the two reports, typeset in bold italics so they would be easy to find.

What's remarkable about these reports was not the facts they contained, although they were jam-packed with new information, culled from more than 40,000 finished intelligence reports produced by the CIA on Iraq in the six years leading up to the war.

The absolutely stunning news was the scurrilous effort by committee Democrats to blatantly falsify the facts, introduce phony and erroneous conclusions, and then jump on their political high horse, confident that journalists would never bother to read the actual documents. It was cynical even by Washington standards. And they almost got away with it.

In an unprecedented move for a committee that until 2004 was known for its bipartisanship, committee chairman Senator Pat Roberts (R-KS) actually *dissented* from the report's published conclusions on intelligence provided by Chalabi's Iraqi National Congress. So did most of his Republican majority.

To understand how the Democrats succeeded in superimposing totally bogus conclusions on an otherwise factual report, you need to skip past the 122 pages of the main text to a section blandly titled "Committee Action." Here you read how Vice Chairman John D. (Jay) Rockefeller IV (D-WV) outvoted Roberts on the wording of key passages and conclusions, thanks to the defection of two Republicans: Senators Olympia Snowe of Maine and Chuck Hagel of Nebraska.[1]

Senator Snowe is a moderate Republican from a predominantly blue state, who has been careful to avoid partisan battles. But Senator Hagel is a special case. He gets a positive thrill out of thumbing his nose at President Bush, and seeks to end the war on terror by unilateral surrender and sucking up to the mullahs in Tehran. I have referred to him elsewhere as the senator from France.[2]

"Paraphrasing the late Daniel Patrick Moynihan," Roberts wrote in his dissent, "everyone is entitled to their own opinion, but not their own set of facts. . . . I will continue to draw the line when it comes to amending conclusions in a way that mischaracterizes or ignores the underlying facts."

Roberts (joined by Republican senators Hatch, DeWine, Lott, Chambliss, and Warner) dissected one by one the "myths" about alleged INC efforts to influence the judgment of the U.S. intelligence community on Iraqi WMD programs and Saddam's ties to terror that the Democrats (plus Snowe and Hagel) adopted in the report's conclusions.

Primary among them was the myth that the INC was "engaged in a disinformation campaign to supply erroneous information to the Intelligence community" that influenced the now infamous October 2002 National Intelligence Estimate on Iraqi WMD programs. (Remember, this was the same NIE that was drafted at the request of congressional Democrats, so they would feel comfortable voting for the war).[3]

"The facts detailed in the findings portion of this report . . . do not support this theory," Roberts stated blandly. In fact, the truth was *precisely the opposite.* "INC information did *not* significantly affect intelligence judgments" on Iraqi WMD programs. "The INC did *not* supply information used to support the Intelligence community's key judgments about Iraq's links to terrorism," Roberts and his colleagues wrote.

For example, "of the 45 human intelligence (HUMINT) sources cited in the WMD NIE, only two were affiliated with the INC—and that does not account for the vast amount of information in the WMD NIE derived from signals intelligence, imagery, and HUMINT sources not specifically cited," they wrote.

But that didn't seem to matter to Senator Rockefeller and his colleagues. They asserted baldly that "false information from the Iraqi National Congress–affiliated sources was used to support key Intelligence Community assessments on Iraq and was widely distributed in intelligence products prior to the war," and cited "over 250 intelligence information reports" based on reporting from just a single INC-affiliated defector.

And who were the chief villains in this enterprise to peddle "false" intelligence from the INC? Why, the Office of Vice President Dick Cheney, and his evil twin at the Pentagon, Doug Feith, whose document forgers had camped out in the now infamous "office in the basement," Rockefeller & Co. claimed.

Even the State Department's Bureau of Intelligence and Research (INR), often cited by the elite media and Intelligence Committee Democrats for its wisdom, couldn't quite stomach this blatant twisting of the truth.

Referring specifically to the two INC-affiliated defectors whose information was included in the 2002 intelligence estimate, INR told the committee that the defectors "did not influence *any* INR assessments relating to prohibited weapons programs." Regarding terrorism, INR said it "did *not* make much use of INC reporting . . . in the years before Operation Iraqi Freedom" (emphasis in the original).

At the request of the intelligence committee staff, the CIA also reviewed how it had used INC defector information and found that, aside from two sources, "most of the other reports were of marginal value to the CIA finished intelligence production and had almost no impact on CIA analytic assessments."

Furthermore, the CIA found "no evidence" that the INC had fabricated information or consciously provided false information aimed at "convincing the United States that Iraq possessed weapons of mass destruction and had links to terrorists," as the Democrats asserted.

"If you're trying to say that the INC is the one that pushed us to go to war because of the WMD reporting, that's wrong," one CIA officer told the committee.

"The facts are clear," Roberts concluded. "The prewar assessments of Iraq's WMD programs were a tragic intelligence failure. However, the real causes of that failure . . . had nothing to do with Ahmad Chalabi and the INC."

You would think such unambiguous findings would lay to rest the old conspiracy-laden allegation that Chalabi's INC concocted a cock-and-bull story at the request of Dick Cheney to sucker the United States into war.

Think again.

In the increasingly vicious election campaign that fall, Democrats behaved as if the Senate intelligence committee investigation had never taken place. They were the ones who initially triggered the committee probe four years earlier, but when the conclusions did not support their political ax, they simply ignored them. And so did their surrogates in the press.

CALLING ALL LEAKERS

For Daniel Ellsberg, the infamous leaker of the Pentagon Papers that exposed U.S. military planning in Vietnam, a "hidden crisis" had begun. "Many government insiders are aware of serious plans for war with Iran," he wrote in a feature story for *Harper's Magazine* in the autumn of 2006, "but Congress and the public remain largely in the dark."

Think of it: The United States government had contingency plans for a "massive air attack" to take out suspected nuclear weapons and missile sites in Iran, and no one knew about it! That was shocking, Ellsberg wrote.

Appearing (appropriately) on Comedy Central to hype his story on September 21, Ellsberg told Stephen Colbert that today was 1964 all over again, with the White House and the Pentagon gearing up for a new war. But Ellsberg had a strategy for sabotaging those plans: he called on government officials with access to secret war plans to leak them to the news media.

"We've gotten very good leaks on Abu Ghraib, on NSA wiretaps," he said. "But they were oral leaks, not documents." To avert war with Iran, he said the shadow warriors needed to come forward with "actual documents."

Colbert joked that by leaking the Pentagon Papers in the 1970s, Ellsberg had prevented him from going to Vietnam when he turned eighteen in 1982. "I was on a show like this and Pat Buchanan told me that I had lost the Vietnam War," Ellsberg replied. "That was a kind of honor that I really didn't anticipate."

Calling on a new generation of leakers to follow his example, Ellsberg added, "Don't wait until the bombs have fallen. Don't wait till years into the war."

In his *Harper's* story, Ellsberg noted that a former CIA official named Philip Giraldi had started to leak the Iran war plans, which of course were being devised by the Evil Dick Cheney. He praised Giraldi for revealing that "several senior Air Force officers" involved in the planning were "appalled at the implications of what they are doing—that Iran is being set up for an unprovoked nuclear attack." Seymour Hersh was writing similar scare-mongering stories in the *New Yorker*, asserting that the United States was planning to launch a tactical nuclear strike on Iran with bunker-busting nuclear warheads. He forgot to mention that the very weapons he claimed were to be used had never been built, because Congress had refused to fund them.[4]

The notion of "patriotic leaking" had by now become second nature to many within the intelligence community, and a subject of smirks from the Left. Steve Clemons, the left-wing activist who claims he played a key role in blocking the Senate confirmation of John Bolton the year before, flagged left-wing bloggers when he noticed a job opening in the State Department's Bureau of International Organization Affairs. "Want to Join Bolton Watch's Secret Team?" his blog entry was headed. "This would be an ideal spot to watch what the U.S. Mission to the UN is doing and particularly the US Ambassador to the UN, John Bolton," he wrote. "Don't tell them I sent you if you apply, but if you get the position, give me a ring."[5] (Clemons told me later that his recruitment effort had paid off, and he had a "well-placed mole" in Bolton's United Nations office who was feeding him inside information.)

On September 24, 2006, the leakers struck again. This time, they gave the *New York Times* portions of the latest National Intelligence Estimate on the worldwide jihadi movement in an attempt to drive home their message that Bush had actually made America less secure during his presidency.

The *Times* knew exactly how to spin this latest leak. "A stark assessment of terrorism trends by American intelligence agencies has found that the American invasion and occupation of Iraq has helped spawn a new generation of Islamic radicalism and that the overall terrorist threat has grown since the Sept. 11 attacks," their page-one story began. The classified NIE "attributes a more direct role to the Iraq war in fueling radicalism than that presented either in recent White House documents or in a report released Wednesday by the House Intelligence Committee," it continued.

One unnamed U.S. intelligence official selectively quoted from the report—on condition, of course, that he not be named, because he had broken the law. He told the *Times* that the report "says that the Iraq war has made the overall terrorism problem worse."[6]

Like the earlier NIE on the global terrorist threat, released at the start of the Iraq War, this document was far more nuanced than the *New York Times* led its readers to believe. Elite media accounts of the NIE focused on one sentence from the report's Key Judgments: "The Iraq conflict has become the cause célèbre for jihadists, breeding a deep resentment of U.S. involvement in the Muslim world and cultivating supporters for the global jihadist movement."

But predictably, no major news organization carried the very next sentence from the NIE, until the White House itself declassified the key judgments and released them several days later. It read, "Should jihadists leaving Iraq perceive themselves, and be perceived, to have failed, we judge fewer fighters will be inspired to carry on the fight."[7]

In other words, the real message of the NIE was that the United States could defeat the global jihadi movement by defeating the terrorists in Iraq. But the media, fueled by selective leaks, twisted the meaning into its direct opposite.

No surprise there.

What was surprising was the way in which Democrats such as Representative Jane Harman, the ranking Democrat on the House intelligence committee, fell lockstep into line behind the skewed interpretation of the NIE presented by the *Times*. After all, Harman had read the NIE in its entirety and knew better.

Yet she told CNN's *Late Edition* on the day the initial leak appeared that "Every intelligence analyst I speak to confirms that" the Iraq War had contributed to the increased terrorist threat. "This administration is trying to change the subject. I don't think voters are going to buy that."

The strategic timing of the leak was clear. Even the *Times* noted that it came "just weeks" before the November 2006 midterm elections, when Democrats appeared poised to take over one or both houses of Congress. Although the White House responded quickly by releasing the key judgments of the report, the damage had been done.

But how did the *New York Times* get access to the NIE? In October, Representative Pete Hoekstra suspended a top Democratic staffer on the committee after receiving a letter from a Republican colleague, Representative Ray Lahood, who said that the staffer had requested and received a copy of the NIE from the office of U.S. intelligence chief John Negroponte just days before the leaks began to appear. "This may, in fact, be only coincidence, and simply look bad. But coincidence, in this town, is rare," Lahood wrote.[8]

Fox News and the *Los Angeles Times* identified the suspended staffer as Larry Hanauer, and noted that he had been fired previously from a Pentagon job by Undersecretary of Defense Bill Luti. Through his lawyer, Jonathan Turley, Hanauer denied any wrongdoing and said he had requested the document from Negroponte's office on behalf of Representative John F. Tierney (D-MA) and simply passed it on. "I didn't talk to the *New York Times*, and I don't think he did either," Representative Tierney said of Hanauer.[9]

After the Democrats won the elections, Hanaeur's security clearances were reinstated and he went back to work at the intelligence committee. For the shadow warriors, it was business as usual.

STATE OF DENIAL

The war in Iraq had been going to hell in a handbasket since February 22, 2006, when al Qaeda terrorists, disguised as Iraqi police commandos, blew up the Golden Mosque in Samarra, one of the most revered shrines in Shia Islam.

Shiites believe that the Imam Mahdi, a descendant of the prophet Mohammad who disappeared in A.D. 941 at the age of five, will reappear at the Samarra mosque, the burial place of his father and grandfather. Iranian president Mahmoud Ahmadinejad frequently evokes the "hidden imam," and said that his role as president of the Islamic Republic of Iran was to "hasten" his return. Shiite Muslims devoted to the 12th Imam believe that the boy-ruler is "hiding" in a well near Tehran, and that he will return to earth during a worldwide conflagration, after which Islam will triumph over other religions and rule the world in perfect "justice."

The bombing of the Shiite shrine triggered a sectarian war in Iraq between Sunnis and Shias that claimed tens of thousands of casualties. Death squads on both sides blew up holy places and attacked schools, mosques, and markets. Americans watched in mounting horror as Iraq descended into chaos. Our troops appeared powerless to stop the mayhem.

Documents captured from Abu Musab al-Zarqawi before the Samarra mosque attack showed that al Qaeda's goal was to ignite a sectarian war between Sunnis and Shiites, in the hopes of so discouraging the United States that we would withdraw our forces from Iraq. And that strategy was working.

The Iraq War became *the* issue in the 2006 congressional elections. Democrats were blasting the Bush administration with all barrels. On September 26, 2006, they convened a panel of retired military officers on Capitol Hill, who accused the administration of bungling the war, lying to the American people, and sending the troops into battle with substandard equipment. Senator John Cornyn (R-TX) dismissed the event as "an election-year smoke screen aimed at obscuring the Democrats' dismal record on national security." But the Democrats' strategy of making the elections a referendum on the Iraq War was working.

By late September, 58 percent of Americans felt the U.S. military effort in Iraq was going "not too well" or "not at all well," while only 37 percent felt it was going "very well" or "fairly well," according to a Pew Research Center poll conducted regularly on war-related issues. This came despite a series of detailed, upbeat speeches by the president on the war, and a U.S. tour by Iraqi deputy premier Barham Salih, who urged Americans to step back and put the Iraq War in perspective, as his government made slow but real progress toward establishing a fledgling democracy after thirty-five years of Baathist dictatorship.*

Washington Post managing editor Bob Woodward weighed in on October 1 with a new book that savaged the president and his top advisors. Woodward appears to have been stung by criticism from Democrats for having written two earlier books on the war on terror that painted a fairly evenhanded picture of Bush and the inner workings of his administration. He wasn't about to make that mistake a third time.

"What's going through my mind is this is just going to be great," he says National Security Advisor Stephen Hadley told a colleague when discussing whether they should cooperate with Woodward's latest project. "So we will go into the '06 congressional elections with a raging debate"

---

*Adding to the Republican woes was the self-destruction of Florida representative Mark Foley, forced to resign for having made sexual advances to underage male pages, and the disgust of the party's conservative base over runaway spending and ballooning budget deficits.

on the war and the "incompetence" of the administration "as demonstrated by the Bremer and the Woodward books."

Hadley "understandably wanted to win the 2006 congressional elections," Woodward wrote. "Having the president answer questions about Iraq was conspicuously inconsistent with that goal. The strategy was denial."

There it was. Cooperate with Bob Woodward, and you looked good. Refuse to cooperate, and you had entered a "state of denial."[10] Woodward let his anger with the White House for refusing to talk to him show repeatedly in the book and in media interviews.

One of Woodward's main themes was that Rumsfeld and U.S. military leaders were sugarcoating the news from Iraq, pretending that the situation on the ground was improving even as the number and lethality of terrorist attacks increased. Their public assessments were "all happy talk," while the secret memos painted a dire picture. Rumsfeld had to go, Woodward argued. Why? Because the defense secretary "could not see his role and responsibility" in key decisions in the Iraq War that Woodward judged to be wrong.

IRAN LENDS A HAND

Arguably the most powerful example Woodward cited of senior U.S. officials refusing to confront reality on the ground in Iraq went totally ignored by the media.

In September 2005, Condoleezza Rice sent top advisor Philip Zelikow on a fact-finding mission to Iraq. He found "strong evidence that starting in mid-2005, there had been a flow of advanced IED components coming into Iraq from Iran," Woodward wrote.

The Iranian assistance was significant because the new shaped charges they were providing insurgents allowed them to build improvised explosive devices that were four times as lethal as previous IEDs. Instead of dissipating in all directions, these specially shaped explosives focused all their blast effect in a narrow radius, transforming the flat metal liner of the bomb into a compact projectile that could pierce most add-on armor used by the Americans. The new IEDs were "capable of killing everyone inside an armored Humvee," Zelikow wrote. Subsequent improvements by Iran of these explosively formed penetrators made them so effective they could take out an Abrams tank.

But Zelikow was worried, because the Iranian action was "arguably an act of war against the United States." He urged Rice to hush it up. "If we start putting out everything we know about these things, Zelikow felt, the administration might well start a fire it couldn't put out."[11]

Would Americans have voted differently on November 7, 2006, had they known the full extent of Iran's involvement in the Iraq War and their covert alliance with al Qaeda? Perhaps not. But had the president ordered a crackdown on the massive Iranian presence in Iraq, it is quite likely that the level of violence in Iraq would have diminished significantly by the time Americans went to the polls. While the overall election results constituted a "thumping" for Republicans, many individual races were quite close. "Nineteen of the seats we lost in the House were decided by fewer than 5,000 votes," a White House official told a conservative gathering the day after the elections.

The CIA and the State Department both sought to downplay Iran's misdeeds in Iraq, as well as their direct material involvement in the September 11 attacks. Iran's role in the Iraq insurgency goes unmentioned in any of the leaked National Intelligence Estimates on Iraq. This is either a deliberate omission by the leakers and complicit reporters, or a failure to gather critical intelligence.

The CIA also attempted to conceal its knowledge of Iran's longstanding ties to al Qaeda from the 9/11 Commission, as documented in seventy-five highly classified U.S. intelligence reports discovered at the last minute by alert commission staffers. Once exposed, 9/11 Commission staff director Philip Zelikow sought to downplay that information in the final commission report, just as he did later in his recommendations to Secretary of State Rice.[12]

Iraqi leaders had been complaining of Iran's involvement in their country for some time. In October 2004, the Iraqi interim interior minister, Falah Naqib, told Al-Hurriya TV that Iranian agents had been arrested with a group of Sunni insurgents in Samarra. The arrest of eighty Iranian fighters posing as Iraqis was confirmed separately that same week by the U.S. military.[13]

Not long afterward, Iraq's national intelligence chief, Muhammad Abdullah Shahwani, told reporters that his men had raided three Iranian safe houses in Baghdad and uncovered documents linking the Shiite Badr militia to al Qaeda *and* to the government of Iran. "Badr and Zarqawi have assassinated eighteen of my men," Shahwani said. He accused the Iranians of aiding Zarqawi's organization, also known as Jama'at al-Tawhid wal Jihad (Monotheism and Holy War group). Just one month earlier, al-Tawhid changed its name to al Qaeda in Iraq.[14]

But this type of information ran counter to the conventional wisdom in the intelligence community and at the State Department, which held that Shiite Iran could never cooperate with Sunnis, let alone Wahhabi extremists. To his credit, former CIA director George Tenet had been trying to crack heads on this subject at the Agency, but he had had little success.[15] State Department spokesman Richard Boucher commented at the time of the October 2004 arrests that if it were "to be found that Iran was providing particular support for [al-Tawhid], obviously that would be a very, very serious matter."[16]

Bit by bit, information trickled out on Iran's deep involvement in Iraq, despite Zelikow's warning to Rice to downplay the connection. In July 2005, Iraqi soldiers confiscated weapons and explosives during a raid on an insurgent warehouse in Basra believed to have originated in Iran. In early August 2005, NBC News reported that the U.S. military had intercepted a large shipment of Iranian-made shaped charges as they were being smuggled across the border from Iran into northeastern Iraq.

All of this occurred under the government of "moderate" mullah Mohammad Khatami, *before* former Revolutionary Guards officer Mahmoud Ahmadinejad assumed power as Iran's president in August 2005. Since then, Iran's involvement in Iraq has deepened and broadened, with the unleashing of the Revolutionary Guards foreign expeditionary army, the Sepah Quds, known in English as the Quds Force or Jerusalem Army.

Iran's goals were clear, according to documents captured during raids on Iranian safe houses and interrogations of Sepah Quds officers:

- to promote chaos and the ultimate collapse of the Iraqi government by stoking the fires of sectarian conflict in Iraq
- to demonstrate the weakness of the United States and promote the global anti-Western jihad
- to force a U.S. withdrawal from Iraq and eventually from the Persian Gulf region
- to preempt U.S. efforts to support regime change in Iran

The U.S. military began arresting a number of Quds Force operatives in Iraq in December 2006. Some had supplied weapons to the Badr militia and to the Jaish al-Mahdi of Muqtada al-Sadr, including the deadly explosively formed penetrators used in roadside bombs to kill American soldiers. Iraqi sources provided me with pictures of Iranian-made 81mm mortars captured during these raids as well as captured electronic mapping and targeting devices bearing the manufacturing stamp of the Iranian

Defense Industries Organization—Electronics and Communications Industries Group. But the Americans found much more than just weapons. One of the Iranians was a senior Quds Force operations officer who was caught with "smoking gun" documents that established beyond any doubt Iran's strategy to provide military and intelligence assistance to both Shiite and Sunni insurgent groups in Iraq. "We found plans for attacks, phone numbers affiliated with Sunni bad guys, a lot of things that filled in the blanks on what these guys are up to," a U.S. official who had seen summaries of the captured documents said.

A senior Quds Force commander, Brig. Gen. Mohsen Shirazi, was captured during a pre-Christmas raid on a compound belonging to Abdul Aziz al-Hakim, a Shiite leader who had visited with President Bush in the White House just weeks earlier, seeking U.S. support. American Enterprise Institute scholar Michael Ledeen called the documents seized from Shirazi a "wiring diagram" of Iran's terrorist networks inside Iraq. Several sources indicated that the documents showed that the Iranians had helped Sunni insurgents to plan and carry out the attack on the Shiite Muslim shrine in Samarra—the same attack that ignited the sectarian war in February 2006.[17]

But wait. I can hear the uncomfortable sighs of "area experts" and "experts on Islam." You're saying that Shiite Iran encouraged the destruction of a Shiite shrine in Iraq to incite Iraqi Shiites to battle Iraqi Sunnis?

You bet.

Remember the August 1978 arson of the Cinema Rex in Abadan, when 400 Iranian moviegoers perished in flames. At the time, Iran's "revolutionaries," led by Ayatollah Ruhollah Khomeini, blamed the shah for mercilessly killing his countrymen, and used the event to spark mass demonstrations against his government. Only two decades later did the revolutionaries admit to what many had suspected for years: that they themselves had planned and carried out the arson attack, in order to ignite the match of revolution.

Since 1979, when Islamic terrorism took off as a religious phenomenon, U.S. intelligence analysts have used exquisite, often twisted rationalizations to differentiate between Shiite Muslim terrorist groups, backed by Iran, and Sunni Muslim terrorist groups, backed initially (during the anti-Soviet jihad in Afghanistan) by Saudi Arabia, Pakistan, and the United States.

But all that began to change in the early 1990s, when Iran took a fresh look at the success of Osama bin Laden's jihad against the Soviets. The Iranians concluded that bin Laden's increasing estrangement from his

Saudi backers presented an opportunity they could exploit. They were right.

In 1993, Iran dispatched its top international terrorist, Imad Mugniyeh, to meet with bin Laden in Khartoum. We know about this meeting because the man who organized it—an Egyptian-born U.S. special forces officer named Ali Mohamed—now sits in a U.S. prison, after copping a plea with prosecutors for his involvement in the 1998 Africa embassy bombings and other al Qaeda operations against the United States.

Ali Mohamed not only arranged that 1993 meeting between bin Laden and Mugniyeh; he continued to broker Iranian assistance to al Qaeda, all the while he duped the FBI and got paid as a confidential informant.

I wrote about Ali Mohamed and the Khartoum meeting in *Countdown to Crisis: The Coming Nuclear Showdown with Iran.* I felt it was essential to show how Iran's Shiite Islamist leaders came to the conclusion that supporting the Sunni Islamist al Qaeda movement served their strategic interests, and how they acted on those interests.

The CIA has consistently attempted to debunk any notion of Shiite-Sunni terror collaboration. From Paul Pillar, the top CIA analyst on Middle East terror until he retired in 2004 (thanks in part to Porter Goss), to Stephen Kappes, the current deputy director of CIA, the Agency establishment has pushed the story that an iron wall exists between Shia and Sunni terrorists.

The documents seized in Baghdad and during subsequent raids provided yet more proof that such a wall does not exist. The Iranians tore it down in 1993, and have never regretted it. The only ones who still failed to recognize that fact were the old guard at CIA and the Arabists at the State Department.

And why do they refuse to recognize the cooperation between Sunni and Shiite terrorists, or between Islamist groups and the secular regime of Saddam Hussein? Because that cooperation proves that President George W. Bush was right—right to strike the terrorists in Afghanistan, right to take out the terrorist-enabling regime of Saddam Hussein, and right to keep the pressure on Iran.

In June 2007, I acquired a nine-page document from sources inside Iran that provided dramatic proof that Bush's military response to 9/11 took the Iranians by surprise—and convinced them to cancel plans then under way to launch follow-up attacks against American civilians.

This document, prepared by the Defense Ministry for the Office of the Supreme Leader of the Islamic Republic of Iran, presents a blow-by-blow account of a meeting of the regime's top security officials that took place in Tehran on October 12, 2001.

The Iranians were stunned by the power and drive of the U.S. special forces Bush had unleashed in Afghanistan, according to the minutes of this meeting. They had never expected Bush to respond militarily to the 9/11 attacks, which the Iranians knew about in great detail because they had helped facilitate the operation. They based that expectation on the behavior of Bush's predecessor, Bill Clinton, who never struck back at them despite direct attacks on U.S. civilians (the World Trade Center, 1993), a U.S. military base in Saudi Arabia (1996), on two U.S. embassies in Africa (1998), and on a U.S. warship, the USS *Cole*, in Yemen in October 2000. The intelligence department of Iran's Revolutionary Guards Corps and the Sepah Quds had been working with al Qaeda to launch a second wave of airliner attacks against the United States, advisors to the Supreme Leader said. But now they couldn't, because the U.S. attack in Afghanistan had taken out all major al Qaeda bases and sent the surviving terrorists scurrying across the border for safe haven in Iran. (As I reported in *Countdown to Crisis*, the Defense Intelligence Agency had satellite imagery and other evidence of Iranian helicopters and fixed-wing aircraft evacuating top al Qaeda operatives from Mazar-e Sharif in northwestern Afghanistan to the Iranian city of Mashad just as this meeting was taking place in Tehran.)

"This document shows beyond any doubt that President Bush saved American lives," said Hamid Reza Zakeri, a former Iranian intelligence operative who had taken part in similar meetings before fleeing Iran in July 2001. That's why the shadow warriors don't want the public to know about it, or about Iranian cooperation with al Qaeda and with other Sunni terrorist groups.

Bush is right: the terrorists have declared a worldwide war against America and our friends and allies, and America must fight back. The war on terror is not a "bumper sticker," as Democratic presidential candidate John Edwards has said. Nor is the war in Iraq "Bush's war," as Senator Hillary Clinton insists. Iraq is just one campaign in a larger war that in all likelihood will continue for a generation. If we surrender now, as the Democratic leadership in Congress has urged, we *will* lose that wider war and our grandchildren will be bowing five times a day toward Mecca.

THE OTHER SHOE DROPS

When President Bush announced his new Iraq strategy on January 10, 2007, it had an immediate impact on the ground. U.S. commanders said that Shiite militia leaders began fleeing Baghdad for Iran, fearing that the U.S. troop surge would spell their doom. That very night, U.S. forces raided an Iranian intelligence headquarters in the northern Iraqi city of Irbil, this time seizing a top strategist to Iranian president Ahmadinejad and four top Quds Force officers.

"Iran is providing material support for attacks on American troops," Bush said. "We will disrupt the attacks on our forces. We'll interrupt the flow of support from Iran and Syria. And we will seek out and destroy the networks providing advanced weaponry and training to our enemies in Iraq."

In Tehran, the new American approach generated immediate panic. Fearing that the confrontational approach taken by President Ahmadinejad and the Quds Force had brought Iran to the brink of a shooting war with the United States military, Supreme Leader Ayatollah Ali Khamenei hastily created a top secret fifteen-man commission to study new strategic and military options. His advisors described the new U.S. strategy as the "cobra standing on its tail," Iranian sources told me. They feared for the first time since the U.S. Navy sank a third of Iran's major surface ships in 1988 that the United States was getting serious about confronting Iran for its aggression. Khamenei was desperate to find a way for Iran to climb down without losing face or losing influence inside Iraq.

But in Washington, top Democrats were more eager to help Tehran's leaders than they were to help their own country. Representative Tom Lantos, the new chairman of the House Foreign Affairs committee, and Senator Joe Biden, his counterpart in the U.S. Senate, argued that the United States should follow the recommendation of the Baker-Hamilton Iraq Study Group and open a "dialogue" with the regime in Tehran. That recommendation was "music to the ears" of Tehran's mullahs, says Iranian exile Shahriar Ahy. "When they heard that in Tehran, they believed they had won."

At the World Economic Forum in Davos, Switzerland, at the end of January 2007, Senator John Kerry shared a platform with former Iranian president Hojjat ol-Eslam Mohammad Khatami, decked out in all his clerical regalia. Kerry said he was personally willing to go to Tehran for talks. As the enturbaned Khatami smiled and nodded, Kerry slammed his own country. "So we have a crisis of confidence in the Middle East—in the world, really," he said. "I've never seen our country as isolated, as much as a sort of international pariah for a number of reasons as it is today."[18] Senator Kerry forgot to mention that it was under Khatami that Iran launched the activities that have sparked today's confrontation with the West.

Former Iranian Revolutionary Guards Corps leader Mohsen Sazegara, who has fled Iran and now teaches at Harvard, told me that such offers of dialogue were "not helpful," and only bolstered the regime. "As preconditions to any such talks, the United States should insist that Iran adhere to internationally recognized standards of human and political rights," he said.

He and other pro-democracy activists I consulted agreed that the United States needed to pressure the Tehran regime, not accommodate it.

On January 31, 2007, the other shoe dropped in Europe, when German prosecutors announced that a court in Berlin had issued arrest warrants for thirteen suspected CIA officers and contractors for the January 23, 2004, rendition and subsequent detention of a German car salesman of Lebanese descent, Khalid El-Masri. Arrested by local authorities while crossing into Macedonia from Serbia by bus on New Year's Eve 2003, he claims he was imprisoned for twenty-three days in a hotel room in Skopje and then turned over to the CIA.

Masri had become a cause célèbre for the Left. After five months of interrogations at an alleged CIA secret prison in Afghanistan known as the Salt Pit, he says his jailers told him that their intelligence tying him to al Qaeda had been wrong. They flew him to Albania, released him on a hillside, and told him to keep his mouth shut about his ordeal.

But Masri didn't keep quiet. As soon as he returned to Germany, he contacted lawyers and human rights groups. The ACLU eventually picked up his case and in December 2005 filed a lawsuit against George Tenet and the CIA. They also sued two private contractors, PETS and Keeler & Tate Management, who allegedly owned and operated the aircraft used in his rendition. On May 12, 2006, U.S. District Court Judge T. S. Ellis III ruled that the case could not go forward because it would jeopardize state secrets.[19]

By this point, the European Union had swung fully behind Masri and helped promote the notion that the CIA had kidnapped and tortured dozens, if not hundreds, of innocents. Claudio Fava, the left-wing politician who spearheaded the European Parliament investigation into the "ghost flights," issued his final report in late November 2006. On January

27, 2007, the European Parliament released a draft resolution condemning the United States as well as European countries that assisted the rendition effort.

In a throwback to the policies of the Clinton administration, the European Parliament insisted that "terrorism must be fought by legal means," and then dropped this extraordinary sentence right into the lap of congressional Democrats. "[T]he so-called 'war on terror'—in its excesses—has produced a serious and dangerous erosion of human rights and fundamental freedoms."[20] Nancy Pelosi, John Conyers, and Jack Murtha couldn't have said it better.

Fava's research found that 336 CIA aircraft had stopped in Germany, 170 in Britain, 147 in Ireland, 91 in Portugal, 68 in Spain, 64 in Greece, and 57 in Cyprus since September 11, 2001. Now all those flights were considered potential "torture taxi" flights, whereas "the overwhelming majority" of them were carrying U.S. military personnel or government officials on trips unrelated to extraordinary renditions or the interrogation of suspected terrorists, a former senior CIA official involved in the program told me.

The Europeans gave a nod to congressional Democrats, by "welcom[ing] the announcement by the new majority . . . that it will investigate the CIA's extraordinary rendition program." In addition, they called on all European countries that have not already done so to "initiate independent investigations into all stopovers made by civilian aircraft carried out by the CIA" since 2001, and called for a review of existing European antiterrorism legislation "to avoid any repetition" of the CIA extraordinary renditions.

It was this pressure from the European Parliament that led to the indictment in Germany of the thirteen CIA operatives in the Masri case. With the help of Human Rights Watch researcher John Sifton, the German court tracked the CIA team to Palma de Mallorca, where they spent the night of January 22, 2004, at the Marriott Son Antem Golf Resort and Spa en route to Macedonia to pick up Masri the next day. Credit card records turned over to the German court showed that one male team member was billed for an $85 massage and a $23 bar tab. After flying Masri to Baghdad and then on to Kabul, the CIA team and their flight crew returned to Mallorca for a three-day holiday at U.S. taxpayer expense.

"I suppose they never expected there would be a flap about all this or else they would have been more cautious," Sifton told reporters. "When you think a local government is cooperating with you in your criminal activities, you're probably less careful."[21]

For Human Rights Watch and, apparently, for the *Washington Post*, the criminals are now the CIA officers waging the war on terror, not the terrorists and their supporters.

LIARS AND CONVICTED FELONS

Democrats in Congress invited the Europeans to present their report at a congressional hearing on April 17, 2007, where they hectored the Bush administration on "human rights," "torture," and the "rule of law."

Not once during the two-hour hearing did Fava or any of his European colleagues pause to say "thank you, America," for helping to keep their citizens safe. That was a point not lost on Representative Dana Rohrabacher, a California Republican, who railed against the "anti-American vitriol" of the European report.

"If you doubt our motives, you're welcome to," Rohrabacher said. "I know there's a lot of people that hate America. But when the pressure's on, quite frankly, we have known all along that at times America has to go it alone, and people will try to find fault with us rather than trying to at least understand our morality."

The Europeans and their Democrat sponsors argued that the rendition program should be abandoned because of occasional "mistakes" such as the one that landed German used-car dealer Khalid El-Masri in a CIA prison in Afghanistan.

And yet, as the "father" of the rendition program, former CIA officer Michael Scheuer told the House Foreign Affairs subcommittee, "Not one single al Qaeda leader has ever been rendered on the basis of any CIA officer's 'hunch' or 'guess' or 'caprice.' These are scurrilous accusations that became fashionable after the *Washington Post*'s correspondent Dana Priest revealed information that damaged U.S. national security and, as a result, won a journalism prize for abetting America's enemies."

Scheuer estimated that of just under a hundred renditions, just three involved mistakes. "And if they're not Americans," he added, "I really don't care."

Scheuer's edgy testimony included moments of high comedy the Democrats clearly hadn't been expecting from someone they had thought was one of them. After accusing the governments of Italy and Sweden of lying about their knowledge of renditions on their soil, he went after former president Clinton, National Security Advisor Sandy Berger, and counterterrorism czar Richard Clarke for having willfully misrepresented the program.

REP. DELAHUNT: So we have a situation where you accuse the Swedes of lying and the Italians of lying.

MR. SCHEUER: Absolutely, sir.

REP. DELAHUNT: And we know that Clinton lied—

MR. SCHEUER: Well, he's—yeah, he's a convicted liar, sir.

REP. DELAHUNT: Okay. And Berger lied.

MR. SCHEUER: He's a convicted felon, sir.

REP. DELAHUNT: And who's the other individual?

MR. SCHEUER: Mr. Clarke.

REP. DELAHUNT: Mr. Clarke, a liar.

MR. SCHEUER: Yes, sir. He hasn't been convicted yet.[22]

A month before this hearing, CIA Director Michael Hayden gave ambassadors from the European Union a detailed briefing on the rendition program that debunked the popular image presented in the Fava report.

First, he said, they needed to understand that the current U.S. approach to the global war on terror was "NOT . . . the product of just one administration or just this president." Just as Scheuer would say publicly, Hayden laid out in detail the origins of the rendition program during the Clinton administration.

He also revealed the extensive legal work that went into each case. For each terrorist, the CIA put together a "comprehensive interrogation plan" that is "approved in detail, for each detainee, by a very senior CIA official." Since 2004, Hayden said, that official has been the CIA director himself. Contrary to urban legends of rogue operators, CIA interrogators "do not freelance."

And then he told the Europeans something they really didn't want to hear: America was at war. "As you enter one of the more operational offices we have at CIA headquarters, visitors are greeted by a sign and a reminder: 'Today's date is September 12, 2001.' We make no apologies for this attitude, for our legal definition of the conflict, or . . . for our actions."[23]

One ambassador I spoke with about Hayden's briefing called it "impressive, detailed, and convincing." Now the Europeans could no longer plead ignorance about the legality of the rendition program, the manner in which CIA interrogations occurred, or the direct involvement of their own governments.

But just like the Democrats, who had also been briefed repeatedly, they ignored it. This was not about the truth, or about security, or about saving lives. It was all about getting Bush.

THE BIG QUESTION

While their election victory in November 2006 gave the Democrats control of Congress, they quickly realized the limits of congressional power. They could cut off funding for the war in Iraq, but under the constitution the president remained the commander in chief and would make the big decisions come what may. After the long standoff between Congress and the White House over Iraq War funding that lasted well into May 2007, Congress finally caved, unwilling to be held accountable by the voters for having cut off funding to the troops.

From the very first days of his presidency, George W. Bush believed he could charm or otherwise bribe his political opponents into cooperation. After all, it had worked in Austin, when he was governor. What was different about the Democrats in Washington? And so he willingly handed out political perks, naming a Democrat (Norm Mineta) to his cabinet and allowing Clinton-era appointees to remain as U.S. attorneys and as top-level bureaucrats throughout his administration, while he continued to appoint Democrats to sensitive positions in Iraq and elsewhere, where they undermined his freedom agenda.

When the perks didn't do the trick, the president resorted to bribery. He initiated vast entitlement programs such as the prescription drug benefit while the nation was at war, and ran up historic deficits. He even acceded to Democrat demands that he federalize the 28,000-plus airport security screeners, the greatest single expansion of the federal workforce in a generation, and to grant them collective bargaining rights.

Similarly, when it came to treasonous revelations of the *New York Times*, the president continued to rail but refused to press charges, apparently fearful of an all-out war with an already hostile press.

If some of these tactics could have been defended early in his administration, I believe that after the staggering losses in the November 2006 elections they must be abandoned if this president wants to maintain any credibility within his own party, let alone with America's foreign foes.

Bush remains adept at laying out the big picture. Speaking to NATO leaders gathered in Latvia just one month after the U.S. elections, he said that the question facing America was this: "Will we turn the fate of millions over to totalitarian extremists, and allow the enemy to impose their hateful ideology across the Middle East? Or will we stand with the forces of freedom in that part of the world, and defend the moderate majority who want a future of peace?"

Osama bin Laden called the battle under way in Iraq "a war of destiny between infidelity and Islam." For al Qaeda, Iraq was not a distraction from their war on America. It was "the central battlefield where the outcome of this struggle will be decided."[24]

Senator Joe Lieberman, now an independent from Connecticut, reminded his colleagues of the stakes of a U.S. retreat from Iraq during their floor debate on the Iraq War on February 5, 2007. "Our enemies believe they are winning in Iraq today. They believe they can outlast us, that sooner or later we will tire of this grinding conflict and go home and leave the field in that country open for them. That is the lesson Osama bin Laden has told us, in his writings and statements, he took from our retreats from Lebanon and Somalia in the 1980s and 1990s. It is a belief at the core of the insurgency in Iraq and at the core of the fanatical goals of radical Islam worldwide."[25]

In "key judgments" of a revised National Intelligence Estimate on Iraq released on February 2, 2007, the U.S. intelligence community warned that the possibility of total collapse of the Iraqi government was very real unless the United States succeeded in moving Iraqis toward political reconciliation. A rapid withdrawal of U.S. forces would create "chaos leading to partition," the National Intelligence Council found.

"If such a rapid withdrawal were to take place, we judge that the ISF [Iraqi Security Forces] would be unlikely to survive as a nonsectarian national institution; neighboring countries—invited by Iraqi factions or unilaterally—might intervene openly in the conflict; massive civilian casualties and forced population displacement would be probable," the NIE stated.[26]

The stakes are equally huge in Iran, where the United States faces a millenarian despot who believes that nuclear war with America and with Israel will hasten the End Times and ultimate redemption.

The big question remains: Will George W. Bush succeed in uniting our government behind him, or will the shadow warriors continue to push their own agendas, undermine his presidency, and put our nation at risk?

APPENDIX

Peering into the Shadows

The shadow warriors have done a remarkable job of obscuring their efforts to undercut the official policy of the United States and sabotage the war on terror. But sometimes the truth peeks through. The documents and photographs included here—many of which have never been published, and some of which were previously classified—show the extent to which Washington Democrats and partisan bureaucrats have put American national security at risk by playing politics. They also reveal the severity of threats that Democrats have tried to downplay in their relentless efforts to subvert the Bush administration.

Readers interested in seeing more of the evidence can visit www.kentimmerman.com/shadow-warriors.htm.

Get Dick Cheney! From Day 1 of the Bush administration, Democrats in Congress have been gunning for the vice president. The grand jury that they hoped would indict Cheney for sanctions violations found no offense.

DICK CHENEY, IRAN AND HALLIBURTON:
A GRAND JURY INVESTIGATES SANCTIONS VIOLATIONS

A REPORT BY THE OFFICE OF
SENATOR FRANK R. LAUTENBERG

The untold Chalabi story: The smear campaign against Iraqi Ahmad Chalabi often highlights a trumped-up indictment handed down in absentia by a Jordanian kangaroo court in 1992. But rarely mentioned is the suit Chalabi himself filed against Jordan for return of hundreds of millions of dollars of bank assets illegally seized in 1989 at the behest of Saddam Hussein's intelligence director. The allegations contained in Chalabi's complaint against King Abdullah II and his father, King Hussein, are stunning and unprecedented.

IN THE UNITED STATES DISTRICT COURT
FOR THE DISTRICT OF COLUMBIA

AHMAD CHALABI, PETRA BANK, and PETRA INTERNATIONAL BANKING CORP., Plaintiffs,	CASE NUMBER 1:04CV01353 JUDGE: Gladys Kessler DECK TYPE: General Civil DATE STAMP: 08/11/2004
v.	
THE HASHEMITE KINGDOM OF JORDAN, THE CENTRAL BANK OF JORDAN, MUHAMMED SAEED EL-NABULSI, AND MUDHAR BADRAN, Defendants.	VERIFIED COMPLAINT FOR DAMAGES CAUSED BY VIOLATIONS OF 18 U.S.C. § 1962; BY INTERFERENCE WITH CONTRACTUAL RELATIONS AND WITH ECONOMIC ADVANTAGE; BY CONVERSION; AND BY FRAUD

Plaintiffs, for their Complaint against the defendants, allege as follows:

COUNT I
(18 U.S.C. §§ 1962 and 1964 – RICO Violations)

Nature of This Action

1. This action is brought under the Foreign Sovereign Immunities Act ("FSIA") (Title 28 U.S.C. § 1602, et seq.) and seeks damages from defendants because they have injured and continue to injure plaintiffs in their business and property in violation of the Racketeer Influenced and Corrupt Organizations Act ("RICO") (Title 18 U.S.C. § 1961, et seq.); and also because defendants have defrauded and continue to defraud plaintiffs, have converted and continue to convert plaintiffs' property, have interfered with and continue to interfere with plaintiffs' contract rights and prospective economic

2. In retaliation for Ahmad Chalabi's tireless efforts to unseat Saddam Hussein from power in Iraq, and for Chalabi's public exposure of Jordan's growing criminal complicity with Saddam Hussein's illegal purchases of embargoed weaponry and with his torture and murder of dissidents, defendants combined and conspired to destroy Ahmad Chalabi in his business and property and his influence, and thus his ability to continue with his efforts against Saddam Hussein and Jordan's complicity with him.

serious financial trouble. Using this false pretense, defendants illegally invoked Martial Law and used it to seize and operate Petra Bank in a way which unlawfully stripped it of its assets (many of which, plaintiffs have recently discovered, defendants still wrongfully hold) and thereby to ruin it. Defendants also seized control of Petra Bank's U.S.

3. Using the contrived Bank failure as a pretext, defendants ordered Chalabi to remain in Jordan supposedly to assist with Bank matters, when, in truth, this order was part of a plot to have him kidnapped by members of the Iraqi Mukhabarat (Saddam's notorious intelligence agency) and taken from Jordan to Baghdad, where, like many other dissidents before him, he would have been tortured and killed. This plot failed when Chalabi was warned about it and left Jordan to save his life.

when in truth, as has been recently discovered, defendants themselves had taken the missing money from the Petra Bank and still hold it today, concealed in a disguised bank charges and, in Chalabi's absence, defendants conducted a sham trial of Chalabi, which defendants said, resulted in Chalabi's "conviction" for "embezzlement." Chalabi was sentenced in absentia to a prison term of 22 years, a sentence they promised to impose if he ever returned to Jordan.

6. In addition to the repeated media dissemination of this sham conviction, defendants have, more recently, and as part of the same scheme to destroy Chalabi's reputation and thus his ability to prevent defendants' ruinous operation of the Bank, repeatedly used the U.S. mails and wire communications in interstate and foreign commerce to falsely implicate Chalabi for a supposed "leak" by him to the Republic of Iran of sensitive U.S. intelligence information, when in truth and in fact Chalabi has never disclosed any such information to anyone. Further, defendants have attempted to induce the United States itself to bring criminal charges against Chalabi on false information; and

2

have submitted false information to be transmitted in interstate and foreign commerce to the United States, and its Executive Branch, which caused the United States to order a destructive and damaging raid on Chalabi's home and offices in Baghdad. Defendants effective voice against the wrongdoing of Jordan both in relation to the Bank, and in relation to its criminal complicity with Saddam Hussein.

7. Many of the actions summarized above and stated with more particularity below have been concealed from plaintiffs and have been only recently discovered. Much of the wrongdoing stated herein is ongoing and thus amounts to continuous violations of the RICO statute, and continuous tortious activity.

Jurisdiction and Venue

8. The subject matter jurisdiction of this Court is conferred by the Foreign Sovereign Immunities Act ("FSIA"), 28 U.S.C. §§ 1605(a)(2) and (3), and 28 U.S.C. §§ 1330(a) and (b), because, as alleged in more detail below, defendants committed the wrongful actions stated herein in the course of engaging in commercial activity in relation to which they are not immune from suit, namely, the seizure and operation of Petra Bank and its United States subsidiary, Petra International Banking Corp. ("PIBC"), and because each of the defendants is either a foreign state, an instrumentality of a foreign state, or an individual employed by a foreign state or an agency or instrumentality thereof, being sued for actions undertaken within his official capacity, all the defendants are foreign states within the meaning of 28 U.S.C. § 1603.

9. The subject matter jurisdiction of this Court is, alternatively, conferred by 28 U.S.C. §§ 1330(a) and (b), and 1605(a)(1) because, as is stated in more detail below, defendants and others acting in concert with them have waived immunity from jurisdiction by attempting to invoke the assistance of the United States courts and the United States Department of Justice to further the wrongful conduct stated herein, to conceal said

Pleasing Saddam: This never-before-released document is a certified translation of the Jordanian government order that illegally dismissed the board of the Petra Bank and expropriated its assets, because Chalabi had become a serious threat to Saddam.

REF: 7020/ 16426
DATE: 2/8/1989

HIS EXCELLENCY THE MINISTER OF FINANCE/ HEAD OF THE ECONOMIC SECURITY COMMITTEE
AMMAN

ITS WITHIN THE GOVERNMENT GENERAL APPROACH TO REGULATE THE BANKING SYSTEM, AND IN LIGHT OF THE CURRANT SITUATION OF PETRA BANK, AND TAKING INTO CONSIDERATION THE FACT THAT PETRA BANK FAILED TO ENSURE THE BALANCE BETWEEN ITS FINANCIAL/FUND RECOURSES AND THE USE OF THE SAME

AND [illegible] OF [illegible] ED BY [illegible]

FOR ALL THE REASONS ABOVE, AND BASED ON PUBLIC INTEREST, I PLEA THE ISSUANCE OF ECONOMIC SECURITY COMMITTEE RESOLUTION PER THE FOLLOWING:

FIRST: **DISMISSING THE BOARD OF DIRECTORS OF THE PETRA BANK CORPORATION P.S.L AND THE JORDAN AND GULF BANK CORPORATION P.S.L AND TO DISMISS THE RESPECTIVE CHIEF EXECUTIVE OFFICERS FOR BOTH.**

SECOND: **DISMISSING THE PETRA BANK CHIEF EXECUTIVE OFFICER FROM HIS POSITION AS THE PRESIDENT OF THE BOARD OF DIRECTORS FOR THE CREDIT AND FUND COMPANY AND THE VEHICLES LEASE AND THE MERGED COMPANY THEREAFTER.**

GOVERNOR

No plan?: The Pentagon was criticized for having "no plan" for the reconstruction of Iraq. But as these unclassified talking points reveal, from the beginning the Defense Department had a very specific timeline in place. This plan called for transitioning to full Iraqi sovereignty somewhere between thirty-three and forty-eight months after the liberation—that is, between January 2006 and April 2007. In fact, Iraq regained full sovereignty with the elections held on December 15, 2005.

UNCLASSIFIED

- Through coordination with JTF-IV and CFLCC, OHRA initiated the process of coordinating and synchronizing the inter-agency effort in support of the reconstruction of Iraq.

- March 2003 - USCENTCOM focused the planning effort to synchronize coalition military efforts with ORHA.
- April 2003 - USCENTCOM finalized ***OPLAN Iraqi Reconstruction*** (nearly 300 pages) to transfer responsibility and control for the reconstruction of Iraq to Iraqi civil authority.
    - ***OPLAN Iraqi Reconstruction*** was activated at the end of April 03 by USCENTCOM OPORD 10-03.

Discussion: (U)
- Adequate planning was accomplished.

- All foreseeable major post-war catastrophes were adequately planned for and completely ameliorated.
    - WMD use, oil well fires, water and food crises, IDP flow to neighboring countries did not occur in large part because of the detailed planning and emphasis placed on preventing these catastrophic events..

- The USCENTCOM OPORD 10-03 included 7 lines of operation of similar tasks to address all known requirements involved in the reconstruction of Iraq:

- Current efforts in Iraq focus on and executing in accordance with the in-depth analysis and anticipated timeline outlined in the OPLAN.
    - The timelines associated with the OPLAN Iraqi Reconstruction were as follows:
        - Phase IV A (Stabilization): 3-6 months.
        - Phase IV B (Reformation) 18-24 months.
        - Phase IV C (Transition) 12-18 months.

- A war plan can never cover all eventualities.
    - Planning is based upon known and forecasted information.
    - Since Iraq under Hussein was virtually a "closed" society, a completely accurate model of Iraq's infrastructure and self-capacity for rebuilding was not available.

Summary: Adequate planning based upon known and projected enemy actions for combat operations in Iraq and Iraq reconstruction was conducted by Central Command and approved by the Joint Chiefs of Staff and the Office of the Secretary of Defense.

The connection: Congressional Democrats insisted there was no proof of Iraqi ties to al Qaeda, but in fact there were extensive ties, as this highly classified June 2002 CIA report shows. Former CIA director George Tenet wrote in his 2007 memoir that "the intelligence did not show any Iraqi authority, direction, or control" over al Qaeda, but that was never the standard set by the president, whose January 2002 State of the Union speech defined the axis of evil as countries that aided, abetted, or harbored terrorists.

Iraq and al-Qa'ida: Interpreting a Murky Relationship
21 June 2002

- In the past several years, Iraq reportedly has provided specialized training to al-Qa'ida in explosives and assistance to the group's chemical and biological weapons program, although the level and extent of this assistance is not clear.

- Ahmad Hikmat Shakir, an Iraqi national in Malaysia, facilitated the arrival in January 2000 of Khalid al-Mihdhar—one of the 11 September hijackers—to Kuala Lumpur for a key operational meeting before Mihdhar traveled to the US. Reporting is contradictory on hijacker Mohammad Atta's alleged trip to Prague and meeting with an Iraqi intelligence officer, and we have not verified his travels.

TOP SECRET

Scope Note (U)

This Intelligence Assessment responds to senior policymaker interest in a comprehensive assessment of Iraqi regime links to al-Qa'ida. Our approach is purposefully aggressive in seeking to draw connections, on the assumption that any indication of a relationship between these two hostile elements could carry great dangers to the United States.

- We reviewed intelligence reporting over the past decade to determine whether Iraq had a relationship with al-Qa'ida and, if so, the dimensions of the relationship.
- Our knowledge of Iraqi links to al-Qa'ida still contains many critical gaps because of limited reporting and the questionable reliability of many of our sources.

Some analysts concur with the assessment that intelligence reporting provides "no conclusive evidence of cooperation on specific terrorist operations," but believe that the available signs support a conclusion that Iraq has had sporadic, wary contacts with al-Qa'ida since the mid-1990s, rather than a relationship with al-Qa'ida that developed over time. These analysts would contend that mistrust and conflicting ideologies and goals probably tempered these contacts and severely limited the opportunities for cooperation. These analysts also do not rule out that Baghdad sought and obtained a nonaggression agreement or made limited offers of cooperation, training, or safehaven (ultimately uncorroborated or withdrawn) in an effort to manipulate, penetrate, or otherwise keep tabs on al-Qa'ida or selected operatives.

The CBRN Angle. The most ominous indications of Iraqi–al-Qa'ida cooperation involve Bin Ladin's chemical, biological, radiological, and nuclear (CBRN) ambitions. Although Iraq historically has tended to hold closely its strategic weapons experts and resources, Baghdad could have offered training or other support that fell well short of its most closely

Contacts: Contrary to the assertions of congressional Democrats such as Senator Carl Levin, Pentagon officials did not claim that Saddam was "responsible" for the 9/11 attacks. As this previously classified briefing provided by Undersecretary of Defense Douglas Feith reveals, the Pentagon concluded that the evidence showed the relationship between Iraq and al Qaeda fell somewhere in between "senior-level contacts" and "cooperation."

DRAFT WORKING PAPERS

Fundamental Problems with How Intelligence Community is Assessing Information

- Application of a standard that would not normally obtain
  - IC does not normally require juridical evidence to support a finding
- Consistent underestimation of importance that would be attached by Iraq and al Qaida to hiding a relationship
  - Especially when operational security is very good, "absence of evidence is not evidence of absence"
- Assumption that secularists and Islamists will not cooperate, even when they have common interests

DRAFT WORKING PAPERS

2

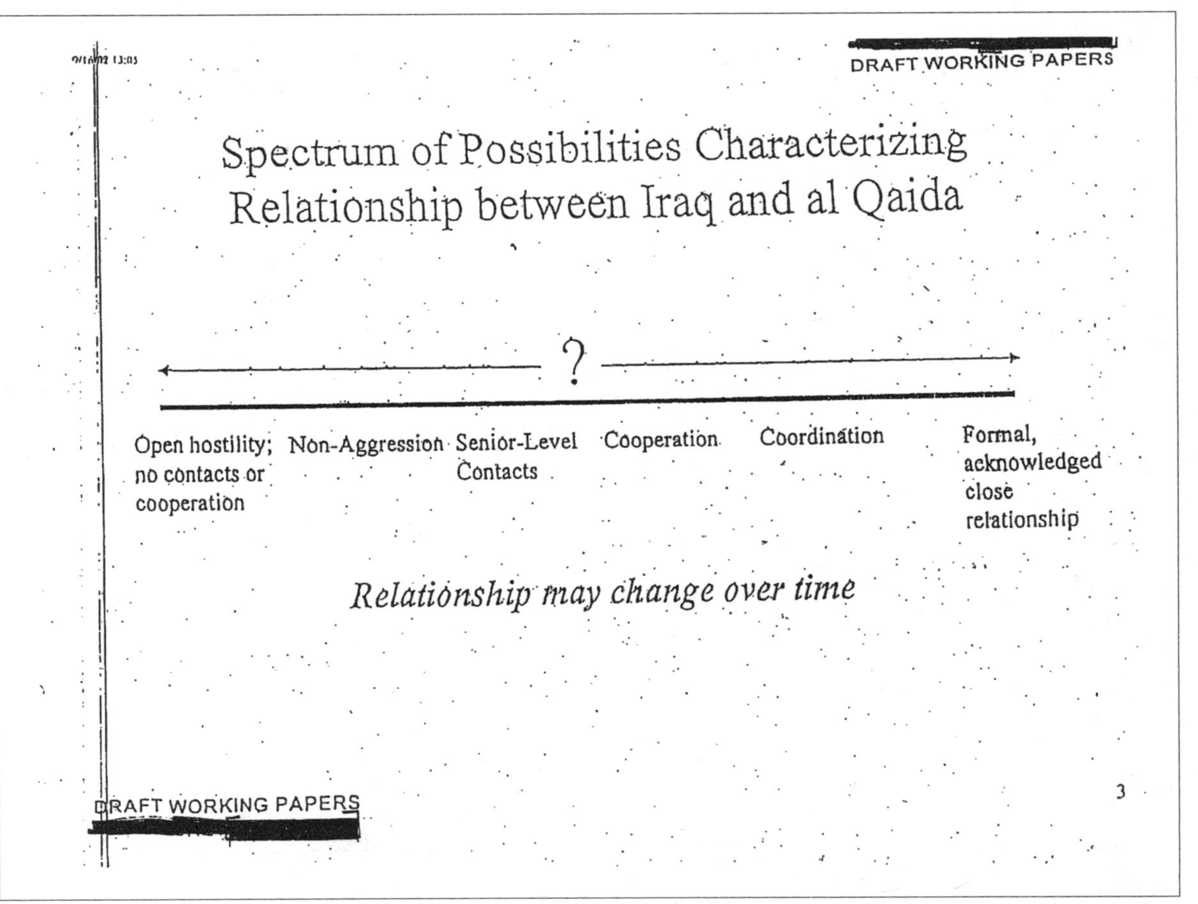
DRAFT WORKING PAPERS
Spectrum of Possibilities Characterizing
Relationship between Iraq and al Qaida
?
Open hostility; no contacts or cooperation
Non-Aggression
Senior-Level Contacts
Cooperation
Coordination
Formal, acknowledged close relationship
Relationship may change over time
DRAFT WORKING PAPERS
3

9/16/02 13:05

DRAFT WORKING PAPERS

Key Questions

- What is the probability that there are contacts between Iraq and al Qaida?
- What is the probability that there is cooperation regarding such support functions as finances, expertise, training and logistics?
- What is the probability that Iraq and al Qaida actually coordinate on decisions or operations?
- What is probability that if a relationship existed, Iraq and al Qaida could conceal its depth and characteristics from the United States?

DRAFT WORKING PAPERS

4

DRAFT WORKING PAPERS

High-Level Contacts, 1990-2002

1990: UBL sends emissaries to Jordan to meet with Iraqi government representatives to avert US attack;

1993: National Islamic Front leader Hassan al-Turabi helps UBL develop relationship with Iraq according to CIA reporting; Iraqi defector later confirms information; UBL "understanding" with Saddam is reached (non-aggression pact and agreement to cooperate on unspecified activities); no al-Qaida attacks against Iraqi regime's interests after that; UBL forbade Iraqi dissidents to attack Iraq

1994-1998: senior Iraqi IIS official Faruq Hijazi met at least twice with UBL

1996: Deputy IIS Director Faruq Hijazi meets with UBL shortly after UBL returns from Qatar

1996: Director of IIS, Mani' abd al-Rashid al-Tikriti met privately with UBL at one of his farms in Sudan several weeks after Khobar Towers attack; used Iraqi delegation travelling to Khartoum as "cover"

1995-1996: UBL requests Iraqi assistance with bombmaking

1998: Hijazi meets with UBL in Afghanistan in late 1998

1998: Zawahiri visits Baghdad and meets with Iraqi Vice President

1998: Senior al Qaida official Zawahiri meets with 2 IIS officers in Afghanistan

1998-1999: Flurry of reported meetings following al Qaida's successful East Africa attacks and ; discussions of safe haven following bombings; Iraq reportedly promises al Qaida training

1999: al Qaida established operational training camp in northern Iraq; also reports of Iraq training terrorists at Salman Pak

1999: IIS officials meet UBL in Afghanistan; additional contacts through Iraq's embassy in Pakistan

2001: Prague IIS Chief al-Ani meets with Mohammed Atta in April

2002: Large number of al Qaida reported operating in northern Iraq;

2002: Zarqawi located in Iraq;

DRAFT WORKING PAPERS

5

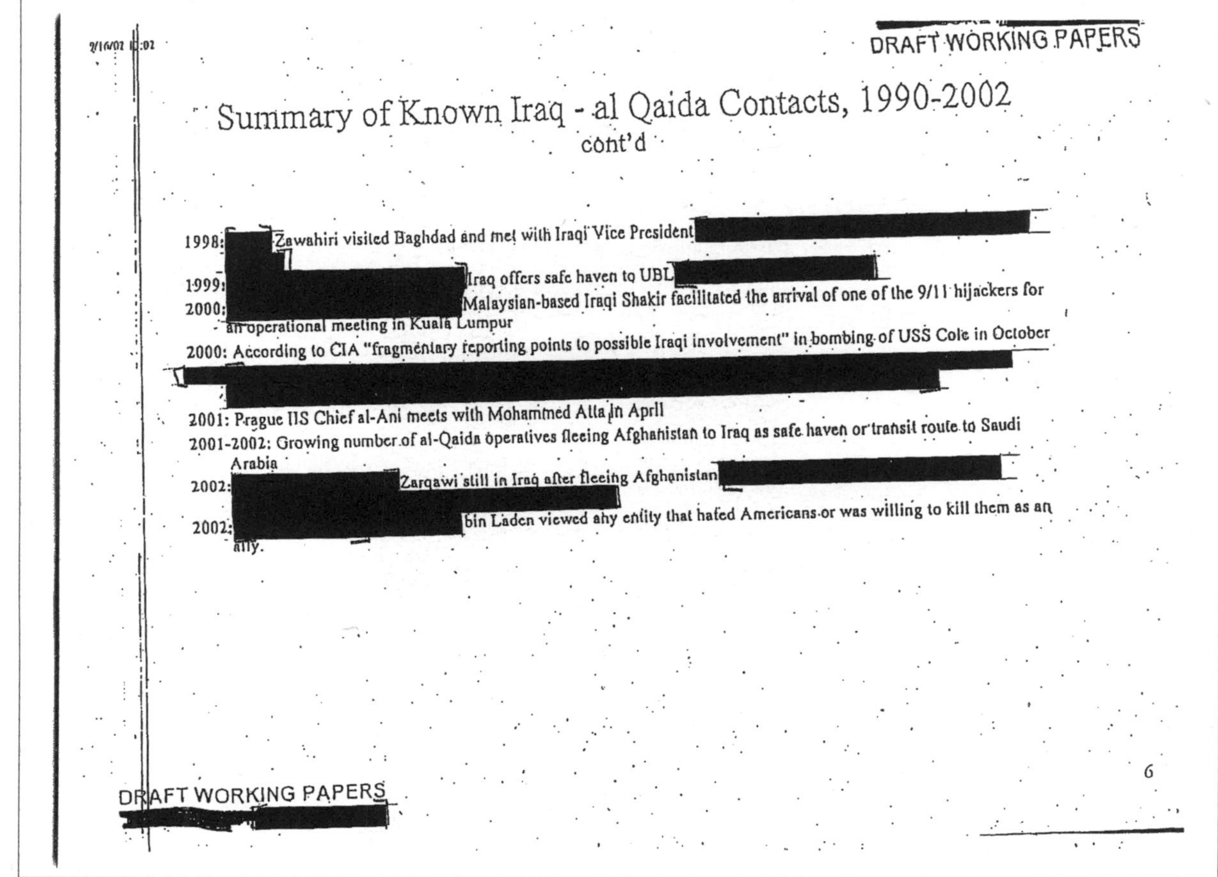

2/16/02 [illegible]:02

DRAFT WORKING PAPERS

Summary of Known Iraq - al Qaida Contacts, 1990-2002
cont'd

1998: Zawahiri visited Baghdad and met with Iraqi Vice President

1999: Iraq offers safe haven to UBL

2000: Malaysian-based Iraqi Shakir facilitated the arrival of one of the 9/11 hijackers for an operational meeting in Kuala Lumpur

2000: According to CIA "fragmentary reporting points to possible Iraqi involvement" in bombing of USS Cole in October

2001: Prague IIS Chief al-Ani meets with Mohammed Atta in April

2001-2002: Growing number of al-Qaida operatives fleeing Afghanistan to Iraq as safe haven or transit route to Saudi Arabia

2002: Zarqawi still in Iraq after fleeing Afghanistan

2002: bin Laden viewed any entity that hated Americans or was willing to kill them as an ally.

6

DRAFT WORKING PAPERS

"The general pattern": This January 29, 2003, report from the CIA's Counter Terrorism Center (CTC), heralded by Democrats as "proof" that the Bush administration lied about Iraqi ties to al Qaeda, actually buttresses the case made by Doug Feith and others. While this CIA report makes every effort to downplay the significance of the intelligence, it states clearly, "The general pattern that emerges is of al-Qai'da's enduring interest in acquiring CBW expertise from Iraq."

TOP SECRET

Iraq–al-Qa'ida Training

After contacts, the reporting touches most frequently on the topic of Iraqi training of al-Qa'ida. Details on training range from good reports varying reliability, often the result of long and opaque reporting chains or discussions of future intentions rather than evidence of completed training. The general pattern that emerges is of al-Qa'ida's enduring interest in acquiring CBW expertise from Iraq.

There have been fewer reports of al-Qa'ida receiving conventional terrorist training from Iraq after Bin Ladin relocated to Afghanistan in 1996, possibly because Bin Ladin's needs were less in this area.

ome of the most ominous suggestions of ossible Iraqi–al-Qa'ida cooperation involve Bin adin's CBW ambitions. Although Iraq istorically has guarded closely its strategic weapons information, experts, and resources, Baghdad could have offered training or other support to al-Qa'ida.

suggesting the involvement of Iraq or Iraqi nationals in al-Qa'ida's CBW efforts.

- Most of the reports do not make clear whethr training initiatives offered by Iraqis or discussed by the two sides remained in the planning stages or were actually implementec
- In about half of the reports, we cannot determine if the Iraqi nationals mentioned hac any relationship with the Baghdad governmen or were expatriate or free-lance scientists or engineers.

OP SECRET

The real *Niger story:* This is one of the documents from the Niger embassy in Rome that Italian intelligence broker Rocco Martino sold to his handlers in French intelligence. The telex shows that top Iraqi nuclear procurement officer Wissam Zahawie planned a trip to Niger. This document is, in fact, *authentic,* and it landed in the hands of French intelligence well before the famed Niger forgeries appeared—forgeries that were successfully planted with the CIA.

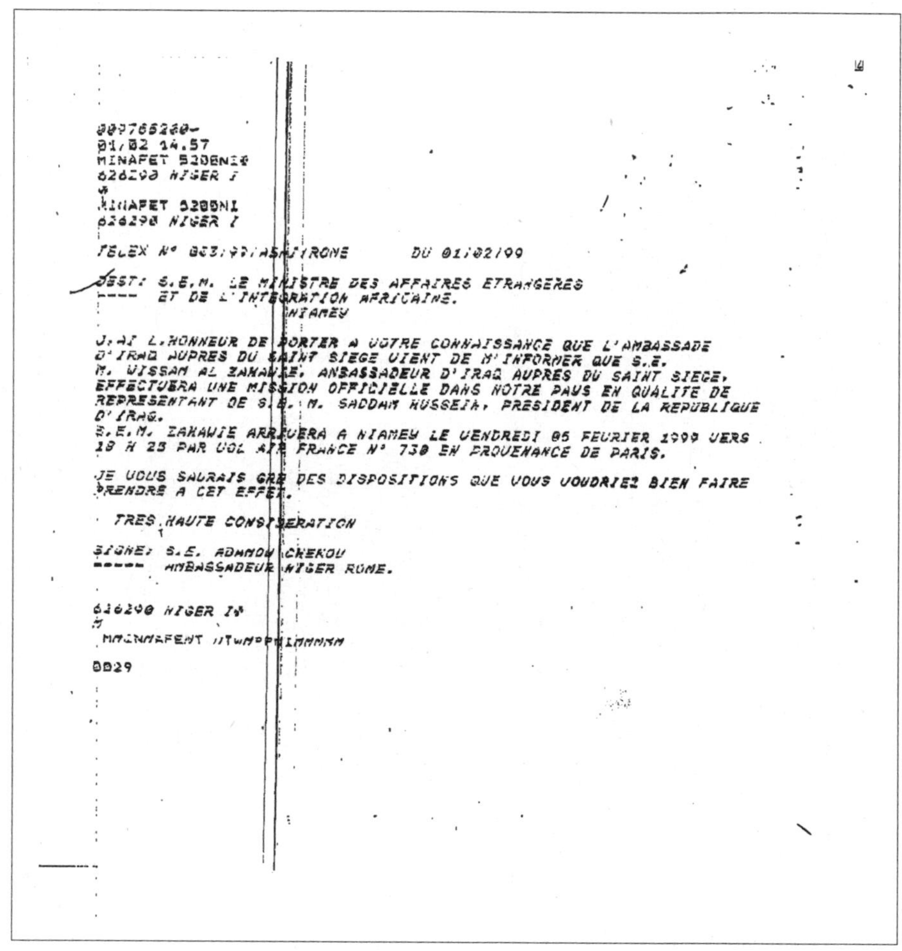

009765260-
01/02 14.57
MINAFET 5208NI
626290 NIGER I

MINAFET 5208NI
626290 NIGER I

TELEX N° 003/99/ASM/ROME DU 01/02/99

DEST: S.E.M. LE MINISTRE DES AFFAIRES ETRANGERES
---- ET DE L'INTEGRATION AFRICAINE.
NIAMEY

J'AI L'HONNEUR DE PORTER A VOTRE CONNAISSANCE QUE L'AMBASSADE D'IRAQ AUPRES DU SAINT SIEGE VIENT DE M'INFORMER QUE S.E. M. WISSAM AL ZAHAWIE, AMBASSADEUR D'IRAQ AUPRES DU SAINT SIEGE, EFFECTUERA UNE MISSION OFFICIELLE DANS NOTRE PAYS EN QUALITE DE REPRESENTANT DE S.E. M. SADDAM HUSSEIN, PRESIDENT DE LA REPUBLIQUE D'IRAQ.
S.E.M. ZAHAWIE ARRIVERA A NIAMEY LE VENDREDI 05 FEVRIER 1999 VERS 18 H 25 PAR VOL AIR FRANCE N° 730 EN PROVENANCE DE PARIS.

JE VOUS SAURAIS GRE DES DISPOSITIONS QUE VOUS VOUDRIEZ BIEN FAIRE PRENDRE A CET EFFET.

TRES HAUTE CONSIDERATION

SIGNE: S.E. ADAMOU CHEKOU
----- AMBASSADEUR NIGER ROME.

626290 NIGER I

MMINMAFENT ITWMPPHIMMMM

0029

Beyond the forgeries: This April 2003 CIA report clearly shows that multiple reporting streams—not just the forged Niger documents—indicated that Iraq was seeking to purchase uranium from Niger. Item 6 refers to Ambassador Joseph Wilson's report to the CIA quoting a former Nigerian official who referred to the 1999 Zahawie trip to Niger as an indication that "Iraq was interested in discussing yellowcake purchases."

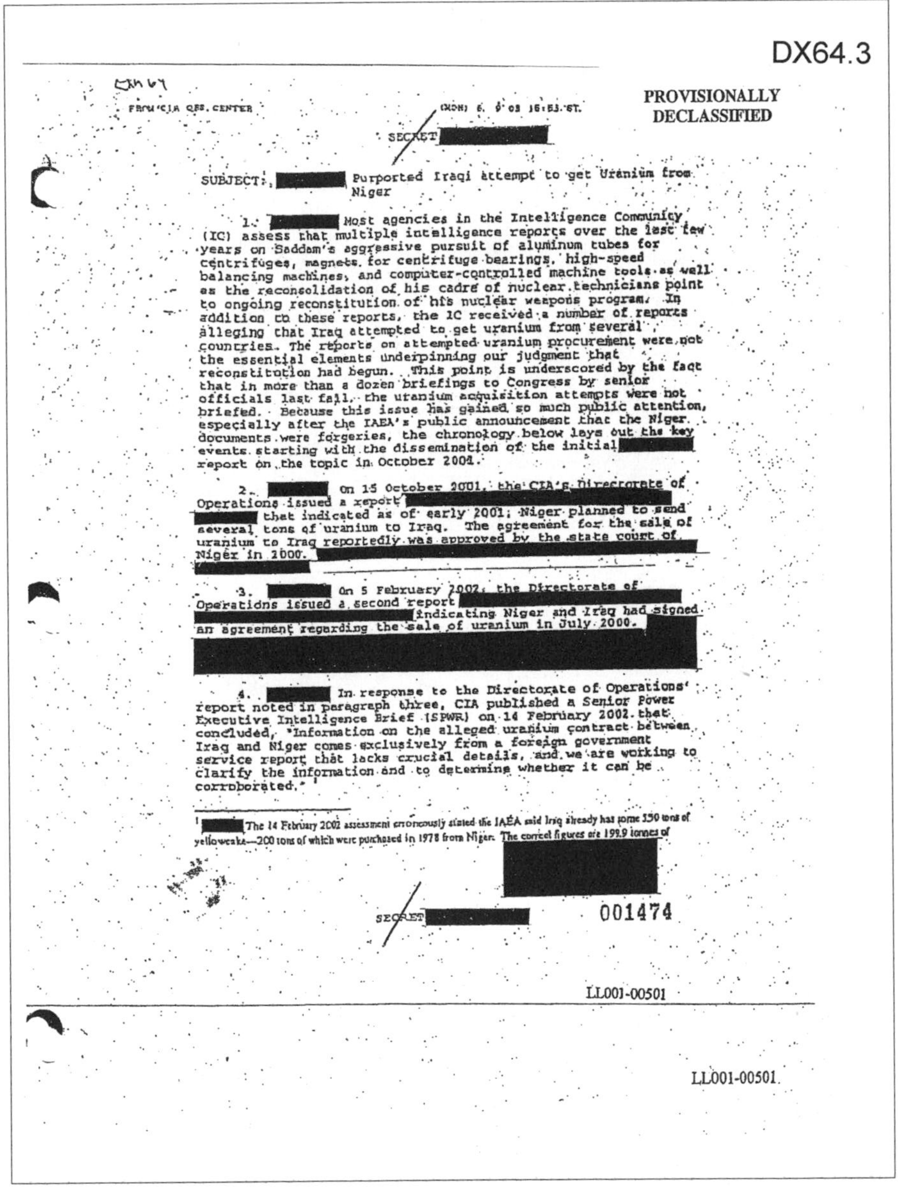

DX64.3

FROM CIA OPS. CENTER (MON) 6. 9 03 16:53 ST.

PROVISIONALLY DECLASSIFIED

SECRET [redacted]

SUBJECT: [redacted] Purported Iraqi attempt to get Uranium from Niger

1. [redacted] Most agencies in the Intelligence Community (IC) assess that multiple intelligence reports over the last few years on Saddam's aggressive pursuit of aluminum tubes for centrifuges, magnets for centrifuge bearings, high-speed balancing machines, and computer-controlled machine tools as well as the reconsolidation of his cadre of nuclear technicians point to ongoing reconstitution of his nuclear weapons program. In addition to these reports, the IC received a number of reports alleging that Iraq attempted to get uranium from several countries. The reports on attempted uranium procurement were not the essential elements underpinning our judgment that reconstitution had begun. This point is underscored by the fact that in more than a dozen briefings to Congress by senior officials last fall, the uranium acquisition attempts were not briefed. Because this issue has gained so much public attention, especially after the IAEA's public announcement that the Niger documents were forgeries, the chronology below lays out the key events starting with the dissemination of the initial [redacted] report on the topic in October 2001.

2. [redacted] On 15 October 2001, the CIA's Directorate of Operations issued a report [redacted] that indicated as of early 2001, Niger planned to send several tons of uranium to Iraq. The agreement for the sale of uranium to Iraq reportedly was approved by the state court of Niger in 2000. [redacted]

3. [redacted] On 5 February 2002, the Directorate of Operations issued a second report [redacted] indicating Niger and Iraq had signed an agreement regarding the sale of uranium in July 2000. [redacted]

4. [redacted] In response to the Directorate of Operations' report noted in paragraph three, CIA published a Senior Power Executive Intelligence Brief (SPWR) on 14 February 2002 that concluded, "Information on the alleged uranium contract between Iraq and Niger comes exclusively from a foreign government service report that lacks crucial details, and we are working to clarify the information and to determine whether it can be corroborated."[1]

[1] [redacted] The 14 February 2002 assessment erroneously stated the IAEA said Iraq already has some 550 tons of yellowcake—200 tons of which were purchased in 1978 from Niger. The correct figures are 199.9 tonnes of [redacted]

SECRET [redacted]

001474

LL001-00501

LL001-00501

DX64.4

FROM CIA OPS. CENTER (MON) 6. 9' 03 15:59

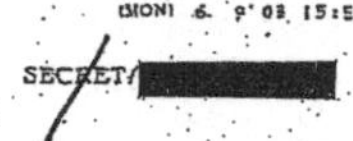
SECRET/[redacted]

PROVISIONALLY DECLASSIFIED

5. [redacted] In early March 2002, the Directorate of Intelligence prepared an analytic update that reported on a meeting between the U.S. Ambassador to Niger, the Deputy Commander-in-Chief of the US European Command, and President Tandja of Niger. The update noted that in this late February 2002 meeting, President Tandja indicated that Niger was making all efforts to ensure that its uranium would be used only for peaceful purposes. We also reported that President Tandja had asked the US for unspecified assistance to ensure Niger's uranium did not fall into the wrong hands. Our analytic update also stated that we had requested additional information from the [redacted] service that provided the original reporting on this topic and that the service currently was unable to provide new information.

6. [redacted]. On 8 March 2002, the Directorate of Operations disseminated information--obtained independently from a sensitive source--that indicated a former Nigerien government official claimed that since 1997, there had been no contracts signed between Niger and any rogue states for the sale of uranium in the form of yellowcake. While also asserting there had been no transfers of yellowcake to rogue states, one subsource—a former senior Nigerien official we are confident would have known of uranium sales--also said that he believed Iraq was interested in discussing yellowcake purchases when it sent a delegation to Niamey in mid-1999. The Directorate of Operations collected this information in an attempt to verify or refute [redacted] [redacted] reporting on an alleged Iraq-Niger uranium deal. The Directorate of Operations assesses their sensitive source to be highly reliable [redacted] [redacted]. The subsources, however, were described in the disseminated report as knowing their remarks could reach the US Government and noted these individuals may have intended their comments to influence as well as inform.

---

uranium contained in 276.8 tonnes of uranium yellowcake, which were imported in the early 1980s. The precise year of import of this material is in question as the IAEA indicates Iraq received 432 barrels of yellowcake (137,435 kgs total) from Niger in 1981. It also lists that in 1982, Iraq received another 426 barrels of the material (139,409 kgs total) from Niger, bringing the total to 276.8 tonnes. The Iraqi declaration from 7 December 2002, however, indicates that two shipments of yellowcake occurred on 8 February 1981 and 18 March 1981. These are the same dates noted by Iraq in one section of its 1998 "Full Final and Complete Declaration" on its nuclear program. These discrepancies in dates have been flagged to the Department of State.

001475

2

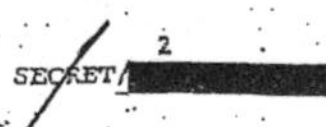
SECRET/[redacted]

LL001-00502

LL001-00502

Mission to Niger: These previously classified CIA documents, presented at the trial of Vice President Dick Cheney's former chief of staff, Scooter Libby, show that Cheney did *not* dispatch former ambassador Joe Wilson to Niger, as the Left has claimed. They also show that Valerie Plame misrepresented her own role during sworn Congressional testimony in March 2007. The Senate intelligence committee found that Wilson's wife, Valerie Plame, "offered up" her husband's name for the Niger mission in a memorandum to her CIA boss on February 12, 2002. But as these documents reveal, Cheney was not briefed on Iraq's uranium purchases until the next day.

DX66.1

UNCLASSIFIED

PROVISIONALLY DECLASSIFIED

SECRET/ [redacted]
CLASSIFICATION

2003 JUN -9 PM 2:42

SITE 3: CIA
MESSAGE NUMBER: 320

MONDAY
6-9-2003

TIME TRANSMITTED 1441

TIME RECEIVED

FROM: [redacted] Office/Desk: OI/OPS/PASS Phone: [redacted]

SUBJECT: IRAQ-NIGER PART II

DELIVERY INSTRUCTIONS: -

Pages: 3 (including Cover)

NOTE: FURNISH AFTER-DUTY-HOURS CONTACT TELEPHONE NUMBER FOR EACH ADDRESSEE REQUIRING AFTER DUTY HOURS DELIVERY.

[X] IMMEDIATE / URGENT *
[ ] HOLD FOR NORMAL DUTY HOURS

SIT ROOM CALL 6900 FOR PICKUP *

TRANSMITTED TO

AGENCY	RECIPIENT	OFFICE / ROOM NUMBER	PHONE NUMBER / SECURE FAX
WH	JENNY MAYFIELD	V.P.'s OFFICE	
		ROOM 276	
	PLEASE PASS TO		
	MR. HANNAH		
	+ MR. LIBBY		
	ASAP		

Remarks:

001791

LL001-0000581

WASHFAX COVER SHEET

SECRET/ [redacted]
CLASSIFICATION

UNCLASSIFIED

LL001-00582

DX66.2

UNCLASSIFIED

PROVISIONALLY
DECLASSIFIED

Office of Deputy Director for Intelligence
President's Analytic Support Staff

Briefer's Tasking for Richard Cheney on 02/13/2002

Briefer:
David D. Terry

Briefing Date:
02/13/2002

Principal:
Richard Cheney

Attendees:

Tasking:
The VP was shown an assessment (he thought from DIA) that Iraq is purchasing uranium from Africa. He would like our assessment of that transaction and its implications for Iraq's nuclear program. A memo for tomorrow's book would be great.

Tasking met: No

001792

LL001-0000582

UNCLASSIFIED

LL001-00583

DX66.3

PROVISIONALLY DECLASSIFIED

14 February 2002

Memorandum for the Vice President

In response to your question on the possible sale of uranium from Niger to Iraq and its implications for Baghdad's nuclear program:

We have tasked our clandestine sources with ties to the Nigerien Government and consortium officials to seek additional information on the contract. We also are working with the Embassy and the defense attache's office in Niamey to verify their reports.

If converted to feed material and enriched, 500 tons of yellowcake could be used to produce enough weapons-grade material for [redacted] nuclear devices. According to our assessment of Iraq's nuclear weapons program, Iraq could produce enough fissile material for a nuclear weapon by mid-decade if it obtains significant foreign assistance [redacted].

— The IAEA says Iraq already has some 550 tons of yellowcake—200 tons of which were purchased in 1978 from Niger—but the material remains in sealed containers subject to annual IAEA inspection.

— The IAEA conducted its most recent inspection last month and has officially verified that the container seals were intact. [redacted]

001793

SECRET [redacted]

LL001-0000583

LL001-00584

Wilson and the Wahhabi lobby: Joe Wilson was ready to stand at the altar for just about any anti-Bush cause, including this fund-raiser held by the Muslim Public Affairs Council, a key component of the powerful Wahhabi lobby in the United States. Preceding Wilson on the schedule was Tariq Ramadan, who had to appear by video because he was denied entry to the United States. A State Department spokesman said Ramadan had "provid[ed] material support to a terrorist organization."

MUSLIM PUBLIC AFFAIRS COUNCIL
Los Angeles | Washington

5th ANNUAL CONVENTION

"Examining Our Role in America"

Long Beach Convention Center / December 17, 2005

-- Program --

10:00 – 10:40 **Welcoming Remarks** — *Grand Ballroom*
Quranic Recitation
Introduction by Dr. Nayyer Ali (Chairman, MPAC Board of Directors)
Dr. Javeed Akhter (President, International Strategy & Policy Institute)
Chaplain James Yee (Author, "For God and Country")

3:05 – 4:35 **Comparing the American & European Muslim Communities** — *Grand Ballroom*
(Moderator: Ahmed Younis)
Mockbul Ali, Islamic Issues Advisor to the Islamic World Group of the Foreign and Commonwealth Office (UK)
Waqqas Khan, President of the Federation of Student Islamic Societies (UK)
Bob Pierce, British Consul General
Dr. Tariq Ramadan, Author of "Western Muslims and the Future of Islam" (video)

4:40 – 4:55 **Maghrib Prayer**

5:00 – 6:00 **Workshop A: Emerging American Muslim Leaders** — *104A*
(Moderator: Dr. Omar Ezzeldine)
Sheikh Yassir Fazaga, Islamic Foundation of Mission Viejo
Farhana Khera (Executive Director, National Association of Muslim Lawyers)
Nahid Qureshi (Safe and Free Western Organizer, American Civil Liberties Union)
Naim Shah (Executive Director, Ilm Foundation)

6:30 – 9:30 **MPAC Fundraising Banquet** — *Grand Ballroom*
Featuring Keynote Speakers:
Dr. Sulayman Nyang (Author, *Islam in the United States*)
Ambassador Joe Wilson (Author of the forthcoming book *The Politics of Truth*)

Plame game: This transcript of a taped interview by the *Washington Post*'s Bob Woodward shows that it was Deputy Secretary of State Richard Armitage, not Scooter Libby, who first revealed to a reporter that Valerie Plame was responsible for sending her husband to Niger, and that she worked at the CIA. The redactions in the text are not classified information, but expletives. The full tape was played at the Libby trial.

BW1

Scene	Designation	Source	Tx
1	**1:14-1:25**	Woodward & Amitage Interview	
		1:14	WOODWARD: ...What's Scowcroft up to?
		1:15	ARMITAGE: [ ] Scowcroft is looking into
		1:16	the yellowcake thing.
		1:17	WOODWARD: Oh yeah?
		1:18	ARMITAGE: As the PFIAB
		1:19	WOODWARD: Yeah. What happened there?
		1:20	ARMITAGE: They're back together. [coughs] They
		1:21	knew with yellowcake, the CIA is not going to be hurt by this
		1:22	one---
		1:23	WOODWARD: I know, that's---
		1:24	ARMITAGE: -- Hadley and Bob Joseph know. It's
		1:25	documented. We've got our documents on it. We're clean as a
2	**2:1-3:2**	Woodward & Amitage Interview	
		2:1	[ ] whistle. And George personally got it out of the
		2:2	Cincinatti speech of the president.
		2:3	WOODWARD: Oh he did?
		2:4	ARMITAGE: Oh yeah.
		2:5	WOODWARD: Oh really?
		2:6	ARMITAGE: Yeah.
		2:7	WOODWARD: It was taken out?
		2:8	ARMITAGE: Taken out. George said you can't
		2:9	do this.
		2:10	WOODWARD: How come it wasn't taken out of the State
		2:11	of the Union then?
		2:12	ARMITAGE: Because I think it was overruled by
		2:13	the types down at the White House. Condi doesn't like being
		2:14	in the hot spot. But she ---
		2:15	WOODWARD: But it was Joe Wilson who was sent by
		2:16	the agency. I mean that's just ---
		2:17	ARMITAGE: His wife works in the agency.
		2:18	WOODWARD: --- Why doesn't that come out? Why does ---
		2:19	ARMITAGE: Everyone knows it.
		2:20	WOODWARD: ---that have to be a big secret?
		2:21	Everyone knows.
		2:22	ARMITAGE: Yeah. And I know [ ] Joe Wilson's
		2:23	been calling everybody. He's pissed off because he was
		2:24	designated as a low-level guy, went out to look at it. So,
		2:25	he's all pissed off.
		3:1	WOODWARD: But why would they send him?
		3:2	ARMITAGE: Because his wife's a [ ]
3	**3:2-3:23**	Woodward & Amitage Interview	

Printed: 2/12/2007 1:27:59PM

Page 1 of 2

BW1

ARMITAGE: Because his wife's a [ ] analyst at the agency.
WOODWARD: It's still weird.
ARMITAGE: It---It's perfect. This is what she does she is a WMD analyst out there.
WOODWARD: Oh she is.
ARMITAGE: Yeah.
WOODWARD: Oh, I see.
ARMITAGE: [ ] look at it.
WOODWARD: Oh I see. I didn't [ ].
ARMITAGE: Yeah. See?
WOODWARD: Oh, she's the chief WMD?
ARMITAGE: No she isn't the chief, no.
WOODWARD: But high enough up that she can say, "Oh yeah, hubby will go."
ARMITAGE: Yeah, he knows Africa.
WOODWARD: Was she out there with him?
ARMITAGE: No.
WOODWARD: When he was ambassador?
ARMITAGE: Not to my knowledge. I don't know. I don't know if she was out there or not. But his wife is in the agency and is a WMD analyst. How about that [ ]?

Total time for all Scripts in this report: 00:01:45

The NIE: The much-disputed October 2002 National Intelligence Estimate on Iraq's WMD programs, like virtually all intelligence estimates, provides heavily caveated conclusions. But the Bush administration and Congress based their assessment that allowing Saddam Hussein to remain in power constituted an unacceptable threat to the United States on key judgments in which the intelligence community had "high confidence."

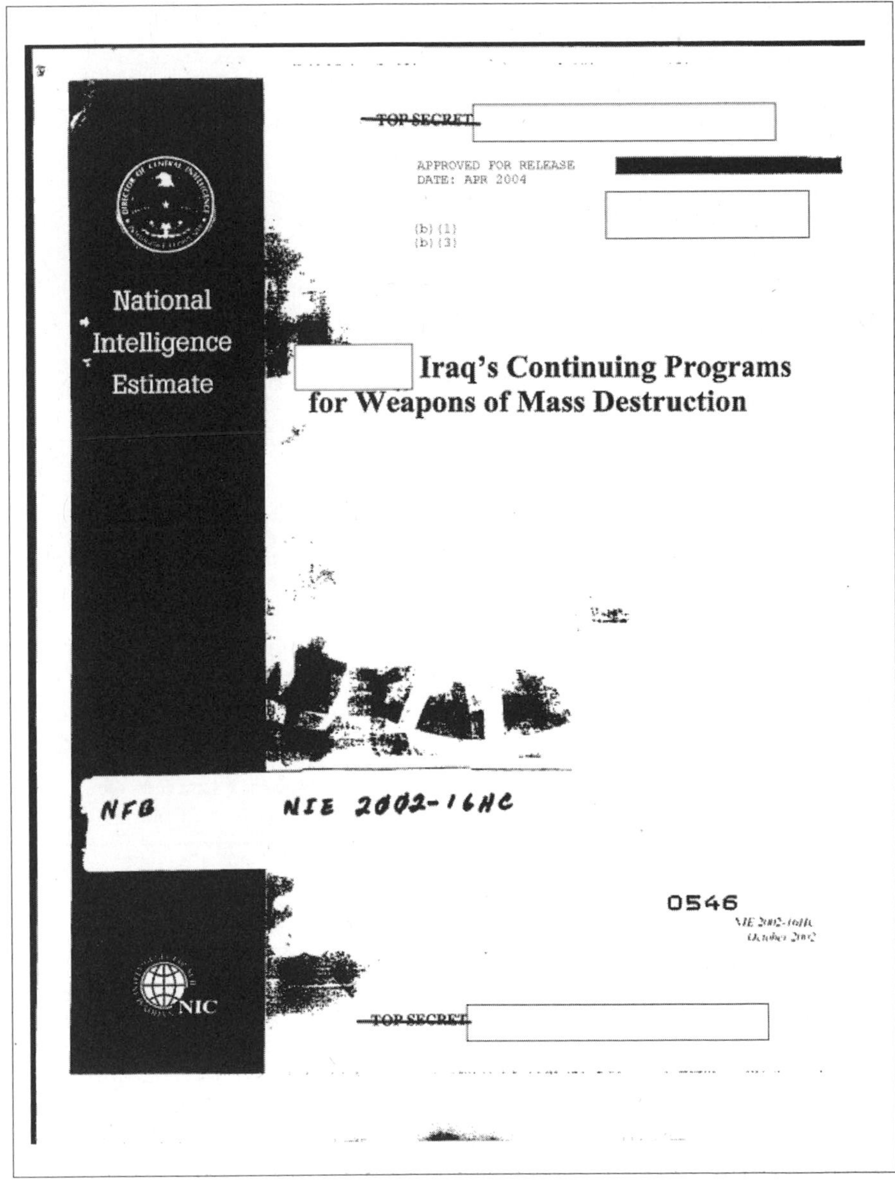

~~TOP SECRET~~

APPROVED FOR RELEASE
DATE: APR 2004

(b)(1)
(b)(3)

National Intelligence Estimate

Iraq's Continuing Programs for Weapons of Mass Destruction

NFB NIE 2002-16HC

0546

NIC

~~TOP SECRET~~

~~TOP SECRET~~

- Saddam might use CBW after an initial advance into Iraqi territory, but early use of WMD could foreclose diplomatic options for stalling the US advance.

- He probably would use CBW when he perceived he irretrievably had lost control of the military and security situation, but we are unlikely to know when Saddam reaches that point.

- We judge that Saddam would be more likely to use chemical weapons than biological weapons on the battlefield.

- Saddam historically has maintained tight control over the use of WMD; however, he probably has provided contingency instructions to his commanders to use CBW in specific circumstances.

Baghdad for now appears to be drawing a line short of conducting terrorist attacks with conventional or CBW against the United States, fearing that exposure of Iraqi involvement would provide Washington a stronger cause for making war.

Iraq probably would attempt clandestine attacks against the US Homeland if Baghdad feared an attack that threatened the survival of the regime were imminent or unavoidable, or possibly for revenge. Such attacks—more likely with biological than chemical agents—probably would be carried out by special forces or intelligence operatives.

- The Iraqi Intelligence Service (IIS) probably has been directed to conduct clandestine attacks against US and Allied interests in the Middle East in the event the United States takes action against Iraq. The IIS probably would be the primary means by which Iraq would attempt to conduct any CBW attacks on the US Homeland, although we have no specific intelligence information that Saddam's regime has directed attacks against US territory.

Saddam, if sufficiently desperate, might decide that only an organization such as al-Qa'ida—with worldwide reach and extensive terrorist infrastructure, and already engaged in a life-or-death struggle against the United States—could perpetrate the type of terrorist attack that he would hope to conduct.

- In such circumstances, he might decide that the extreme step of assisting the Islamist terrorists in conducting a CBW attack against the United States would be his last chance to exact vengeance by taking a large number of victims with him.

State/INR Alternative View of Iraq's Nuclear Program

The Assistant Secretary of State for Intelligence and Research (INR) believes that Saddam continues to want nuclear weapons and that available evidence indicates that Baghdad is pursuing at least a limited effort to maintain and acquire nuclear weapon-related capabilities. The activities we have detected do not, however, add up to a compelling case that Iraq is currently pursuing what INR would consider to be an integrated and comprehensive approach to

(continued on next page...)

~~TOP SECRET~~

(continued ...) **State/INR Alternative View**

acquire nuclear weapons. Iraq may be doing so, but INR considers the available evidence inadequate to support such a judgment. Lacking persuasive evidence that Baghdad has launched a coherent effort to reconstitute its nuclear weapons program, INR is unwilling to speculate that such an effort began soon after the departure of UN inspectors or to project a timeline for the completion of activities it does not now see happening. As a result, INR is unable to predict when Iraq could acquire a nuclear device or weapon.

In INR's view Iraq's efforts to acquire aluminum tubes is central to the argument that Baghdad is reconstituting its nuclear weapons program, but INR is not persuaded that the tubes in question are intended for use as centrifuge rotors. INR accepts the judgment of technical experts at the U.S. Department of Energy (DOE) who have concluded that the tubes Iraq seeks to acquire are poorly suited for use in gas centrifuges to be used for uranium enrichment and finds unpersuasive the arguments advanced by others to make the case that they are intended for that purpose. INR considers it far more likely that the tubes are intended for another purpose, most likely the production of artillery rockets. The very large quantities being sought, the way the tubes were tested by the Iraqis, and the atypical lack of attention to operational security in the procurement efforts are among the factors, in addition to the DOE assessment, that lead INR to conclude that the tubes are not intended for use in Iraq's nuclear weapon program.

(U) Confidence Levels for Selected Key Judgments in This Estimate

High Confidence:

- Iraq is continuing, and in some areas expanding, its chemical, biological, nuclear and missile programs contrary to UN resolutions.
- We are not detecting portions of these weapons programs.
- Iraq possesses proscribed chemical and biological weapons and missiles.
- Iraq could make a nuclear weapon in months to a year once it acquires sufficient weapons-grade fissile material.

Moderate Confidence:

- Iraq does not yet have a nuclear weapon or sufficient material to make one but is likely to have a weapon by 2007 to 2009. (See INR alternative view, page 84).

Low Confidence:

- When Saddam would use weapons of mass destruction.
- Whether Saddam would engage in clandestine attacks against the US Homeland.
- Whether in desperation Saddam would share chemical or biological weapons with al-Qa'ida.

~~TOP SECRET~~

"Extraordinary renditions": On May 21, 2002, the State Department's Counterterrorism coordinator released the following list of individuals who were extradited or "rendered" to other countries prior to the September 11 attacks—proof positive that so-called extraordinary renditions were not invented by the Bush administration, but in fact began under Clinton. These renditions have been called "kidnappings" by Bush administration critics such as Human Rights Watch.

Appendix D

Extraditions and Renditions of Terrorists to the United States

Extraditions and Renditions of Terrorists to the United States, 1993-2001

Date	Name	Extradition or Rendition	From
March 1993	Mahmoud Abu Halima (February 1993 World Trade Center bombing)	Extradition	*
July 1993	Mohammed Ali Rezaq (November 1985 hijacking of Egyptair 648)	Rendition	Nigeria
February 1995	Ramzi Ahmed Yousef (January 1995 Far East bomb plot, February 1993 World Trade Center bombing)	Extradition	Pakistan
April 1995	Abdul Hakim Murad (January 1995 Far East bomb plot)	Rendition	Philippines
August 1995	Eyad Mahmoud Ismail Najim (February 1993 World Trade Center bombing)	Extradition	Jordan
December 1995	Wali Khan Amin Shah (January 1995 Far East bomb plot)	Rendition	*
September 1996	Tsutomu Shirosaki (May 1986 attack on US Embassy, Jakarta)	Rendition	*
June 1997	Mir Aimal Kansi (January 1993 shooting outside CIA headquarters)	Rendition	*
June 1998	Mohammed Rashid (August 1982 Pan Am bombing)	Rendition	*
August 1998	Mohamed Rashed Daoud Al-Owhali (August 1998 US Embassy bombing in Kenya)	Rendition	Kenya
August 1998	Mohamed Sadeek Odeh (August 1998 US Embassy bombing in Kenya)	Rendition	Kenya
December 1998	Mamdouh Mahmud Salim (August 1998 East Africa bombings)	Extradition	Germany
October 1999	Khalfan Khamis Mohamed (August 1998 US Embassy bombing in Tanzania)	Rendition	South Africa
September 2001	Zayd Hassan Abd al-Latif Masud al-Safarini (1986 hijacking of PanAm 73 in Karachi, Pakistan)	Rendition	*

* Country not disclosed

Lady left out to dry: In 2005, an Italian judge issued arrest warrants for nineteen CIA officers and military personnel in connection with the disappearance of suspected al Qaeda operative Abu Omar in Milan. Most of the names, revealed here for the first time, are pseudonyms—with the exception of the CIA's chief of station for Milan, Robert Seldon Lady.

TRIBUNALE DI MILANO

Sezione Giudice per le indagini preliminari

n. 10838/05 R.G.N.R.

n. 1966/05 R.G.GIP

THE JUDGE PRESIDING OVER PRELIMINARY INVESTIGATIONS

Having examined the Prosecutor's request, in which custodial measures are sought for:

1) ADLER Monica Courtney, born in Seattle (Washington - USA) on 02/02/1973, US citizen with US passport n. 017017139 (issued on 07.25.01), international driver's licence (copy acquired) n. 66605387, issued by US Authority in Heatrow (Florida) on 04.03.2002, Diners Club credit card n. 38541798540000 (expiry date May/2004), resident at *2001 N.Adams, Arlington – VIRGINIA – 22201*;
2) ASHERLEIGH Gregory, born in Hyattsville – Maryland (USA) on 12/23/1955, *Coachmen Enterprises Washington, DC P.O. Box 91228 Washington DC (USA)* or *STS Inc. P.O. Box 1606 Hyattsville (Maryland) 20788 (USA)*, telephone number 3015953823; US citizen with US passport n. 015135635, issued on 06.04.96; US driver's licence n. 66605685; Visa Card credit card n. 4118160311575248 (expiry date June/2005)
3) CARRERA Lorenzo Gabriel, born in Texas (USA) il 01.29.71, US citizen with US passport n. 016422583, issued on 02.12.95, or n. 016422583, issued on 01.28.00; Visa Card credit card n. 4118160306976955 (expiry date October/2005) and Diners Club credit card n. 38502203140000 (expiry date October/2004)

13) IBANEZ Brenda Liliana, born in New York (USA) on 01.07.60, *Coachmen Enterprises Washington, DC P.O. Box 91228 Washington DC (USA)*. Telephone number in Washington DC. 2026823098; US citizen with US passport n. 017018953; Visa Card credit card n. 4118165007635784 (expiry date aprile/2003) and Delta Airlines *Frequent flyer* card n. 2349251336;
14) LADY Robert Seldon, born in Tegucigalpa (Honduras) on 21.05.54, US citizen, domiciled or residente in via Don Bosco n. 40, in Penango (AT), Italy;
15) LOGAN Cyntia Dame, born in Maryland (USA) on 05/01/1960; *Coachmen Enterprises Washington, DC P.O. Box 91228 Washington DC (USA)*. US citizen with US passport n. 016430730 (copy acqured), issued on 01.03.2000 by the *Passport Agency* in Washington, Visa Card credit card n. 4118165007635768 (expiry date April/2003), SPG card (Special Preferred Guest Westin Hotel), type "A", n. 50556297010, United Airlines *Frequent flyer* card n. 01394828870;
16) PURVIS L. George, born in China on 05.29.59, 21008 Matchlock Ct 20147 Ashburn – Virginia (USA), US citizen with US passport n. 015645726, issued on 05.20.97; Master Card credit card n. 5466160067501849 (expiry date March/2003); e-mail address "loiep53@aol.com"; United Airlines *Frequent flyer* card n. 01208942316; Hilton Honors card n. 441369809

ARE UNDER INVESTIGATION
For the following offences:

Felony ex Arts. 110, 112 n° 1, 605 criminal code, whereby among themselves and together with others (also Egyptian nationals), including ROMANO Joseph L. III - with the consequent aggravating circumstance of the offence being committed by over five persons - for having kidnapped, depriving him of personal freedom, Nasr Osama Mustafa Hassan alias Abu Omar, apprehending him by force and forcibly making him enter a van, thereafter taking him first to the US military airbase at Aviano,

Going after the Americans: Italian prosecutors went to extraordinary lengths to track down and expose the CIA team that operated in Milan to capture al Qaeda suspect Abu Omar, pulling cellphone records and cross-referencing them to identify members of the CIA team. If only they would go to such lengths to identify and arrest suspect terrorists, the CIA wouldn't be carrying out these operations in Italy!

Call Made	Call Received	Date, Time	Duration	Cell
3473204821	**3480614737**	20/02/2003 20:43:34	38	MILANO - Via Marco Aurelio 26 - Centrale Telecom Italia Mil, Sett. 9
3477619320	**3480614737**	20/02/2003 22:16:29	28	MILANO - Via Marco Aurelio 26 - Centrale Telecom Italia Mil, Sett. 3
3477619320	**3480614737**	21/02/2003 08:44:04	113	MILANO - C.so di P.ta Nuova, 7/ V. Cernaia, 10, Sett. 8
3478344302	**3480614737**	21/02/2003 08:57:26	67	MILANO - C.so Garibaldi 68 (Hotel Ritter), Sett. 8
3478344302	**3480614737**	21/02/2003 09:05:02	11	MILANO - C.so di P.ta Nuova, 7/ V. Cernaia, 10, Sett. 2
3480614737	043426764	21/02/2003 17:34:41	43	VI - MONTECCHIO MAGGIORE - Via Madonnetta, Sett. 1
3480614737	3331729183	22/02/2003 09:52:44	22	VI - GRUMOLO DELLE ABBADESSE - A4 - km 121,3, Sett. 7
3478344302	**3480614737**	22/02/2003 10:13:42	23	VE - VENEZIA – Via dei Salici 32, Sett. 7
3480614737	3331729183	22/02/2003 11:01:14	105	VE - PORTOGRUARO - Viale Trieste, 3, Sett. 9
3480614737	3331729183	22/02/2003 11:27:34	22	GO - MONFALCONE - Terreno in loc. Cima di Pietrarossa, Sett. 1
3480614737	3331729183	22/02/2003 11:31:17	15	GO - MONFALCONE - Via Terza Armata, 21, Sett. 3
3480614737	335204587	03/03/2003 09:35:51	10	
	3480614737	03/03/2003 11:34:23	30	**Egypt**
	3480614737	03/03/2003 11:35:13	165	**Egypt**
3480614737	3477619320	15/03/2003 10:29:58	42	CO - CARIMATE - Via Stazione, Sett. 3
3480614737	3477619320	15/03/2003 10:31:28	43	MI - MEDA - Via S. Maria c/o Torre acqua comunale, Sett. 3
3480614737	3483948952	15/03/2003 10:34:28	38	MI - SEREGNO - Via S.Stefano da Seregno, 39 c/o centrale Telecom, Sett. 3
3478344302	**3480614737**	15/03/2003 10:46:23	9	MI - MILANO – Viale Monza 139, Sett. 3
3478344302	**3480614737**	15/03/2003 11:56:18	63	MI - MILANO - Via de Alessandri, 11, Sett. 1

Lady Robert Seldon has long since retired from diplomatic service, and taken up residence it Italy. Indeed, he purchased a farmhouse in the hamlet of Penango (Asti), and lives together with his family in via Don Bosco nr. 40.

The investigation: The Italian prosecutors constructed flow charts showing the relationship of each member of the CIA team, their location at the time of the arrest, and which cellphone they used, after identifying the specific cellphone relay towers in the vicinity of the arrest.

- *Also the number **3480614737** (registered under the name of Suddath Barbara) has contacted several times the staff of Milan Digos;*
- *From October 15, 2001 at 10.04.43 am till February 18, 2003 at 7.44.22 pm, the number **3357504143** has deviated, at irregular intervals, but more frequently during December 2002, the phone calls to number **3480614737.** For example, the calls made by the phones registered under the name of HARBAUGH (See following graphic) during the month of December 2002 were directed to number **3357504143** that deviated them to number **3480614737.***

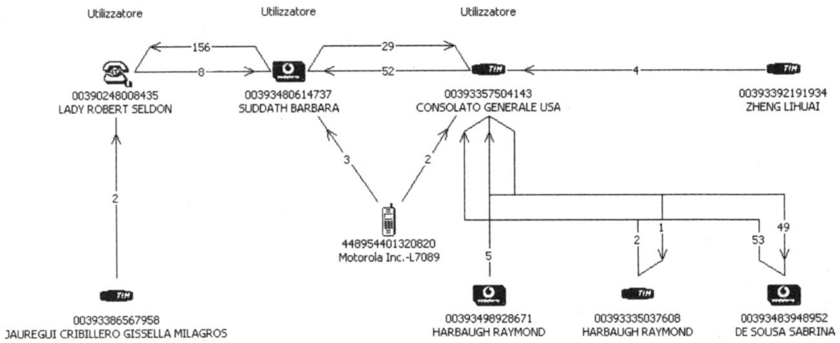

*After verifications made on the cells that were more frequently activated between 9pm and 10am by number **3480614737**, we individuated the cells listed in the following table. We note that during the evenings and nights, the number has used **270 TIMES** the cell in Via de Alessandri, at about 100 meters from **Lady's** old address: Via Cimarossa 22; and **49 times** the cell in Moncalvo (AT) situated at less than 2km from the actual address of Mr Lady, in Penango (AT), via Don Bosco 40. The Digos also points out that the first time that this phone has activated this cell, was on **September 10, 2003** at 3.12.21pm, and the change of address is dated **September 9, 2003. So, this coincides with Seldon's change of residence.** As for cells numbers 2, 4 and 5, those are the ones that cover the zone where the US Consulate is situated in Milan, via Principe Amedeo 10.*

Address of the cell	*Number of contacts between 9 pm and 10 am*	*First Contact*	*Last contact*
1. MI - MILANO - Via de Alessandri, 11, Sett. 1	***270***	*16/10/2000 21.05.13*	*02/08/2003 22.19.53*
2. MI - MILANO - C.so di P.ta Nuova, 7/ V. Cernaia, 10, Sett. 2	***57***	*14/12/2000 22.29.44*	*21/09/2004 09.15.50*

103

Valerie Plame perjury?: In sworn testimony to Congress, Valerie Plame insisted she never recommended her husband to the CIA to investigate reports that Iraq was seeking to purchase uranium from Niger. This previously classified memo suggests otherwise.

~~SECRET~~

12 February 2002

MEMORANDUM FOR: [Redacted]

FROM: [Valerie Wilson]

OFFICE: DO/CP/[office 1]

SUBJECT: Iraq-related Nuclear Report Makes a Splash

REFERENCE:

The report forwarded below has prompted me to send this on to you and request your comments and opinion. Briefly, it seems that Niger has signed a contract with Iraq to sell them uranium. The IC is getting spun up about this for obvious reasons. The Embassy in Niamey has taken the position that this report can't be true – they have such cozy relations with the GON that they would know if something like this transpired.

So, where do I fit in? As you may recall [redacted] of CP/[office 2] recently [2001] approached my husband to possibly use his contacts in Niger to investigate [redacted] [a separate Niger matter]. After many fits and starts, [redacted] finally advised that the Station wished to pursue this with liaison. My husband is willing to help if it makes sense, but no problem if not. End of story.

Now, with this report, it is clear that the IC is still wondering what is going on... my husband has good relationships with both the PM and the former Minister of Mines (not to mention lots of French contacts), both of whom could possibly shed light on this sort of activity. To be frank with you, I was somewhat embarrassed by the Agency's sloppy work last go round and I am hesitant to suggest anything again. However, [my husband] may be in a position to assist. Therefore, request your thoughts on what, if anything to pursue here. Thank you for your time on this.

~~SECRET~~

(end memo)

Page 207 of 226

Saddam's chemical weapons: After the war, investigative reporters from Cybercast News Service gained access to several caches of documents from Saddam's intelligence service and the presidential office, showing contracts to purchase chemical weapons protection gear. This is one of the reasons why CENTCOM commander General Tommy Franks was convinced his troops would face Iraqi chemical weapons on the battlefield.

Saddam's Possession of Mustard Gas:

(Table specifying contracts for mustard gas and protective equipment)

Sequence	**1**	**2**	**3**
Contract's date & number	**450/TT/1999 Sept.6th.1999**	**5460/TT/2000 May.20th.2000**	**983/TT/2000 Aug.21st.2000**
The company's name	**Jaber Ibn Hayan general company**	**Jaber Ibn Hayan general company**	**Saddam's company**
The item mentioned in the contract	**A- Military face uniform B- Filter CF4 C- Mask bag D - Expiratory valve E - Viewer glass F - Wooden boxes**	**A - Prophylactic gloves B - Leg protectors C - Wooden boxes**	**Mustard**
The quantity mentioned in the contract	**A-10000 B-10000 C-10000 D-5000 E-5000 F-200**	**A- 50000 pairs. B- 40000 pairs C- 500**	**5 kgms**
The quantity supplied	**A-10000 B-10000 C-10000 D-5000 E-5000 F-200**	**A- 47000 B- 40000 C- 500**	**5 kgms**
The quantity left	Non	A- 3000 pairs B - Non. C- 6	Non

The "secret flights": Italian leftist Claudio Fava dumped a huge amount of data on the press in June 2006 exposing CIA aircraft and CIA proprietaries he claimed were associated with the rendition of suspected terrorists. In fact, as the U.S. government has acknowledged, fewer than 100 prisoners were rendered using CIA aircraft, far fewer than the 1,254 "secret flights" Fava revealed.

Claudio Fava

CONTRIBUTION OF THE RAPPORTEUR:

RESEARCH ON THE PLANES USED BY THE CIA

N8183J[i]

- ***N8183J*** *is a cargo plane Hercules Lockheed C-100-30 (L382G), owned by the CIA shell company Rapid Air Tran (Transport). Tepper Aviation, Inc., maintains and operates these planes out of the Bob Sikes Airport in Crestview (a CIA hub). The European base of the Lockheeds N8183J is Rhein-Main, Germany. According to Der Spiegel, and the New York Times, Tepper is linked to CIA.*[ii] *Tepper Aviation is also listed as a CIA company in the Amnesty report.*[iii]
- *According to European flight records, Tepper C-130 N8183J's favourite route seems to be* ***Frankfurt-Tashkent; Frankfurt-Luxor; Frankfurt-Baku****. It is spotted in other European places as Shannon, Antalya, Prestwick, Iraklion.*
- *It has been object of a query to the House of Common.*[iv]

DEPARTURE AIRPORT	*ARRIVING AIRPORT*	*DATES*
Baku (Azerbaijan)	***Frankfurt(Germany)***	*15/12/2001*
Frankfurt (Germany)	***Shannon (Ireland)***	*16/12/2001*
Shannon(Ireland)	*Gander(Canada)*	*17/12/2001*
Gander (Canada)	***Shannon(Ireland)***	*27/03/2002*
Shannon(Ireland)	***Antalya(Turkey)***	*28/03/2002*
Antalya (Turkey)	*Tashkent (Uzbekistan)*	*29/03/2002*
Tashkent(Uzbekistan)	***Antalya(Turkey)***	*09/04/2002*
Antalya(Turkey)	***Frankfurt(Germany)***	*10/04/2002*
Frankfurt(Germany)	*Baku(Azerbaijan)*	*12/04/2002*
Baku(Azerbaijan)	***Frankfurt(Germany)***	*19/04/2002*
Frankfurt (Germany)	***Ramstein(Germany)***	*21/04/2002*
Ramstein(Germany)	*Baku(Azerbaijan)*	*21/04/2002*

N 313P + N4476S (BOEING 737)

∞ **N313P - N4476S** is a Boeing 737-7ET aircraft.[1] It can make non-stop from Dulles (Washington DC) to Tashkent (Uzbekistan) in 11 hours, and can transport up to 127 passengers.

∞ First registered by **Stevens Express Leasing Inc**, and then re-registered, on 1st May 2002 by **Premier Executive Transport Services**. On 1st December 2004 **Keeler & Tate Management** re-registered the aircraft as N4476S. The three companies are all CIA shell companies.[2] Stevens Express Leasing Inc. and Premier Executive Transport Services were both permitted to land at US military bases worldwide.[3]

∞ Human Rights Watch has identified it as the "*plane that the CIA used to move several prisoners to and from Europe, Afghanistan, and the Middle East in 2003 and 2004*".[4] According to EuroControl records, the jet has flown regularly between destinations that are known for or suspected of being used for the detention or rendition of prisoners. From 2002 to 2005, it made at least three stops at **Guantanamo**, nine stops in **Kabul**, seven in **Morocco**, 13 in **Jordan**, five in **Pakistan**, three in **Kuwait**, ten in **Baghdad**, and eleven in **Libya**.

∞ Flight records show that it was the plane that took **Khaled el-Masri** from Skopje to Afghanistan in January 2004. El Masri was transferred to U.S. custody

Aereoporto partenza	**Aereoporto arrivo**	**Data**
Camp Spring (Usa)	**Frankfurt (Germany)**	22/11/2002
Frankfurt (Germany)	Amman (Jordan)	24/11/2002
Amman (Jordan)	**Frankfurt (Germany)**	24/11/2002
Frankfurt (Germany)	Camp Spring (Usa)	24/11/2002
Camp Spring (Usa)	**Pisa (Italy)**	01/12/2002
Pisa (Italy)	**Frankfurt (Germany)**	01/12/2002
Frankfurt (Germany)	**Mildenhall (UK)**	04/12/2002
Mildenhall (UK)	Camp Spring (Usa)	04/12/2002
Washington (Usa)	**Frankfurt (Germany)**	15/12/2002
Frankfurt (Germany)	Islamabad (Pakistan)	16/12/2002
Islamabad (Pakistan)	**Frankfurt (Germany)**	23/12/2002
Frankfurt (Germany)	Washington (Usa)	23/12/2002
Washington (Usa)	**Shannon (Irlanda)**	11/01/2003
Shannon (Irlanda)	Parnu (Estonia)	11/01/2003
Parnu (Estonia)	**Frankfurt (Germany)**	11/01/2003
Frankfurt (Germany)	Parnu (Estonia)	12/01/2003
Parnu (Estonia)	**Frankfurt (Germany)**	12/01/2003
Frankfurt (Germany)	Washington (Usa)	14/01/2003
Washington (Usa)	**Ramstein (Germany)**	30/01/2003
Ramstein (Germany)	Washington (Usa)	01/02/2003
Washington (Usa)	**Frankfurt (Germany)**	06/02/2003
Frankfurt (Germany)	Amman (Jordany)	06/02/2003
Kuwait	**Ramstein (Germany)**	06/02/2003
Ramstein (Germany)	Washington (Usa)	10/02/2003
Washington (Usa)	**Frankfurt (Germany)**	15/02/2003
Frankfurt (Germany)	Islamabad (Pakistan)	15/02/2003
Islamabad(Pakistan)	**Frankfurt (Germany)**	27/02/2003
Frankfurt (Germany)	Washington (Usa)	28/02/2003
Washington (Usa)	**Luton (UK)**	11/03/2003

Democrats play politics: Senate intelligence committee chairman Pat Roberts slammed Democrats on his committee for skewing the facts on Ahmad Chalabi and the Iraqi National Congress, and ripped apart their report. His blistering dissent is one of the most stunning documents to have emerged from a congressional debate in many years.

ADDITIONAL VIEWS OF CHAIRMAN ROBERTS JOINED BY SENATORS HATCH, DEWINE, LOTT, CHAMBLISS, AND WARNER

If you're trying to say that the INC is the one that pushed us to go to war because of the WMD reporting, that's wrong.
— CIA Officer, Directorate of Operations

Over thirty years ago, the Select Committee on Intelligence was established to "oversee and make continuing studies of the intelligence activities and programs of the United States Government." To meet our obligations to the Senate and the American people, the members of this Committee are provided with access to some of the most sensitive intelligence information possessed, and reporting produced, by the United States Government. We have a responsibility to ground our oversight in fact. Recommendations or conclusions drawn from our oversight should be based on these facts and sound intelligence policy – free from partisan political bias.

We met our obligations and responsibilities when the Committee produced the first phase of its review of prewar intelligence on Iraq. The Committee employed an exacting and thorough methodology in the first phase of our review. The hard work of members and staff culminated in the adoption of a unanimous report. That report identified significant, systemic failures in prewar intelligence on Iraq, and its conclusions contributed to needed reforms of our Intelligence Community. When we expanded the scope of our review, Committee staff were instructed to use that same approach for all five elements of "Phase II."

Regrettably, with the adoption of the amended conclusions now contained in this report, the Committee has failed to meet its obligations and responsibilities as they relate to our review of the use by the Intelligence Community of information provided by the Iraqi National Congress (INC). These failures are

Page 127

borne out by the sharp divide between the findings and conclusions adopted by several members of the Committee, and the findings and conclusions – drawn from the fine work of Committee staff – that I, along with several of my colleagues, supported as the Committee considered this report. This failure led several members to vote against the adoption of the findings and conclusions of the report.

Despite many misgivings, the adoption of the findings and conclusions of this report allows the facts and circumstances to be presented to the entire Senate and, in unclassified form, to the public. Together with these additional views, this report represents a comprehensive understanding of the relationship of the Intelligence Community to the INC.

The Committee's review focused on how information provided by the INC was used by the Intelligence Community. Was the information included in Intelligence Community assessments? Did the information play a role in the Intelligence Community's judgments about Iraq's weapons of mass destruction (WMD) capabilities or its links to terrorism?

Understanding the role of INC information in Intelligence Community assessments was critical to the Committee's efforts. As the Committee began its review, there seemed to be a growing number of individuals charging that the INC engaged in a disinformation campaign to supply erroneous information to the Intelligence Community and that such information led to the Intelligence Community's failures in its prewar assessments on Iraq, particularly in its WMD assessments.

The facts detailed in the findings portion of this report (and outlined more briefly below) do not support this theory. Information supplied by the INC played only a minor role in the Intelligence Community's prewar judgments concerning

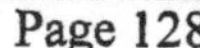

Iraq's WMD programs or links to terrorism. As it relates to prewar assessments of Iraq's WMD programs, INC information did not significantly affect intelligence judgments. Only one key judgment in the October 2002 National Intelligence Estimate (NIE), *Iraq's Continuing Programs for Weapons of Mass Destruction* contained corroborating information from an INC-affiliated source and, according to the CIA, that judgment would not have changed had the information from that source not been considered. Indeed, of the 45 human intelligence (HUMINT) sources cited in the WMD NIE, only two were affiliated with the INC – and that does not account for the vast amount of information in the WMD NIE derived from signals intelligence, imagery, and HUMINT sources not specifically cited. The INC did not supply information used to support the Intelligence Community's key judgments about Iraq's links to terrorism.

These facts should be sufficient to lay to rest the myth that INC information led to the intelligence failure on Iraq. Indeed, the popular misconception is likely based on past, and continued, media reporting on these INC sources. Given the level of media attention the INC sources have received, it would be quite easy for an uninformed observer to conclude that these sources formed the bulk of intelligence supporting prewar intelligence assessments on Iraq. The conclusion is seemingly buttressed by several media organizations that reported the accounts that INC sources had provided to the Intelligence Community, often with embellishments that never made their way into intelligence products. Although the media chose to highlight the information provided by these INC sources, the facts demonstrate that the Intelligence Community did not.

Unfortunately, if the public focuses only on the conclusions adopted by several members of this Committee, they will not get the full story. ***The adopted conclusions are not supported by fact.*** Taken as a whole, they misrepresent the INC's relationship to the Intelligence Community, leaving the impression that the INC (with the knowledge and acquiescence of intelligence officials and policy

makers) intentionally provided the Intelligence Community with false information in an effort to push the United States to war with Iraq. These conclusions – and the misconceptions they support – are a myth. The reality – while politically unappealing for some – is quite different.

To correct these errors, these additional views set forth the most troubling and significant examples of how the adopted conclusions misrepresent the relationship of the INC to the Intelligence Community and how the Intelligence Community used the information provided by the INC in prewar assessments.

The Intelligence Community's Use of INC Information

The amended conclusions suggest that the INC intentionally provided false information to the Intelligence Community and that the Intelligence Community used that information to support key judgments about Iraq's WMD programs and links to terrorism. These conclusions not only distort the extent to which the Intelligence Community used INC information, they mischaracterize the significance of the information that was used. As with most HUMINT reporting, some of the information provided by the INC was inaccurate, some was accurate, and some remains ambiguous, even today. The Committee, however, has no evidence to suggest that the INC intentionally provided false information.

The following section addresses the myths – either expressed or implied – in the amended conclusions.

Myth: **The Intelligence Community made extensive use of INC information and that information played a key role in assessments about Iraq's WMD programs and links to terrorism.**

Reality: **INC information was not widely used by the Intelligence Community and played little role in the Intelligence Community's judgments about Iraq's WMD programs and links to terrorism.**

The Intelligence Community agencies told the Committee that INC-affiliated reporting had a minimal impact on prewar judgments about Iraq. Despite evidence to the contrary, amended Conclusion 1 suggests that INC information played a significant role in the Intelligence Community's judgments about Iraq, particularly in judgments about Iraq's WMD capabilities and links to terrorism.

The Defense Intelligence Agency (DIA) told the Committee that INC sources and collected material were not instrumental in shaping DIA assessments of the former Iraqi regime's terrorist connections or the terrorist threat the regime presented. The DIA said it "considered this information – as well as other information of uncertain quality – as background information which had the potential of earning more credibility as additional data was collected, though it played no direct role in forming our assessments."

The State Department's Bureau of Intelligence and Research (INR) told the Committee that it viewed all reporting on Iraq from HUMINT sources with skepticism. The INR said "this reporting was seldom, if ever, used as the basis for judgments unless corroborated by other sources that INR deemed credible." With regard to the two INC-affiliated defectors whose information was included in the WMD NIE, the INR said their reports "did not influence any INR assessments relating to prohibited weapons programs." Regarding terrorism, INR said it "did *not* make much use of INC reporting on terrorism issues related to Iraq in the years before Operation Iraqi Freedom." (Emphasis in original).

The CIA told the Committee that its analysts tended not to rely on non-specific prewar opposition reporting alleging WMD or terrorism-related activities "because they were not first-hand accounts from sources with verifiable access." A CIA review of 23 INC-affiliated defector reports which contained WMD, terrorism, or other potentially significant information, said "few of the 23 reports were cited in CIA finished intelligence production or affected prewar assessments. As [the Committee] is already aware, reporting from [two sources] was used in assessments of Salman Pak, but our analytic judgments on those substantive issues did not rely solely on reports from those sources. Aside from those two sources, most of the other reports were of marginal value to the CIA finished intelligence production and had almost no impact on CIA analytic assessments."[342]

The CIA comments corroborate the finding of the Commission on the Intelligence Capabilities of the United States Regarding Weapons of Mass Destruction (WMD Commission). In its report, the WMD Commission wrote, "Over all, CIA's post-war investigations revealed that INC-related sources had a minimal impact on pre-war assessments." The WMD Commission noted that two INC-affiliated defectors whose information was included in the WMD NIE "had a negligible impact on the overall assessments."

The Committee's review supports the comments of the WMD Commission and the responses from the Intelligence Community. For example, as the findings portion of this report shows, the Committee found that only one Intelligence Community assessment used INC-affiliated reporting at all – the WMD NIE. In that NIE, the Intelligence Community used information from ***only one*** INC-affiliated source in support of ***only one*** key judgment – that Iraq had a mobile

[342]The CIA initiated this review at the request of Committee staff. Committee staff did not request that the CIA review reporting from the two defectors used in the WMD NIE because at this request, Committee staff was already aware that the reporting from these two sources had been used.

biological weapons capability. According to a CIA review of this issue, "even without [that source's] reporting, the bottom-line judgment at the time on Iraq's overall mobile BW program would have remained the same." The Intelligence Community used information from ***only one other*** INC-affiliated defector in the NIE in a separate text box which described a possible suspect nuclear facility. The information about the possible suspect facility was not included anywhere in the text or key judgments of the NIE and ***played no role*** in the NIE judgment that Iraq was reconstituting its nuclear program.

Intelligence Community agencies attached even less significance to INC-affiliated sources in their terrorism assessments. The CIA included intelligence reporting from only two INC-affiliated sources in its key terrorism assessment, *Iraqi Support for Terrorism*. The information was used in ***only one paragraph*** of the 32-page document. Furthermore, the paragraph described one defector's information as "exaggerated," and the other's as not first-hand.

In addition to the key products described above, Intelligence Community agencies used INC-affiliated reporting in ***less than 20 other products*** about Iraq's WMD programs and links to terrorism. By comparison, the Committee's request for CIA's assessments on Iraq's WMD programs and Iraq's links to terrorism from 1997 to March 2003 yielded over 40,000 finished intelligence products. ***In other words, when compared to more than 40,000 finished CIA intelligence products, INC information was included in about 20 Intelligence Community reports – a minuscule 0.05% of CIA's intelligence products on these issues and an even smaller amount of community products.***

Two conclusions drafted by the Committee's investigative staff more accurately reflect the extent to which the Intelligence Community used INC information in key assessments. The conclusions accurately detail the lack of impact that this information had on prewar intelligence assessments.

Accordingly, we would have concluded the following with respect to the use of INC information concerning Iraq's WMD programs:

✱ **Conclusion: Information from the INC and INC-affiliated defectors was not widely used in Intelligence Community products and played little role in the Intelligence Community's judgments about Iraq's WMD programs.**
The Intelligence Community used information from two INC-affiliated defectors in the NIE, but the information was not used as the primary basis for any of the key judgments about Iraq's WMD capabilities. In one case, analysts assessed reporting from an INC-affiliated defector as corroboration of other primary source reporting about Iraq's mobile biological weapons production capabilities. In the other case, a defector's information formed the basis for Intelligence Community concerns that an Iraqi facility may have had a nuclear association. Of the thousands of reports sent to the Committee as supporting documentation for the October 2002 NIE, only five were from these two sources.

With respect to the use of INC-related information concerning Iraq's links to terrorism, we would have concluded:

Conclusion: The Intelligence Community made little use of INC-affiliated defector information in its assessments about Iraq's links to terrorism. Some of these assessments mischaracterized the content and the credibility of the reporting. The CIA and the DIA used intelligence reporting from two INC-affiliated defectors in intelligence assessments discussing alleged special operations training of non-Iraqi Arabs at Iraq's Salman Pak Unconventional Military Training Facility. Most of the assessments describe the defectors as not having direct access to the information and in some cases described the information they provided as "questionable" or "exaggerated." Ironically, despite describing that reporting as exaggerated, three of the CIA assessments which used INC-affiliated information actually mischaracterized both the content and some of the concerns about the reporting, making it appear more sensational and questionable than it was. The CIA assessments said the defectors alleged that "al-Qa'ida and other non-Iraqis engaged in special operations training at Salman Pak," but the defectors had reported the training of only non-Iraqi Arabs, not al-Qa'ida members. In addition, the assessments said that two of the defectors did not have direct access to the reporting they provided. In one case, the defector did have direct access. In the other case, the CIA was not in a position to judge the access of the defector because the CIA had never spoken to the defector and did not know his identity. The analysts used the information from a magazine article which described an unnamed defector.

Characterization of INC-related Sources and Information

As with most HUMINT reporting, information provided by INC sources to the Intelligence Community was a mixed bag – some was accurate, some inaccurate, and some, even in hindsight, remains ambiguous. What is clear, however, is that the Intelligence Community used information from ***only one*** INC-affiliated defector to support ***only one*** key assessment in prewar intelligence products. No other INC information, inaccurate or accurate, was used to support any other key assessments.

The Iranian connection: These photographs, taken by Iraqi police in late 2006, show an Iranian-manufactured range-finding computer and an Iranian-made mortar, seized from Iraqi Shiite insurgents. Both show markings clearly establishing that they were made in Iran. Despite this and other evidence, congressional Democrats continue to dispute Iran's involvement in Iraq.

NOTES

PROLOGUE: THE UNDERGROUND

1. Kenneth R. Timmerman, *Shakedown: Exposing the Real Jesse Jackson* (Washington, DC: Regnery, 2002), p. 385.

CHAPTER ONE: A BATTLE ROYAL

1. Ricciardone told me he couldn't recall how Quality Support, Inc., was selected by the State Department to run the Iraqi programs, but one official working on the project was less coy. "This was a no-compete contract hot-wired to a minority business that was a recognized State Department vendor." For more details, see Kenneth R. Timmerman, "State Saddamists," *Insight* magazine, March 19, 2001.
2. Jane Mayer, "The Manipulator," *The New Yorker*, June 7, 2004. Evan Thomas and Mark Hosenball, "The Rise and Fall of Chalabi: Bush's Mr. Wrong," *Newsweek*, May 31, 2004. The *Newsweek* cover showed a picture of Chalabi behind broken glass and was titled "Our Con Man in Iraq."
3. Steve C. Clemons, "New Yorkers: Arrest Ahmad Chalabi on Friday," Nov. 18, 2005, http://www.thewashingtonnote.com/archives/001079.php.
4. *Ahmad Chalabi et al v. Hashemite Kingdom of Jordan*, U.S. District Court for the District of Columbia, Civil Complaint, Aug. 11, 2004. Case 1:04CV01353; pp. 2–4, 27.
5. Bob Baer subsequently published his own account of these events, including the text of the cable, in *See No Evil* (New York: Crown, 2002). See *inter alia* chapters 15–16. The cable appears on p. 173.
6. Steven C. Clemons, "If You're Blocked from Ahmad Chalabi's Event, Try Judith Miller for $375," Nov. 8, 2005. http://www.thewashingtonnote.com/archives/001078.php.
7. Quoted in Jeffrey Goldbert, "Breaking Ranks: What Turned Brent Scowcroft Against the Bush Administration," *The New Yorker*, Oct. 31, 2005.

CHAPTER TWO: THE SPOOKS' WAR

1. Interview with Gary Berntsen. For a complete account, see Gary Berntsen with Ralph Pezzullo, *Jawbreaker* (New York: Crown, 2005), p. 290.
2. Barton Gellman and Thomas E. Ricks, "U.S. Concludes Bin Ladin Escaped at Tora Bora Fight," *Washington Post*, Apr. 17, 2002.
3. A bin Ladin cook, Haji Mohamad Akram, told Philip Smucker of the *Christian Science Monitor* that bin Ladin had fled Tora Bora for Pakistan, and then made his way to Iran. Smucker spoke to Haji Akram in Ghazni, Afghanistan, where he was being held captive by Afghan tribals. Philip Smucker, "An Al Qaeda Chef, Captured and Tortured by Afghans, Begged Tuesday to Be Handed Over to US Officials," *Christian Science Monitor*, Feb. 6, 2002.
4. Quoted by Ron Suskind, *The One Percent Doctrine* (New York: Simon & Schuster, 2006), p. 77.
5. CNN first reported al-Libi's arrest on Jan. 5, 2002, and cited his interrogation on board the USS *Bataan* on January 9, 2002. See also "Myers: Intelligence Might Have Thwarted Attacks: Senior Taliban Fighters Taken into Custody," CNN.com, Jan. 9, 2002. http://www.cnn.com/2002/WORLD/asiapcf/central/01/08/ret.afghan.attacks/.
6. Michael Hirsh, John Barry, and Daniel Klaidman, "A Tortured Debate," *Newsweek*, June 21, 2004.
7. Suskind, *The One Percent Doctrine*, p. 55.
8. Senator Bob Graham, with Jeff Nussbaum, *Intelligence Matters* (New York: Random House, 2004), pp. 125–26.
9. The White House released the PDB article on April 10, 2004, with three deletions—the names of foreign intelligence services that had provided the CIA with information. Here is the complete text (italics in original):

> BIN LADIN DETERMINED TO STRIKE IN US
>
> *Clandestine, foreign government, and media reports indicate Bin Ladin since 1997 has wanted to conduct terrorist attacks in the US.* Bin Ladin implied in U.S. television interviews in 1997 and 1998 that his followers would follow the example of World Trade Center bomber Ramzi Yousef and "bring the fighting to America."
>
> After U.S. missile strikes on his base in Afghanistan in 1998, Bin Ladin told followers he wanted to retaliate in Washington, according to a [redacted] service.
>
> An Egyptian Islamic Jihad (EIJ) operative told an [redacted] service at the same time that Bin Ladin was planning to exploit the operative's access to the U.S. to mount a terrorist strike.
>
> *The millennium plotting in Canada in 1999 may have been part of Bin Ladin's first serious attempt to implement a terrorist strike in the U.S.* Convicted plotter Ahmed Ressam has told the FBI that he conceived the idea to attack Los Angeles International Airport himself, but that Bin Ladin lieutenant Abu Zubaydah encouraged him and helped facilitate the operation. Ressam also said that in 1998 Abu Zubaydah was planning his own U.S. attack.
>
> Ressam says Bin Ladin was aware of the Los Angeles operation.
>
> *Although Bin Ladin has not succeeded, his attacks against the U.S. Embassies in Kenya and Tanzania in 1998 demonstrate that he prepares operations years in advance and is not deterred by setbacks.* Bin Ladin associates surveyed our embassies in Nairobi and Dar es Salaam as early as 1993, and some members of the Nairobi cell planning the bombings were arrested and deported in 1997.
>
> *Al Qa'ida members—including some who are US citizens—have resided in*

or traveled to the US for years, and the group apparently maintains a support structure that could aid attacks. Two al-Qa'ida members found guilty in the conspiracy to bomb our embassies in East Africa were US citizens, and a senior EIJ member lived in California in the mid-1990s.

A clandestine source said in 1998 that a Bin Ladin cell in New York was recruiting Muslim-American youth for attacks.

We have not been able to corroborate some of the more sensational threat reporting, such as that from a [redacted] service in 1998 saying that Bin Ladin wanted to hijack a U.S. aircraft to gain the release of "Blind Sheikh" Omar Abdel Rahman and other U.S.-held extremists.

Nevertheless, FBI information since that time indicates patterns of suspicious activity in this country consistent with preparations for hijackings or other types of attacks, including recent surveillance of federal buildings in New York.

The FBI is conducting approximately 70 full-field investigations throughout the US that it considers Bin Ladin–related. CIA and the FBI are investigating a call to our embassy in the UAE in May saying that a group of Bin Ladin supporters was in the US planning attacks with explosives.

10. Graham, *Intelligence Matters*, p. 80–82.
11. Senator Graham, who chaired the Joint Inquiry, agreed with Levin that the committee should reveal not only KSM's name but the CIA's top secret file on his activities as well. Graham, *Intelligence Matters*, p. 172.

CHAPTER THREE: SECRET OFFICE IN THE BASEMENT

1. Karen Kwiatkowski, "In Rumsfeld's Shop," *The American Conservative*, December 1, 2003.
2. Lyndon H. LaRouche, Jr., "Rumsfeld as Strangelove II," in *Children of Satan*, a 32-page pamphlet distributed by the LaRouche organization, p. 3. See http://larouchein2004.net/pdfs/pamphletcos.pdf.
3. Michael Rubin, "Web of Conspiracies," *National Review Online*, May 18, 2004.
4. I detailed these plans in articles for *Insight* magazine before and after the 2003 war. Cf. inter alia, "Justice looms for Saddam, cronies," *Insight* magazine, Feb. 18, 2003. http://www.kentimmerman.com/news/insight_iraq2003_02_18.htm; and "Democrats Target Pentagon Planning," *Insight* magazine, Nov. 24, 2003. http://www.kentimmerman.com/2003_11_24planning1.htm. Josh Bolten testified on these plans before the Senate Foreign Relations committee on July 29, 2003.
5. Cited in "Smearing Mr. Chalabi," lead editorial, *Wall Street Journal*, April 10, 2003.

CHAPTER FOUR: PREPARING FOR WAR

1. David L. Phillips, *Losing Iraq* (New York: Basic Books, 2005), p. 90.
2. General Tommy Franks, *American Soldier* (New York: Regan Books, 2004), paperback edition. Citations respectively from p. 468 (the 3x5 cards), p. 418 (King Abdallah II), p. 419 (Hosni Mubarak), pp. xiv–xv (Franks's thoughts on the day the war began), and p. 514 (April 1 events). And these are just selections. Franks mentions the fear of WMD attacks, and hard intelligence on WMD deployed with Iraqi units, throughout his memoir.

3. Kanan Makiya, "Our Hopes Betrayed," *The Observer*, Feb. 16, 2003.
4. Adnan Pachachi, "Iraq's Route to a Democratic Future" *Financial Times*, March 3, 2003. Predictably, Pachachi also said that any future Iraqi government must take "a forthright stand" in favor of the Palestinians.
5. Cited in Bradley Graham, "U.S. Airlifts Iraqi Exile Force for Duties Near Nasiriyah," *Washington Post*, Monday, April 7, 2003; p. A01. http://www.washingtonpost.com/wp-dyn/articles/A42859-2003Apr6.htm.

CHAPTER FIVE: THE NIGER CAPER

1. Department of State transcript of Powell's Feb. 5, 2003, presentation to the UN Security Council.
2. *Report to the President of the United States* by the Commission on the Intelligence Capabilities of the United States Regarding Weapons of Mass Destruction (hereafter, Robb-Silberman Commission report), p. 213, text of footnote 210.
3. Zahawie's close association with Iraq's nuclear weapons programs was pointed out by Christopher Hitchens, "Wowie Zahawie," *Slate* magazine, April 10, 2006.
4. Transcript of ElBaradei's March 7, 2003, presentation to the UN Security Council courtesy of CNN.
5. Felicity Barringer, "Forensic Experts Uncovered Forgery on Iraq, an Inspector Says," *New York Times*, March 9, 2003.
6. Citations drawn from *Report on the U.S. Intelligence Community's Prewar Intelligence Assessments on Iraq*, July 7, 2004, Select Committee on Intelligence, U.S. Senate. (Hereafter: SSIC 7/2004.) The President's sixteen words were: *The British government has learned that Saddam Hussein recently sought significant quantities of uranium from Africa.*
7. George Tenet, *At the Center of the Storm* (New York: HarperCollins, 2007), p. 461.
8. Robb-Silberman Commission report, op cit, p. 78.
9. Senate Select Committee on Intelligence, *Report of the Select Committee on Intelligence on Prewar Intelligence Assessments about Postwar Iraq*, May 25, 2007, p. 217.
10. Carlo Bonini and Giuseppe d'Avanzo, "Berlusconi Behind Fake Yellowcake Dossier," *La Repubblica*, Oct. 24, 2005.
11. The leaked transcripts were published by *Il Giornale*, a Berlusconi daily, in February 2006. See "Il Giornale Transcripts of Rocco Martino Testimony" for translations and links to the originals. http://www.eurotrib.com/?op=displaystory;sid=2006/2/22/202646/733, accessed Nov. 10, 2006.
12. SSIC 7/2004, p. 59.
13. Carlo Bonini and Giuseppe d'Avanzo, "Nigergate, French Spymaster Debunks Sismi Version," *La Repubblica*, Dec. 1, 2005. English translation by blogger de Gondi at http://www.eurotrib.com/story/2005/12/1/95016/1741, accessed Nov. 10, 2006. Chouet was deputy director of the DGSE in charge of counterintelligence.
14. Vaiju Naravane, "Protests in Italy as PM Meets Bush," *The Hindu*, Oct. 16, 2001. http://www.hinduonnet.com/2001/10/16/stories/03160007.htm, accessed Nov. 11, 2006.
15. SSIC 7/2004, p. 36.
16. "The CIA had still not evaluated the authenticity of the documents when it coordinated on the State of the Union address, in which the president noted that the 'British government has learned that Saddam Hussein recently sought significant quantities of uranium from Africa.' Although there is some disagreement about the details of the coordination process, *no one in the Intelligence Community had asked that the line be removed* [emphasis mine]. At the time of the State of the Union speech, CIA analysts continued to believe that Iraq probably was seeking uranium from Africa, although there was growing concern among some CIA analysts that there were problems with the report-

ing." Robb-Silberman Commission report, p. 78. In Britain, the Butler commission found in 2006 that British intelligence reports on Iraqi attempts to purchase uranium in Africa were "well founded" and did not rely on the fake Niger documents. That conclusion was repeated by former MI6 director Richard Dearlove to Richard Perle in early 2007, as I reported earlier in this chapter.

17. It is worthwhile noting that in his anti-Bush memoir, *On the Brink* (New York: Carroll & Graff, 2006), Drumheller claims that he only learned of the Niger forgeries in July 2003—well after the damage to the president had been done. "I was not involved directly in the story behind those famous 'sixteen words,' " Drumheller wrote (p. 119). If this is true, then Drumheller is guilty of gross incompetence, for having allowed three reports from a subordinate on such a sensitive topic to make their way into the system as finished intelligence products.
18. Senate Select Committee on Intelligence, "Postwar Findings About Iraq's WMD Programs and Links to Terrorism and How They Compare with Prewar Assessments," Sept. 8, 2006; additional views, pp. 143–44.
19. Byron York, "Mr. Counterterrorism Guru," *National Review*, June 5, 2006.
20. Senator Bob Graham with Jeff Nusbaum, *Intelligence Matters* (New York: Random House, 2004), p. 162.
21. As author Ron Kessler, who has written several books sympathetic to the CIA, put it, "the FBI's counterterrorist effort was hampered by lack of technology, analysis, and manpower. In contrast, the CIA had been in the forefront of the fight against al Qaeda." Kessler, *The CIA at War* (New York: St. Martins-Griffin, 2003), p. 254.
22. John J. Lumpkin, "Ex-CIA Officers Defy Bush Administration," Associated Press, March 14, 2003, posted at http://www.voxfux.com/features/cia_agents_defy_bush.html. See also "Berg Beheading Is a Bush "Psy Op" on their main website, www.voxfux.com, accessed Nov. 15, 2006.
23. *Vanity Fair* writer Craig Unger would later cite VIPS members and other former officials who believed that the Niger documents were a neo-con "black operation." The nine were former CIA Soviet operations director Milt Bearden (who was sanctioned by R. James Woolsey for his role in the Aldrich Ames spy case); Colonel W. Patrick Lang, a rabidly anti-Israel, anti-neocon former DIA analyst; Larry Wilkerson, former chief of staff to Secretary of State Colin Powell; VIPS members Melvin Goodman, Ray McGovern, and Larry C. Johnson; Karen Kwiatkowski, whose anti-Bush screeds regularly appeared on a Lyndon Larouche website; former CIA official Philip Giraldi, later praised by Vietnam War leaker Daniel Ellsberg for leaking the Iraq War plans; and Vincent Cannistraro, a former operations officer at the CIA's counterterrorism center, who left the Agency under a cloud. Craig Unger, "Former US Intelligence Officials Say Niger Documents Were 'Black Op,' *Vanity Fair*, June 6, 2006. http://www.truthout.org/docs_2006/060706N.shtml, accessed Nov. 13, 2006.
24. Polling data from PollingReport.com.

CHAPTER SIX: LIBERATION WOES

1. Celeste J. Ward, "The Coalition Provisional Authority's Experience with Governance in Iraq," U.S. Institutes of Peace, Special Report 139, May 2005; p. 3.
2. Raphel was debriefed by the U.S. Institutes for Peace after returning from Baghdad for their "Iraq Experience Project." Her complete interview can be accessed via the USIP website at http://www.usip.org/library/oh/iraq.html. Condoleezza Rice promoted her to become the head of the State Department's Office of Iraq Affairs.
3. George Tenet, *At the Center of the Storm* (New York: HarperCollins, 2007), p. 387.
4. L. Paul Bremer III, *My Year in Iraq* (New York: Simon & Schuster, 2006).
5. General Tommy Franks, *American Soldier* (New York, Regan Books, 2004), p. 441.

6. Rowan Scarborough, "Rebuilding in Iraq Tops 4,000 Projects," *Washington Times*, Nov. 20, 2006.
7. National Intelligence Council, "Principal Challenges in Post-Saddam Iraq," January 2003, p. 30. Included in *Report of the Select Committee on Intelligence on Prewar Intelligence Assessments about Postwar Iraq*," Senate Select Committee on Intelligence, May 25, 2007. Tommy Franks discussed his decision not to destroy Iraqi infrastructure in Franks, *American Soldier*, op cit, p. 480.
8. Garner and Bush quotes from the *News Hour with Jim Lehrer*, April 28, 2003.
9. Author's notes of comments by Kanan Makiya, National Press Club, Washington, DC, April 23, 2003.
10. Raphel interview.
11. Rajiv Chandrasekaran, *Imperial Life in the Emerald City* (New York: Knopf, 2006), p. 81.
12. Jonathan Foreman, "Bad Reporting in Baghdad: You Have No Idea How Well Things Are Going," *The Weekly Standard*, May 12, 2003.
13. Bill Gertz and Rowan Scarborough, "Rumsfeld Departure," Inside the Ring, *Washington Times*, Dec. 8, 2006.

CHAPTER SEVEN: THE VICEROY COMETH

1. Bremer, op cit, p. 12.
2. Ibid., pp. 14–15.
3. Ibid., p. 40
4. Ibid., p. 44. Bremer claims that the decision to fire the ILC was taken by NSC principals back in Washington.
5. Ibid., p. 49.
6. "Truth, War, and Consequences," PBS's *Frontline*, Oct. 3, 2003.
7. Bob Woodward, "Secret Reports Dispute White House Optimism," *Washington Post*, Oct. 1, 2006.
8. Special Defense Department Briefing with L. Paul Bremer. Subject: Reconstitution of Iraq, 10:49 A.M. EDT, Thursday, June 12, 2003.
9. *Report of the Select Committee on Intelligence on The Use by the Intelligence Community of Information Provided by the Iraqi National Congress*, 109th Congress, 2nd session, Sept. 8, 2006; pp. 40–56. A July 2002 classified memorandum from the National Intelligence Council, "The Iraqi National Congress Defector Program," described this defector as "the most successful INC referral" with "exceptional access to information of interest to the U.S. Intelligence Community." His information was "deemed highly credible and includes reports on a wide range of subjects including conventional weapons facilities, denial and deception; communications security; suspected terrorist training," and more. "Many reports included geo-coordinates, diagrams, and hand drawings." P. 44.
10. Cited in Daniel Henninger, "Baker-Hamilton Won't Stop Beltway Bloodshed," *Wall Street Journal* editorial page, Dec. 8, 2006.

CHAPTER EIGHT: JOE WILSON LIES

1. "U.S. Diplomat Launched a 'Bush Lies' Campaign in June '03," *Insight* magazine, May 5, 2005.
2. "Pro and Con: Local Voices Join the Global Debate on War," *Island Packet*, Sunday, March 23, 2003.
3. Walter Pincus, "CIA Did Not Share Doubt on Iraq Data," *Washington Post*, June 12, 2003.
4. SSIC 7/2004, p. 45.
5. Ibid., pp. 36–83.

6. "A Good Leak," lead editorial, *Washington Post*, April 9, 2006.
7. Wilson wrote to the Senate intelligence committee after it issued its July 2004 report, stating that several conclusions reached in the additional views of Chairman and Senators Bond and Hatch were "not true." Specifically, he disputed the conclusion that "the plan to send the former ambassador to Niger was suggested by the former ambassador's wife, a CIA employee." In an exhaustive reexamination of all the evidence, Republicans on the committee not only reaffirmed their earlier conclusions *in toto*, they accused Wilson of making statements that were "not true." Regarding the faked Niger documents, which he initially said he had reviewed, they concluded: "We agree that Ambassador Wilson is confused." As for his allegation that an earlier report from U.S. ambassador to Niger Barbro Owens-Kirkpatrick "indicated that there was nothing to the Niger-Iraq uranium story," the senators wrote, "This too is untrue." Senate Select Committee on Intelligence, *Report of the Select Committee on Intelligence on Prewar Intelligence Assessments about Postwar Iraq*, May 25, 2007; minority views of Vice Chairman Bond, joined by Senators Hatch and Burr, p. 206.
8. Howard Fineman, "Rove at War," *Newsweek*, July 25, 2005; Nancy Gibbs, "Karl Rove on the Spot," *Time* magazine, July 25, 2005. See also David Broder, "One Leak and a Flood of Silliness," *Washington Post*, Sept. 7, 2006.
9. Larry C. Johnson, "The Law Is On the Side of Valerie Plame," Oct. 17, 2005. Available at www.noquarter.typepad.com, accessed May 30, 2006.
10. Larry C. Johnson, "Who Told Dick Cheney," Oct. 24, 2005. http://www.truthout.org. Accessed Dec. 20, 2005.
11. Ronald Kessler, *The CIA at War* (New York: St. Martin's-Griffin, 2004), p. 344.
12. Senate Select Committee on Intelligence, *Report of the Select Committee on Intelligence on Prewar Intelligence Assessments about Postwar Iraq*, May 25, 2007; minority views of Vice Chairman Bond, joined by Senators Hatch and Burr, p. 212.
13. Sarah Kelley, "Fitzgerald Leads Legion of Lawyers to Libby Indictment," *Legal Times*, October 31, 2005, http://www.law.com/jsp/article.jsp?id=1130499505379, accessed June 12, 2007.
14. Jack Cashill, "Why Bush Justice Rolled Over for Sandy Berger," *WorldNetDaily*, January 25, 2007.
15. SSIC 7/2004, p. 39.
16. Zell Miller, "Rule Can Head Off Dirty Tricks at CIA," *Atlanta Journal and Constitution*, Nov. 2, 2005.
17. "Disclosure of CIA Agent Identity," House Oversight and Government Reform Committee hearing , March 16, 2007. At the time this book went to press, the CIA had not responded to Waxman's request that they provide the alleged memo written by Plame's colleague.
18. SSIC 7/2004, p. 39.
19. Byron York, "Scootergate," *National Review*, April 2, 2007. The CIA document, dated Feb. 13, 2002, was a tasking memo generated by David D. Terry, Cheney's CIA briefer, relaying the vice president's request for additional information. Labeled Defense Exhibit (DX) 66.3, it includes a follow-on briefing, dated February 14, 2002, that outlines what the intelligence community knew at that time about alleged Niger uranium shipments to Iraq.
20. Senate Select Committee on Intelligence, *Report of the Select Committee on Intelligence on Prewar Intelligence Assessments about Postwar Iraq*, May 25, 2007, minority views of Vice Chairman Bond, joined by Senators Hatch and Burr, p. 206.
21. Cited in Bruce Johnston, "Agent Behind Fake Uranium Documents Worked for France," *Daily Telegraph*, Sept. 19, 2004.
22. James Lewis, "Joseph Wilson IV: The French Connection," *The American Thinker*, Nov. 7, 2005. Available at http://www.americanthinker.com/articles.php?article_id=4970, accessed Jan. 12, 2006.

23. Wilson was speaking with former Defense Intelligence Agency analyst Pat Lang, another dedicated opponent of the Bush administration. It can be viewed at http://webstorage1.mcpa.virginia.edu/library/mc/forums/audio/for_2003_1031_lang.mp3.
24. "Diplomat's 'Outrage' Finds Political Outlet," *Boston Herald,* Oct. 25, 2003, archived at FreeRepublic.com, http://www.freerepublic.com/focus/f-news/1007776/posts; Wilson, *The Politics of Truth,* pp. 410–11, 442; cited in "What Wilson Didn't Say About Africa: Joseph Wilson's Silent Partner," Oct. 25, 2004, by Fedora at www.freerepublic.com.
25. Ambassador Joseph C. Wilson, IV, "A State of the Movement Address," The 2003 Iraq Forum: June 14, 2003, audio online at Education for Peace in Iraq Center. http://www.epic-usa.org/Default.aspx?tabid=68&showlogin=1.
26. *Los Angeles Times,* Aug. 24, 1990.
27. Wilson, *The Politics of Truth,* p. 69.
28. Department of Justice, Foreign Agents Registration Act, Biannual report January–June 1998. Jacqueline Wilson first registered as an agent for Gabon on June 16, 1998. http://www.usdoj.gov/criminal/fara/fara1st98/country/gabon.htm, accessed Nov. 25, 2006. Jacqueline Wilson's last filing as an agent for Gabon was in June 2002.
29. Joseph Wilson, "A State of the Movement Address." Wilson, *The Politics of Truth,* pp. 290–92, 294–97. Cited in "What Wilson Didn't Say About Africa: Joseph Wilson's Silent Partner," Oct. 25, 2004, by Fedora at www.freerepublic.com.

CHAPTER NINE: POLITICIZING INTELLIGENCE

1. Transcript of remarks by David Kay, Iraq Survey Group, before the House Committee on Appropriations, Subcommittee on Defense and the Senate Select Committee on Intelligence, Oct. 2, 2003.
2. "The Hunt for Iraq's Weapons," letter from David Kay to the *Washington Post,* Nov. 1, 2003, p. A21.
3. Bill Gertz, "Syria Storing Iraq's WMDs," *Washington Times,* Oct. 29, 2003.
4. "King Abdullah: Al-Qaida WMDs came from Syria," newsmax.com, April 17, 2004. http://www.newsmax.com/archives/ic/2004/4/17/141224.shtml, accessed April 18, 2004.
5. "Saddam Had WMD (the continuing account)," *Investor's Business Daily,* lead editorial, Feb. 27, 2006, http://www.investors.com/editorial/IBDArticles.asp?artsec=20&artnum=2&issue=20060227, accessed Feb. 28, 2006.

CHAPTER TEN: AIR CIA

1. Stephen Grey, "America's Gulag," *New Statesman,* May 17, 2004.
2. Swedish TV4 *Kalla Fakta,* "The Broken Promise," broadcast May 17, 2004. English transcript by Human Rights Watch. Al-Zery claimed he was tortured by the Egyptians and eventually released without trial, but banned from leaving Egypt.
3. Stephen Grey, *Ghost Plane,* (New York: St. Martin's Press, 2006), pp. 112–14.
4. In *Ghost Plane,* Grey presents excruciating detail on individual cases of rendition. But he is less forthcoming about his source for the flight logs. In the book, he describes the person as "my Deep Throat . . . a man in the aviation industry I'd known all along" (p. 116). But Italian investigators who interviewed him in November 2004 in connection with the kidnapping of Egyptian exile Abu Omar in Milan told an Italian judge that Grey had described his sources to them as "ex-CIA agents." Arrest warrant issued in case n. 10838/05—R.G.N.R. and n. 1966/05/R.G.GIP by Judge Dr. Chiara Nobili,

Tribunale di Milano, June 22, 2005; p. 191. English translation provided by the Public Prosecutor.

CHAPTER ELEVEN: THE "CABAL"

1. *Ahmad Chalabi et al. v. Hashemite Kingdom of Jordan*, U.S. District Court for the District of Columbia, Civil Complaint, Aug. 11, 2004. Case 1:04CV01353; p. 46. One such article, "Jordan tip exposed Chalabi as Iran 'spy,' " appeared in the *New York Post* on May 23, 2004. Citing unnamed "diplomats," the *Post* said that King Abdullah presented a file compiled by his intelligence service to President Bush that "detailed Mafia-style extortion rackets and secret information on U.S. military operations being passed to Iran" by Chalabi.
2. Bremer, op cit, p. 364.
3. " 'Raw Deal' for Chalabi, According to Friends," *Special Report with Brit Hume*, Fox News, June 3, 2004. http://www.foxnews.com/story/0,2933,121702,00.html, accessed June 3, 2004.
4. *United States of America v. Lawrence Anthony Franklin*, affidavit filed by FBI Special Agent Catherine M. Hanna in support of Criminal Complaint, May 3, 2005; U.S. District Court for the Eastern District of Virginia, 1:05:mj309.
5. See James Bamford, "Iran: The Next War," *Rolling Stone*, July–August, 2006. Bamford began his career as a writer of insightful and well-informed books on the NSA, but in recent years has become a shrill figure, joining forces with the anti-Bush, anti-Israel crowd.
6. *United States of America v. Lawrence Anthony Franklin*, Steven J. Rosen, Kieth Weissman, United States District Court for the Eastern District of Virginia, 1:05CR225, Superseding indictment, Aug. 4, 2005, p. 10–11.
7. "To Catch a Spy," CBS's *60 Minutes*, Aug. 24, 2003.
8. Bamford, "Iran: The Next War."
9. Stephen Green, "Serving Two Flags: Neo-Cons, Israel and the Bush Administration," counterpunch, Feb. 28–29, 2004. http://www.counterpunch.org/green02282004.html, accessed April 15, 2007.

CHAPTER TWELVE: CIA INSURGENCY

1. "Sources: Goss Front-Runner for CIA Post," CNN, June 24, 2004.
2. Intelligence Authorization Act for Fiscal Year 2005, Report 108-558, June 21, 2004; p. 26.
3. Intelligence Authorization Act for Fiscal Year 2005, p. 23.
4. Goss's remarks were declassified and released by the CIA in July 2005. Cf. "DCI Goss Addresses Employees," MORI DocID: 1227720.
5. I tell the story of this Iranian opposition group, the Flag of Freedom Organization, in more detail in *Countdown to Crisis: The Coming Nuclear Showdown with Iran*, pp.139–42.
6. Vernon Loeb, "At Hush-Hush CIA Unit, Talk of a Turnaround," *Washington Post*, Sept. 7, 1999.

CHAPTER THIRTEEN: "ROGUE WEASELS"

1. "The CIA's Insurgency," *Wall Street Journal*, lead editorial, Sept. 29, 2004.
2. Bill Gertz, "CIA Funds Liberal Efforts," *Washington Times*, Sept. 7, 2004.

3. Jack Wheeler, "Porter at the Pass: Heading Off the CIA's October Surprise," *To the Point News*, Oct. 20, 2004, http://www.tothepointnews.com/content/view/1559/2/.
4. Robert Novak, "Tension Is Rising Between CIA, Bush," *Washington Post*, Sept. 26, 2004.
5. Paul R. Pillar, *Terrorism and U.S. Foreign Policy* (Washington, DC: Brookings Institution Press, 2001; paperback edition, 2003), p. 218.
6. See, for example, a compilation of freshly translated HARMONY documents published in April 2007 by a former member of the Iraq Survey Group. Ray Robison, *Both in One Trench*. Available online at http://rayrobison.typepad.com/ray_robison/2007/04/announcement_a_.html.
7. Douglas Jehl and David E. Sanger, "Prewar Assessment on Iraq Saw Chance of Strong Divisions," *New York Times*, Sept. 28, 2004, p. A1.
8. Reuel Marc Gerecht, "Intelligence Deficit Disorder," *Wall Street Journal*, May 9, 2006.
9. Richard Perle, Q&A with the author, Intelligence Summit, Feb. 28, 2006.
10. "The CIA's Insurgency," *Wall Street Journal*, lead editorial, Sept. 29, 2004.
11. Tyler Drumheller, *On the Brink* (New York: Carroll & Graff, 2006), pp. 175, 179.
12. "There are far far fewer clandestine service personnel serving overseas as I speak now than are on the payroll of the faculty of the University of Virgina," Hart told an audience at UVa's Miller Center on Dec. 3, 2004. "Let's get it in perspective. Far far fewer. The New York field station of the Federal Bureau of Investigation is bigger than our entire overseas worldwide presence." Hart's videotaped presentation was broadcast in early January 2005 by C-SPAN2 and is available digitally from the Miller Center website. http://millercenter.virginia.edu/scripps/diglibrary/forums/forum_detail.php?forum_gid=1816.
13. See Walter Pincus and Dana Priest, "Goss Brings 4 Staffers from Hill to CIA," *Washington Post*, Oct. 1, 2004.
14. Jack Wheeler, "Porter at the Pass." Kostiw was never prosecuted on the shoplifting charges.
15. Kappes spun the Belgrade incident furiously in his favor. See, for example, Mark Hosenball, "Belgrade Meltdown," *Newsweek*, May 24, 2006.
16. Judith Miller, "Intelligence Success: How Gadhafi Lost His Groove: The Complex Surrender of Libya's WMD," *Wall Street Journal*, May 16, 2006. Miller claimed that Kappes declined to be interviewed for her article. Her slap at administration neo-cons came after former colleagues on the Left had accused her of becoming too close to top White House aide Scooter Libby in her reporting on prewar intelligence on Iraq. An equally glowing account of Kappes's role in Libya's disarmament can be found in anti-Bush writer Ron Suskind's "The Tyrant Who Came in from the Cold," *Washington Monthly*, October 2006.

CHAPTER FOURTEEN: OCTOBER SURPRISE

1. Mary Louise Kelly, "More CIA Resignations Come Amid Shake-Up," National Public Radio's *All Things Considered*, Nov. 15, 2004.
2. Michael Duffy, "In Your Face at the CIA," *Time*, Nov. 29, 2004. With reporting by Timothy J. Burger, Matthew Cooper, Elaine Shannon, and Adam Zagorin.
3. Julia Borger, "CIA Memo Urging Spies to Support Bush Provokes Furore," *The Guardian*, Nov. 18, 2004.
4. Duffy, "In Your Face at the CIA."
5. Ibid.
6. Borger, "CIA Memo."
7. David Ignatius, "The Langley Labotomy," *Washington Post*, Nov. 30, 2004.
8. John Diamond, "Goss Conspicuously Mum About CIA Turmoil," *USA Today*, Dec. 13, 2004; statement by Representative Jane Harman of California, May 5, 2006.
9. Diamond, ibid.

CHAPTER FIFTEEN: PEOPLE ARE POLICY

1. J. Michael Waller, "Holdovers Held Up Security Strategy," *Insight* magazine, March 29, 2004.
2. The February 1999 incident is described on page 137 of the 9/11 Commission Report, although Clarke's role in calling off the air strike against bin Ladin is relegated to footnote 163 on page 486 of the report. See also Kenneth R. Timmerman, "Did Richard Clarke Save Osama?" NewsMax.com, April 12, 2006. http://www.newsmax.com/archives/articles/2006/4/11/124637.shtml?s=lh.
3. Private communication with the author, April 17, 2007. Substantial background information on Sheikh Hamdan and the Sheikh Ali hunting camp can also be found on the group's website, SaveTheFalcons.org.
4. J. Michael Waller, "Kerry Partisan Blocks Iran Democracy Funds," Fourth World War blogspot, July 11, 2005. http://fourthworldwar.blogspot.com/2005_07_01_archive.html.
5. J. Michael Waller, " 'Witch Hunt' at State Department," Fourth World War blogspot, July 13, 2005.
6. See also Kenneth R. Timmerman, "The State Department's Dead Parrot," *Frontpage* magazine, April 20, 2006. http://www.frontpagemag.com/Articles/ReadArticle.asp?ID=22127.
7. "Treasury Cuts Iran's Bank Saderat Off from U.S. Financial System," Department of Treasury press release, September 8, 2006.
8. Congressional Record, Intelligence Reform and Terrorism Prevention Act of 2004—Conference Report, Dec. 8, 2004, p. S11957.
9. Katherine Pfleger Shrader, "Lawmaker Says Mystery Spy Program 'Dangerous to National Security'," *Washington Post*, Dec. 9, 2004.
10. Dana Priest, "New Spy Satellite Debated on Hill," *Washington Post*, Dec. 11, 2004.
11. Douglas Jehl, "New Spy Plan Said to Involve Satellite System," *New York Times*, Dec. 12, 2004.
12. William Douglas and Warren P. Strobel, "Bush Nominates Controversial Bolton for UN Ambassador Job," *Detroit Free Press*, March 8, 2005.
13. Nomination of John R. Bolton to Be U.S. Representative to the United Nations, Senate Foreign Relations committee, April 11, 2005, p. 40.
14. Humberto Fontova, "Castro Bashes John Bolton as 'Gangster,' " *Human Events*, Aug. 5, 2005.
15. John R. Bolton, "Beyond the Axis of Evil: Additional Threats from Weapons of Mass Destruction," Heritage Lecture #743, May 6, 2002. Also available at http://www.state.gov/t/us/rm/9962.htm, accessed Jan. 11, 2007.
16. Ibid.
17. Scott Carmichael, *True Believer* (Annapolis, MD: Naval Institute Press 2007), p. 138.
18. Humberto Fontova, *Fidel: Hollywood's Favorite Tyrant* (Washington: Regnery Publishing, 2005), p. 9.
19. Armstrong's trip to Atlanta to brief Carter was revealed by Christian Westermann under questioning by Democratic staff member Janice O'Connell.

> MS. O'CONNELL: When Carter was about to go to Cuba, shortly after this speech, he was briefed by people within the U.S. Government. Was he briefed by anyone to your knowledge in INR?
>
> MR. WESTERMANN: INR was not involved in the briefing.
>
> MS. O'CONNELL: Was INR aware? Were you aware he was about to go to Cuba?
>
> MR. WESTERMANN: No, I was not aware. I was aware that some friends of

mine at CIA were part of a team that went to Atlanta. That was just friends. We were not asked to participate.

SFRC Staff interview with Christian Westermann, April 11, 2005, p. 50.

20. "Carter Backs Castro on 'Lie,' " *Washington Times*, May 14, 2002.
21. *SFRC Staff interview with Frederick Fleitz*, Thursday, April 7, 2005, pp. 70–72.
22. Ibid., p. 71.
23. Ibid., p. 78.
24. *SFRC Staff interview with Lawrence Wilkerson*, May 6, 2005; pp. 39–40.
25. Wilkerson went on to write an outraged op-ed, which appeared in the April 23, 2006, edition of the *Baltimore Sun*, that raises questions about why he worked for the Bush administration to begin with.

> In January 2001, with the inauguration of George W. Bush as president, America set on a path to cease being good; America became a revolutionary nation, a radical republic. If our country continues on this path, it will cease to be great—as happened to all great powers before it, without exception.
>
> From the Kyoto accords to the International Criminal Court, from torture and cruel and unusual treatment of prisoners to rendition of innocent civilians, from illegal domestic surveillance to lies about leaking, from energy ineptitude to denial of global warming, from cherry-picking intelligence to appointing a martinet and a tyrant to run the Defense Department, the Bush administration, in the name of fighting terrorism, has put America on the radical path to ruin.

26. Martin Arostegui, "Castro Weaponizes West Nile Virus," *Insight* magazine, Oct. 1, 2002 (posted Sept. 16, 2002).
27. Per Ahlmark, "Let the Nobel Go Nuclear," *Wall Street Journal*, Feb. 6, 2006. Only current and former members of Scandinavian parliaments have the right to legally nominate candidates for the Peace Prize. As a former deputy prime minister and member of the Swedish Parliament (and head of Sweden's Liberal Party), Per Ahlmark fit that bill.
28. The CIA inspector general report was completed in August 2005 and censured Tenet for failing to develop a strategic plan to crush al Qaeda before 2001, but it was never released publicly. Portions of the report were leaked to *New York Times* reporter James Risen at the time, but Tenet managed through surrogates—including his former deputy, John McLaughlin—to keep a lid on it. Two years later, over the objections of CIA director General Michael Hayden, CIA Inspector General John Helgerson released a nineteen-page executive summary of the report, which Democrats in Congress promptly spun as new evidence of the failures of the Bush administration, even though the overwhelming majority of failures noted by Helgerson occurred prior to 2001. The report is available at www.kentimmerman.com/shadow-warriors.htm.
29. CNN's *Late Edition with Wolf Blitzer*, May 7, 2006.
30. In April 1968, Negroponte was named to the U.S. delegation to the Paris peace talks with the North Vietnamese. Shortly afterward, a network of South Vietnamese operatives working for the Phoenix program was rounded up and executed by the Vietcong. Former CIA paramilitary officers involved in Operation Phoenix have long suspected that someone at the peace talks leaked the names to the French, but no hard proof has ever surfaced to confirm the allegation or that Negroponte was in any way involved.
31. In a written question submitted as part of his confirmation hearing as DNI, Senator Carl Levin dredged up the story of the disappearance of Father James Carney, an American priest who was allegedly murdered by a right-wing death squad in 1983 while Negroponte was serving as ambassador to Tegucigalpa. Others dwelled on Negroponte's alleged indifference to human rights violations. But they were old allegations, and the Democrats raised them to please their constituents, little more.

Nomination of John Negroponte to be Director of National Intelligence, Senate Select Committee on Intelligence, April 12, 2005 (Senate hearing 109-79); See inter alia pp. 16–18, 42–43, 161.

32. Negroponte confirmation hearing, p. 41.
33. In a specific reference aimed at the "sixteen words" spoken by President Bush on Saddam Hussein's alleged attempts to acquire uranium from Africa, Levin asked, "Do you agree that there should be a formal review process for major statements by senior policymakers about intelligence matters, and that the head of the U.S. Intelligence Community should be aware of such public statements about intelligence and aware of Intelligence Community concerns that a major source may be a fabricator?" Negroponte supplied the necessary weasel words in reply: "I would work with the president's staff to ensure that any portions of his speeches referring to intelligence information would be double-checked with the intelligence-community beforehand." Negroponte hearing, p. 159.
34. Dafna Linzer, "Iran Is Judged 10 Years from Nuclear Bomb," *Washington Post,* Aug. 2, 2005. http://www.washingtonpost.com/wp-dyn/content/article/2005/08/01/AR2005 080101453.html, accessed Aug. 2, 2005.
35. Even the IAEA determined (in February 2006) that evidence it had discovered in Iran demonstrated clearly that Iran had a nuclear *weapons* program, not just a civilian research program. I have written several articles discussing the NIE that lay out evidence apparently rejected by Fingar. See, inter alia, "That Nuclear Dance of 1,000 Veils," *Washington Times,* Aug. 5, 2005. http://kentimmerman.com/news/wt-2005_08_06nie.htm; "IAEA Says Iran Is Working on 'Nuclear Weapons,' NewsMax.com, Feb. 3, 2006. http://newsmax.com/archives/articles/2006/2/2/221519.shtml?s=lh%0D; "Israeli Official: Iran Could Have Nukes in 2007," NewsMax.com, June 27, 2006. http://newsmax.com/archives/articles/2006/6/26/152424.shtml?s=lh; "IAEA State of Denial," *FrontPage* magazine, Oct. 5, 2006. http://www.frontpagemag.com/Articles/ReadArticle.asp?ID=24778; "Showdown with Iran," *Frontpage* magazine, Dec. 27, 2006. http://frontpagemag.com/Articles/ReadArticle.asp?ID=26150.
36. I described Brill's tepid performance while he was enjoying Vienna in *Countdown to Crisis,* p. 285.
37. House National Security Committee hearing on Whistleblower protection and Special Access Programs, Feb. 15, 2006. Van Hollen warned that "a court of law may determine that an individual NSA employee could be held criminally liable for violating the Foreign Intelligence Surveillance Act" if he took part in the NSA terrorist surveillance program.

CHAPTER SIXTEEN: THE DAILY LEAK

1. Witness statement by Mohamed Reda Elbadry to Italian prosecutors, June 15, 2004. Elbadry said he had learned of Abu Omar's fate just two months earlier from the missing cleric's wife, Ghali Nabila. His account of the timing of Abu Omar's arrest did not tally with flight records of the aircraft the prosecutors examined. They attributed this to the fact that Elbadry was a "third-hand" witness, while not impeaching his good faith. Arrest warrant issued in case n. 10838/05-R.G.N.R. and n. 1966/05 /R.G.GIP by Judge Dr. Chiara Nobili, Tribunale di Milano, June 22, 2005; pp. 7–8, 189–90.
2. Milan arrest warrant, p. 190. Scarpolini testimony, p. 183. Flight logs, p. 187.
3. This information also was known to Italian prosecutors. See, inter alia, Milan arrest warrant p. 57, witness statement from Mohamed Elbadry.
4. Kenneth R. Timmerman, "This Man Wants You Dead," *Reader's Digest,* July 1998. This was the first mass media profile of Osama bin Laden that appeared in America. It

hit the newsstands just three weeks before bin Laden blew up two U.S. embassies in Africa and became a household name.

5. Stephen Grey, *Ghost Plane* (New York: St. Martins Press, 2006), p. 196.
6. Grey describes the search and reproduces the entire e-mail in *Ghost Plane*, p. 208.
7. See, inter alia, Dana Priest, "CIA Holds Terror Suspects in Secret Prisons," *Washington Post*, Nov. 2, 2005, which refers to an ongoing IG investigation into renditions, and "Covert CIA Program Withstands New Furor," *Washington Post*, Dec. 30, 2005, which specifically mentions the spring 2004 IG report on torture. Her repeated references to the CIA inspector general should have raised eyebrows, but did not.
8. Frances D'Emilio, "Italian Resists Pressure on CIA Case," Associated Press, March 2, 2006.
9. Grey, *Ghost Plane*, p. 194.
10. Milan arrest warrant, p. 24.
11. Ibid., p. 5.
12. The Milan arrest warrant does not reproduce the telegram or identify Castelli by name. Both can be found in Grey, *Ghost Plane*, p. 195.
13. Grey, *Ghost Plane*, p. 197.
14. Representative Pete Hoekstra, "Secrets and Leaks: The Costs and Consequences for National Security," July 29, 2005, Heritage Webmemo #809 and Heritage Lecture #897. http://www.heritage.org/Research/HomelandDefense/wm809.cfm, accessed Sept 9, 2005.
15. Scott Shane, "Official Reveals Budget for U.S. Intelligence," *New York Times*, Nov. 8, 2005, p. A18. Graham said the total intelligence budget was $44 billion.
16. Priest, "CIA Holds Terror Suspects in Secret Prisons."
17. John Hinderaker, "Leaking at All Costs: What the CIA Is Willing to Do to Hurt the Bush Administration," *Daily Standard*, Nov. 30, 2005.
18. Rebecca Carr, "GOP Seeks Source of CIA Prison Story," *Atlanta Journal and Constitution*, Nov. 9, 2005.
19. Dana Priest, "Covert CIA Program Withstands New Furor," *Washington Post*, Dec. 30, 2005.
20. Doug Mellgren, "Scandinavian Countries Investigating Reports of Secret CIA Prisoner Flights," Associated Press Worldstream, Nov. 17, 2005.
21. Daniel Woolls, "Canary Islands Probes CIA Questions," Associated Press—AP Online, Nov. 16, 2005.
22. See, inter alia, Seth Hettena, "Navy Is Linked to Planes in Torture Cases," *St. Louis Post Dispatch* (AP), Sept. 25, 2005, for the mention of plane spotters in Afghanistan.
23. "CIA Prison Flights Hypocrites Gripe On? Jose Rodriguez, CIA DDO, Made Deals for Them!" Posted by CHallmark on Nov. 29, 2005 at 10:17 P.M. MST. http://www.phxnews.com/fullstory.php?article=28832, accessed Sept 23, 2006.
24. Tracy Wilkinson, "Ex-CIA Agent in Milan Asks for Immunity," *Los Angeles Times*, Dec. 5, 2005.
25. Condoleezza Rice, remarks on extraordinary renditions, Dec. 5, 2005. http://www.state.gov/secretary/rm/2005/57602.htm, accessed 11/30/2006.
26. Wilkinson, "Ex-CIA Agent."
27. For Human Rights Watch funding sources, I am indebted to Joe De Feo and the Capital Research Center in Washington, DC.
28. See, for example, "U.S. Operated Secret 'Dark Prison' in Kabul," Human Rights Watch, Dec.19, 2005. http://www.hrw.org/english/docs/2005/12/19/afghan12319.htm. The group also provided assistance to the American media by posting an English-language transcript of the seminal Swedish television *Kalla Fakta* show from May 17, 2004, which was the first to detail the use of proprietaries and to publish aircraft tail numbers.
29. Jack Kelly, "CIA Moonbats Sabotage Bush," *Washington Times*, Oct. 12, 2005.

30. Jennifer Verner, "Post Reporter Dana Priest's Troubling Connections," Accuracy in Media Special Report, May 9, 2006. Verner notes that in 2002, Goodfellow teamed with Fenton Communications, a public relations firm whose client list read like a Who's Who of the anti-Bush Left (MoveOn.org, George Soros's Open Society Institute, the Marxist-inspired Institute for Policy studies, etc.) to establish the Iraq Policy Information Project. Their goal was to promote information that would change public perception of the war in Iraq.
31. Justin Stares, "EU Deal Secretly Let in US Flights," *Washington Times (London Sunday Telegraph)*, Dec. 12, 2005.
32. Paul Farhi, "At the Times, a Scoop Deferred," *Washington Post*, Dec. 17, 2005.
33. James Risen and Eric Lichtblau, "Bush Lets U.S. Spy on Callers Without Courts," *New York Times*, Dec. 16, 2005 (print edition). An Internet version of the story was released the night before with the title "Bush Secretly Lifted Some Limits on Spying in U.S. After 9/11, Officials Say."
34. "Initial Reactions to NSA Spying Report," NewsMax.com, Dec. 16, 2005.
35. "Kerry Wants Bush Impeached," NewsMax.com. Dec. 16, 2006. http://www.newsmax.com/archives/ic/2005/12/16/112423.shtml, accessed Dec. 17, 2005.
36. "Sen. Accuses Times of Endangering U.S.," Associated Press, Dec. 17, 2005.
37. Jonathan Alter, "Bush's Snoopgate," *Newsweek* Web commentary, Dec. 19, 2005. http://www.msnbc.msn.com/id/10536559/site/newsweek/, accessed Dec. 20, 2005.
38. Michael A. Fletcher, "President Takes the Offensive with Press," *Washington Post*, Dec. 20, 2005, p. A8. Boxer quote: Peter Baker and Charles Babington, "Bush Addresses Uproar Over Spying," *Washington Post*, p. A1.
39. Joseph Curl, "Bush Calls Leak 'Shameful,' " *Washington Times*, Dec. 20, 2005.
40. Michelle Malkin, "A Leak Is a Leak Is a Leak," *Jewish World Review*, Jan. 7, 2006. http://jewishworldreview.com/michelle/malkin010406.php3, accessed Jan. 10, 2006
41. Michael Barone, "So Much for Democracy," *U.S. News & World Report*, Jan. 9, 2006. http://www.usnews.com/usnews/opinion/baroneblog/archives/060109/so_much_for_dem.htm#more, accessed Jan. 10, 2006.
42. Carol D. Leonnig, "Surveillance Court Is Seeking Answers," *Washington Post*, Jan. 5, 2006.
43. Andrew McCarthy, "Now Judges Are Leaking," *National Review Online*, Jan. 5, 2006. http://www.nationalreview.com/mccarthy/mccarthy200601051559.asp, accessed Feb. 4, 2006.
44. Bill Gertz, "NSA Whistleblower Asks to Testify," *Washington Times*, Jan. 5, 2006.
45. Bill Gertz, "Ex-official Warned Against Testifying on NSA Programs," *Washington Times*, Jan. 12, 2006.
46. *National Review Online* media blog, Jan. 5, 2006. http://media.nationalreview.com/, accessed Jan. 9, 2006.
47. The Clinton wiretaps were carried out under the Echelon program and were described by NSA operator Margaret Newsham in an interview with CBS's *60 Minutes* that aired in February 2000. See "Clinton NSA Wiretapped Top Republican," NewsMax, Jan. 6, 2006.
48. "Wiretaps for Me, Not Thee?" *Washington Times*, lead editorial, Dec. 23, 2005.
49. Dan Eggen and Walter Pincus, "Campaign to Justify Spying Intensifies," *Washington Post*, Jan. 24, 2006, p. A4.

CHAPTER SEVENTEEN: THE MISSING WMDs

1. See also, Jamie Glazov, "Where the WMDs Went," *FrontPage*magazine.com, Nov. 16, 2005.

2. David Thibault, "CNSNews.com Publishes Iraqi Intelligence Docs," Oct. 11, 2004. Twenty-eight pages of Arabic-language originals and English translations can be viewed starting at http://www.cnsnews.com/specialreports/2004/exclusive1.asp.
3. "Saddam's Documents," *Wall Street Journal* lead editorial, Jan. 13, 2006, p. A12. http://online.wsj.com/article/SB113711497850845516.html?mod=opinion&ojcontent=otep, accessed Jan. 13, 2006. The documents were first bruited by Stephen Hayes in *The Weekly Standard* (see below).
4. Stephen F. Hayes, "New Documents Reveal Saddam Hid WMD, Was Tied to Al Qaida," *The Weekly Standard*, Nov. 18, 2005.
5. Stephen F. Hayes, "Saddam's Terror Training Camps," *The Weekly Standard*, Jan. 16, 2006, http://www.weeklystandard.com/Content/Public/Articles/000/000/006/550kmbzd.asp, accessed Jan. 11, 2006.
6. Charles Duelfer et al., "Comprehensive Report of the Special Advisor to the DCI on Iraq's WMD," Central Intelligence Agency, Sept. 23, 2004; Vol. 2, p. 51.
7. Stephen. F. Hayes, "Down the Memory Hole: The Pentagon Sits on the Documents of the Saddam Hussein Regime," *The Weekly Standard*, Dec. 19, 2005.
8. Jerry Seper, "Clinton White House Axed Terror-Fund Probe," *Washington Times*, April 2, 2002.
9. In fact, Shaw was investigating allegedly improper contract awards to Nadmi Auchi, an Iraqi exile whose corporate empire was based in Luxembourg and who had long been cited for his ties to Saddam Hussein. "The winners of the Iraqi cellular tender were Saddam's most senior financiers, their Egyptian, Kuwaiti and Iraqi supporters, the bank BNP Paribas, European cellular corporations, particularly Alcatel and the European GMS technology it depends on, and Chinese telecom interests, such as Huawei, which had been active in breaking the Iraqi embargo," Gertz quoted an unnamed defense official as saying. "The losers were American bidders," the official added. Bill Gertz, "Iraqi Probed in Rigging of Cell-Phone Pacts," *Washington Times*, May 9, 2004.
10. Georges Hormuz Sada, *Saddam's Secrets* (Nashville: Thomas Nelson, 2006).
11. Ira Stoll, "Saddam's WMD Moved to Syria, an Israeli Says," *New York Sun*, Dec. 15, 2005. http://www.nysun.com/article/2448, accessed Dec. 16, 2005.
12. Nayouf's information was published on Jan. 5, 2003, at reformsyria.com.
13. Charles Duelfer, *Addendums to the Comprehensive Report of the Special Advisor to the DCI on Iraq's WMD*, Central Intelligence Agency, March 2005, p. 4.

CHAPTER EIGHTEEN: SINKING THE SHIP

1. "Iraqi Diplomat Gave U.S. Prewar WMD Details," by Aram Roston, Lisa Myers, and the NBC Investigative Unit, MSNBC.com, March 20, 2006.
2. Walter Pincus, "Ex-Iraqi Official Unveiled as a Spy," *Washington Post*, March 23, 2006.
3. Porter Goss, "Loose Lips Sink Spies," *New York Times* op-ed, Feb. 10, 2006. http://www.nytimes.com/2006/02/10/opinion/10goss.html?ex=1297227600&en=3e6d549a42e100dc&ei=5090&partner=rssuserland&emc=rss, accessed 4/22/2006.
4. Kenneth R. Timmerman, "CIA Sabotage," *Frontpage* magazine, April 27, 2006. http://frontpagemag.com/Articles/ReadArticle.asp?ID=22241. See also Walter Pincus, "Democrats Suggest Double Standard on Leaks," *Washington Post*, April 24, 2006; p. A2.
5. According to Weldon, Able Danger had identified al Qaeda cells operating in the United States, and produced a chart that included a photograph of 9/11 hijacker Mohammed Atta. But the Able Danger team was ordered to destroy the charts and all their data by Clinton administration officials. After the 9/11 attacks, Weldon claimed that Bush Pentagon officials stymied efforts by members of the Able Danger team to cooperate with the FBI, although they denied it in public hearings. See, inter alia, Kenneth

R. Timmerman, "Rep. Weldon: Pentagon Report a Whitewash," Newsmax.com, Sept. 22, 2006. http://www.newsMax.com/archives/articles/2006/9/22/90332.shtml?s=lh. On Mary McCarthy's contributions to the Sestak campaign, see Timmerman, "Curt Weldon, the Man the Left Wants to Beat," *Frontpage* magazine, Sept. 28, 2006. http://www.frontpagemag.com/Articles/ReadArticle.asp?ID=24655.

6. R. Jeffrey Smith, "Fired Officer Believed CIA Lied to Congress," *Washington Post*, May 14, 2006.
7. Mary Louise Kelly, "In Latest Setback, No. 2 Man at CIA Quits," *All Things Considered*, National Public Radio, Sept. 15, 2005.

CHAPTER NINETEEN: THE EMPIRE STRIKES BACK

1. Robb-Silberman Commission, op cit, p. 798.
2. Ed Bradley, "A Spy Speaks Out," CBS *Sixty Minutes*, April 23, 2006. http://www.cbsnews.com/stories/2006/04/21/60minutes/main1527749.shtml, accessed April 25, 2006.
3. *Report of the Select Committee on Intelligence on Postwar Findings about Iraq's WMD Programs and Links to Terrorism and How They Compare with Prewar Assessments*, together with *Additional Views*, Sept. 8, 2006; p. 144. Also known as Iraq Phase II accuracy.
4. In his bitter memoir, *On the Brink*, Drumheller explained how his wife, who was a CIA analyst, had gone from being a "Reagan Republican" to become an active campaign worker for Senator John Kerry in 2004. "Many CIA families found this conflict at that time. We had always believed that patriotic citizens were supposed to support their president at war," he wrote. "But, like many of my colleagues, knowing what we did, I found this increasingly difficult to do" (p. 128).
5. George Tenet, *At the Center of the Storm*, op cit, pp. 377–83.
6. Despite this, Scheuer remained a dedicated enemy of Goss. "Hearing of the International Organizations, Human Rights and Oversight Subcommittee and the Europe Subcommittee of the Hosue Foreign Affairs Committee. Subject: Extraordinary Rendition in U.S. Counterterrorism Policy: The Impact on Transatlantic Relations," April 17, 2007.
7. Sally Quinn, "From Her Lips to His Ear," *Washington Post*, March 24, 2006, p. C1.
8. "Pesticides are the key elements in the chemical agent arena," Hanson says. "In fact, the general pesticide chemical formula (organophosphate) is the 'grandfather' of modern-day nerve agents." Cf. Kenneth R. Timmerman, "Saddam's WMD Have Been Found," *Insight* magazine, April 25, 2004.
9. Cf. Kevin McCullough, "WMDs: The Real Scandal," Townhall.com, June 26, 2006.
10. "Liars," editorial by *Frontpage*mag.com, June 22, 2006.
11. "Fox Makes Up News, NY Times Editor Says," Newsmax.com, June 23, 2006.
12. "Report: Hundreds of WMDs found in Iraq," Fox News, June 21, 2006.
13. Exchange between Representative Nadler and former CIA official Michael Scheuer, Hearing of the International Organizations, April 17, 2007, op. cit.
14. "Verbatim Transcript of Combatant Status Review Tribunal Hearing for ISN 10024," March 10, 2007, U.S. Naval Base Guantánamo Bay, Cuba, p18.; http://www.defenselink.mil/news/transcript_ISN10024.pdf, accessed April 16, 2007.
15. "New York Times Buries King Prosecution Story," NewsMax.com, June 27, 2006.
16. "Ed Meese: NY Times Aiding the Enemy," NewsMax.com, Jun 26, 2006.
17. Letter from Treasury Secretary John Snow to *New York Times* executive editor Bill Keller, June 26, 2006.

CHAPTER TWENTY: LAME DUCK NATION

1. "Report on the Use by the Intelligence Community of Information Provided by the Iraqi National Congress, together with Additional Views, Senate Select Committee on Intelligence," Sept. 8, 2006; p123. Hereafter, SSIC Phase II INC report. http://intelligence.senate.gov/phaseiiinc.pdf.
2. Cf. "Democrats Target Pentagon Planning," *Insight* magazine, Dec. 9, 2003; and "Dealing with the Devil," *FrontPage* magazine, May 18, 2006, available at http://frontpagemag.com/Articles/ReadArticle.asp?ID=22513.
3. Available at https://www.cia.gov/cia/reports/iraq_wmd/Iraq_Oct_2002.htm.
4. Daniel Ellsberg, "The Next War," *Harper's Magazine*, October 2006. http://harpers.org/TheNextWar.html, accessed Nov. 13, 2006; The Colbert Report, Comedy Central, Sept. 21, 2006. Seymour Hersh, "The Iran Plans," *The New Yorker*, April 17, 2006.
5. http://boltonwatch.tpmcafe.com/node/29928, accessed June 4, 2006.
6. Mark Mazzetti, "Spy Agencies Say Iraq War Worsens Terrorism Threat," *New York Times*, Sept. 24, 2006, p. A01.
7. "Declassified Key Judgments of the National Intelligence Estimate on Global Terrorism," *New York Times*, Sept. 27, 2006.
8. "Hoekstra Suspends Dem Staffer Over Leak," NewsMax.com, Oct. 20, 2006. http://www.newsmax.com/archives/ic/2006/10/20/135230.shtml?s=lh, accessed 10/21/2006.
9. See Michelle Malkin, "Dem Leak Suspect Identified," Oct. 21, 2006. http://michellemalkin.com/archives/006166.htm, accessed 10/23/2006.
10. Bob Woodward, *State of Denial: Bush at War, Part III* (New York: Simon & Schuster, 2006), p. 491.
11. Ibid., pp. 415, 474.
12. Cf. *Countdown to Crisis: The Coming Nuclear Showdown with Iran*, pp. 7–18, 268–71; and pp. 240–41 of the 9/11 Commission Report.
13. "Armed Iranian Fighters Arrested in Samarra," *Iran Focus*, Oct. 4, 2004. http://www.marzeporgohar.org/index.php?action=news&n_id=17648&l=1, accessed Oct. 6, 2004.
14. "Iraq spy chief accuses Iran embassy of killing agents," Agence France-Presse/*Jordan Times*, Oct. 15, 2004. Shahwani was involved in the aborted 1995 coup against Saddam by Iyad Allawi and has been falsely accused by the American left as being a tool of former Baathists. But during his tenure, he helped *dismantle* former Baathist networks, in addition to exposing Iran's involvement in the insurgency.
15. "The distinction between Sunni and Shia that have traditionally divided terrorist groups are not distinctions you should make anymore, because there is a common interest against the United States and its allies in this region, and they will seek capability wherever they can get it," Tenet told the Senate Armed Services committee on March 19, 2002. Cf. Bill Gertz, "CIA Won't Rule Out Iraq, Iran," *Washington Times*, March 20, 2002.
16. "US Warns Iran Against Any Support for Zarqawi," Agence France-Press/Iranmania, Oct. 19, 2004. http://www.iranmania.com/News/ArticleView/Default.asp?ArchiveNews=Yes&NewsCode=26234&NewsKind=CurrentAffairs, accessed Feb. 22, 2005.
17. Eli Lake, "Iran's Secret Plan for Mayhem," *New York Sun*, Jan. 4, 2007.
18. CBS News, Jan. 27, 2007. http://www.cbsnews.com/stories/2007/01/27/politics/main2404562.shtml.
19. *Khaled El-Masri v. George Tenet et al.*, Order to Dismiss, May 12, 2006; United States District Court for the Eastern district of Virginia, Case No. 1:05cv1417. Available at http://www.aclu.org/pdfs/safefree/elmasri_order_granting_motion_dismiss_051206.pdf. The court ruling followed filings by CIA Director Porter Goss, who asserted state secrets would be jeopardized if the case was heard. The CIA could not defend itself, he

said, because they did "not, however, have the luxury of denying unfounded allegations of clandestine intelligence activities without serious adverse consequences. The denial of CIA involvement may, by itself, provide the informed intelligence analyst useful information about the CIA's capabilities and the scope and thrust of CIA activities." *Masri v. Tenet et al.*, Goss declaration, March 8, 2006, p. 8.

20. "Report on the alleged use of European countries by the CIA for the transportation and illegal detention of prisoners," Temporary Committee on the alleged use of European countries by the CIA for the transportation and illegal detention of prisoners, Rapporteur Giovanini Claudio Fava, European Parliament, Jan. 26, 2007; reference A6-9999/2007, p. 6.
21. Craig Whitlock, "Travel Logs Aid Germans' Kidnap Probe," *Washington Post*, Feb. 2, 2007.
22. "Extraordinary Rendition in U.S. Counterrorism Policy: The Impact on Transatlantic Relations," transcript of an April 17, 2007, hearing of the International Organizations, Human Rights, and Oversight Subcommittee of the House Foreign Affairs Committee.
23. Kenneth R. Timmerman, "Trans-Atlantic Terror Divide," *Frontpage* magazine, April 20, 2007. http://www.frontpagemag.com/Articles/ReadArticle.asp?ID=27949.
24. "President Discusses Global War on Terror," Bush speech to the Military Officers Association, White House, Office of the Press Secretary, September 5, 2006.
25. Senator Joe Lieberman, floor debate on S470, Feb. 5, 2007; *Congressional Record* p S1562.
26. "Prospects for Iraq's Stability: A Challenging Road Ahead," National Intelligence Estimate, January 2007; Key judgments released by the director of national intelligence on Feb. 2, 2007. http://www.dni.gov/press_releases/20070202_release.pdf.

ACKNOWLEDGMENTS

Any book that describes the inner workings of government while that government is still in power must rely on confidential resources. While this certainly is not a journalist's first choice, it is necessary if one wants to peer beneath the happy face the administration displays to the public and to its supporters.

Most of the information in these pages has not been reported previously and will come as a surprise to readers who have become accustomed to the conventional wisdom versions purveyed by the press. When I have relied on public documents, such as the reports from the Senate Select Committee on Intelligence or from the Scooter Libby trial, it is because these documents were ignored by the elite media in their efforts to paint a uniformly uncomplimentary picture of the Bush administration.

While all the sources whose information is included in this book knew the project to which they were contributing, in almost every single case they insisted that I not tie their names to specific comments or information. I interviewed many of these sources repeatedly, some more than two dozen times. I have used direct quotation marks for speech that has been reported publicly, or when quoting directly from a source. As a general rule, I have used indirect speech to relay conversations described to me by one or several direct participants. Similarly, the thoughts or reflections ascribed to participants in these events were conveyed to me directly or by eyewitnesses. Because all of this material is original to this book, it does not appear in the notes.

I have shared the most controversial passages of this book with these sources, to ensure that the details and the quotes printed here are rigorously accurate.

This book couldn't have been written without Richard Perle, one of that rare Washington species who will speak his mind honestly and on the record. Dr. Ahmad Chalabi, whom I have known for nearly two decades, also collaborated freely and unconditionally and in many cases provided documents to back up his version of events. Zaab Sethna, Intifad Qanbar, Francis Brooke, Tamara Chalabi, Peg Bartell, Linda Flahr, Aras Karim Habib, Frank Ricciardone, Qobad Talabani, Sherry Kraham, Barham Salih, Hoshyar Zebari, Jalal Talabani, Warren Marik, R. James Woolsey, Hamad Bayati, Bakhtiar Amin, Claude Hankes-Drielsma, Bill Luti, David Kay, Sherif Ali bin Hussein al Hashimi, Michael Rubin, and John Markham also helped at various points.

Thanks to Bill Tierney, Robert Reilly, Jack Shaw, Gary Berntsen, Stephen Grey, Ken deGraffenreid, Adam Ciralski, General Georges Sada, and the head of Company X for sharing their stories. Thanks to JINSA, Finmeccanica, Paul Wolfowitz, Hal Koster, and Stephen Bryen for all you have done to help handicapped veterans from the Iraq War, and shame on the Hilton hotel chain for closing down the dinners in their honor.

Thanks to Margaret "Ducky" Hemenway, Michael Stransky, Bob Thompson, and Ed Corrigan for opening doors. Representative Pete Hoekstra, and former congressmen Curt Weldon and Christopher Cox also deserve special thanks for their service to the truth. And thanks to the more than two dozen congressional staffers, and several dozen executive branch employees at State, DoD, Treasury, and the White House, who provided insight and information: you know who you are.

J. Michael Waller, Wayne Simmons, Victoria Toensing, Peter Huessy, Michael Scheuer, and John McLaughlin all shared ideas and helped to steer me back on track. In addition, more than three dozen current and former CIA officials—including some who served in Iraq and witnessed the events described here firsthand—contributed information and comments for this book. Although none of them would discuss classified information, they have all asked to remain anonymous. Thank you for your service to our country.

My editor, Jed Donahue, and my agent, Mel Berger at William Morris Agency, kept this project on track, while Random House lawyer Matthew Martin helped to clarify the line between fact and opinion. Your skill and insights are much appreciated. Any mistakes are all mine.

Since his arrest on what I believe were trumped-up charges, I have lost touch with former DIA officer Larry Franklin, whom I have known since

1995. Larry, just like Scooter Libby, you deserve a medal for all you have done for your country, not jail time. Thanks to Plato Cacheris for giving me access to the court record.

As a president, George W. Bush has demanded absolute loyalty from his top advisors. While not unusual in itself, when exercised by a president who rightly suspects the elite media of seeking his defeat, it makes the task of a conservative reporter such as myself more difficult than it might otherwise be. As one senior White House official told me when I asked him to comment on actions by State Department officials that went directly counter to stated administration policies, "As far as the president is concerned, Condi is in charge. He has zero tolerance for executive branch officials dumping on others in the executive branch."

As *Shadow Warriors* makes clear, if this president believes that the permanent bureaucracy is committed to his agenda, he is truly living in a fantasy world.

INDEX